AF553929

# MORAL JUDGMENT OF INTERMEDIATE STUDENTS

# MORAL JUDGMENT OF INTERMEDIATE STUDENTS

*By*
**Dr. B.Yella Reddy**
*Deptt. of Education*
*S.V. University*
*Tirupati - 517 502*
*&*
**Dr. V.Dayakara Reddy**
*Deptt. of Education*
*S.V. University*
*Tirupati - 517 502*
*(India)*

**DISCOVERY PUBLISHING HOUSE PVT. LTD.**
**NEW DELHI-110 002**

*Published by:*
**Tilak Wasan**

**DISCOVERY PUBLISHING HOUSE PVT. LTD.**
4831/24, Ansari Road, Prahlad Street
Darya Ganj, New Delhi-110002 (India)
Phone: +91-11-23279245, 43764432
Fax: +91-11-23253475
E-mail: parul.wasan@gmail.com
info@discoverypublishinggroup.com
discoverypublishinghouse@gmail.com
web: www.discoverypublishinggroup.com

***First Edition:* 2011**
**ISBN: 978-81-8356-800-5**



***Printed at:***
***Shree Balaji Art Press***
***Delhi***

*Dedicated to My*

*Beloved Parents*

*SMT. B. PADMAVATHAMMA*

*SRI B. VISWANATHA REDDY*

# FOREWORD

At present the nations across the globe are finding it difficult to solve the problem of mismatch between the moral judgment of their populace and positive human capital development. Due to the surge of print and electronic media sensationalizing the infraction of moral judgment making mountain out of anthill, industrialization, globalization, the moral judgment in every society are taking a nosedive. This trend is spreading like a virulent virus across mankind and national governments. It is also learnt that some national Governments are sponsoring terrorism resulting in loss of innocent lives. To obviate all these ills in the society the government is promoting national integration through songs, dances, dramas, youth festivals, etc. Even some of the school children are kept in schools of other States for considerable period of schooling to integrate their cultures and augment national integration.

This study assumes transcending importance since it has embarked on the attitude of intermediate students on moral judgment, who are at the transitional stage of concretizing their moral judgment which act becomes the bedrock of societal building. The objectives of the study are apt and non-pedestrian. The antecedent variables such as socio-demographic, psychological, and academic achievement are well conceived which have a bearing on moral judgment. The subjects (Intermediate students) included for probing come from variegated backgrounds (rural and urban) and colleges manned by government, aided and private managements thus nullifying danger of getting one-sided responses due to mono-cultural situations.

The findings of the study and suggestions given to inculcate moral judgment in students of different educational institutions would provide food for thought for the policy-makers and administrators if they heed and put them into practice. As the plant creeper behaves on how to occupy the gradient of a mesh or ladder provided by the Gardner, the children can be moulded on values, as they are tender enough to internalize them. As the adage - charity begins at home; imbibing moral judgment should start at home, schools and colleges concomitantly.

Finally, this book is of immense value to teachers and educational administrators who can take a cue out of it to imbibe moral judgment in student fraternity who eventually occupy the positions in legislatures, judiciary and executive echelons of governance.

**Dr. V. DAYAKARA REDDY,**
*M.A.(Eco.), M.A.(Soc.), M.Ed., Ph.D.,*
*Professor, Head and Chairman,*
*Board of Studies (Comb.),*
*Department of Education,*
*S.V. University,*
*Tirupati-517502,*
*Andhra Pradesh, INDIA.*

# PREFACE

Modern mass society presents a sharp contrast, as the young grow up. They are faced with confusions, delays and discontinuities. Adolescents in particular are uncertain about themselves. Some are in conflict with themselves, bewildered an insecure.

Moral judgment is usually influenced by the changing philosophical ideologies, cultural and religious perspectives, social, political and geographical conditions. In modern emerging society, there has been a revolutionary change in the field of values due to many factors in addition to the influence of modern culture, industrialization, modernization, urbanization, globalization and multinationals.

Moral judgment is the guiding principles, decisive in day-to-day behaviours as also is critical life situations. Values are a set bring of principles or standards of behaviour. Values are regarded desirable, important and held in high esteem by a particular society in which a person lives.

Today, there is lot of degradation of values in every walk of human life. Individuals are crazy for material wealth. Money making is the main motive of the initial stages of the child. Schools and Colleges are institutions which can shoulder the responsibility of including moral judgment among the people and students. Though there are considerable numbers of studies on moral judgment in relation with certain psycho-sociological variables at school and college level. The present study is concentrated on Intermediate students. Intermediate students are adolescents and they are the citizens of future generation. It is necessary to know what is right and wrong; which is good and bad; which is good way and bad way and how to behave with others especially with elders. Hence, there is a need to take research activities in the area of moral values.

There are so many factors influencing moral judgment, i.e. psychological factors, academic achievement and socio-demographic factors/variables. In this study different types of statistical techniques were used-critical ratio, one-way ANOVA, multiple regression and factorial analysis. The main aim of the study is to predict the multiple effects of the independent factors on attitude of Intermediate Students towards moral judgment.

The present book is aimed to identify the influence of certain psycho-sociological factors on moral judgment of Intermediate students. data were collected from 1080 Intermediate students.

Subject-matter of the book has been divided into six chapters. In the first chapter brief introduction of the topic is given. Chapter 2 deals with a brief review of related literature. Chapter 3 deals with the present study, chapter 4 gives an account of methods employed in the investigator. Chapter 5 consists of analysis of the data, results and discussions. Chapter 6 gives the summary, major findings, conclusions, educational implifications, recommendations and suggestions for further research.

This book is prepared to know the moral judgment of Intermediate students. This book is more useful not only for teachers but also parents. The present government is planning to introduce philosophy/psychology at intermediate level to develop moral judgment in the students. I do not know to what extent I have succeeded in my attempt, but I feel this book is more useful for all.

Any suggestions and criticisms will be gratefully welcomed and acknowledged.

**Dr. B. YELLA REDDY**

# ACKNOWLEDGEMENTS

Fervently and modestly, I extol the genuine co-operation, inspiration and affection offered by my Teacher and Research Supervisor **Dr. V. Dayakara Reddy,** M.A. (Eco.), M.A. (Soc.), M.Ed., Ph.D., Professor, Chairman, Board of Studies in Education (Comb), Department of Education and Principal, Institute of Advanced Studies in Education (IASE), Sri Venkateswara University, Tirupati; right from the initiation of the work to ship – shaping of manuscript. The present work bears at every stage the impression of his wise counsel and concrete suggestions, criticism and meticulous attention to details. It is indeed a rare privilege for me to work under his unending inspiration and indomitable spirit.

I express my deep sense of gratitude to **Dr. B. Ramachandra Reddy**, M.A., M.Sc., M.Ed., M.Phil., Ph.D., B.L., Dip. In Adult Education, Dip in Statistics, Professor and Head, Department of Education, Sri Venkateswara University, Tirupati; for his constant encouragement and valuable suggestion throughout the study.

I wish to express my deep sense of gratitude to **Dr. M. Syamala**, M.A. (Soc.), M.A. (Edu.), M.Phil., Ph.D., Associate Professor, Department of Education, S.V. University, Tirupati; for her constant encouragement and valuable suggestions throughout the study.

I wish to express my deep sense of gratitude to **Dr. C.D. Swarna Latha,** M.Sc., M.Ed., Ph.D., Lecturer, Sri

Padmavathi Women's Degree College, Tirupati; **Kum. V. Sushma** and **Mr. V. Sreekar** for their constant encouragement and valuable help throughout the study.

I sincerely wish to tender my heartfelt gratitude to **SRI Mannem Rami Reddy**, M.A., H.D.C., Chairman, Rami Reddy Rayalaseema Vidyasamsthalu, Tirupati; and his family members for their constant encouragement and good wishes to complete this work.

I wish to express my deep sense of appreciation to **Dr. K. Jagannadhan**, M.A., M.Ed., Ph.D., Associate Professor, Sree Rama College of Education (M.Ed.), Tirupati; **Dr. Shaik Shamshuddin**, M.A., M.Ed., Ph.D., Lecturer, DIET, Thandrapadu, Kurnool; **Dr. M.T.V. Nagaraju**, M.Sc., M.Ed., Ph.D., Assistant Professor, Dr. B.R. Ambedkar Open University, Hyderabad; **Dr. G. Ranga Swamy**, M.A., M.Ed., Ph.D., Assistant Professor, St. Paul's College of Education (M.Ed.), Giddalur; **Sri A. Ranganath**, M.Sc., M.Ed., (Ph.D.), Assistant Professor, ICFAI University, Agarthala; and **Sri K. Sekhar**, M.A., M.Ed., (Ph.D.), Principal, Sree Rama College of Education (B.Ed.), Tirupati; for giving me the source of strength and moral support throughout the course of my study.

I wish to express my deep sense of appreciation to all the Teaching Faculty, Research Scholars and Non-Teaching Staff of the Department of Education and IASE, Sri Venkateswara University, Tirupati; for giving me the source of strength and moral support throughout the course of my study.

I am thankful to the Authorities of Sri Venkateswara University, Tirupati; for providing and extending the facilities to complete my Ph.D. programme.

I wish to express my thanks to all the Teaching and Non-Teaching Staff of Rami Reddy Rayalaseema Vidyasamsthalu, Tirupati; for their co-operation throughout this investigation.

I place on record my special thanks to Principals, Staff and Students of Intermediate colleges, for unstrained help, constant encouragement and co-operation in collecting the research data.

I am highly thankful to **Sri G. Sridhar Reddy**, Proprietor, Laxmi University Xerox, Prakasam Road, Tirupati; for timely computer typing, xeroxing and binding.

I am highly indebted to my Parents, Sisters, Brothers-in-law, Sister-in-law, Daughters-in-law, Son-in-law, Uncle, Aunt and my Relatives, for their affectionate blessings without which it could not be possible for me to complete this work.

I have pleasure to express my thanks to my Colleagues, Friends and Well wishers for their co-operation in completing this investigation.

With immense pleasure, I express my profound sense of gratitude and thanks to my wife **Smt. N. Kavitha**, M.Sc., M.Ed. and my daughter **Kum. B. Neeharika**.

Finally, I am thankful to all those who have helped me in completing this investigation.

Above all, I am indebted to the **Lord Varasiddi Vinayaka** and **Lord Almighty** for whose benevolent blessings this endeavour would not have been completed.

**B. YELLA REDDY**

# CONTENTS

# LIST OF ABBREVIATIONS

| | | |
|---|---|---|
| ANOVA | : | Analysis of Variance |
| BC | : | Backward Caste |
| B.Ed | : | Bachelor of Education |
| BiPC | : | Biological sciences, Physics, Chemistry |
| BIE | : | Board of Intermediate Education |
| B.P. Ed | : | Bachelor of Physical Education |
| CEC | : | Commerce, Economics, Civics |
| D.Ed | : | Diploma in Education |
| df | : | Degrees of freedom |
| Ed | : | Editor |
| Eds | : | Editors |
| *et al* | : | And others |
| Fig | : | Figure |
| HEC | : | History, Economics, Civics |
| HSPQ | : | High School Personality Questionnaire |
| IASE | : | Institute of Advanced Studies in Education |
| Ku | : | Kurtosis |
| IQ | : | Intelligence Quotient |
| M | : | Mean |
| Md | : | Median |
| M.Ed | : | Master of Education |

| | | |
|---|---|---|
| M.P.Ed | : | Master of Physical Education |
| Mo | : | Mode |
| MPC | : | Mathematics, Physics, Chemistry |
| N | : | Number of sample subjects or Number of observations |
| NPE | : | National Policy on Education |
| OC | : | Open Category |
| Ph.D | : | Doctor of Philosophy |
| $Q_1$ | : | First Quartile |
| $Q_2$ | : | Second Quartile |
| $Q_3$ | : | Third Quartile |
| QD | : | Quartile Deviation |
| R | : | Range |
| RPM | : | Raven's Progressive Matrices test |
| SC | : | Scheduled caste |
| SD | : | Standard Deviation |
| $SE_M$ | : | Standard Error of Mean |
| SES | : | Socio-Economic Status |
| Sk | : | Skewness |
| Ss | : | Sample Subjects |
| SSC | : | Secondary School Certificate (X Class) |
| SVU | : | Sri Venkateswara University |
| SVUCEES | : | Sri Venkateswara University College of Education and Extension Studies |
| ST | : | Scheduled Tribe |
| UGC | : | University Grants Commission |
| USA | : | United States of America |
| VN | : | Variable Number |

# Chapter 1

# INTRODUCTION

*"Education is not merely a means for earning a living or an instrument for the acquisition of wealth. It is an initiation into life of spirit, a training of the human soul in the pursuit of truth and the practice of virtue."*

**—Vijaya Lakshmi Pandit**

The chief aim of education is not merely the acquisition of knowledge but also the proper utilization of knowledge for the improvement of the quality of human life. True education should be concerned with the development of right conduct. If education has to fulfil this function, it is imperative that it should promote good conduct and values through the transaction of school and college curriculum. Cultivation of moral and social values and bringing a closer relationship between education and life of the people become important.

Morality is concerned with beliefs and actions, which are in conformity with the social norms shaped, modified and chiseled over a length of time. In ancient Greece, there was an emphasis on beliefs where as in ancient India; the stress was on an action. However, action had to be in conformity with *dharma*. Thus, action itself had moral and spiritual base. Manu, the great Indian Codifier, on the strength of the *Vedas* and the *Smritis*, said that doing noble actions is the higher duty (*dharma*) of man. To be frank, it is difficult to precisely define the philosophical and abstract concept of morality. One may attempt to understand this term in the following ways:

1. The basis of morality is right belief and right action.
2. The element of free – will of the dos is fundamental to any moral act. The dos must adhere to the moral act in spite of a temptation to deviate from it.
3. Moral act extends both over physiological and psychological domains.

The study of moral development in children has long been recognized as a key problem in the field of child development and education. One reason for this sustained and continued interest is that morality and character are considered to be the part and parcel of the personality of the individual and their social significance, especially in the field of education. Moral development is a complex area of human development and an objective analysis of its nature and processes is crucial to moral education.

There has been a dramatic growth of interest in the area of moral growth and development of children and youth in the past two decades. This trend is mainly evident from the research reports on various aspects of moral development and moral education and also the schools interest in meeting the moral and ethical needs of students through several activities. The assumption that moral education is not simply giving information on moral principles, but also the formation of moral attitudes and moral values and their associated factors in children and youth.

The problem of inculcating ability among children to judge morality is infested with many problems. Moral judgment is the result of a complex and interactive process of many psychological, social, cognitive and emotional factors. It is a by-product of many other learning conditions. It is made up of self-control, awareness of self, and skill and insight reaction of authority of parents and of cultural mores.

Although moral development and judgment in children and adolescents have been mainly studied from the perspective of cognitive development, the influence of socializing agents on the development of moral judgment has become an undisputed fact. How children acquire a sense of right and wrong from their interaction with socializing agents, particularly family, parents and peers has been studied extensively by developmental and social psychologists. Studies on social influences on moral development and judgment are numerous and extremely heterogeneous in the measures of moral judgment used and the variables studied. Indeed different foci and methodology have been followed resulting in contradictory perspectives on the extent of influences of these socializing agents on moral judgment.

Behavioural scientists have often remarked that adolescence is a stormy period characterized by cross pressures, conflicts between the practices advocated in the family and those endorsed by peers. How do children react to these conflicting situation depends much upon the characteristics of socializing agents, cultural sanctions, personality factors and situational determinants. The changes that occur in moral judgment during late childhood, pre-adolescence and adolescence reflect gains in both cognitive maturity and characteristics of social development.

As the social horizons broaden in adolescence, the individual is faced with inconsistencies in moral values in much the same manner as he is faced with inconsistencies in religious values. No longer do the moral values learned in the narrow environment of his childhood days apply to all the new social groups in the school, neighborhood, and community with which he affiliates himself. He discovers variations according to socio-economic status, sex, national origin and many other factors. This, combined with the greater sensitivity to inconsistency that results from his higher value of intelligence, causes confusion, which not only complicates the learning of moral values appropriate for his level of development but which also has a marked influence on his behaviour.

The adolescent of today is faced with more moral alternatives than members of the older generations ever had to face. This is due to many causes, the most important of which are:

(a) Movement in modern society, which results in he adolescent's leaving the neighborhood and family group early in life;

(b) Rapid change in all phases of life, which has resulted in the breakdown of well - established moral standards, with the result that parents lack positive ness in their teaching of moral percepts or they neglect it entirely; and

(c) Adolescent codes holding way in many of the youth groups, with little chaperonage by adult codes (Landis, 1952). When the moral values of the adolescent's peer group differ markedly from those of his parents, the parents refuse to accept these new moral values, with the result that there is constant friction between the adolescent and his parents (Kuhlen, 1952).

In meeting the problem of conflicting moral values, the adolescent must first know what values to accept and then have sufficient experience in meeting such conflicts, so that he will be able to do so when he is independent of adult guidance and help. The role of parents and teachers is very crucial at this stage of moral development of adolescents. They must therefore, pay special attention during this period.

Moral reasoning in children and youth is a complex, multidimensional process whose development is differentially influenced by socio-cultural environment. It involves not only human intellect, but also appetite and desires, feelings and stunning emotion and will. Moral judgment involves the entire person, when elicited from genuine, often deeply held attitudes and powerful motivation.

## MEANING OF MORALITY

The word 'moral' comes from the Latin word 'Mores' which means custom, practice, a way of accomplishing things.

Therefore, it has come to mean "Belonging to manners and conduct of men" or "Pertaining to right and wrong and well conduct".

According to *Webster's Dictionary* (1972) of Synonyms, "moral, ethical, virtuous, righteous, noble are synonyms only when they mean conforming to a standard of what is right and good. In all its pertinent sense moral implies a relationship to character and conduct viewed as good or bad, right or wrong."

According to *Oxford Talking Dictionary*, morality is noun with the meaning of:

1. The morality of abortion ethics rights and wrongs.
2. A man/woman of morality ethics, goodness, virtue, righteousness, rectitude, uprightness, integrity, principles, honour, honesty, justness, decency, chasteness, chastity, purity, blamelessness.
3. Discuss morality morals, moral code, moral standards, ethics, principles of right and wrong and standards/ principles of behaviour.

According to *Webster's Online Dictionary*,

"Morality is a complex of concepts and beliefs by which an individual determines whether his or her actions are right or wrong. Oftentimes, these concepts and beliefs are generalized and codified in a culture or group, and thus serve to regulate the behaviour of its members."

*Chamber's 20th Century Dictionary* describes morality as

"That in action which renders it right or wrong, the doctrine treats actions as being right or wrong."

In the popular sense, morality, which consists of certain dos and don'ts, depends on the existence of a large area of agreement in respect of moral principles or rules in conformity with customs or usual popular standards of morality. Good and bad are terms of evaluation, by which we assess the worthiness or unworthiness of an action and we clearly see the right action from the wrong and one, which we should or should not do.

Westermark (1912) explained the nature of moral values in terms of pleasant and unpleasant emotions.

According to Earnest Hemingway (1955) the test list in the effect of an action on one's feelings, he lies down that "What is moral is what you feel good after and what is immoral is what you feel bad after."

In the *Encyclopaedia of Social Sciences*, Kaileen (1968) explains,

> "Until rather recent times morals were not distinguished from manners. Together with a ceremonial they were techniques of behaviour believed to be efficacious in securing good and averting evils . . . they were called not morals but morality and were ascribed to universal principles of right conduct endemic to mankind. Right in the differential of the moral of a term of selection, it designates group approval as against group disapproval and implies instrumentalities to enforce the approved and to punish the disapproved."

The term 'Moral' are used in three main senses:

1. It may be used to refer to 'resistance to temptation', or the inhibiting of behaviour, which is regarded as 'wrong' through perhaps pleasurable or profitable. In the sense, an immoral person is one who does not inhibit such impulses but pursues the immediate satisfaction of his desires. However, one may refrain from socially disapproved actions because one is afraid of the consequences. In this case, whether an action is regarded as moral will depend entirely on the social definition of the behaviour as 'good' or 'bad'.

2. It may refer to the control of behaviour by reference to 'internalized' standards rather than by reference to the possible consequences of the behaviour for the actor. In the sense, one must have regard for the motives and

intentions of the actor; actions carried out or not carried out because of fear of consequences are not moral – actions carried out or not carried out because of prescriptions or prohibitions accepted as compelling, are. However, insofar as these prescriptions are prescriptions have been internalized, they represent the acceptance of external authority. They are accepted as 'naturally' right without any genuine understanding of reasons for their acceptance.

3. It may indicate behaviour, which is carried out by reference to rules, or principles, which are rationally accepted in the sense that reasons for accepting them are understood and felt to be legitimate. Immoral behaviour in this sense is behaviour, which is carried out in the pursuance of ends, in spite of the fact that the behaviour or the ends conflict with the requirements of such rules or principles. In the sense, moral behaviour is behaviour consequent upon a moral decision, which itself entails a moral judgment as to what is the right thing to do. The main basis of such judgment is the golden rule that one should take full account of the rights of other people, and apply to one's own behaviour the rules of right and wrong which one holds to be applicable to other's behaviour. To be immoral is to fail in this sense to take full account of the rights of others, or to claim special privileges for oneself, which one does not allow to others. Something like this last use of the term 'moral' indeed is frequently regarded as the only proper use. It implies that, to be capable of a high level of morality, one must have sufficient intellectual capacity to understand the nature of moral rules or principles, and the capacity to analyze problems and dilemmas in terms of these rules or principles, and decide how they should properly be applied.

It is however, arguable that 'morality' in the first two senses may be a prerequisite for the development of the capacity for both moral judgment and moral behaviour in the third sense.

Following the three-fold division made by Aristotle, who may be viewed human conduct as having three aspects or dimensions-the cognitive, the affective and the behavioural. The cognitive aspect refers to such processes as perceiving, judging, knowing and thinking. In the moral sphere, this includes such things as knowledge of moral rules, understanding of the nature and the 'why' or moral rules, and moral judgment, i.e., the capacity for deciding, in terms of general principles, whether a given action or course of action is good or bad, and for deciding which of alternative courses of action are most defensible in moral terms. It also includes the capacity for self-criticism by reference to principles, as distinct from feelings of remorse or guilt. The affective aspect refers to the kind of feeling which in relation to actions that is considered right or wrong in particular, to feelings such as anticipatory anxiety, guilt, remorse and shame, which are experienced in relation to the temptations and transgressions. It also includes the positive feelings of satisfaction, which is experienced when, for example, the feelings of human sympathy, which is induced to respond to others in need, even at a cost of one's own self-interest. It may further be extended to include feelings of moral indignation, which may be experienced, when one believes that some kind of injustice appears to be flourishing. The behavioural aspect refers, as the term indicates, to overt behaviour - resistance to temptation, taking steps to put up right, if one can, the wrongs to others which have resulted from one's transgressions, confessing one's guilt and on the positive side, not merely the avoidance of what is considered to be wrong, but the performance of those actions which is believed to be right, for example helping others. In so far as it is believed that the 'conscience' forms a single more or less organized and self-consistent system, and that it makes sense to talk of a general 'moral character', that should expect to find a fair degree of consistency both within each area and between areas. Those with the highest level of moral judgment, for example, should, in general, also be those who act in the most moral way.

Morality thus consists of universal principles of conduct, which teach the distinction between good and evil, between proper and improper actions and it is a doctrine or right or wrong.

Morality involves consistency, regularity of conduct: what is moral today must be moral tomorrow. It also invariably involves some sense of authority: constrained to act in certain ways; a resistance to strictly idiosyncratic impulses (Durkheim, 1961).

In the popular sense, morality which consist of certain do's and don'ts depends on the existence of a large area of agreement in respect of moral principles or rules in conformity with customs or usual popular standards of morality.

Good and bad are terms of evaluation, by which the worthiness or unworthiness of an action is assessed and one can clearly see the right actions from the wrong and one that should or should not be.

Often acts, which arouse feelings of pleasure, are described as moral, while those which produce feelings of remorse and repentance are considered immoral (Westermark, 1912).

According to Earnest Hemingway (1955), "What is moral is what one feels well after and what is immoral is what one feels that is bad after."

## MORAL DEVELOPMENT

Moral science gives ample justification for concern, and for the growing interest in moral education in schools. Such education bristles with difficulties. It must clearly be educationally sound, broad based and rooted in reason, not in any form of authoritarianism. Above all it must be closely geared to the moral development of the child. It must therefore be based upon solid, empirical evidence of the stages through which the child passes in his moral growth, and of the key factors that influence and shape it. The fact is however that the moral field is one of the most neglected areas in the study of child development.

A more serious difficulty is that of securing evidence of moral development. There are two broad approaches that might be used, the theoretical and the practical. The more theoretical approach seeks the child's judgment upon hypothetical, realistic, moral situations. It is open to the obvious criticism that a child's cognitive judgment upon theoretical situations may bear little or no relation to his actual conduct. The practical approach observes the child's actual behaviour in concrete fabricated moral situations.

## THEORIES OF MORAL DEVELOPMENT

If the task of moral education is to help children to develop appropriate skills and judgment capacity to cope with variety of moral choices they have to face in their life, it goes without saying that every one concerned with moral education must play a significant role in understanding how children develop morally. To plan any kind of moral education, whether formally or informally requires a proper insight into the child's level of moral development.

Attempts have been made by developmental psychologists over the past few decades to explore the nature and content of moral development in children and adolescents. As a result of continuous research the issue of moral development and judgment has received a new impetus in the field of developmental psychology. Many research studies have been generated covering a wide variety of issues and concepts on the moral development and judgment.

Moral development is a comprehensive process whereby individuals learn to consciously adopt the norms of moral conduct and behaviour. The true end of this development is to make the individual morally autonomous, leading to a state where the individual is able to act in accordance with universal moral principles, which he accepts in relation to the larger society. Kohlberg considered conscience or morality to be a set of cultural rules of social action, which have been internalized by the individual. Moral development has been conceived as increase in such internalization by basic cultural rules. The process of internalization of moral values involves three essential components:

(1) The behaviour component,

(2) The emotional and learning component and

(3) Judgmental component.

The behavioural criterion may be used to refer to resistance to temptation or the inhibiting of behaviour, which is regarded as wrong through perhaps pleasurable or profitable. The emotional aspect of internalization refers to emotion of guilt. The individual behaves morally to avoid guilt. The third component is the ability to make moral judgments in terms of standards and justify maintaining the standards to one and others. The main basis of such judgment is the golden rule that one should take full account of the rights of other people. These three components have been the basis for most of the research studies in the field of moral development.

Moral development is itself an omnibus term containing a number of related ideas. There is interplay between the quantitative and qualitative elements which makes it difficult to analyze this development with complete certainty but in general one may trace a frame work of moral growth through a series of sequential, qualitatively different stages and also along a line of growth marked by quantitatively increasing stability and complexity.

A comprehensive analysis of moral development from the content and principles of growth and development point of view may be considered, firstly as a sequential process which passes through different stages and that the behaviour pattern of each stage could be clearly described. Secondly moral development can be better understood in terms of social and cultural sanctions, which govern moral behaviour. This is an elaborative process and involves a study of the strength of motives underlying moral behaviour at different stages of growth and development. Thirdly, moral development is viewed as a process of analyzing the reasons for moral actions and fourthly moral development is viewed as an integral part of psychosocial development.

Moral development is an integral part of the personality development. But moral development is mainly studied from the viewpoints of cognitive and social development. The cognitive aspect mainly refers to such process as perceiving, judging, knowing and thinking. When applied to moral behaviour, these cognitive components together constitute the moral judgment of a person. Moral judgment is the decision making process, the capacity for deciding, in terms of general moral principle whether a given action is good or bad, and for deciding the alternative course of action morally acceptable.

Psychologists concerning the nature and process of moral development have expressed several views:

1. The simple view that moral development, like intellectual development, passes through different stages of development and the behaviour characteristic of each stage of moral development can clearly be described.
2. Moral development can also be studied in terms of sanctions of the cultural, which govern moral behaviour of the individual. The approach requires a study of the varying motives for moral development and action at different stages of development.
3. The study of moral development as a result of moral judgment. Moral judgment action is basically a part of intellectual development.

Moral development is also studied as part and parcel of personality development. The moral behaviour and judgment is viewed as a function of psychosocial development of the individual. Thus it is evident that morality is partly intellectual, partly social, shaped and directed by environmental considerations.

Based on the analysis of the relationship between morality and the individual, three basic components of morality have been suggested, an affective or emotional component a cognitive or intellectual component and a behavioural component. And this analysis has resulted in the formulation of three important theories concerning the nature of moral development and judgment:

(a) Psychoanalytic theory emphasizing the affective or the emotional aspects of moral development,

(b) Cognitive developmental theory emphasizing the intellectual or cognitive component of moral judgment and its development,

(c) The social learning theory, helps us to understand how children are able to resist temptation and inhibit the behaviour that violates the established moral standards.

A further analysis of the major issues on moral development provides us with the necessary generalizations, methodological consideration consists the relationship between social, emotional and intellectual aspects involved in the process of moral development adjustment and its implications to the role of parents and teachers.

The study of moral development takes different forms depending upon the area selected for the investigation. Indeed, different methods of investigations based on various theories of moral development have yielded often-contradictory perspectives on the origin of moral.

Many theories of moral development have contributed to an understanding of the child's cognitive development. An examination of the three main psychological approaches of moral development-the psychoanalytic view point, the learning theory approach and the cognitive development view-will offer insight into different aspects of a child's moral growth.

The psychoanalytical approach as manifested by Freud's work sees morality as conforming to cultural standards through a process of internalization. The acquisition of morality was for Freud, the development within the child's personality of the super-ego, the agency which issues moral imperatives derived from standards of adults close to him which the child has internalized. Like the conscience, super-ego represents the voice of parents and thus of society, giving some guidance on moral conduct (Freud, 1914).

Learning theories, as reflected in the work of Sears (1957), Bandura (1963), Eysenck (1960), assume that moral behaviour is the results of reinforcement, rewards or punishments and modeling or imitating an admired adult. Eysenck (1960, 1964) suggested that the learning of moral values is based on the formation of a conscience in terms of conditional responses. Bandura and Walters (1963) says that moral values are learnt by imitation or modeling, Cross-cultural studies (Nash, 1958; Bronfenbrenner, 1976) substantiate the fact that children not only learn from what they are told to do but also from what they see the adults doing.

Cognitive-development theorists on the other hand (Piaget, 1932; Kohlberg, 1964) view moral development as an active, dynamic constructive process leading to a state where the individual is able to act according to moral principles which he either accepts because he understands them and agrees with them or which he has worked out for himself.

## Piaget's Theory on Stages of Moral Development (1932)

Piaget from his extensive interviews and observations of children concluded that their conception of morality shifted at about seven years of age from a rather primitive view dominated by obedience and unilateral respect for adults to a more mature one characterized by cooperation and mutual trust.

Piaget's (1932) development theory, the child first moves a moral a stage to Durkheim's stage of respect for sacred rules. Piaget believes that intellectual growth and experiences of role taking in the peer group naturally transform perceptions of rules from external authoritarian commands to internal principles. In essence he views internal moral norms as logical principles of justice. Justice means a concern for reciprocity and equality between individuals.

Piaget evolved a system of two broad stages of moral development, which encompass both the respect for rules, and sense of justice. The earlier stage referred to variously as moral realism, morality of constraint or heteronymous morality. Heteronymous morality develops from four years to about eight years. The term 'heteronymous' means, "subject to another's law", i.e., subject to the law of adult authority. In the heteronymous stage the child judges the rightness or wrongness of an act on the basis of the magnitude of its consequences, the extent to which it conforms exactly to established rules, and whether or not elicits punishment.

The child in the more advanced stages was called autonomous morality. It develops after eight years. The word autonomous means subject to one's own law. The autonomous child was more apt to revolve around conforming to peer expectations and considering their welfare, expressing gratitude for past affection and favours and, above all, putting one self in the place of others. From Piaget (1928), the progression from the child continuing effort to comprehend one system of his total moral experience. Moral development springs largely from the general development of the child's conception of the world.

## Kohlberg's Theory on Stages of Moral Development (1958)

Kohlberg (1958) delineated six qualitatively different modes or stages of thinking about morality that extend beyond childhood, through adolescence and well into adulthood. They are:

1. Punishment obedience orientation
2. Instrumental relativist orientation
3. Good boy, good girl orientation
4. Law and order orientation
5. Social contractual orientation
6. Universal ethical principle orientation

Both Piaget and Kohlberg view their stages as forming an invariant sequence, which an individual must pass through each preceding stage in the sequence in order to progress to the next stage.

Varying stages of moral judgment in the child and varying levels of judgment in the adult both reflect differences in the shaping of moral concepts. Their complexity as well as their variety, suggest the different influences at work. These vary from one individual to another, and these variable factors must be taken into account while seeking to trace the development. They key variables are relationships at home, the pattern of discipline in the home, the school environment, religious influence, intelligence and last but not the least significant, sex. All such factors are involved in the moral development. No part of it can opt out of moral responsibility. Thus, it could be seen that moral judgment is a blanket term covering a number of related factors.

The concept of stages implies the following characteristics:

1. The stages are organized systems of thought and people are consistent in their level of moral judgment.
2. The stages form an unchanging sequence. A person always moves forward, and while one can never skip stages, one may fixate at one stage level.
3. A particular stage is seen as being integrated into the next stage and finally replaced by it.

Many attempts have been made to study the types and stages of moral development by various developmental psychologists. A brief study of some of the types and stages provides the data necessary for proper understanding of the nature and factors of development of moral judgment in children and adolescents.

Both empirically derived and theoretically derived types of moral character have been evolved. The most popular study on types of character has been the one carried out by Havighurst and Taba (1949), character according to this study is a word with many meanings. Character is that part of personality of the individual which is most subject to social approval. Character develops as a results of three forces, rewards and punishments, unconscious imitation and reflective thinking. They postulated two levels of character, social expectation and the second control the first by moral ideals. Character is an amalgam of moral traits. They suggested four character types:

(a) The deviant person - openly hostile to society, unable to cooperate with other people in the pursuit of any social end,

(b) The submissive type - is one who will not initiate action, relies mainly on authority and tends to have strong moral standards, a well developed sense of duty and obligation,

(c) The adoptive type is sociable, friendly with pleasant manners, adaptable to social situations, conforms to social norms and

(d) The self-directive type - conscious orderly, and persistent. He sets high standards for himself and is seldom satisfied with his performance.

## Bronfenbrenner's Theory on Stages of Moral Development (1962)

In contrast to Kohlberg's stage approach, Bronfenbrenner's analysis in 1962(a) described five types of moral judgment:

1. **Self-oriented:** In which the individual is motivated primarily by impulses of self-gratification without regard for the desires or expectations of others, except as objects of manipulation.

2. **Authority-oriented:** In which the individual accepts parental structures and values as immutable and generalizes this orientation to include moral standards imposed by other adult authority figures.

3. **Pre-oriented:** In which the individual is an adaptive conformist who goes along the peer group which is largely antonymous of adult authority and ultimately of all social authority and in which behaviour is guided by momentary shifts in group opinion and interest.

4. **Collective-oriented:** in which the individual is committed to a set of enduring group goals, which take precedence over individual desires, obligations, etc.

5. **Objectively-oriented:** In which the individual's values are functionally autonomous but are no longer dependent, on a day-to-day basis.

## Kohlberg's Extension of Piaget's Theory on Stages of Moral Development (1963)

Kohlberg (1963) has criticized much of the substance of Piaget's theory and development. In developing his stages, Kohlberg's aim was to retain the best of Piaget's scheme and fit it into a more refined, comprehensive and logically consistent framework. His final system consists of six development stages. The six stages are ordered into three levels of moral orientation.

| | | |
|---|---|---|
| **Level 1** | **:** | **Pre-Moral** |
| Stage 1 | : | Punishment and obedience orientation |
| Stage 2 | : | Native instrumental hedonism |
| **Level 2** | **:** | **Morality of conventional role conformity** |
| Stage 3 | : | Good boy morality of maintaining good relations, approval by others. |
| Stage 4 | : | Authority maintaining morality. |
| **Level 3** | **:** | **Morality - of self-accepted moral principles** |
| Stage 5 | : | Morality of contract, of individual rights, and of democratically accepted law. |
| Stage 6 | : | Morality of individual principle and of conscience. |

It is evident that this aspect of moral development represents successive degrees of internalization of moral sanctions. Other aspects of moral development involve successive cognitive reorganization of the meaning of culturally universal values. As an example, in every society human life is a basic value, even though cultures differ in their definition of the universality of this value or of the conditions under which it may be sacrificed for some other values. With regard to the value of life, the six stages are defined as follows:

| | |
|---|---|
| Stage 1: | The value of a human life is confused with the value of physical objects and is based on the social status of physical attributes of its possessor. |

| | |
|---|---|
| Stage 2: | The value of a human life is seen as instrumental to the satisfaction of the needs of its possessor or of other persons. |
| Stage 3: | The value of a human life is based on the sympathy and affection of family members and others towards its possessor. |
| Stage 4: | Life is conceived as sacred in terms of its place in a categorical moral or religious order of rights and duties. |
| Stage 5: | Life is valued both in its relation to community welfare and as a universal human right. |
| Stage 6: | Life is valued as sacred and as representing a universal human value of respect for the individual. |

It is evident that these stages represent a progressive disentangling or differentiation of moral values and judgments from other types of values and judgment.

In this sense we can define a moral judgment as 'moral' without considering its content (the action judged) and without considering whether it agrees or not with our own judgments or standards.

**Kay's Theory on Stages of Moral Development (1968)**

Based on the sanctions of the society, Kay (1968) suggested five stages in moral development based on 'dominant sanctions'.

1. At the first stage child is controlled simply by the necessity of complying with externally imposed restrains.
2. At the second stage control is though interjected irrational values, which seems to mean the unquestioned obedience to restriction and demands imposed by authority.
3. Third stage is the stage of control by group opinion.

4. There is then a stage when control is thought an ego ideal or ideal self-image.
5. Finally, 'reasonable, personal moral principles control the individual's behaviour'.

Kay (1968) suggested that these five stages could be reduced to three, which will almost correspond to Kohlberg's three levels, pre-moral, conventional and post-conventional.

**Kohlberg's Theory on Stages of Moral Development (1969)**

Lawrence Kohlberg's (1969) Theory of Moral Development is one of the most widely used approaches to the examinations of moral reasoning. This stage theory is based on various responses to scenarios, which involved a moral dilemma. Kohlberg recognized three levels of moral development, which encompassed six stages.

A brief description of the levels and stages are as follows:

**Level 1, The Pre-Conventional Level**

Children at this level respond to moral cues from their social reference group, most commonly parents. At this level children are extremely self - involved and moral behaviour is only in response to sanctions and reward based on behaviour.

*Stage 1, Obedience and Punishment Orientation*

Avoidance of punishments and unquestioning deference to power are valued in their own right.

*Stage 2, Obedience Relativism Orientation*

That which instrumentally satisfied one's own needs and occasionally the needs of others is considered right.

**Level 2, The Conventional Level**

Moral reasoning is now based on existing social norms as well as the rights of others. Kohlberg asserts that most adolescents and some adults operate at this level of reasoning.

*Stage 3, Interpersonal Concordance Orientation*

This stage indicates that the individual has developed the ability to empathize and is no longer selfish in their moral reasoning.

*Stage 4, Law and Order Orientation*

At this stage moral activity becomes a function of following rules and has no association with the need for personal approval.

*Stage 4A, Anti-Establishment Orientation*

This stage involves rejection of conventional morality by late adolescents.

**Level 3, The Post-Conventional Level**

This is the most advanced level of moral reasoning which relies on universal principles in approaching moral problems.

*Stage 5A, Social Contract Legalistic Orientation*

This stage identifies right action as that which is defined in terms of general individual rights and in terms of standards which have been critically examined and agreed upon by the society.

*Stage 5B, Morality of Intuitive Humanism Orientation*

At this stage obligations stem from "certain ideals".

*Stage 6, Universal Ethical Principles Orientation*

This stage is rarely reached. The orientation relies on principles that are self-generated and universally applicable.

According to Kohlberg (1969) Education plays a major role in moral development. His strongest statement to this effect is that moral reasoning stops at the same point that formal education stops. Although this assertion has stimulated much needed discussion above moral education, there ahs been a great deal of resistance.

## Bull, Norman's Theory on Stages of Moral Development (1969)

Bull, Norman (1969) based on McDougall's (1960) and Kay's (1968) theory defined moral development in terms dominant sanctions.

1. The stage of anomie or pre-morality where the individual's moral sanctions are guided not by rules and standards, rather by the principles of pleasure and pain. This stage is also known as 'animal stage'.
2. The stage of heteronomy or external morality, in which others impose rules, especially parents, teachers, police and religious heads. Rewards and punishments are associated with rules. This stage is also known as externally imposed discipline stage.
3. The stage of sociology, in which there is increased sensitivity to opinion of others. This stage is also known as 'external - internal morality', in which the main sanctions essentially the social sanctions of public praise and blame.
4. The stage of autonomy or internal morality, morality guided by one's own standards. The contribution of Bull is highly significant especially in describing the three essential characteristics of the stage of autonomy: (a) Freedom from restrictive emotional ties to one's family. (b) Freedom to criticize the conventions and the values of others. (c) Freedom to apply one's own standards or principle in action. In addition to the four stages, Bull suggested intermediate levels in the assessment of children's moral judgment.

## Damon's Theory on Stages of Moral Development (1971)

Kohlberg's research primarily concentrates on late childhood, adolescence, and adulthood. The validity of Kohlbergian theory for children younger than ten years of age was questioned by Damon who redefined Kohlberg's pre-moral and pre-conventional levels of moral reasoning. Damon (1971) considered positive justice specifically, the justice of distribution, determining who in society should get what share of the available resources to be the code structure of moral cognition in young children. Damon used this concept to provide a more detailed structural analysis of the young child's moral reasoning than did earlier versions posited by Kohlberg.

Damon (1973) analyses that moral reasoning for children between the age of four and then may be categorized in to three major stages 0, 1, and 2, each of which may be divided into two sub stages 'A' and 'B', each of Damon's major stages roughly parallels Kohlberg's sub-stages, having the same numerical designation.

The developmental progression described by Damon's (1974) series of sub stages revolves around four related aspects of the child's reasoning in the area of positive justice. These aspects are:

(a) The type of justice conflict recognized by the child,

(b) The means that the child constructs to resolve these conflicts,

(c) The persons considered to be significant in determining a 'fair' resolution of the conflict, and (d) The nature of the justification that the child used to support his position.

The six sub-stages of moral reasoning for children between the ages of four and ten presented by Damon are:

1. Sub stage 0 - A,
2. Sub stage 0 - B,
3. Sub stage 1 - A,
4. Sub stage 1 - B,
5. Sub stage 2 - A,
6. Sub stage 2 – B.

## Gilligan's Theory on Stages of Moral Development (1977)

According to Kohlberg (1969), more males than females move beyond stage 4 of their moral development. There appeared to be deficiencies in females' ability to reason morally. This deficiency was accepted and confirmed by other theorists until Carol Gilligan of Harvard University supplied an alternative explanation. Gilligan demonstrated through several studies that males and females approach moral issues from completely different perspectives. The most significant difference in the females' approach was the inclination to emphasize interpersonal relationships (Gilligan, 1977). Females tend to base their moral actions on responsibility towards specific others more than on abstract principles. Gilligan described the stages of female moral development in terms of levels and transitions.

### Level 1: Orientation toward self-interest

The First Transition: from selfishness to responsibility

### Level 2: Identification of goodness with responsibility for others

The Second Transition: from conformity to a new inner judgment

### Level 3: Focusing on the dynamics between self and others

This stage theory suggests that we seriously consider gender differences when evaluating moral reasoning, judgment, and actions.

The implications of Gilligan's research go beyond the domain of psychology to reach into any field that theorizes about people as an intelligent and respectful effort to provide an empirical basis for differences that are discovered between genders. In an educational context this would suggest that different types of behaviour should be expected from boys and girls. There is also the implication that moral education interventions should be tailored to the appropriate gender.

## MORAL JUDGMENT

Moral education as the stimulation of natural development is widely accepted in the area of Moral judgment, where there appears to be considerable regularity of developmental sequences and directions in various cultures. Because of this regularity, it is possible to define the maturity of a child's moral judgment without considering whether it agrees with the teacher's own particular moral judgment or values.

According to Piaget, the development of moral judgment is a direct consequence of cognitive development: the moral cannot be understood or explained without a complete comprehension of the cognitive.

Play is the best laboratory where a child's judgment and behaviour can be explored in relation to rules. Two aspects can be studied: the practice of rules and awareness of them. In relation to practice, it is observed how children apply and adapt rules in terms of age and cognitive development. In relation to conscience, emphasis is placed on observing how they represent the obligatory character of the rules and what level of awareness they have concerning their obligation to follow them.

After several years of longitudinal and cross-sectional studies, Piaget concluded that children pass through two stages:

1. Rules are imposed from the outside, and are considered to be sacred.
2. Later, a process of internalization, mutual consent and autonomous conscience occur.

Each stage leads to a certain type of behaviour. In the first stage, any of these two behaviors can take place: rebellion or obedience. In the second, cooperation is a conviction of individual and social utility.

Mifsud (1985) proposes three behavioural laws, motor, egocentric and cooperative which coincide with three types of rules:

(a) The motor rule (preverbal) is independent from all social relation and is governed by reflex schemes and circularity of movements;

(b) The rule due to one-sided respect restrictive; and finally

(c) The rational rule is governed by mutual respect and reciprocity.

Each of the steps in the development of moral judgment represents a step towards a more genuinely or distinctly moral judgment. That is not to say that a more moral judgment is more moral in the sense of showing closer conformity to the conventional standards of a given community. Philosophers do not agree with the principles of the good that would define correct moral judgments. According to Hare (1952), Frankena (1962), moral judgments are judgments about the good and right of action. Not all judgments of good or right are moral judgments. However, many are judgments of aesthetic, prudential, technological goodness or rightness.

Hare (1952) argues that the value judgments of low stage subjects about moral issues are not genuine moral judgments. The genuinely moral judgment of the high stage subject is a judgment of principle, and to become a morally conscious adult is to learn to make decisions of principle it is to learn to use 'ought' sentences verified by reference to a standard or set of principles which one has accepted by his own decision and made his own.

The developmental conception of moral education does not imply the imposition of a fixed system of values by teachers. It does demand that the educator achieves some clarity in his understanding of the nature of moral development and of the appropriate methods of moral communication with children at given developmental levels. Developmental findings on moral stages, moral philosophic conceptions of principles, and the tenets of constitutional democracy cohere to define a philosophically and psychologically viable conception of moral education. This conception though outlined in 1959 by John Dewey, has only recently gained the research support needed to make it truly convincing.

## DETERMINANTS OF MORAL JUDGMENT

While the findings stressed so far suggest the determination of moral action by non-moral situational and personality forces, there are also some findings suggesting the determination of action by specifically moral values. Subjects which say that cheating is very bad or that they would never cheat are as likely to cheat in an experimental situation as are subjects which express a qualified view as to the badness of cheating (Kohlberg, 1966), the same willingness deceives in order to make a good appearance which implies cheating also impels the child to make pious moral statements about cheating.

The basic social science problem of moral development is not that of accounting for individual differences in moral character as revealed in behaviour. Moral behaviour that involves conformity to social rule is on the whole, to be explained as the result of the same situational forces, ego variables and socialization factors that determine behaviour, which has no direct moral relevance. A more distinctive focus of analysis centers instead upon the direct study of the development of moral values, judgments and emotions. The study of actual conduct becomes relevant to problems of moral development in so far as research is able to find links between the child's conduct and the development of his moral values and emotions. The major questions are: what is the origin of distinctively moral concepts and emotions in the child? To what extent does the child's development indicate typical or regular trends of change in these concepts and statements? What causes or stimulates these developmental changes in moral concepts and sentiments? To what extent are these developmental changes in moral concepts and attitudes reflected in developmental changes in the child's moral action under condition of conflict or temptation.

Hobhouse (1906) points out that psychological as well as sociological thought has assumed that the problem of the origin of moral values was a culture problem. It has been assumed that morality was a system of rules and values defined by the culture and that the individual child acquires these ready made values by general cultural transmission mechanism such as reinforcement learning or identification.

Durkheim (1953) observes the following four phenomena:

(1) Morality is basically a matter of respect for fixed rules,

(2) Morality seems universally to be associated with punitive sentiments, sentiments incompatible with the notion that the right was a matter of human welfare consequences,

(3) Nature of rules arousing moral respect, punitive ness and the sense of duty,

(4) Modern western societies divorce morality from religion and the basic moral rules and attitudes in many groups are those concerning relations to God, not men.

In respect of general developmental approach to moral psychology, Baldwin (1906), Mead (1934), Mc Dougall (1908), Hobhouse (1906), Piaget (1932), Kohlberg (1966), have attempted to mediate between the extreme positions represented by the futilitarians and by Durkheim (1953). Moral judgment and emotion based on respect for custom, authority, and the group are seen as one phase or stage in the moral development of the individual rather than as the total definition of the essential characteristic of morality. Judgment of right and wrong in terms of the individual's consideration of social welfare consequences, universal principles, and justice was shown as a later phase of development. This phase depends upon and integrates many of the emotional features of the earlier customary phase and does not spring directly from the minds of unsocial zed rational adults, as it did for the futilitarians. Both a morality of respect for social authority and an autonomous rational morality are to be understood as arising from the development of a self through the process of taking the roles or attitudes of other selves in interactions occurring in institutionalized patterns.

Moral development was studied in three separate stages. These approaches are derived from social, developmental and clinical psychology.

### Religion and Moral Judgment

History of mankind reveals that religion has been the chief agent in promoting morality. Among all human races, from the primitive times to the modern age, religion has striven to point the way and strengthen the impulse to moral conduct. Religion was, thus the main spring of moral values.

In the early stages, people in the society were not discriminating about moral principles. The religious teachers and prophets seemed to have confined themselves to laying down commands to do or not to do certain specified acts only, without going into the final moral principles and distinctions.

### Personality and Moral Judgment

There are so many definitions of personality as it covers a varied and complex domain. As Allport (1937) listed there exists some 50 meanings of the term personality and no doubt even this list is not all-inclusive. In his words, "Personality is a dynamic organization with in the individual of those psycho-physical systems that determine his unique adjustment to his environment".

According to Gage (1983), the term personality derived from the Latin word 'Personal'. One meaning of personality is the appearance (even false appearance) of the individual as socially perceived. As used in 'dramatic personal', personality has another meaning, that is, the role or function of an individual as in a group. In this sense the personality of the teacher may be defined narrowly by what he does as a teacher. In a third and broader sense, personality means the person as a psychological or unique whole and refers to the dynamic organization of motives with in the individual.

While consolidating the definitions of personality Gage (1983) wrote that the definitions of personality were often contradictory and observations based on one definition will contradict observations based on another definition. He classified the more common definitions under three main categories:

1. Behavioural definitions treating personality as the totality of a person's usual behaviour,
2. Social stimulus definitions treating personality as the response made by others to the individual as the stimulus, and
3. Depth definitions treating personality as the dynamic organization with in the individual that determined his unique behaviour.

Guilford (1964) says that an individual's personality is "An integrated pattern of traits". Kaul (1974) defined personality, as it is now generally meant, that "It is an organization and integration of a large number of human habits". Crowne's (1979) definition of personality is a brief. "Personality is the organised system of potentialities for behaviour". According to Cattell (1950), "Personality is that which permits a prediction of what a person will do in a given situation". His theory is based on personality sphere concept (Cattel, 1946, 1965) a design to ensure initial item coverage for all the behaviour that commonly enters rating and the dictionary of a personality. It focuses heavily on source traits.

## Intelligence and Moral Judgment

On one issue there is a little theoretical dispute. Intelligence relates strongly to moral judgment and behaviour as it does to a great many other dimensions of human functioning. The disagreement about the role of intelligence in morality turns on the issue of how much part intelligence has, and whether high intellectual capacity ensures high moral development.

Mischel and Mischel (1962) surveyed a variety of studies showing a clear relation between the cognitive competence and general adequacy of social functioning. Maturity on Piagetian moral judgment is positively correlated with IQ and IQ and dishonest behaviour have been found to be negatively related, on the basis of such data. Aronfreed (1968) and Mischel and Mischel (1962) accent the role of sheer cognitive power is the operation of conscience and question whether children comparable in general cognitive capacity would show any significant variation in principles of conscience.

Is conscience no more than a matter of intelligence. Behavioural evidence show that something else is involved as suggested by Burton's (1963) review of studies showing for example, that the relation between IQ and honesty declines or disappears when the context is non-academic or when the risk of getting caught is low. Turning to the realm of judgment, one finds while high IQ children do better than low IQ subjects on most Piaget tests of moral judgment, for some dimensions the reverse is true. Cognitive development theories such as Kohlberg and Selman have offered a way of clarifying the intelligence morality relation. A given stage of cognitive development is a necessary but not sufficient condition for the parallel morality stage. The relevant data are generally supportive. Ninety-three per cent of all five to seven year olds who passed a moral reasoning task at Kohlberg's stage (which involves primitive social reciprocity) passed a correspondence task of logical reciprocity, where as fifty two percent of the children who passed the logical task and did not pass the moral test. The necessary but not sufficient relationship appears to hold at the higher levels as well. All adolescents and adults who score at stages, five or six are capable of formal reasoning on Piaget's pendulum and correlation problems, but many persons who are formal operational on these logical problems fail to show any moral reasoning at the highest, post-conventional stages.

The research then appears to be conform a common institution, being smart and being moral are not the same? Cognitive powers may be needed for principled moral thought, but it is not enough. History is full of examples of how human intelligence can be turned to great evil, the understanding of which stands the next critical challenges to a science of morality.

Thus a commonly accepted finding in moral conduct studies is that intelligence and academic ability are positively correlated with honesty.

Judgments of right-wrong comprise an important aspect of morality. An evaluative dimension consistently emerges when people rate each other's traits and attributes as well as when they rate meanings of words and events.

Moral judgment is an aspect of intellectual activity. The study of moral judgment inevitably leads one to consider the relatively clear and comprehensible activity of human thought. Here the individual is primarily involved in cognitive activity. He is applying his mind to a moral problem, just as he would solve a logical problem and reach a decision by purely intellectual means, so he applies the same mental apparatus to a moral problem and reaches a decision by almost exactly the same process.

Moral judgments are clearly made without emotional involvement of some kind. The moral judgment is usually accompanied by objectives describing human states and verbs describing human behaviour.

The child's moral judgment changes, as he grows older. Child begins with a morality of constraint in which moral judgments are based on external authority and rigid interpretation of rules and regulations, and passes finally to a morality of co-operation in which judgments are based on social consideration and a flexible interpretation of previously inflexible rules.

Piaget's view is that the society of the older children achieves an organic unity, with laws and regulations and often even a division of social work. Morality is only possible where there is co - operation between equals leading to voluntary restraint on their behaviour.

Piaget frequently makes it perfectly clear that moral judgments are only really valid when they are made from a position of moral independence. At the stage of equality both logical processes are involved in the judgments made. The whole process is clearly cognitive in form, is revealed by a consideration of the origin as well as the evolution of moral judgment.

Moral judgment has a number of constituent parts. Native intelligence has a key place, not only in making a moral analysis of the concrete situation but also in bringing to bear upon in such non-moral knowledge as has been acquired in other life experiences and in other areas of education.

Moral judgment also involves, secondly critic factors, and not least the emotional, which is found to heavily tune the moral concepts of children and so to colour their moral judgments. Moral judgments thus become a shorthand term for the various aspects of the total personality expressed in its encounter with other persons.

Moral judgment is essentially an end product of cognitive process. One would expect to find correlation between intelligence and moral judgment. Durkheim (1925) for example found hardly any evidence at all that a child's intelligence was correlated with the level of his moral judgment.

The problem of inculcating the ability among children to judge morally is infested with many problems. Even though the individuals innate intelligence mat be quite substantial, whether he is helped to use it for the purpose of development of moral judgment and ethical and social values is another question. The student when uses his intelligence for other purposes, then his intelligence becomes a prevent intelligence. An immoral person is not intelligent but his intelligence is being used for other dubious purposes.

The factors that affect the moral judgment among children are the home background, school environment and also peer influence.

The religion provides a common ground for development of moral sense. But the system of education must take a positive action in properly directing the development of moral values among children for which it has to assess the judgment of students in respect of their own moral perception. It is this aspect of the need to identify and clarify the level extent of moral judgment among children that must get sustained attention and action of the educators.

Moral judgment is important, as it is a process of defining a happening in terms of moral justifiability. It is the ability to evaluate the situation as right or wrong. It is the cognitive capacity, which helps the child to evaluate the worthiness or unworthiness of an action. Children in this modern society of technological and scientific advancement are at conflict to choose the moral values from among the existing of values. Value is not just a preference but is a preference, which is felt and considered to be justified - "Morally or by reasoning or by aesthetic judgments usually by two or all three of these". One of the increasingly important tasks of education is to help children develop the appropriate skills and judgment to cope up with the variety of moral choices they have to face in today's complex world. As the intellectual capacity of an adolescent increase the judgment on morality also increases. Therefore, intelligence is treated as one of the independent factors in the study.

## Education and Moral Judgment

Education is above all a social means to a social end - the means by which a society guarantees its own survival (Durkheim, 1961).

Education must help the child to understand at an early point that beyond certain contrived boundaries that constitute the historical framework of justice, there are limits based on the nature of things, that is to say in the nature of each of us.

The public schools are the general education system, which develops national character. Therefore, attention should be focused on them and consequently on moral education as it is understood and practiced in them and as it should be understood and practised.

In the school, there is a whole system of rules that predetermine the child's conduct. He must come to class regularly; he must arrive at a specified time and with an appropriate bearing and attitude. He must not dispirit things in class. Therefore, there are a host of obligations that the child is required to shoulder. Together they constitute the discipline of the school. It is the morality of the classroom.

The class is a miniature society. It is therefore both natural and necessary that it will have its own morality corresponding to its size, the character of its elements, and its functions. Several commissions and committees on education in the post-independence period of our country have pointed out the need for education in values.

The Report of the Secondary Education Commission (1952-53) was of the view that the attitudes, values and modes of behaviour of the society were bound to be reflected in the school as it was a smaller society. There might be indiscipline in the society, but the school had to take the responsibility of its removal from the society. The commission felt that it was the responsibility of the headmaster and teachers to set a high standard of work and conduct. The activities of the school should be planed to create congenial environment for training of right character. The purpose of education is fulfilled only if certain definite moral values are inculcated in the minds of the youth of the country.

The Report of the Committee on Religious and Moral Instruction (1959) examined the desirability and feasibility of making specific provision for moral and spiritual values in educational instructions. Many ills of our society are disturbing and dislocating the entire social life. The old bonds between people are last loosening. New ideologies with new meanings are worsening the situation. The committee was of the opinion that the cure of the phenomenon lay in the inculcation of moral and spiritual values right from the childhood. The committee further opined about moral values and it referred to the conduct of man towards man in different situations like home, social and economic fields. The committee defined moral values as 'anything that helps us to behave properly towards others'. Similarly, spiritual values were explained as "anything that takes us out of ourselves and inspires us to sacrifice for the good of others or for a great cause".

The Report of the Education Commission (1964-66) pointed out the major weakness of India and particularly of Hindu society as lack of equality and social justice. Serious social and ethical conflicts are being created in the younger generation by the weakening of social and moral values. Further modernization did not man avoiding the inculcation of moral and spiritual values. The society of the future should strengthen the sense of social responsibility and appreciation of moral and spiritual values. The expanding knowledge and the growing power, which had been placed at the disposal of modern society, should be combined with a sense of social responsibility and appreciation of moral and spiritual values. The lack of essential values in younger generation is dangerous for the society. The commission recommended the inculcation of right values among the students of all stages of education. The inculcation of values may be based on our national traditions. The commission made a reference to father of the Nation, Mahatma Gandhi, who had striven for social justice and social reconstruction.

The Report of the Committee of Members of Parliament on National Policy of Education (1967) emphasized the cultivation of moral, social and spiritual values. The most important reforms suggested by the committee were to transform the existing system of education, promote social integration, accelerate economic growth and generate moral, social and spiritual values.

The Report of the Curriculum for the Ten-year School (1976) emphasized the importance of developing values among the future citizens through education. The school curriculum should be related to the cultivation of moral and social values. The entire life of the school in which a child lives should provide social, intellectual and moral environment. The future citizens should learn how to cooperate with others for the common good. The school should develop a will in every pupil to participate in the task of the reconstruction of our society. Thus, education should foster universal and values (National Policy on Education, 1986).

The Report of the Indian Education Commission, Kothari Commission (1964-66) and Sri Prakasha Committee on Moral Education as one of the main included in the 10+2. But no extra time table for the same nor was any attempt made to integrate moral education with the existing courses. It is heartening to note that Central Ministry of Education (December 1981) is taking due interest in this domain.

A conference on moral education was held in Simla, July (1981), wherein the significance and value-oriented education was discussed. Various issues on socio-political and religious arising out of the subject were discussed thoroughly and consensus obtained.

As a follow-up measure of the same, NCERT (December 1981) had a special seminar from 10th to 12th November 1981 in which five Cardinal human values - truth, right conduct, love, peace and non-violence - were discussed. Guidelines were prepared for the development of curriculum and value - oriented education in schools.

Thus, it was hoped, would help an individual to internalize the moral values in order to develop within himself a fine character and an integrated personality.

The moral degradation of youth causes serious concern to parents, teachers and community members. The National Policy of Education (1986) observed that the growing concern over the erosion of essential values and increasing cynicism in society has brought to focus the need for readjustments in the curriculum in order to make education a powerful toll for the cultivation of social and moral values which would ultimately need to ethical decision making and acceptable moral judgment.

The Review Committee on National Policy on Education (1990) has pointed out that "In addition to the techno-informative base and the opportunity to acquire skills, education must further provide for a climate for the nurturance of values both forming one's character and for inculcating the necessary social, cultural and national values, so as to have a context and meaning for actions and decisions and in order to enable the person to act with conviction and commitment."

This revival of interest in education in moral value in recent years in our country appears to have arisen from the growing realization that the complexity of Indian society with a heterogeneous population belonging to diverse religions, castes and creeds preludes the provision of religious education in the state schools and that this situation can be met by the Introduction of moral education. Moral education under its umbrella includes every thing that is considered to be valuable in the education of the young people such as training in appropriate social behaviour and discipline, character and personality, citizenship and purposeful living.

One of the major tasks of school education is to pass on each succeeding generation what is best in the nation's heritage including the essential value. It is said that values are inseparable from the process of education and all activities of the school have a value dimension in them. The purpose of moral education is to provide opportunities for young people to imbibe essential values through planed activities and also to help them to develop the ability to deal effectively with issues related to values in their life.

The aims of secondary education are defined in terms of the needs of growth and development of young people. The idea of giving suitable experiences to learners according to their developmental requirement is evident in all the recorded practice of secondary education. This is evidently the kind of education that emerges when principles of moral development are applied to learning of moral attitudes and values. Education for moral development Point of view is a scientific process of developing a desirable from of thinking and the ability to deal with issues related to values. Moral development has been viewed as a part of total personality development of the individual. It is a multidimensional and a continues process leading to the state where the individual is able to understand, imbibe and act according to universal principles and values which he accepts in relation to the larger society.

If education in moral, social and ethical values is to be undertaken as seriously as any other aspects of school curriculum, the first essential requirement is that one should know how the development of these values takes place in the individual at different stages of growth and development. Moral education should be viewed from the developmental perspective if it is to serve its purpose in school education.

A developmental dimension of moral education implies the growth of moral judgment. The ultimate aim of moral education is to raise the level of moral judgment and behaviour is based to as great extent as possible upon general moral principles. The main reason is that moral judgment is the only distinctively moral factor among all the factors, which influence moral behaviour. Therefore, it is only by virtue of this factor that behaviour may be called genuinely moral.

The basic assumption of moral judgment is that human beings generate behaviour but also categories, evaluate and judge them. Any comprehensive theory of morality must consider judgments about moral behaviour. Moral judgment and moral conduct involve one's effort to deal with moral components of human actions.

# CHAPTER 2

# REVIEW OF RELATED LITERATURE

This chapter deals with the internal review of the literature. It is an attempt to discover relevant material published in the problem area under study. This covers the empirical research studies done previously in the problem area. The studies conducted during the past few decades in the field of Moral Judgment that are more relevant and pertinent to the present investigation are discussed in this chapter.

## NEED TO KNOW ABOUT RELATED LITERATURE

For any worth while study in any field of knowledge, the research worker needs an adequate familiarity with the library and its many resources. Only then will an effective search for specialized knowledge be possible. The search for reference material is a time consuming, but very fruitful phase of a research programme. Every investigator must know what sources are available in his field of enquiry, which of them he/she is likely to use and where and how to find them. (Sukhia, *et al.,* 1980).

The related literature forms the foundation upon which all future work will be built. It enables the investigator to know the means of getting to the frontier in the field of his research. It also provides idea, theories, explanations, hypotheses or methods of research, valuable in formulating and studying the problems. It furnishes the researcher with indispensable suggestions about comparative data, good procedures, likely methods and tried techniques. The information about the activities of previous investigations, stimulate the researcher to use each bit of knowledge as a starting point for new and further progress.

There are number of studies relating to the moral judgment done in the past. However, only the literature pertaining to the independent variables used in the present study is referred in the succeeding pages.

Therefore, the studies are presented under the following sub-headings:

- Studies related to sex and moral judgment.
- Studies related to year of study and moral judgment.
- Studies related to management and moral judgment.
- Studies related to academic achievement and moral judgment.
- Studies related to personality and moral judgment.
- Studies related to intelligence and moral judgment.
- Studies related to caste and moral judgment.
- Studies related to religion and moral judgment.
- Studies related to locality and moral judgment.
- Studies related to socio-economic status and moral judgment.
- Studies related to residence and moral judgment.
- Studies related to age and moral judgment.
- Studies related to birth order and moral judgment.
- Studies related to father's education and moral judgment.

- Studies related to size of the family and moral judgment.
- Studies related to medium of the study and moral judgment.
- Studies related to course of the study and moral judgment.
- Studies related to moral judgment among students in general.

The trend studies in moral judgment are reviewed for their coverage of research done in this area in the past few decades both in India as well as abroad. Through this the research gap can be identified and also one can focus on the areas which have received priority and attention in this area. Therefore, the relationship of moral judgment and many different factors have been explored and considered.

Moral development cannot be studied in isolation from other aspects of development, viz., physical, intellectual, emotional and social, because some extent of intellectual maturity and emotional balance is necessary for moral understanding and its judgment.

In the fifth survey of educational research, six or seven researches have been indicating on the moral judgment and its dimension. Researches on the process of value inculcation or on the moral instructional materials are meager. Majority of the available researches have used survey method rather than of experimental designs. A number of researches should be done on the development of strategies for moral awareness among students, teachers and parents so that in turn by inculcating moral values and moral behaviour among children, the society can be transferred into a better society.

## STUDIES RELATED TO SEX AND MORAL JUDGMENT

In a male dominated society, girls are deprived in the society in all aspects partiality in treatment - predetermined notion of parents - restrictions in their mobility - lack of freedom of girls - partiality of parents - social evils like dowry have been biggest impediments for girls to progress in the field of education compared to boys. Sex is one of the important variable in the reasoning of moral judgment. The following are some of the studies revieneed on this aspect:

Researches by Maccoby (1966), Anastaci (1966) and Horner (1972) had demonstrated that females scored equally well or slightly above males on a number of developmental measures at an early age but the female's score tended to stabilize prematurely during the adolescent period.

Wright and Cox (1967) conducted a research on relationship between moral judgment and religious belief on a sample of 2276 pupils of whom 49.6% were boys and 50.4% girls from 6$^{th}$ forms of 96 maintained grammar schools in England were found that on nearly all items, girls were more severe in their judgments than were boys. (N = 2276)

Parikh (1968) conducted a study on development of moral judgment and its relation to family environmental factors in Indian and American families. The findings have indicated that the difference in the level of moral judgment development, between the mother and fathers suggest a possible sex difference but the results do not show any significant difference between boys and girls.

In terms of moral reasoning, proportionately more females remained at the conventional level than males and lesser percentage reached the post conventional level (Hunn, 1971; Kohlberg and Turiel, 1971; Holstein, 1973). One explanation for this difference was that limitations were imposed on female's growth by social conventions and Behavioural expectations.

Freeman (1974) conducted a study to investigate individual differences in moral judgment in relation to age and sex. It was found that female more than males were influenced by the sex of the story model in their judgments. Females showed more mature judgments than males.

Ravan Hashim Rowahan (1974) found that sex has no effect on moral judgment.

Benniga (1976) indicated that there is no significant sex difference in moral judgment scores.

Meera Varma (1976) in his study the following results were found, when the relationship between moral judgment and sex was established. It was found that there was hardly any difference in the children below 9 years. The coefficient of correlation's being 0.91 and 0.75 in two groups. But in the 10 to 11 age group, the coefficient was only 0.44. It is reported that at this level, the girls gave a higher value to animas, duty, respect and sin than the boys and a lower value for forgiveness, anger and revenge than the boys. The above findings proved that girls showed a better moral judgment than boys.

Schruner (1976) investigated moral reasoning on 50 female and 50 male college undergraduates in education, between the age 19 and 25 years and also examined in the interaction of various personality characteristics with attained level of moral reasoning, across and between sexes. The study revealed differences in favour of males over females in the attained level of moral reasoning. The reasoning of young women was more pragmatic, stereotyped to immature. The reasoning of men was more vigorous, autonomous and independent. Certain personality variables were significantly correlated with the moral maturity score. (N = 100)

Gupta (1977) studied individual differences in value pattern and personality type of the school going adolescents (400 boys and 400 girls were taken from the secondary schools of Eastern U.P.). The major findings of the study were boys and girls differed significantly in their values. (N = 800)

Fifis Daniel Francis (1978) investigated that correlations between sex and moral judgment scales did not reach a statistically significant level when classed by sex, it was found that the correlation and 0.64 for empathy and moral judgment was significant for males at the 0.05 level. (N = 39)

Toai Ton (1978) investigated the relationship of age, sex and adult authority figure to the moral judgment in Vietnamese immigrant children. It was found that there was no sex difference despite the traditional sex dichotomy in Vietnamese culture.

Dockstander (1979) made a comparative study of developmental sex differences in moral reasoning. The findings of this study showed no significant differences between males and females in the levels of moral development at the 7th and 11th grade, using the Rest Defining Issues test. At the 7th grade level there was a significant difference at the 0.05 level between the moral reasoning of female experimental students and female control group students, but no such difference was shown at the 11th grade level.

Evans (1980) concluded that do not permit conclusions regarding the relationship of stages of development of knowledge of Kohlberg's theory and sex.

Bandopadhyay (1981) observed that seven areas of moral judgment girls showed more maturity than boys in three areas viz., attitude towards justice, equality and authority and collective responsibility, imminent justice and guilt, there was no sex bias, but inefficiency of punishment, girls have mature responses than thc boys.

Bush (1981) investigated the validity of Kohlberg's measure of moral reasoning from a role - identification stand point. The findings revealed that males and females staged significantly higher on the Alternative Dilemma Questionnaire (ADQ) than on the Defining Issues Test (DIT).

Gopalaiah (1981) did a study on moral judgment in children. The sample consisted of 60 boys and 60 girls belonging to 6 different age groups with equal number in each constituted subjects for this investigation. He investigated that the moral judgment did not depend on sex. (N = 120)

Gorgre (1981) found that significant relationships did not exist between DIT scores and the sex.

Johnston (1981) concluded that sex does not have significant difference in moral growth.

Kenvin (1981) revealed that there is no significant difference between the levels on which female and male high school students make moral judgment.

Siefering (1981) investigated that sex does not have significant difference in moral reasoning.

Bannon (1982) conducted a study on sex differences in parental press at several socio-economic levels. The study was conducted to know the parental involvement and their contribution to the education of the child. The major findings of the study were: (1) The distribution of scores of boys and girls in all the five areas (educational, social, physical, emotional and moral) of parental press showed lack of symmetry, (2) The girls secured better points in educational and physical areas whereas boys exhibited better scores in the emotional and moral areas, (3) Sex did not affect the parental press scores.

O' Connor (1982) studied sex and leadership differences in moral perspective, field dependence and moral judgment. Female leaders were significantly more likely to be scored as demonstrating principled thinking in Defining Issues Test. It was suggested that the Defining Issues Test was possible tapping reasoning other than formal deductive logic. Examination of female protocols indicated; support for the idea that female reason inductively about moral problems rather than deductively applying the rules to fairness.

Sipaur (1983) compared educated boys and girls of 9$^{h}$ and 11$^{th}$ grade. For moral development and self-concept, he found that the moral development scores of the girls were significantly higher than those of boys for overall sample and for 9$^{h}$ grade level. But no such significant difference was found at the 11$^{th}$ grade.

Begum Shahina (1983) studied that sex does not have significant influence on moral judgment.

Singh (1983) inferred that the correlation between moral judgment and sex was significant.

Jennifer (1984) conducted a study to know the sex difference in the expression of moral judgment, a current issue in the question of sex differences in moral judgment. One concern has been that females were assessed in Kohlberg's moral stage theory as developmentally inferior, because their pronounced orientation to empathy and caring is associated with stage-3 (a less-advanced stage) charges of a possible gender bias have been mitigated by the absence of sex differences in stage level in the preponderance of studies. Nevertheless, emphatic and sex role difference between males and females could be reflected in the expression - if not stage level - of moral judgment . In this study, a significant difference favoring females was found in the proportion of appeals to emphatic role taking used among those subjects making stage 3 justifications.

Marrie and Elliot (1984) conducted a study to know the children's (90 subjects (ages 6, 8 and 10 years)) concepts of moral and prudential rules were assessed in this study. Moral and prudential events are similar in that they may involve consequences to persons, but also differ in that morality bears upon social relations and prudence does not. The findings showed that most subjects regard moral and prudential rules as useful their violation as wrong, the validity of the actions as non-contingent on rules or authority, and as generalisable; these effects were stronger for the moral than the prudential rules, with older children distinguishing the 2 male types. However, the reasons given in justification of moral rules focused on both consequences. Moral rules were attributed more importance than the prudential rule. The pattern of findings indicated that children differentiate between consequences and regulation of social interactions. Intelligence and value of superior boys was higher than that of superior girls. (N = 19)

Singh (1984) investigated that there was no sex difference between government and convent school so far as the moral judgment was consent.

Soni (1984) conducted a study judgment in school going children of rural area of Delhi belonging to different castes and sexes. She found that In all the caste groups as well as in the whole groups, girls were better than boys in moral judgment.

Sreedharamurthy (1984) observed that sex was not effecting on moral judgment of high school students.

Vanaja (1984) observed that girls were significantly better in their moral judgment.

Bhargava (1986) investigated that boys and girls scored equally well on moral judgment.

Dayakara Reddy, V. (1987) found that sex has significant influence on the reasoning of moral stage 3 and pre-conventional level of moral judgment. (N = 900)

Geethanath, P.S. (1987) found that sex has significant influence on the reasoning of moral stage 2, moral stage 5, pre-conventional level and conventional level of moral judgment. (N = 1400)

Stiller and Forrest (1990) examined differences in self-description (SD) moral reasoning (MR) in 45 female and 32 male undergraduates, extending research by Gilligan (1982) and Lyons (1984). Questionnaire results indicated that women used the connected mode in SD's significantly more frequently than men. In MR, men used the justice/rights mode significantly more frequently than women, and women used the care/response mode more frequently than men. Results generally support the theoretical constructs of Gilligan's Lyons's work and show that differences exist between male and female use of SD and MR, implying gender differences in conceptions of choices of modes. (N = 77)

A care-based measure of levels of moral thought, based on Gilligan's (1982) theorizing was developed by Skoe and Marcia (1991) to investigate the relationship between moral reasoning and identity in women. Sample subject (Ss) were 86 female students, aged 17-26 yrs. Also, as hypothesised, women high on the ECI were higher in identity status than were women low on the ECI. One conclusion is that woman's development of moral reasoning and self concept of self are intricately linked. (N = 86)

Chaya (1993) investigated that boys were significantly higher than girls in the "non-violence" dimension of moral judgment.

Narayanaswamy (1994) examined that sex is not significantly related to moral judgment.

Sridhar (1994) inferred that boy and girls have shown similarly in their adult and peer approved moral judgment.

Solomon (1995) designed a study to examine the relationship between children's moral reasoning maturity and their legitimacy judgments about gender stratification. He revealed that no significant relationship between children's moral reasoning maturity and their legitimacy judgment about gender stratification.

Chaya (1996) indicated that sex was not related to moral judgment.

Prabhu (1996) investigated that sex did not affect moral judgment of student's ninth standard. (N = 400)

Pradhan and Pande (1996) were studied the independent and interactive effects of tribal, non-tribal difference and sex on moral judgment of secondary school children. The study revealed that: (1) Tribal, non-tribal difference and sex has significant effect on moral judgment of secondary school children independently, but interaction of sex and tribal, non-tribal difference has no significant effect; (2) Tribal, non-tribal and sex have neither independent nor interactive effect on attainment of autonomous level of moral judgment of secondary school children.

Wark and Krebs (1996) investigated the effects of gender, gender role, and type of moral dilemma on moral maturity and moral orientation on 55 female and 55 male university students. Moral stage, moral orientation, and the relation between them varied across dilemmas. Females were more consistent than males in moral stage; males were consistent in moral orientation. Females made higher stage and more care-based moral judgment than males made on personal real-life dilemmas. The observed variations occurred primarily because males reported moral stage 2, justice pulling anti-social dilemmas than females, and females reported moral stage 3, care-pulling pro-social dilemmas than males.

Elbedour *et al.* (1997) examined the moral development of 3 groups of children, who had been subjected to varying degrees of political violence and economic advantage, in an attempt to determine if group membership or gender influenced the level of moral reasoning or orientation. Ninety-three students (8-13 year old Israel Jewish and Bedouin school children and Palestine west bank school children) were asked various moral reasoning questions based on an animal fable involving a moral dilemma fewer than 3 (hypothetical, role-taking, political) conditions. Results indicate that mutually solutions to moral dilemmas were given more frequently by Israel Jewish children than Israeli Bedouin or Palestinian children as the questions shifted from abstract to real life situations. No significant gender differences were found between Jewish children and Bedouin children in hypothetical issues; however, violence and limited resources were found to affect moral judgment in real life situations for boys, but not for girls.

In an extension of a previous study, Burke (1998), at school-based intervention in socio moral reasoning was evaluated. Comparison was made between middle-school students 266 sixth - grades (135 boys and 131 girls) and 279 eighth-grade (149 boys and 130 girls) receiving in-class mentoring and those not receiving the intervention. Significant result found included an interaction between gender and grade of participants for socio moral reasoning scores, a significant improvement in the mentor's moral reasoning and significant correlation between teacher ratings of peer social skill for boys and for girls. Socio-moral reasoning was significantly and negatively correlated with personal distress for boys. (N = 279)

Lagerspetz (1998) administered a moral approval of aggression (MAA) inventory and the Bem sex-role Inventory to 48 military officer trainers (OTs), 35 conscientious objectors (COs) to armed service, and 32 women of comparable age. Aggression was mostly approved of among the OTs and least among the COs, with the women scoring in the middle somewhat closer to OTs. Differences in sex-role identity emerged, so that OTs often chose a masculine sex role, whereas for COs, the choice of an androgynous role was most frequent. Women chose feminine and androgynous roles with equal frequency. MAA could not be explained on the basis of sex role identification.

Deguchi and Ohkawa (2000) examined the characteristics of empathy with age and the relationship between empathy and moral judgment on 1148 male and 170 female juvenile delinquents (14-19 yrs) in Japan. The results showed that the female Sample subject (Ss) showed higher empathy rates and moral judgment rates than male Ss, but females' in group B showed a lower empathy rate than any other group. (N = 1318)

Humphries *et al.* (2000) examined the ways in such gender, empathy and cultural orientation (communalism and competitive individualism) influence the moral judgments of urban 5th and 8th grade African American children. Pencil and paper measures of these constructs were completed by 44 5th 46 8th graders. Results revealed greater endorsement of communalism among girls than boys. Separate correlation matrices and path analysis models were computed for girls and boys. Communalism, empathy, and grade emerged as significant correlations and predictors moral reasoning among boys. Empathy emerged as a mediator between communalism and moral reasoning for boys. Grade was the only significant correlate and predictor of moral reasoning for girls.

Ayesha Noor (2001) examined that sex difference was not significant on any dimension of moral judgment.

Chaya (2001) observed that girls were significantly better in the honesty, truthfulness dimensions and in total moral judgment.

Suma Rani (2001) concluded that sex does not have significant difference in any dimension of moral judgment.

Dawson (2002) examined the four sets of data, collected by four different teams over a period of 30 yrs. Common item equating, which yielded correlations from 94 to 97 across data sets, was employed to justify the data for a new analysis. Probabilistic conjoint measurement was used to model the results. The detailed analysis of these pooled data confirms results reported in previous research about the ordered acquisition of moral stages and the relationship between moral stages and age, education, and sex. New findings include:

(1) Empirical evidence that transitions between "childhood" and "adult" stages of development involve similar mechanisms; (2) Support for the notion of stages as qualifiedly distinct modes of reasoning that display properties consistent with a notion structure d ensemble; and (3) Evidence of a stage between Kohlberg's stages 3 and 4. Consist with reports from earlier research, the relationship between age and moral development is curvilinear. The relationship between educational attainment and moral development is linear, suggesting that educational environments have an equivalent impact across the course of development. Older males have slightly higher score than older females after age and education are taken into account.

Thakur and Kang (2002) studied that the development of both the moral values and judgment in both the males and females, rural pre-adolescents along with changes related to the age. The findings of the study were: female showed higher levels of significantly as compared to males of the same age. Girls also significantly showed higher level of moral values than boys.

Sabitha Reddy (2003) concluded that girls were significantly better in their moral judgment than boys.

Raaijmakers, *et.al.* (2005) investigated that no substantial gender differences were obtained for either moral reasoning or its relationship with delinquency.

Comunian *et al.* (2006) studied that an active orientation toward role-taking opportunities were related to higher levels of moral judgment among both men and women.

Rangaswamy, G. (2006) inferred that sex has significant influence on the reasoning of moral stage 3, moral stage 4, moral stage 6, conventional level, post-conventional level and moral judgment scores. (N = 900)

Talwar and Sheela (2006) concluded that female students have scored significantly higher than the male students on moral judgment. (N = 169)

## STUDIES RELATED TO YEAR OF STUDY AND MORAL JUDGMENT

The year of study may have influence on the reasoning of moral judgment of the students. Some of the related studies are given below:

Prahalladha (1982) has investigated moral judgment of junior college students and their relationship with the socio-economic status, intelligence and personality adjustment. He found that there was significant difference in the moral judgment scores of junior college in India (Mysore) and senior high school students in the United States.

Dayakara Reddy, V. (1987) inferred that class has significant influence on the reasoning of moral stage 1, moral stage 4, moral stage 4A, moral stage 6, pre-conventional level and conventional level of moral judgment (N = 900).

Geethanath, P.S. (1987) inferred that class has significant influence on the reasoning of moral stage 1 moral stage 2, moral stage 3, moral stage 4, moral stage 5, moral stage 6, pre-conventional level, conventional level, post-conventional level and moral judgment (N = 1400).

Bhattacharya (2002) designed to understand the nature of social life adjustment pattern and moral behaviour of group of students studying in secondary and higher secondary level at West Bengal. The findings revealed that both the groups possess: (1) A healthy psycho-physical make up favorable for gaining self confidence and developing a rationale for optimism. (2) A right attitude to perform with best of loyalties, the functions of task expected of him by his family, community and country of large and (3) A capability of playing a competent social role for attaining objectives of national interest but, there is variation between these two groups in certain degree. The findings have also revealed that the students of higher secondary level are more peer-oriented than the students of secondary level.

Rangaswamy, G. (2006) concluded that class has significant influence on the reasoning of moral stage 1 moral stage 2, moral stage 3, moral stage 4, moral stage 4A, moral stage 5A, moral stage 5B, moral stage 6, pre-conventional level, conventional level, post-conventional level and moral judgment. (N = 900)

## STUDIES RELATED TO MANAGEMENT AND MORAL JUDGMENT

The management may have influence on the reasoning of moral judgment of the students. Some of the related studies are given below:

Kenvin (1981) conducted a study to determine the relationship among systematic secular value education, programmed religious education and secular general education in terms of levels of moral development on a sample of three groups of high school students, each of which included fifteen females and fifteen males. It was found that there is no significant difference in the levels on which public school students who receive systematic value instruction private religious school students who received programmed religious instructions and public school students who have not been exposed to any systematic value instruction make moral judgments. (N = 90)

Bandopadhyay (1981) observed that the moral judgment was positively related with type of school.

Prahalladha (1982) investigated that significant difference was not reported between students studying in junior colleges and composite colleges as for as their moral judgment was concerned.

Singh (1983) examined that insignificant positive correlation was found between type of school and children's moral judgment.

Gupta (1984) concluded that the children from co-educational schools showed lower reformatory zeal in comparison to the children from non co-educational schools.

Singh (1984) conducted a comparative study on 180 children studying I grade in three different types of schools: Saraswati

Shishu Mandir, Convent School and Government Schools of Uttar Pradesh on moral judgment. The results revealed that null hypothesis regarding the difference between the Government schools and Saraswathi Shishu Mandirs and Convent schools in respect of moral judgment were rejected. (N = 180)

Vanaja (1984) investigated that students studying in government school were significantly better in their moral judgment than the students studying in private schools.

Schrmdt (1988) studied moral values of adolescents studying in Public versus Christian schools. 118 students in Public high school and 73 students in Christian schools completed a true false test measuring 8 pairs of moral and immoral attitudes. Findings indicated that there is significant difference on a "total morality index" favoring the Christian school students. Significant differences were obtained in 3 particular areas: money, body/health, and sexuality. Christian school students were more inclined than Public school students to be aware of and confess their minor character flaws, contracting the view that Christian students tend to present themselves in a socially desirable light. (N = 191)

Narayanaswamy (1994) concluded that students studying in Government school were significantly better in their moral judgment than the students studying in Private schools.

Chaya (1996) studied that the type of school was not a significant factor for moral judgment.

Prabhu (1996) investigated that students studying in Government school have better moral judgment than the students studying in Private school.

Good and Cartwright (1998) examined the effort of the university environment on the moral judgment development of students (360 undergraduate students attending a state university in Arkansas, a Christian liberal arts university in Oklahoma and a Bible university in Texas). Results show significant freshman to senior gains in principled thinking among the Ss attending the state and Christian liberal arts universities; whereas, no significant freshman to senior gains in principled thinking was found among the Ss attending the Bible University. (N = 360).

Ayesha Noor (2001) did a study on the effect of personality traits on the moral judgment of 310 tenth standard students in Bangalore Urban secondary schools. She found that the type of school did not significantly affect any dimension of moral judgment. (N = 310)

Chaya (2001) observed that students studying in Unaided private schools were significantly better in honesty, dimension and in total of moral judgment that students studying in government and Aided private schools.

Suma Rani (2001) conducted a study on the five dimensions of moral judgment among students of ninth standard of Kolar district in relation to their gender, type of school, urban and rural background and social maturity. It found that type of school did not significantly affect any dimension of moral judgment.

McPherson, Michael; Schapiro, Morton Owen (2007) investigated that the enrolment management in higher education, that has significant value dimensions.

## STUDIES RELATED TO ACADEMIC ACHIEVEMENT IN MORAL JUDGMENT

Academic Achievement is of paramount importance, particularly in the present socio-economic and cultural contexts obviously, in the school/college, great emphasis is placed on achievement right from the beginning of formal education. The school/colleges has its own systemic hierarchy which is largely based on achievement and performance rather than ascription. The school/colleges performs the function of selection and differentiation among students on the basis of their academic and other attainment and open avenues for advancement primarily in terms of achievement. Some of the related studies are given below:

Evans (1980) concluded that do not permit conclusions regarding the relationship of stages of development of knowledge of Kohlberg's theory and academic achievements.

Gorgre (1981) found that significant relationships did not exist between DIT scores and the terminal and continuous status on moral judgment.

Bannon (1982) concluded that the emotional, educational and moral areas of parental press appeared to make major contribution in the predication of academic achievement of boys whereas in the case of girls, moral, social and education areas of parental press seemed to contribute much in the predication of academic achievement.

Zupanic and Horvat (1990) examined the role of moral judgment components in a child's school functioning in the 2$^{nd}$ grade 176 Slovenian City children. Results suggest that children's ability of logical judgment in moral situations significantly contributes to their school achievement in the 2$^{nd}$ grade of primary school.

Schoffner (1997) was examined decision making in the area of moral reasoning and its relationship with identity development,. emotional super sensitivity, and gender role flexibility gifted high academically gifted adolescents. Results indicated that there were several main effects by gender, with gifted adolescent females tending to score higher on measures of super sensitivity, expressiveness, and ideological identity formation than gifted adolescent males.

Mc Pherson, Michael; Schapiro, Morton Owen (2007) investigated that the college rankings in higher education has significant value dimensions.

## STUDIES RELATED TO PERSONALITY FACTORS AND MORAL JUDGMENT

Personality is a significant psychological factor that has a very significant impact on all aspects of children's learning and motivation, growth and development. As moral judgment, it is an inherent and cognitive activity. There is a possibility that a grater level of personality would make sensitive to the moral issues as compared with one who may not be good personality. It is also possible that the personality may lead to high understanding of morality, belief and spiritual aspects of societal situations and in turn better moral judgment. Therefore, the present study attempts to examine the relationship of personality and moral judgment.

Agrawal (1985) concluded that personality was not related with moral development.

Bartar (1985) examined the relationship between cognitive ability to consider a variety of alternatives, social perspectives ability to recognize other person's need, and moral judgment, subjects were 72, 5$^{th}$ graders aged 10-11 and the data regarding helping behaviour and the abilities were collected during 5-month period. Regression analysis showed that the level of helping behaviour development was related to the ability to consider a variety of alternatives and marginally and significantly related to moral judgment. The level of expressed motives and the quantity of helping behaviour were not related to any of the cognitive, social perspective and moral skills. The results were discussed within framework of the proposed cognitive model of helping behaviour development. (N = 72)

Kohlberg (1986) in his one of the fundamental theoretical assumptions is that of parallelism between the cognitive and the moral domain. That means that cognitive and moral development is closely related.

Dayakara Reddy, V. (1987) conducted a research on "A study of moral judgment in relation to intelligence, personality and other variables". He concluded that the factors A, B, D, G, H and $Q_3$ in 14 personality factors of HSPQ were significantly related to moral judgment scores of subjects. (N = 900)

Popovix (1992) explained the cognitivistic approach is a typical example of the so-called error of splitting in the field of morality. More precisely, the cognitivistic approach is considered to be a narrowing of the morality domain because all morality is reduced to moral judgment.

Aleixo and Norris (2000) examined personality, moral reasoning maturity, intellectual capacity, and family back ground in 101 convicted male young offenders (aged 16-21 yrs). Results suggested that both official and self-reported measures of offending were related to high psychoticism and extraversion.

While lower levels of moral reasoning maturity were found, no relationship to self-reported offending was apparent.

The Kohlbergian approach also has spun of heretical research programs focused on the apparent development of moral conventions and traditions, independent of post-conventional reasoning development (Turiel Vol. 2, 5), moral reflectivity, that occurs within seeming first-order moral judgment, not moving to the meta - cognitive level (Gibbs Vol. 2), moral and political ideology, that often mires and masks moral reasoning within attitude schemes that bias its workings (Emler 1983), faith development that surprisingly mirrors moral cognition in its conceptualization of divinity and religious devotion (Fowler 1981, Oser 1980), and moral perception, one of several skills that enable the onset of moral deliberation, negotiation and reasoning (Rest, Narvaez, Bebeau and Thoma, 2000).

Ayesha Noor (2001) concluded that generally higher the personality traits, higher were their level of moral judgment.

Chaya (2001) studied the moral judgment of 800 $10^{th}$ standard students Bangalore district in relation to their parental behaviour, child-rearing practices, emotional maturity and personality traits. The following were the findings of the study. (N = 800)

- Study belonging to high parental behaviour group was having higher mean score in all the dimensions of moral judgment than the students belonging to low parental behaviour groups.
- Students belonging to high emotional Maturity were having higher mean score in all the dimensions of moral judgment than the students to low emotional Maturity.
- Ambient students had higher mean score in the moral judgment than the extroverts and introverts.

Shira Haviv and Patrick, J. Leman (2004) conducted the study addresses two separate but related issues in connection with peoples' real life moral decisions and judgments. First, the notion of moral orientation is examined in terms of its consistency across varying contexts, its relation to gender and to gender role. Second, a new aspect of moral reasoning is explored - the influence on moral decision-making of considering the consequences of an action. Fifty-eight undergraduate students were asked to discuss two personal and two impersonal real life moral dilemmas. The results reveal a significant interaction between gender role and type of dilemma. However, moral orientation was not consistent across various dilemmas and gender was not related to any particular orientation. Also the results indicate a significant difference between the reasoning of consequences of personal-antisocial conflicts and impersonal-antisocial conflicts. These findings suggest that different moral orientations may be embedded in life experience and connect with an individual's sense of his or her moral identity in real-life situations.

Gillian Wark (2006) examined the relations among personality, gender, and the ways people perceive moral dilemmas in their everyday lives participants were 117 young women and men who responded to Gibbs, Basinger, and Fuller's (1992) socio moral reflection measure and to anti-social, protocol, and social pressure types of real - life moral dilemma. Participants completed measures assessing shame and guilt (Harder, 1987; Tangney, 1990) and identity (Bennion and Adams, 1986). The female participants reported feeling more guilt about the protocol dilemma and viewed the social pressure dilemma as more care-oriented than males did. Scores on the shame and guilt measures were not related to guilt associated with the real-life dilemmas. Identity-achieved scores were negatively related to feeling guilty about social pressure dilemmas involving parents. Discussion focuses on the relevance of personality, gender, and family influences for a model of real-life moral reasoning, with implications for development and education. In other words, pervasive personality characteristics, such as personal attributions of shame, guilt, and identity, may influence people to view different situations in similar ways because they may project particular issues onto most situations (Wark and Krebs, 2000). Personality measures on shame and guilt (Harder, 1987; Tangney, 1990) and identity. (Bennion and Adams, 1986) (N = 117).

Rangaswamy, G. (2006) concluded that the factors E and G in 14 personality factors of HSPQ were significantly related to moral judgment scores of subjects. (N = 900).

## STUDIES RELATED TO INTELLIGENCE AND MORAL JUDGMENT

Intelligence is a significant psychological factor that has a very significant impact on all aspects of children's learning and motivation, growth and development. As moral judgment itself is an intellectual activity there is a possibility that a grater level of intelligence would make sensitive to the moral issues as compared with one who may not be too intelligent. It is also possible that the intellectual ability may lead to high understanding of morality, belief and spiritual aspects of societal situations and in turn better moral judgment. Therefore, the present study attempts to examine the relationship of intelligence and moral judgment.

Heishman, Helen Mane (1973) found that I.Q is directly related to moral judgment.

Rowahan, Ravan Hashim (1974) conducted a study to find the relationship between moral judgment and age, sex, intelligence and social class. It was found that intelligence has no effect on moral judgment.

Dolores (1977) conducted a study on the effect of two methods of training upon the development of moral judgment in young children The results revealed that moral judgment as developed in a cognitive conflict model was not distinguishable from a cognitive model among seven years old children as predicted. The lack of change in classroom climate scores may have been functions of the consistency of children's preconceived perceptual view of teach attitude and behaviour. The age of seven is perhaps too early for measurable growth to be expected.

Francis, Fifis Daniel (1978) investigated the relationship between predictive ability, empathy, intelligence and sex to moral judgment in adolescents. The subjects were 39 high school students, aged 17 years of age and above, reading in ninth grade level. Correlation between intelligence and moral judgment scale do not reach a statistically significant level. (N = 39).

Hilton (1978) conducted a study to examine the relationship between the criterion variable of moral judgment and three independent variables of interpersonal trust socio-economic status and intelligence quotient of 195 $11^{th}$ grade students from an urban Denver high school. He found that the combination of IQ and socio-economic status proved to be the best predictor of level of moral judgment and were significant at 0.01 level. (N = 195).

Kalra (1978) found that intelligence was positively related with the level of moral judgment at all the three levels of socio-economic status.

In a study by Kenney, James, Francis (1980) the relationship between cognitive, role-taking and moral judgment abilities of adolescents was examined. Results of this study indicated no difference between the two samples for mental and chronological ages or for intellectual abilities. A significant difference was found between the role-taking abilities of each sample and only a slight difference noted between the moral judgment skills of both groups with the emotionally disturbed adolescents being the weaker in each category.

Marrie and Elliot (1984) concluded that intelligence and value of superior boys was higher than that of superior girls.

Dayakara Reddy, V. (1987) found that intelligence does not have significant influence on reasoning of moral judgment. (N = 900).

Geethanath, P.S. (1987) found that intelligence has significant influence on reasoning of moral judgment. (N = 1400).

Al-Deen (1991) examined the relationship between intelligence and moral development and judgment in 20 mentally retarded Egyptian children with mental ages between 2 and 7 yrs. Mental age was positively correlated with moral judgment. The only correlation between intelligence and moral judgment was the conceptualization of lying. (N = 20).

Dentici and Pagnin (1992) studied the relationship between reasoning ability (verbal, abstract, mathematical, semantic) and moral judgment and problem solving. It is concluded that the type of moral reasoning of the gifted does not necessarily yield better personal and social consequences; it may lead to grater moral flexibility and fewer moral inhibitions.

Sharma and Kaur (1992) investigated the effect of intelligence, birth order, and age of the children on the moral judgment of 150 boys. The factorial design of the study was 2×2×2, with 2 levels of intelligence (higher/lower), 2 birth-orders (first born/last born in the family) and age were important factors in influencing moral judgment. None of the interactions were significant. (N = 150)

Chaya (1993) investigated that moral judgment in its five dimensions among students of eighth standard in relation to their sex, intelligence, religiosity and socio-economic status. It found that the group with 'high intelligence and low socio-economic status had the highest 'obedience' dimension of moral judgment.

Sridhar (1994) investigated that their level of intelligence does not influence moral judgment orientation of high school students.

Frisancho (1996) studied the efficiency of an educational program in improving moral reasoning and cognitive complexity levels in 18 male and female high school students (aged 15-16 yrs) in Peru. Results show that no structural advances in terms of moral reasoning level but do demonstrate an increase in reasoning complexity and in the number of elements of social situations students were able to identify. (N = 18)

An exploratory, descriptive investigation into the relationship between college student's critical thinking ability and their development with in the academic, personal, and moral domains was done by Hill (1996). Results of this study indicate that student's critical thinking ability levels are positively associated with their measured levels of academic, personal and moral development. Student's critical thinking ability levels were also found to be positively.

Debruin and Van-Large (1999) studied few studies and showed how behavioural information about the morality or intelligence of another person influences impressions, exceptions of cooperative behaviour, and own cooperation in a mixed motive interdependence situation. Results (for 125 undergraduate Ss) revealed morality and intelligence had more impact (for 164 Ss) on impressions and interactions relevant measures than positive information. (N = 289)

The study by Hagelskamp (2001) examined the influence of the method by which critical thinking of secondary students included 92 U.S. History students from an all-male, college - preparatory high school in northern California. The findings provide compelling evidence that by an infusion method to teach critical and by practicing transfer of those skills, teachers may be assisting students in improving their critical thinking and faceting their moral development in a significant way. (N = 92)

Reddy, Sabitha (2003) concluded that the main effect of intelligence on the moral judgment was found to be significant indicating that the students having high and moderate intelligence were found to be significantly better in their moral judgment than the students having low intelligence.

Lee, Seon-Young and Olszewski-Kubilius, Paula (2006) examined that using 3 psychological scales, this study examined the level of emotional intelligence, moral judgment, and leadership of more than 200 gifted high school students who participated in an accelerative academic program or an enrichment leadership programme through a university based gifted institute. Major findings include that on emotional intelligence, gifted males were comparable to students in the age normative sample, while gifted females lagged behind the norm group, Regardless of gender, gifted students had higher scores on adaptability but lower scores on stress management and impulse control ability compared to the normative sample. On moral judgment, gifted students were comparable to the level of individuals with master's or professional degrees, and they showed an above-average level of leadership compared to the normative sample. No differences were found in students' scores on the 3 scales by the type of programme (academic versus leadership)

Rangaswamy, G. (2006) inferred that intelligence has significant influence on the moral judgment scores of students. (N = 900).

Derryberry, W. Pitt and Barger, Brian (2008) investigated that to assess reaction time and attributional complexity as factors contributing to the relatively high moral judgment of gifted youth, a sample of 30 gifted youth and 30 college students responded to a computerized measure of moral judgment development, which also indexed reaction time. Additionally, participants completed a measurement of attributional complexity and reported American College Test (ACT) scores. Statistically significant differences favored the gifted in moral judgment development reaction time, and attributional complexity. Regression analysis revealed that attributioanal complexity explained a significant amount of variance, whereas ACT scores and reaction times accounted for minimal variance. Although reaction time did not predict moral judgment developmental difference, discussion is offered to suggest how gifted youth, such as those in this study, might benefit from using their reaction time when considering moral situations. (N = 60).

## STUDIES RELATED TO CASTE AND MORAL JUDGMENT

Caste system is a special social condition prevailing in India. Surprisingly for one cause or the other almost all the Indian researchers neglected this variable in their studies relating to reasoning of moral judgment. There are reservations of seats in the name of caste in educational institution; reservations of jobs are there in the name of caste. There are so many associations in the name of castes for upliftment of the people. Then why this variable is neglected in the field of educational research is not known. So, in the present investigation, the investigator is interested to include this variable also. Some of the studies showing the relationship between caste and moral judgment of students are presented here under:

Soni (1984) conducted a study judgment in school going children of rural area of Delhi belonging to different castes and sexes, found that in both sexes as well as combined group, each of the caste groups - Brahimins, Vaishyas and Kshtriyas had done better than the Shudras.

Pradhan and Pande (1996) were concluded that the interaction of sex and tribal, non tribal difference has no significant effect and tribal, non tribal and sex have neither independent nor interactive effect on attainment autonomous level of moral judgment of secondary school children.

## STUDIES RELATED TO RELIGION AND MORAL JUDGMENT

Cultural background of the students may influence their reasoning of moral judgment community/religion may have impact on the reasoning of moral judgment. Studies related to community/religion are shown here under:

Wright and Cox (1967) investigated that the more ascetic the moral issue, the stronger than association with religious belief and practice on moral judgment. (N = 2276)

Gopalaiah (1981) concluded that there was no difference between the levels of moral judgment of children and their religious back ground. (N = 120)

Gorgre (1981) inferred that the significant relationship did not exist between the DIT scores and religion.

Rao (1984) observed that there was significant relation ship between levels of family religious practices and moral judgment scores, the latter being higher in the case of subjects coming from less rigid religious practices.

Kapur (1986) studied the moral education of primary school children in eight sociological perspectives. The findings of the study were that the learning of religious believes and practices consisted of adult demonstration of the correct observance of certain events. Hindu religious values were a part of the children primary socialization in their homes and villages. Text books were a major repository of Hindu religious value.

Geethanath, P.S. (1987) investigated that religion has significant influence on the reasoning of moral judgment. (N = 1400)

Bruggman (1996) concluded that examined the relationship between moral reasoning and the incidence of cheating and lying in a sample of 90 religious Vs 131 secular (Public) 9$^{h}$-12$^{th}$ grade high school students. Religious and secular school students did not differ in moral reasoning level or in levels of cheating and lying. Level of moral reasoning was not correlated with behaviour. Surprisingly high levels of dishonest behaviour were noted in all subjects. (N = 221)

Talwar and Sheela (2006) investigated that students from Christian Community scores higher moral judgment than students from Hindu community.

Rangaswamy, G. (2006) investigated that religion has significant influence on the reasoning of moral judgment. (N = 900).

## STUDIES RELATED TO LOCALITY AND MORAL JUDGMENT

Boys and girls at the adolescent stage studying in urban and rural schools may be having different moral views. Because of the technological advancement the urban environment may be more modern and sophisticated where as the rural environment may be more agriculture oriented. Therefore, this background itself might affect the moral judgment among students of secondary schools. Hence, urban or rural locality is treated as one of the independent variables in the present study.

Bannon (1982) concluded that locality did not effect the parental press scores on moral judgment.

Begum Shahina (1983) studied on the effect of personality traits on the moral judgment of 300 tenth standard students of Bangalore district. The study has revealed the following findings (N = 300):

- ❖ Rural students are having better moral judgment than the urban students in the honest, non-violence dimensions and *in toto.*

- Rural boys and rural girls did not significantly differ in their moral judgment.
- Rural boys are having better moral judgment than the urban boys in the dimensions of honesty, obedience, and justice and *in toto*.
- Rural boys and urban girls did not significantly differ in their moral judgment.
- Rural girls having better moral judgment than the urban boys in the dimensions of honesty, obedience, justice and *in toto*.
- Rural girls and urban girls did not significantly differ in their moral judgment than urban girls.
- Urban boys have got better moral judgment than urban girls.

Singh (1983) ventured to study of 350 (216 male and 134 female) children studying in the fifth grade on moral judgment in relation to prolonged deprivation and parental attitudes. He concluded that insignificant correlation was obtained between residential (Urban/rural) area and moral judgment. (N = 350).

Sreedharamurthy (1984) did a study on the moral judgment among ninth standard high school students in relation to their religiosity. He found that the students studying in urban schools were significantly better in truth dimension of moral judgment whereas students studying in rural schools were significantly better in non-violence dimension.

Young and Thomson (1984) administered the Defining Issues Test to 240 female and 240 male $6^{th}$, $8^{th}$, $11^{th}$ grade and college students in Korea. Among the Korean subject's females, subjects reared in urban areas and older and showed significantly more responses demonstrating principled mortality than did males subjects reared in rural areas or younger subjects. (N = 480).

Dayakara Reddy, V. (1987) investigated that locality has significant influence on the reasoning of moral stage 3, and pre-conventional level of moral judgment. (N = 900).

Geethanath, P.S. (1987) investigated that locality has significant influence on the reasoning of moral stage 2, moral stage 5, pre-conventional level, conventional level and moral judgment. (N = 1400).

Suma Rani (2001) inferred that urban and rural background did not significantly influence any dimension of moral judgment.

Yadava, Sharma and Gandhi (2001) investigated on a sample of 200 male/female students (aged 15-17) of IX and X classes and sub-cultural difference in aggression and moral values. Results indicated that the aggression was not influenced by gender or area. However, moral disengagement was found to be higher in males and in rural subjects as compared to their female and urban counterparts. Further, moral disengagement could be an important mediator of aggression, at least in rural and female subjects. (N = 200).

Reddy, Sabitha (2003) investigated that there was no significant difference between the locality and moral judgment.

Rangaswamy, G. (2006) observed that locality does not have significant influence on the reasoning of moral judgment. (N = 900).

## STUDIES RELATED TO SOCIO-ECONOMIC STATUS AND MORAL JUDGMENT

The appraisal of the effect of socio-economic status is of immense importance since one's position in the social hierarchy is correlated with a number of crucial variables. The factor of socio-economic status as also the social interaction appears to be positive in their influence in moral judgment of students. Role playing technique as a method for developing moral judgment among students seem to have some virtue, it is not conclusive. However, social dimension in terms of socio-economic status in the school and at home seem to be important in the process of moral judgment. Therefore, socio-economic status is treated as one of the independent variables in the present study.

Heishman, Helen Mane (1973) conducted a study to investigate the relationship between the moral judgment and the age, IQ and three levels of socio-economic status of 120 subjects. He found that Increases in socio-economic status are related to increases in moral judgment. The effect is more significant when comparing middle to upper than when comparing lower to middle socio-economic status.

Rowahan, Ravan Hashim (1974) concluded that the relationship between moral judgment and social class it was found that social class has no effect on moral judgment.

Mohundro (1976) attempted to determine a relationship between kohlberg's stages of reasoning expressed in the justification of values with the value hierarchy sex and socio-economic status and it was found that socio-economic status is related to the stages of moral reasoning and value positions.

Hilton (1978) observed that the combination of IQ and socio-economic status proved to be the best predictor of level of moral judgment and were significant at 0.01 level.

Kalra (1978) conducted a study on the moral judgment in children belonging to different mental and socio-economic levels. The sample comprised of 1000 girls from fifteen schools of the Western Zone of Delhi. The finding of the study was: Socio-economic status was positively related with the level of moral judgment at all levels of intelligence. ( N = 1000).

Johnson (1979) was found that there was relationship regarding socio-economic status and the stages of moral development and moral judgment.

Evans (1980) conducted a study to investigate whether having knowledge of Kohlberg's theory of moral development was a factor in predicting stage development. The findings do not permit conclusions regarding the relationship of stages of development of knowledge of Kohlberg's theory and socio-economic status.

Gopalaiah (1981) examined that there was no difference between the moral judgment and socio-economic status of children. (N = 120).

Gorgre (1981) found that significant relationships did not exist between the DIT scores and socio-economic status.

Johnston (1981) conducted a study to determine whether selected children's stories can be utilized to increase on Kohlberg's moral development scale for 6th grade sample. The findings revealed that there was a significant difference mean gain score changes of the low socio-economic group and the middle socio-economic groups.

Bannon (1982) observed that socio-economic status did not affect the parental press scores on moral judgment

Lewis (1982) compared the moral development of gifted students with the moral development of regular ability students. The findings indicated that a positive correlation between cognitive and moral development and between cognitive development and socio-economic status. Gifted students were found to be significantly different from regular students in their socio-economic status.

Tripathi and Girishwar (1982) studied development of moral judgment in 120 Indian children 6-11 of age. It was concluded that although the capacity for moral judgment increases with age, the pattern was significantly medicated by factor of socio-economic status. ( N – 120).

Garg (1983) has made an attempt to study the main effect of parental disciplinary practice and social class on personality needs, moral judgment and problem solving ability of children belonging to the 10-15 years age group. The findings were:

- Children belonging to moderate as well as low social class families had more for achievement in comparison with high school class family. Children of high social class or moderate social class had more need for change in comparison with those social class families.
- Children of 10-11 years belonging to high social class had more need for change when they got moderately disciplinary practices from their parents, 14 - 15 years old children showed more need for when they got strict disciplinary practices from their parents.

Rao (1984) conducted a study of moral judgment in children. The sample included 200 boys and 200 girls drawn from different classes. The findings of the study were home variable was the significant predictor of moral judgment in terms of socio-economic status of the formal operation stage. (N = 400).

Sreedharamurthy (1984) observed that the students from high socio-economic status were significantly better in truthful ness dimension of moral judgment were as students from low socio-economic status were significant better in non - violence dimension of moral judgment.

Vanaja (1984) found that socio-economic status did not significantly brought out any variation in the moral judgment.

Bhargava (1986) in his study he found that the effect of home and educational environment on moral judgment. The findings of the study were:

- The measures of home variables were positively related with moral judgment at the concrete as well as the formal operational stage. This measure was socio-economic status.
- The measures of socio-economic status correlated significantly with moral judgment at concrete and formal operational stage.
- Home variables were significant predictors of moral judgment in terms of mother-acceptance socio-economic status and moral attitude of the formal operational stage home environment was significant predictor of moral judgment with respect to socio-economic status.

Dayakara Reddy, V. (1987) found that socio-economic status does not significant influence on the reasoning of moral judgment. (N = 900).

Geethanath, P.S. (1987) found that socio-economic status has significant influence on the reasoning of moral judgment. (N = 1400).

Chaya (1993) investigated that the socio-economic status was not found a significant factor contributing for moral judgment among students.

Sridhar (1994) observed that the moral judgment orientation of high school students is influenced by the socio-economic status peer approved moral judgment is positively correlated to peer group status.

Chaya (1996) found that socio-economic status was not a significant factor for moral judgment

Prabhu (1996) investigated that the socio-economic status did not have any effect on moral judgment of students of ninth standard. ( N = 400).

Loos *et al.* (1999) studied the relation of (SES) moral development, disciplinary methods, and emergence of guilt feelings. The results were evaluated according to group, identification of character, emotional recognition, character judgment in conditions of intentional and accidental damage, and conceptions of guilt. Results indicate that age but not social group is associated with guilt conceptions.

Chaya (2001) observed that there was no significant effect of socio-economic status on the moral judgment scores of students

Koexig (2001) to expand the limited knowledge on moral development in abused, neglected and non maltreated children from low socio-economic backgrounds. Findings showed that, contrary to predictions, neglected children engaged in significantly less rule-compatible behaviour compared to non-maltreated children. In addition, maltreatment status differences interacted with gender on several of the moral paradigms. Abused girls displayed significant less guilt and fewer donation behaviors than neglected girls. Finally, results revealed that both abusive and neglectful mothers are more likely to depict a power assertive discipline style, whereas comparison mothers are likely to employ an inductive style of discipline. However, no evidence was found that maternal discipline styles act as a moderator in relation between maltreatment and moral development.

Reddy, Sabitha (2003) investigated that socio-economic status of the students was significantly affecting the moral judgment.

Commons, Michael lamport; Galaz-Fontes, Jesus Francisco; Morse, Stanley Jay (2006) investigated that those who were of high socio-economic status reasoned at higher stages than those who are not.

Rangaswamy, G. (2006) observed that socio-economic status does not significant influence on the reasoning of moral judgment. (N = 900).

Talwar and Sheela (2006) inferred that students from high socio-economic status or less than obedient and morality than student of low socio economic status.

## STUDIES RELATED TO RESIDENCE AND MORAL JUDGMENT

Residence means hostler or day scholar of the students. Residence of the students may have relationship with their reasoning of moral judgment of the students. Some of the studies related to residence are shown here under:

Merrie and Elliot (1984) concluded that residence did not link with emotional maturity on moral judgment.

## STUDIES RELATED TO AGE AND MORAL JUDGMENT

Age of the students may have relationship with they reasoning of moral Judgment of the students. Some of the related studies are presented bellow:

Wright and Cox (1967) concluded that age was not found to be related to moral judgment. (N = 2276)

Heishman, Helen Mane (1973) investigated that younger subject score significantly lower than older subjects on moral judgment tasks.

Rowahan, Ravan Hashim (1974) observed that there is no relation ship between age and moral judgment.

Gopalaiah (1981) studied that between the ages of 7 and 17 years a vivid development was traced in moral judgment. As the age increased, the level of moral judgment reached higher and higher level. (N = 120)

Devendra and Mishra (1981) conducted a study on development of moral judgment in Indian children and found that the main effect of age was significant. Also age X sex and age X socio-economic status interaction yielded significant effect. The interaction of the three independent factors was also found to be significant. It was concluded that although the capacity for moral judgment increases with age, the pattern is significant mediated by factors of sex and socio-economic status.

Gorgre (1981) concluded that significant relationship did not exist between the DIT scores and age.

Bandopadhyay (1981) has studied the effects of socio-economic status conditions, sex, type of school and parental discipline on moral judgment. The major finding is of seven areas of moral judgment girls showed more maturity than boys in three areas viz., attitude towards justice, equality and authority and collective responsibility, imminent justice and guilt, so that the moral judgment was positively related with irrespective of age.

Prahalada (1982) investigated that significance difference was not reported between the students belonging to four difference age groups.

Tripathi and Grishwar (1982) observed that although the capacity for moral judgment increases with age.

Gupta (1984) were to find out the stages of moral development of school children and also to study the moral reasoning of children of various age groups. The tools for the data collection were Moral Reasoning Scale, Moral Dilemmas Scale and the Personal data sheet. The following were the main findings of the study. Reasoning was used by the children at the age of 12, the use of which declined sharply with the increase in age. As the child matured, he had fewer and fewer arguments of reward and punishment.

Marrie and Elliot (1984) observed that age wise (four age levels 13, 14, 15 and 16 years) there were no significant difference on moral judgment.

Rao (1984) concluded that there was a significant development of moral judgment from one age group to the next successive age group.

Bhargava (1986) inferred that there was a significant development of moral judgment from one age group to the next successive age group.

Sharma and Kaur (1992) investigated that age was important factor in influencing moral judgment.

Schoffner (1997) was examined decision making in the area of moral reasoning and its relationship with identity development, emotional super sensitivity, and gender role flexibility gifted high academically gifted adolescents. Results indicated no statistically significant effects by age for any of the dependent variables.

Deguchi and Ohkawa (2000) examined that the males subjects empathy rate and moral judgment rate increased with age and the female subjects empathy rate and moral judgment rate did not show significant difference between ages.

Eisenberg *et al.* (2005) conducted a study on Age changes' measures of pro-social responding and reasoning were examined. Participants' reports of helping, empathy-related responding, and pro social moral reasoning were obtained in adolescence (from age 15-16 years) and into adulthood (to age 25-26 years) Perspective taking and approval/interpersonal oriented stereotypic pro social moral reasoning increased from adolescence into adulthood, whereas personal distress declined. Helping declined and then increased (a cubic trend) pro social moral judgment composite scores (and self-reflective empathic reasoning) generally increased from late adolescence into the early 20s age 17-18 to 21-22) but either leveled off or declined slightly thereafter (i.e., showed linear and cubic trends); rudimentary needs-oriented reasoning showed the reverse pattern of change. The increase in self-reflective empathic moral reasoning was for females only. Thus, perspective taking and some aspects of pro social moral reasoning - capacities with a strong socio cognitive basis - showed the clearest increases with age, whereas simple pro-social proclivities (i.e., helping, sympathy) did not increase with age.

Raaijmakers *et al.* (2005) investigated that multi group analysis for three different age cohorts revealed a consistent negative effect of previous delinquency on moral reasoning between the ages of 21-23 years. Between the ages of 24-26, however, delinquency scores were, in turn, negatively affected by previous moral reasoning.

Commons *et al.* (2006) investigated that the stage of reasoning increased with age.

Helwing *et al.* (2007) examined that at all ages Adolescents appealed to fundamental democratic principles, such as representation, voice and majority rule, to justify their judgments. Similar age-related patterns in judgments and reasoning were found across cultures and across diverse setting within China.

## STUDIES RELATED TO BIRTH ORDER AND MORAL JUDGMENT

The birth order means first or second or third etc., born child to the parents. It is assumed that birth order may have relationship with moral judgment of the students. Some of the related studies are presented bellow:

Sharma and Kaur (1992) investigated that birth order (first born/last born) in the family was important factor is influencing moral judgment.

## STUDIES RELATED TO FATHER'S EDUCATION AND MORAL JUDGMENT

Father's education may be related to the reasoning of moral judgment of the students their may be necessary guidance and counseling from the educated members of the family. Some of the related studies are presented bellow:

Singh (1983) observed that the boys and girls belonging to fathers with high education status had the highest mean moral judgment scores followed by those belonging to fathers with middle and low educational status respectively.

## STUDIES RELATED TO SIZE OF THE FAMILY AND MORAL JUDGMENT

The size of the family may have influence on the reasoning of moral judgment of students. Some of the related studies are presented below:

Rangaswamy, G. (2006) investigated that size of the family does not significant influence on the reasoning of moral judgment.(N = 900).

## STUDIES RELATED TO MEDIUM OF THE STUDY AND MORAL JUDGMENT

The medium of the study may have influence on the reasoning of moral judgment of students. Some of the related studies are presented bellow:

Prabhu (1996) investigated that the students studying in Kannada medium have better moral judgment than the students studying in English medium

## STUDIES RELATED TO COURSE OF THE STUDY AND MORAL JUDGMENT

The course of the study may have influence on the reasoning of moral judgment of students. Some of the related studies are presented bellow:

Wright and Cox (1967) concluded that the subject studies was not found to be related to moral judgment. (N = 2276)

Talwar and Sheela (2006) investigated that science students have scored higher in the components of moral judgment than arts students.

## STUDIES RELATED TO MORAL JUDGMENT IN GENERAL

Wright and Cox (1967) concluded that experience of co-education was not found to be related to moral judgment and consistency; indices of religiosity were found to be severity of moral judgment. (N = 2276).

Saraswathi (1978) did a study to know the relationship between various maternal disciplinary practices, as reported by children and the development of moral judgment. The major findings were: there was a trend of negative correlations between maternal power assertion and Moral Maturity Scores (MMS) of children and positive correlation between maternal induction and moral maturity scores of children.

Gopalaiah (1981) observed that the high achievers were characterized by higher level of moral judgment of socionomy and autonomy, the low achievers had equal levels of judgment among heteronomy, socionomy and autonomy, the low achievers were characterized by heteronomy levels of moral judgment. (N = 120).

Siefering (1981) investigated the relationship between moral reasoning and intelligence. In addition, sex and behaviour correlates impulse control and social conformity were also explored. It indicated that both social conformity and impulse control were significantly related to moral reasoning.

Singh (1983) observed that there was a significant negative correlation between moral judgment and prolonged deprivation and Duncon's range test applied to the mean moral judgment scores showed a significant difference between high and low, and high and medium deprived groups.

Sreedharamurthy (1984) concluded that high religiosity students were found to be significantly better in their moral judgment than moderate or low religiosity students.

Kitchener *et al.* (1984) investigated longitudinal changes in moral development of undergraduates and 20 graduate students, using a concurrent measure of verbal abilities as a statistical control. A significant increase was found between the 2 moral judgment scores and between groups at both testings. Females scored higher than the males; however, these differences were accounted for by their overall higher level of verbal ability. Overall subjects showed a significant increase in their use of principled moral reasoning over the 2 year old follow up period. Findings suggest that moral development continues into the adult years and that verbal abilities may moderate sex differences in moral judgment.

Vanaja (1984) studied the moral judgment among 300 ninth and tenth standard students of Bangalore city in relation to their self confidence, sex, socio-economic status and type of school. Results of the study were indicated that self confidence was significantly and positively related with moral judgments.

Agarwal (1985) conducted a study of feeling of security in morally developed and under developed adolescents as related to their self-concept and personality pattern. The important findings were the adolescents were found to be secure. Moral development was related to the feeling of security. Self-concept was not related with moral development.

Schliefli (1985) reviewed 55 students of education interventions designed to stimulate development in moral judgment. The principle findings from data analysis indicated that the dilemma discussion and psychological development program produce modest overall effect age sizes, the treatment of about 3-12 weeks are optional and that programs with adults (24+ years) produce larger effect sizes than with younger subjects. However, significant effect sizes were obtained with all groups. (N = 55)

Seigal (1985) did two studies to compare the conceptions of moral and social rules in 20 pre-scholars (aged 2 years 11 months to 5 years to 3 months) who had attended day care fir at least 18 months and 20 pre-scholars who were newly enrolled (aged 3 years 1 month to 5 years 5 months). Results provided a basis for previous findings that day care children are more independent tin their compliance with adult directives than are their noonday care counterparts.

Frank, Arsenio Willian (1986) explored the role of affective information in children's conceptual and behavioural distinction among six perspective socio-moral rule systems i.e., inhibitive morally, active morality destructive justice, prosaically morality and conventional and personal. The results indicate that children had highly differentiated conceptions of the affective consequence of socio-moral events. Overall, pro-social morality and distributive justice events were perceived as having positive affective consequences, while conventional personal active and inhibitive morality was viewed as having progressively negative consequence. Children's affective conceptions also differed for each character and for particular rule system and character role combinations.

Derr (1986) investigated how 25 Learning Disabled (LD) and 25 average achieving male high school students (age 14.3 = 18.5 years) formulated moral judgments were administered individually Kohlberg's moral judgment interview. Results showed that, compared with average achieving subjects, the LD group less evidence of being able to view moral dilemmas from a community or societal perspective. Further the LD group exhibited a substantial amount of reasoning from an egocentric perspective that focused on the needs and desires of the self. It is suggested that teachers implement strategies to facilitate the development of social and moral reasoning in LD students. (N = 50)

Gibbs *et al.* (1986) examined the relationship or moral judgment to moral action and to certain cognitive style variables in 10th, 11th and 12th grade students. Results were consistent with explorer hypothesis that type B is a social cognitive manifestation of field independence and is conductive to socially independent and ethically ideal action (moral courage). Both moral judgment type B and moral judgment stage maturity were related to moral courage and field independence but not to internal locus of control.

Parmar (1986) made a sociological study of social values and aspirations of children of rural background. Sample consisted of 250, 10th standard children coming from the rural background. The important findings of the study was the personality development, educational performance, values, attitudes etc., of children coming from different socio-economic status and culture are influenced by their society as well as by the climate to which they belong to. (N = 250)

Feather (1988) investigated relations between principled moral judgment as assessed by the defining issues test, the importance for self of the terminal and instrumental values form the Rokeach value survey, and general conservation as measured by a conservatism scale. The Ss were 133 south Australian students in year 11 course in 4 high schools. Results show that principled moral judgment (stages 5 and 6) was positively linked to the importance assigned by Ss to inner harmony, being broadminded and being logical, and negatively related to the importance they assigned to being clean and obedient. Stage 4 moral judgment and general conservation were positively related, and both were related to a similar (but not identical) subset of values.

Kennedy *et al.* (1988) examined the relationship between 2 aspects of social competence - moral reasoning (moral judgment scale) and Interpersonal Cognitive Problem-solving Skills (ICPS) - in 14-18 year old inner-city, minority Ss from low Socio-Economic Status (SES) backgrounds. Two new ICPS components proposed and employed in the present study were consistently related both to family functioning patterns and to indices of subject adjustment.

Sigman and Erdynast (1988) concerning the moral judgment of adolescents suffering from emotional and cognitive disorders. It is concluded that social involvement is critical for the development of social and moral judgment.

Henry (1989) conducted a study on levels of emotional development with experienced levels of emptiness and existential concerns. Summary of his study reveals using a sample of 61 male students, the relations between level of emotional development, according to Dabrowski and Piechowski theory of positive disintegration, and experienced levels of emptiness, existential concerns, and depression were examined to see if earlier findings are supported. A positive correlation was noted between level of emotional development and emptiness, confirming the earlier study.

Panigua (1989) conducted a study on Lying by children. Why children say one thing, do another? The summary of his study is as follows. Lying constitutes a problematic behaviour for parents and other social agents involved in children's development of effective behaviours. This analysis suggests that lying is in part, the name for a lack of correspondence between saying and doing, and that effective correspondence training procedures can be designed to teach truthfulness in children through the teaching of either promise-then-do correspondence or do-then-report correspondence.

Das (1990) conducted a study on existing programs for moral development in selected secondary schools in India. The results revealed that out of 78 schools, only 12 replied in the affirmative and 8 schools considered moral education as a subject of study and this provided periods fit it in the school time table. This shows that majority of the schools do not regard moral education as a subject of study and do not provide for it in school time table.

Macek and Osecka (1990) used a questionnaire with 313 high school students (150 boys and 163 girls, mean age 16-9 yrs) to examine (1) The more general dimensions considered important by the Ss assessed themselves in reality (real self) and how they wished to be (ideal self). Results of the semantic differential were factor analyzed. Four typical configurations in self-evaluation and self-ideal, somewhat different for boys and for girls, are described.

Glover (1991) conducted a study on applying Neo Piagetian theory to the moral reasoning process. The summary of the study was that this study examined moral reasoning process and patterns of skills underlying a moral dilemma through use of K.W. Fischer's theory for cognitive skill acquisition. Kohelberg's Heinz dilemma issues of life and law were hypothesized as scable within task-domains pertaining to familial relationship, sickness/death, law/rules and fairness. About 80, 4-12 years old were interviewed regarding these issues. Guttmann scale analysis examined scalability of their responses to items in each task and skill domain.

Shweder (1991) suggest that cultural norms and culturally shaped emotions have a substantial impact on the domain of morality and the process of moral judgment.

Richards *et al.* (1992) compared the moral reasoning predicts classroom behaviour problems. He conducted problems of decline monotonically with increasing moral maturity. Their moral reasoning assessed by using the Colby *et al.* (1987) interview method and standard issue scoring. Trend analysis failed to support that they recorded well with the alternative.

Chaya (1993) investigated that higher the religiosity, higher was the moral judgment in all its dimensions and boys having high religiosity had the highest 'honesty' and 'obedience' dimension of moral judgment

Haidt (1993) explored whether disgusting or disrespectful actions are judged to be moral violations, even when these actions are harmless. Stories about victimless yet offensive actions (such as cleaning ones toilet with a flag) were presented to Brazilian and US adults and children of high and low SES (N = 360). Results show that college students at elite universities judged these stories to be matters of social convention or personal preference.

Narayanaswamy (1994) examined the moral judgment of higher primary students (240 higher primary standards from 8 different higher primary schools of Bangalore city) in relation to their sex, type of school, standard and self-concept. He indicated that self concept is significantly and positively related to moral judgment among higher primary children. (N = 240)

Chaya (1996) studied moral judgment of ninth standard students in relation to their parental behaviour, values, socio-economic status and type of management. It was found that valued found to be affect moral judgment of students. Higher the value, higher was the moral judgment also.

Yeh (1996) investigated on culturally grounded conceptualization of self and morality of 60 college students of each country namely Japan and the United States. Japanese respondents were found to have an interpersonally oriented morality: their story completions were significantly more likely than the American's to (1) Focus on the relationship in the story, (2) Maintain harmony in the relationship, (3) Have altruistic motivations for the morally questionable act, (4) Portray the main character sympathetically and (5) Center on emotional and feelings rather than factual details. Part two examines the relationship between interpersonal obligations in morality and culturally based interdependent and independent self - concepts. Ten respondents from each country were administered altered versions of the story completion exercise, with the respondents identified as the moral actors. Respondents were subsequently interviewed about their conceptualizations and their understanding of self and morality. Japanese respondents constructed their understanding of self and morality. Japanese respondents constructed their commission of morally dubious acts as the consequents of betrayal or victimization by a friend. American respondents, in contrast, constructed the acts as altruistic or heroic efforts to protect others from harm. Qualitative data from the story completions and interviews indicate that American respondents understand morality in terms of abstract principles and religious and legal codes. They emphasis personal freedom and responsibility to one self morality is the sum of societal and individually derived moral constructs. The Japanese respondents consider morality to be situation specific, depending on relationships.

Ostini and Ellerman (1997) investigated the relationship between values and moral judgment, which was conducted using 124 Australian university students. Analysis confirmed only some of the predicted relationships between values and the moral reasoning measure and indicated some that had not been predicted.

Schoffner (1997) inferred that the interpersonal identity level explained 12 per cent of the variance in moral reasoning.

Mestre *et al.* (1998) studied the university students of psychology (N = 22) participated in 10 weekly moral discussion/ debate sessions of 80 min, preceded and followed by completion of rest's defining Issues test, Tennessee self-concept scale, and Rokeach's scale of values. They and another group (N = 24) participated in a 6 session, twice weekly programme to improve self-concept. The control group of 22 completed the instruments at the same time. Results showed significant improvement in physical, personal and social self-concept among the self-concept only group. Moral maturity increased among participations in analysis and discussion of moral dilemmas, although self-concept measures did not.

Myyry and Helkama (1998) investigated on the sensitivity to moral issues from a story in a professional context and development of the ability to interpret moral situations in a sample of 50 social psychology students participating in a one-semester course on professional ethics. The relationships between initial value priorities measured by Schwartz value survey (1992) and moral sensitivity were also explored. No gender differences were found in the focus partially sensitivity score. However, females and males seemed to focus partially on different issues while interpreting the situation. Concerning the value priorities, respondents with higher regard for the power, hedonism and stimulation value types were lower on sensitivity, whereas the universalism value type was positively related to the sensitivity level.

Piaget and Wright's (1998) did research study was to look more closely at the moral reasoning abilities of children who have experienced physical neglect. The study has revealed two key findings:

- Elementary school age children who are experiencing neglect are less able to distinguish between right and wrong parenting behaviours than equally poor, non-neglected children;
- Mothers who have an open neglect case with the department of social services rate improvement in their own morality as less important than do equally poor mothers who have a closed case with the department and than who never have had a neglect case.

Batson *et al.* (1999) investigated how can people appear moral to themselves when fail to act morally? Overall, results showed three different faces of moral hypocrisy.

Millis (1999) explored the role that dilemma context had on children's moral judgment responses. Students in grades six and twelve were presented with four school based and four non-school-based socio moral dilemmas, and asked to select a course of action for each, and a reason for their selection. Findings of this study revealed that slight developmental changes in moral maturity occurred between grade six and grade twelve. Grade six students evidenced a preference for stage 1 moral reasoning while grade twelve students chose more stage 2 responses. Hence, the growth observed in moral maturity occurred within the lowest two stages of moral reasoning. The differences in response patterns between the two grade levels did not depend on the context of the dilemma.

Day, Laura (2000) investigated the experiences of, and interactions between participations of a forum theatre workshop, which addressed the issue of the refugee child at school, staged by a UK theatre company, whose actors had, in their own lives, experienced being homeless and/or refugees, the workshop was investigated as it was performed in three London secondary state schools. Findings revealed that the workshop was highly relevant to the students, reflecting moral dilemmas, which they faced in their everyday lives, as they encounted refuge students at school.

Pasupathi *et al.* (2001) examined adolescents wisdom related knowledge and judgment with a heterogeneous sample of 146 adolescents (ages 14-120 years) and a comparison sample of 58 young adults (ages 21-37). The findings confirmed that in contrast to adulthood, adolescence is a major period for normative age-graded development in knowledge about difficult life problems. Adolescents performed at lower levels than young adults but also demonstrated substantial age increments in performance. As expected, adolescent's performance varied as a function of criteria and gender.

Rani, Suma (2001) conducted a study on the five dimensions of moral judgment among students of ninth standard of Kolar district in relation to their gender, type of school, urban and rural background and social maturity. She found that social maturity in its low, moderate and high levels also did not significantly contribute for moral judgment.

Bhattacharya and Mukhopadhyay (2002) designed to understand the nature of social life adjustment pattern and moral behaviour of group of students studying in secondary and higher secondary level at West Bengal. The findings reveal that both the groups possess (1) A healthy psycho-physical make up favorable for gaining self confidence and developing a rationale for optimism. (2) A right attitude to perform with best of loyalties, the functions of task expected of him by his family, community and country of large and (3) A capability of playing a competent social role for attaining objectives of national interest but, there is a variation between these two groups in certain degree.

Bunch, Wilton H. (2005) conducted a study on gains in moral judgment, as measured by the Defining Issues Test (DIT), correlated strongly with advancing education. Curricula that are strongly biblically based may not promote, and students with a strong fundamentalist orientation may not demonstrate, such moral growth. Students at an interdenominational, but very conservative seminary completed the DIT before and after ethics courses conducted in three different formats. Those students who spent 30 hours in small-group discussions of ethical dilemmas improved their moral reasoning scores, while those who had fewer hours of discussion or lectures did not. It would appear that small group discussions, shown to improve moral reasoning scores in other educational setting, are also successful in a strongly biblical environment.

Derryberry, W. Pitt and Thoma, Stephen, J. (2005) conducted a study on current models of moral function such as those of Rest (1983) and Damon and Hart (1988) have maintained that optimal moral development and consistent moral action require the presence of multiple construct. In order to examine the importance of the presence of multiple variables relevant to moral functioning, structural equation modeling was used in addressing relationships among measurements of moral judgment development, self-understanding, and three distinct forms of moral action. A sample of 167 college students responded to measure of moral judgment, self-understanding, and moral action in three data collection sessions. Models generated of these data revealed that three different forms of moral action were statistically distinct and were differentially related to moral judgment development and self - understanding. The results are discussed in terms of the importance and contributions of multiple moral developmental constructs in the production of moral action.

Derryberry, W. Pitt and Thoma, Stephen, J. (2005) examined that applying Synder and Feldman's 1984 consolidation-transition model to moral judgment development has enabled further understanding of how moral judgment translates to moral functioning. In this study, 178 college students were identified as being in consolidated versus transitional phases of moral judgment development using Rest's Defining Issues Test (DIT). Participant moral functioning was inferred through an honest decision-making index along with Attitudes Towards Human Rights Inventory (ATHRI) and Volunteer Functions Inventory (VFI) scores. Multivariate analyses of variance revealed that the consolidated group was significantly more honest than the transitional group. No differences attributable to moral judgment phase were seen for ATHRI and VFI scores. Findings support the claim that consolidated phases improve the explanatory power of moral judgment for certain moral functional outcomes particularly those involving ambiguity and minimal time for decision-making.

Comunian, Anna L. and Gielen, Uwe, P. (2006) examined that social role-taking and moral judgment improvement after an educational group oriented intervention emphasizing guided reflection and role-taking dimensions among 11 groups, made up of a total of 61 female and male Italian university students. They were compared to a control group of 59 students. We twice applied Italian adaptations of two role-taking and two moral development measures, originally developed by Gibbs and by Lind respectively in the USA and in Germany. Good empirical support for the reliability and validity of the American and German instruments was noted in the Italian setting. Students assumed more responsibility in a variety of social roles, exposed themselves increasingly to social role - taking opportunities, and showed increased moral judgment maturity after the educational intervention.

John, C. Gibbs (2006) examined that Krebs and Denton (2005) proposed that Kohlberg's cognitive developmental approach to morality be replaced by a pragmatic approach more relevant to everyday social behaviour and the cooperative moral orders of society. Although the Krebs and Denton article raises some legitimate questions, their proposal is at best premature and provokes some serious concerns. Their starting point, that Kohlberg's model of morality is inadequate, is an evolution shared by many Neo-Kohlbergians. Before the cognitive developmental approach is replaced, however, important contributions (e.g., Rest's schema interpretation of the stages) toward refining or improving the approach must be adequately considered. Evidence suggests that Krebs and Denton may have underestimated relations between moral judgment stages and social behaviour, including sudden behaviour in emergency situations.

Morton *et al.* (2006) inferred that moral motivation (spirituality), moral sensitivity (post – formal skills) and moral reasoning are operationalized to examine the mediational effects of moral sensitivity of medical students. In the complex moral environment of medical students opportunities arise to question values and develop cognitive - affective skills, among them spirituality and post-formal thinking which are linked to increases in post - conventional moral reasoning. The models tested indicated that moral sensitivity mediates the relationship between moral motivation and moral reasoning.

Talwar and Sheela (2006) conducted a research on a study of moral judgment of 169 I$^{st}$ year pre-university students in Government and Private colleges in Bangalore city in relation to gender, socio-economic status, course of study, religion and moral judgment of their teachers. It found that the moral judgment of students is highly correlated to that of their teachers.

Wilhelm, William J. and Czyzewski, Alan, B. (2006) it found that either of the interventions positively affected levels of moral reasoning in students. Intrinsic motivation to engage in substantial ethical analysis was found to be lacking if grade points were not related to the effort.

Boom *et al.* (2007) concluded that proposals to replace Kohlberg's characterization of moral development are premature.

Herigton, Carmel and Weaven, Scott (2007) inferred that the findings indicate that marketing students do not exhibit a lower level of MRA than other business disciplines. Marketing students are no less ethical in their thinking than those pursuing other business careers. The perception of unethical behaviour is more likely to be a product of the visible nature of marketing activities to consumers.

Marx *et al.* (2007) conducted a study on comprehension of moral reasoning is important both for successful moral education and for Kohlbergian claims that moral reasoning development is cognitive in nature. Because a psychometrically appropriate moral comprehension instrument does not appear to exist, the Moral Comprehension Questionnaire (MCQ) was constructed in study 1 and displayed some positive reliability and validity findings. Study 2 used this questionnaire to examine whether the increased Defining Issue Test (DIT) p scores shown by liberals is indicative of increased cognitive development. While liberals displayed slightly greater moral comprehension than conservatives, moral comprehension and political orientation mostly appear to contribute independently to high p scores. Additionally, consistent with Kohlbergian theory, comprehension of Stage 5 moral reasoning is more challenging than comprehension of Stage 3, 4 reasoning. Consequently, while p scores are somewhat cognitive development in nature, they also are independently predicted by political orientation.

Mc Pherson, Michael S. and Schapiro, Morton Owen (2007) found that the examples of issues in higher education that have significant value dimensions. These issues are: (1) Early admissions, (2) Needs analysis in student aid, (3) Need-based aid packages and (4) Admissions decisions.

Steve and Maddux, Cleborne D. (2007) indicated that moral reasoning levels of in-service and pre-service teachers are relatively low but can be increased through proper intervention.

Bartels, Daniel M. (2008) revealed that, in study 1, judgments were affected by rated agreement with moral rules proscribing harm, whether the dilemma under consideration made moral rules versus consequences of choice salient, and by thinking styles (intuitive Vs. deliberative). In studies 2 and 3, participants evaluated policy decisions to "knowingly do harm" to a resource to mitigate greater harm of to "merely allow" the greater harm to happen. When evaluated in isolation, approval for decisions to harm was affected by endorsement of moral rules and by thinking style. When both choices were evaluated simultaneously, total harm - but not the do/allow distinction influenced rated approval. These studies suggest that moral rules play an important, but context sensitive role in moral cognition, and offer an account of when emotional reactions to perceived moral violations receive less weight than consideration of costs and benefits in moral judgment and decision making.

Danielle, E. Warren and Kristin Smith-Crowe (2008) investigated that previous research has overlooked the pervasive ambiguity in ethical situations organizations, as well as how people pierce through this ambiguity to realize new distinctions between right and wrong. Focusing on well-intentioned individuals who unknowingly transgress, we present theory of how they come to recalibrate their moral judgments. Finally found that internal emotional responses to sanctions (name embarrassment) will facilitate this shift by triggering a sense of moral deficiency. More specifically, we assert that embarrassment will focus the transgressor's attention on what went wrong. This reflection provides an opportunity for the recalibration of the initial moral judgment.

Greene *et al.* (2008) conducted a study on traditional theories of moral development emphasize the role of controlled cognition in mature moral judgment, while a more recent trend emphasizes intuitive and emotional processes. Here we test a dual-process theory synthesizing these perspectives. More specifically, our theory associates utilitarian moral judgment (approving of harmful actions that maximize good consequences) with controlled cognitive processes and associates non-utilitarian moral judgment with automatic emotional responses. Consistent with this theory, we find that a cognitive load manipulation selectively interferes with utilitarian judgment. This interference effect provides direct evidence for the influence of controlled cognitive processes in moral judgment, and utilitarian moral judgment more specifically.

Grunwald, Heidi E. and Mayhew, Matthew J. (2008) Investigated that the study was to illustrate the use of propensity scores for creating comparison groups, partially controlling for pretreatment course selection bias, and estimating the treatment effects of selected courses on the development of moral reasoning in undergraduate students. A sample of convenience for comparing differences in moral reasoning development scores among students enrolled in inter group dialogue, service learning, psychology and philosophy courses with those of an introductory sociology course. Adopting a propensity score approach include reviewing the empirical literature for its guidance in substantiating the reasons for including pretreatment variables (i.e., pretreatment course taking behaviors, race, sex, political identification, need for cognition, major pretreatment moral reasoning scores) in our analysis, measuring these variables, and reducing them into a single composite propensity score for each student in our analytic sample. This score then served as the basis for creating a new comparison group and for allowing us to estimate unbiased (or less biased) course-related treatment effects on moral reasoning development. Implications for higher education researchers are discussed.

Mayhew, Matthew J. and King, Patricia (2008) Investigated that college instructors uses a variety of approaches to teach students to reason more effectively about issues with a moral dimension and achieve mixed results. This pre-post study of 423 undergraduate students examined the effect of morally explicit and implicit curricular content and of selected pedagogical strategies on moral reasoning development. Using causal modelling to control for a range of student background variables as well as time 1 scores, 52% of the variance in moral reasoning scores was explained; we found that these scores were affected by type of curricular content and by three pedagogical strategies (active learning, reflection and faculty

- student interaction). Students who experienced more negative interactions with diverse peers were the least likely to show positive change in moral reasoning as a result of participating in any course, Implications for the design of intervention studies are discussed, including the need to attend to selection and attenuation effects.

Eyal, Tal *et al.* (2008) investigated that people judge immoral acts as more offensive and moral acts as more virtuous when their acts are psychologically distant than near. This is because people construe more distant situations in terms of principles, rather than attenuating situation - specific considerations. Results of four studies support these predictions. Study 1 show that more temporally distant transgressions (eg. eating one dead dog) are construed in terms of moral principles rather than contextual information. Study 2 and further show that morally offensive actions are judged more severely when imagined from a more distant temporal (Study 2) or social (Study 3) perspective. Finally, Study 4 shows that moral acts (e.g., adopting disabled child) are judged more positively from temporal distance. The findings suggest that people more readily apply their moral principles to distant rather than proximal behaviors.

Turiel and Elliot (2008) examined that Lawrence Kohlberg first published details of his research on the development of moral judgments in "Vita Humana" (later titled "Human Development") Along with a series of other articles and essays; he greatly influenced research on moral development. He was instrumental in moving the field out of the narrow confines of analyses of psychological mechanisms to inclusion of substantive philosophical definitions of the domain. He persuaded many researchers to take morality seriously as a realm pertaining to people's thinking about how they ought to relate to each other and how social systems should be organized. Although several aspects of Kohlberg's theoretical formulations are now not widely accepted, most researchers (though not all) are concerned with combining epistemological considerations with psychological analyses and view children as possessing moral capacities not solely imposed by adults.

One of these theoretical perspectives, discussed in this easy, is based on distinctions among social domains.

Brimi, Hunter (2009) examined that the role that teachers play in the moral development of American students. Historically, one of public education's purposes in America has been the development of moral citizens. However educators currently face more academic accountability due to no child left behind. Consequently, teachers must strike a balance between achieving quantifiable academic standards and assisting with students' character development.

Fowler *et al.* (2009) studied that how teaching a year long curriculum using Socio-Scientific Issues (SSI) learning out comes. In this report, the effects of a SSI driven curriculum on the development of student's moral sensitivity. Results indicated that development of moral sensitivity can be promoted through science learning experiences embedded in SSI. Moral sensitivity is contextually dependent.

CHAPTER 3

# THE PRESENT STUDY

This chapter deals with the statement of the problem, need for the study, purpose of the study, scope of the study, definition of the terms, objectives and hypotheses of the study, variables included in the study and limitations of the study.

## INTRODUCTION

Study at college level are expected to acquire and assimilate the basic moral values, which help shape their conduct and make moral judgment in accordance with the socio-cultural standards of the society of which they are members. The problem chosen for investigation is to study moral judgment of students from different year of study at Intermediate level.

The present study is concerned with the reasoning of moral stages, moral levels and moral judgment of Intermediate students. It examines the main and interaction effects of sex, year of study, management and region on the reasoning of moral stages, moral levels and moral judgment. It establishes the relationship between the moral stages, moral levels and moral judgment and other variables namely, academic achievement, personality factors, intelligence, socio-economic status scale, socio-demographic and personal variables. It is also predicted the moral judgment with the help of different sets of psycho-sociological variables.

## STATEMENT OF THE PROBLEM

The present study entitled "Moral Judgment of Intermediate Students".

## NEED FOR THE STUDY

The need for the present study arises out of the fact that the actual imparting or moral values in our schools and colleges are very nebulous and the students are left to their own devices to acquire at large, without any direction.

In recent trends, there has been a great debate regarding the need for inculcating moral and religious values in the context of scientific and secular temperament.

The studies available in this area have shown that many factors that contribute to the development of moral and spiritual values and a capacity to judge morally an ethically. In Indian context, not much work has been done to examine the need and the mode of providing moral education to students. In order to do this, one need the background information about the moral views and temperaments among the school going children, so that one can identify the gaps in the knowledge, so that while planning proper attention to be given to these dimensions.

However, no effective attempt is actually made to evaluate the moral judgment among the students so far. Thus to bring about such changes there is a need to know what the adolescents actually have in mind concerning various issues of moral judgment.

The main focus of the present study was, "A Study of Moral Judgment of Intermediate Students in Relation to Certain Factors".

## PURPOSE OF THE STUDY

The purpose of the study is to find out:

1. Whether there is any significant influence of main and interaction effects namely sex, year of study,

management and region on the reasoning of each moral stage, each moral level and moral judgment of Intermediate students?

2. Whether there is any relation between academic achievement and each moral stage, each moral level and moral judgment of Intermediate students?
3. Whether there is any relation between 14 personality factors (HSPQ) and each moral stage, each moral level and moral judgment of Intermediate students?
4. Whether there is any relation between intelligence and each moral stage, each moral level and moral judgment of Intermediate students?
5. Whether there is any relation between socio-demographic variables and each moral stage, each moral level and moral judgment of Intermediate students?
6. Whether there is any relation between personal variables and each moral stage, each moral level and moral judgment of Intermediate students?
7. Whether it is possible to predict moral judgment with the help of psycho-sociological factors?

## SCOPE OF THE STUDY

The main intention of the study is to find the relation of moral judgment of Intermediate students with academic achievement, personality, intelligence, socio-demographic variables and personal variables. Board of Intermediate Education and Board of Secondary Education examinations marks are taken as academic achievement, the personality factors, intelligence, socio-economic status, moral judgment, socio-demographic and personal variables are measured by the relevant instruments. The study attempted to predict the moral judgment of Intermediate students with the help of different psycho-sociological variables.

## OBJECTIVES OF THE STUDY

The study is designed in three purposeful ways. Those are:

1. Moral Stages
2. Moral Levels
3. Moral Judgment (MMQ).

**Moral Stages**

The moral stages deals with the following objectives:

1. To study the influence of sex, year of study, management and region on the reasoning of each moral stage.
2. To study the influence of academic achievement on the reasoning of each moral stage.
3. To study the influence of personality on the reasoning of each moral stage.
4. To study the influence of intelligence on the reasoning of each moral stage.
5. To study the influence of socio - demographic variables on the reasoning of each moral stage.
6. To study the influence of personal variables on the reasoning of each moral stage.

**Moral Levels**

The moral levels deals with the following objectives:

1. To study the influence of sex, year of study, management and region on the reasoning of each moral level.
2. To study the influence of academic achievement on the reasoning of each moral level.
3. To study the influence of personality on the reasoning of each moral level.
4. To study the influence of intelligence on the reasoning of each moral level.
5. To study the influence of socio - demographic variables on the reasoning of each moral level.

6. To study the influence of personal variables on the reasoning of each moral level.

**Moral Judgment**

The moral judgment deals with the following objectives:

1. To know the moral judgment of intermediate students.
2. To study the influence of sex, year of study, management and region on the reasoning of moral judgment.
3. To study the influence of academic achievement on the reasoning of moral judgment.
4. To study the influence of personality on the reasoning of moral judgment.
5. To study the influence of intelligence on the reasoning of moral judgment.
6. To study the influence of socio - demographic variables on the reasoning of moral judgment.
7. To study the influence of personal variables on the reasoning of moral judgment.

## HYPOTHESES OF THE STUDY

Based on the above objectives the following hypotheses are formulated.

**Moral Stages**

The moral stages deals with the following hypotheses:

1. There would be no significant influence of sex, year of study, management and region on the reasoning of each moral stage.
2. There would be no significant influence of academic achievement on the reasoning of each moral stage.
3. There would be no significant influence of personality on the reasoning of each moral stage.

4. There would be no significant influence of intelligence on the reasoning of each moral stage.
5. There would be no significant influence of socio-demographic variables on the reasoning of each moral stage.
6. There would be no significant influence of personal variables on the reasoning of each moral stage.

## Moral Levels

The moral levels deals with the following hypotheses:

1. There would be no significant influence of sex, year of study, management and region on the reasoning of each moral level.
2. There would be no significant influence of academic achievement on the reasoning of each moral level.
3. There would be no significant influence of personality on the reasoning of each moral level.
4. There would be no significant influence of intelligence on the reasoning of each moral level.
5. There would be no significant influence of socio-demographic variables on the reasoning of each moral level.
6. There would be no significant influence of personal variables on the reasoning of each moral level.

## Moral Judgment

The moral Judgment deals with the following hypotheses:

1. There would be no significant influence of sex, year of study, management and region on the reasoning of moral judgment.
2. There would be no significant influence of academic achievement on the reasoning of moral judgment.

3. There would be no significant influence of personality on the reasoning of moral judgment.
4. There would be no significant influence of intelligence on the reasoning of moral judgment.
5. There would be no significant influence of socio-demographic variables on the reasoning of moral judgment.
6. There would be no significant influence of personal variables on the reasoning of moral judgment.
7. None of the 39 independent variables in this study turn out to be significant predictor of moral judgment of Intermediate students.

## VARIABLES STUDIED

The following variables were taken into consideration in this study.

### Independent Variables

1. Academic achievement
2. Psychological variables

   Personality and Intelligence
3. Socio-demographic variables

   Caste, Religion, Native place, Socio-economic status and Residence.
4. Personal variables

   Age, Birth order, Annual income, Father's education, Mother's education, Father's occupation, Mother's occupation, Size of the family, Economic position of the family, Type of the family, Region, Sex, Management, Year of study and Course of the study.

## Dependent Variables

*Moral Stages*

Moral Stage 1, Moral Stage 2, Moral Stage 3, Moral Stage 4, Moral Stage 4A, Moral Stage 5A, Moral Stage 5B and Moral Stage 6.

*Moral Levels*

Pre-conventional level, Conventional level and Post-conventional level.

## MORAL JUDGMENT

### Definitions of the Terms

*Morality*

The word moral comes from the Latin word 'mores' which means custom, practice, a way of accomplishing things. Therefore, it has come to mean 'belonging to manners and conduct of men.'

—*Chambers 20th Century Dictionary*

A Morality is a complex of concepts and beliefs by which an individual determines whether his or her actions are right or wrong. Often times, these concepts and beliefs are generalized and codified in a culture or group, and thus serve to regulate the behaviours of its members.

—*Webster's Online Dictionary*

### Moral Stage

The scores of the subject on any one moral stage represents the students' ability to reason with principles of the particular moral stage in dealing with right or wrong conduct of the given situation.

### Moral Level

The subjects score on any one moral represents the students' ability to reason with principles of the particular moral level in dealing with right or wrong conduct of the given situation.

### Moral Judgment

The moral judgment score indicates the student's ability to reason with principles of all stages together in dealing with right or wrong conduct of the given situation. The study also attempts to study moral judgment interms of Kohlberg's moral stages, which are grouped into three levels. Pre-conventional level with stage 1 and 2, conventional level with stage 3, 4 and 4A and post-conventional level with stage 5A, 5B and 6.

### Academic Achievement

Knowledge attained or skills developed in the school subject usually designated by test scores or by marks assigned by teachers or by both (Good, 1973).

A measures of knowledge gained informal education usually indicated by test scores, grade points, averages and degrees. (Raj, 1996; Bellingham, 2004).

### Psycho-Sociological Factors

Behavioural and societal indicators of individuals.

### Socio-Economic Status

The back ground or standing of one or more persons in the society on the basis both of social class and financial situation (Bellingham, 2004).

### Factor

A cause or determiner, which may be unique to one variable or common to several variables, that may be used to account for the correlations among a set of variables (Good, 1973).

i) An element in the composition of anything, or in bringing about a certain result.

ii) A fact which has to be taken into account or which affects the course of events (Davidson *et al.*, 1988)

**Variable**

Any trait that changes from one case or condition to another; more strictly, the representation of the trait, usually in quantitative form, such as a measurement or an enumeration (Good, 1973).

In educational research, any entity that can vary. An "independent" variable is one that the researcher manipulates e.g., a type of instructional programme. A " dependent" variable is one that changes in consequence with changes in the independent variable (Bellingham, 2004).

**Personality**

A psychological term that refers to the predictable and unique indicators of the way an individual might respond to the environment. A personal reference that usually connotes acceptability and likeability (Raj 1996; Bellingham 2004).

**Study**

Application of the mind to a problems or subject.

**Student**

A person attending an educational institution or enrolled in educational programmes; also pupil, any individual of a bookish, thoughtful, or studious bent. An individual for whom instruction is provided in an educational programme under the jurisdiction of a school system, or other educational institution (Bellingham, 2004).

**Caste**

Caste is a system of stratification in which mobility up and down the status ladder, at least ideally may not occur (Green, 1943).

### Locality

A place considered with reference to some particular events or circumstances with it, a quarter in which certain things are done or which chosen for particular operations (Ridler, 1961).

### Region

Defined portion of the earth's surface now especially as distinguished by certain natural features, climatic conditions a special fauna or Flora, or the like. A separate par t or division of the world or Universe as the air, Heaven, etc. (Ridler, 1961).

## LIMITATIONS OF THE STUDY

1. The study is confined to Andhra Pradesh State of India only, Intermediate academic schedule during 2006-08.
2. The study is limited to Intermediate students only. i.e., (2006-08)
3. Moral judgment of Intermediate students depends on number of psychological, sociological, demographical and personal factors. It is not possible to include each and every factor in this investigation.
4. It is only a prestage product study in the area of moral judgment.
5. Due to laborious calculations, only certain factors are studied in this investigation.
6. It is only study based on survey research wherein the techniques of analyzing data based on Questionnaires and records are adopted.

CHAPTER 4

# METHODS OF INVESTIGATION

This chapter deals with the tools used in the study, scoring of the tools, sample selection, collection of data and statistical techniques used.

The following tools were used in the study:

- ❑ Moral Judgment Questionnaire (MMQ)
- ❑ Ravens Standard Progressive Matrices (RPM)
- ❑ Cattell's 14 Personality Factors Questionnaire (HSPQ), form 'A'
- ❑ Socio-Economic Status scale (SES).
- ❑ The Board of Intermediate Education examinations marks and the Board of Secondary Education examinations marks were taken as the indices of the level of academic achievement of the students.
- ❑ Socio-Demographic scale

The description of the above tools is given in the following pages in detail.

## MORAL JUDGMENT QUESTIONNAIRE

As the present study mainly seeks to describe students nature of moral judgment in terms of Kohlberg's developmental stages, the moral judgment questionnaire constructed, based on the theoretical constructs of Kohlberg's stage topology in connection with the advanced U.G.C. major research project "A study of moral judgment in children" by Srinivasa Rao *et al.* (1987) was adopted. The development and the description of the moral judgment questionnaire adopted are as follows:

### Description of the Development of Moral Judgment Dilemmas

In the past twenty years the outstanding work on moral development was initiated and inspired by Lawrence Kohlberg. Kohlberg's work may be seen as a continuation of Piaget's work in moral development. It extends and refines Piaget's basic notions of the development of moral judgment and introduces new methods of study. Many important findings and ideas have come from Kohlberg's research.

Piaget and Kohlberg gathered data by asking subjects to respond to hypothetical stories. These stories raised moral judgment issues and asked subjects to explain and justify their views.

### Piaget's Method of Data gathering

Piaget characteristically employed a dilemma pair in which both stories were similar except in one aspect. In a typical Piaget item, for instance, one dilemma depicts a boy who walks into a dining room and accidentally knocks over a tray of cups hidden by the door, breaking fifteen cups. The other dilemma of the pair depicts a boy who is trying to seek some jam out of the cupboard and knocks over and breaks one cup. The subject is asked first to judge which boy is naughtier, the one in the first dilemma or the one in the second dilemma and then explain his judgment and answer following-up probe questions, such as if you were the daddy, which one would you punish most. These stories are designed to find out whether the child bases his moral judgment on the amount of physical damage done (a purely objective notion of responsibility) or on the intentions of the actor (a subjective notion of responsibility).

Piaget's stories focused more on data gathering procedure. The set of constructing Piaget's stories was designed to highlight one aspect of moral judgment, and questioning was aimed at eliciting information for a specific scoring decision (e.g., whether the subject judge in terms of objective responsibility or subjective responsibility). The subject was essentiality in a forced choice situation, where he must choose which boy was naughtier.

## Kohlberg's Method of Data Gathering

Kohlberg's method of data gathering was much more open than Piaget's and the method of characterizing a subject though was much more complex Kohlberg employs a single dilemma, raising a dilemma in which an actor has two choices of action. One of the typical Kohlberg's stories depicts the dilemma of Heinz, a man whose wife was dying of cancer and needs a drug that the town druggist will sell only at an exorbitant price. Subjects are asked to tell whether it was right for Heinz to steal the drug from the druggist and justify his answers. The subjects responses are then classified by trained judges according to whether the answer was oriented towards avoidance of punishment and difference to authority (stage 1), towards prudent and purely self – centered concerns (stage 2), towards a husband's natural love and affection for his wife (stage 3) towards the necessity of unwavering adherence to society chaos (stage 4) and so on.

Almost all research based on Kohlberg's stage topology has used method of assessment devised in his 1958 dissertation with modified version of it. In Kohlberg's according system the subject's responses are characterized in terms of a two dimensional scoring grid of 25 aspects and 6 stages, approximately 125 scoring possibilities. Obviously this system which requires the scorer classifies a response into one or more of 125 categories were more complicated than a system demanding only a simple dichotomy decisions in Piaget's method.

The advantage of Kohlberg's open - end method of data gathering was that it leads to the postulations of many new developmental characteristics of moral judgment beyond those brought to light by Piaget. Since Kohlberg's stories are more complex and have gathered interviews from older subjects than Piaget, Kohlberg has lead information on which he postulated more advanced development than those embodied in Piaget's scheme.

The problem in Kohlberg's scoring system was that the subject's thinking was not decisive or completes enough for a scorer to decide clearly into which of the categories the response was to be classified. When the subject does not give sufficient clues to apply a scoring guide or when the subject's responses do not seem to fit very well into any of the scoring categories there is not much a scorer can do but guess.

This method of scoring produces material that is not strictly comparable from subject to subject, the assessments are vulnerable. To interviewer and scorer, biases and scoring the material involve complex interpretations and rather great inferential leaps from the data.

The test-retest reliability in several studies has been poor (Blatt and Kohlberg, 1975; Gilliland, 1971; Tureen, 1966). Correlations of Kohlberg's measure with other sets of moral dilemmas that use a similar interview method and similar scoring guides have been only moderate (Gilligen, Kohlberg, Lerner and Belenky, 1975; Lockwood, 1974). Further more, Kohlberg's measure was very time consuming.

Against these problems, many a major methodological interest in the studies of moral judgment has been conducted to see whether a standard, objectively scorable measure of moral judgment may be devised.

## James, R. Rest's Method of Data Gathering (1979)

For a number of years James, R. Rest and his colleagues have been studying how people choose important issues of moral dilemmas and they devised a procedure called the Defining Issue Test (DIT). The test presents six moral dilemmas; each moral dilemma has 12 prototypic issue statements. Each statement represents a moral judgment stage of Kohlberg's stage characteristics.

The DIT requires a subject to read a hypothetical moral dilemma and then evaluate the set of twelve issue statements and to rate how important each statement was in deciding what ought to be done (most important, much, some, little and no). He/She was also requested to select best four issues among the twelve and rank them to his/ her choice. As the subjects rank the issue statements in terms of their importance in making a decision about the moral dilemma, he or she has to indicate the effect the importance of various stage characteristic way of viewing moral dilemma.

In the case of Heinza's dilemma, the dilemma of whether to steal the drug, for example the subject may be asked to consider issue statement as "Is Heinza willing to risk getting shot as a burglar or going to jail for the chance that stealing the drug might help" (stage 2 statement). Is it not only natural for a loving husband to care so much for his wife that he did steal (stage 3 statement), whether or not community laws are going to be upheld (stage 4 statement) and whether the law in his case was getting in the way of the most basic claim of any member of the society (stage 5A statement).

Since each issue statement represents moral judgment stage characteristics, subject choices of the most important issues over six moral dilemmas are takes as a measure of his grasp of different stages of moral reasoning.

### Using Prototypic Statements

In considering the various ways that moral judgment data can be collected one should note that when subjects are reacting to hypothetical stories and neutral probe questions, they are reporting their own spontaneous view on the problem. The subject's own thinking was deliberately sought.

People also make judgment about moral judgments of others, when a person is faced with moral dilemma, he often seeks the advice of others rather than acting on his own immediate solution to the dilemma. In taking or not taking others advice we are making judgments about their judgments.

### Advantages

The advantages of this type of methodological test formats were as follows:

- It was highly structured so that the information from each subject was comparable.
- It minimizes variances in stage scores caused by individual difference in verbal expressivity
- It was recognition task rather than a production task.
- It can be objectively scored (can be computerized).
- It saves time and minimize scorer bias. The subject's response on test item is discrete and can be analyzed separately.

Each part of the test can be checked for reliability. This method involves writing statements which exemplify.

### Adoption of Moral Judgment Questionnaire

The manuals of Lawrence Kohlberg (1975), James R. Rest (1979), Brain Burnham (1976), Seetharamu, A.S. (1974) and Srinivasa Rao, R., Dayakara Reddy, V. and Geethanath, P.S. (1987) were carefully studied and eight situational moral dilemma stories were developed by Srinivasa Rao *et. al.* (1987) was adopted for the present study. To ensure that the situations were appropriate to Indian conditions and especially to suit the present population under this investigation. These moral dilemma situations were reflective of life incidents in the children's day-to-day activities.

### Dilemma 1: Ramu's Dilemma

Ramu and Shyam were friends. Ramu was good in studies and Shyam was good in games and sports. Both were studying in the same class and in the same school.

One day, their class teacher said "there will be examinations in the forth-coming week; those who pass all the examinations, will be taken on an excursion for two days".

As Shyam was interested in games he was practicing for a match and completely forgot about the examinations.

On the day of mathematics examination Shyam went to Ramu and requested him, "Ramu, I did not prepare for the mathematics examinations. If I fail, the teacher will not take me on excursion. Hence, I will sit beside you in the hall, and you allow me to copy two or three answers. That is enough to pass the examination".

Ramu wondered whether to allow Shyam to copy or not.

| Stage No. | Sl.No. | Considerations |
|---|---|---|
| 1 | 1. | Ramu would not allow Shyam to copy because he would be punished if caught while copying the answers. |
| 2 | 2. | Ramu would allow Shyam to copy because, if he helped him now, Shyam might help him in future. |
| 3 | 3. | Ramu would not allow Shyam to copy because Shyam being selfish, was trying to satisfy himself. |
| 4 | 4. | Ramu would not allow him to copy because as a responsible student he would like to uphold school's rules and regulations. |
| 1 | 5. | Ramu wouldn't allow Shyam to copy because if caught both would be dropped of the tour. |
| 2 | 6. | Ramu would help Shyam because, if not helped he might loose his friendship. |
| 3 | 7. | Ramu would not help Shyam because it was not proper to help anyone who was being tested on his ability. |
| 4 | 8. | Ramu would not help Shyam, thinking that no real good would come to the school if copying the examinations was practiced. |
| 4A | 9. | Ramu would help Shyam because he |

| | | |
|---|---|---|
| | | thought that school rules regulations were worthless and regiment the lives of the students. |
| 5A | 10. | Ramu would not help Shyam by allowing him to copy because it would go against the rights of other students. |
| 5B | 11. | Ramu would allow Shyam to copy because he thought Shyam was free and unique individual with independence. |
| 6 | 12. | Ramu would help Shyam's because Shyam's rights and freedom more worth respected. |

From the four best decisions you have just made, rank them of your choice.

| | ITEM NO. |
|---|---|
| Rank I | |
| Rank II | |
| Rank III | |
| Rank IV | |

**Dilemma 2: Suresh Dilemma**

Ravi was Suresh's brother. Ravi having planned to go to a movie had some money. One afternoon, Ravi's friend decided to go a movie. They persuaded Ravi to accompany them.

Ravi accordingly sought the permission of his parents. But they refused to give him permission and said that he could go on some other day. After a while, Ravi informing his parents that he was going to his friend's house went to a movie along with his friends.

Next day Ravi's elder Suresh came to know that despite his parents' refusal to permit him to go, Ravi had gone to the movie with his friends.

Would Suresh inform about Ravi to his parents?

| Stage No. | Sl.No. | Considerations |
|---|---|---|
| 3 | 1. | Suresh would not inform his parents because Ravi was not really a bad person and he had gone to the movie on friends' compulsion |
| 2 | 2. | Suresh would inform his parents because Ravi might repeat the act again and again and deceive them every time. |
| 5A | 3. | Suresh would inform his parents to consider Ravi as a free individual, had rights and independence. |
| 1 | 4. | Suresh would inform his parents because if parents had come to know, that he was hiding the facts, he might get punished for it. |
| 4 | 5. | Suresh would inform his parents because; they were the authority in the family and responsible for family welfare. |
| 5B | 6. | Suresh would not inform his parents about Ravi because; he was independent and capable of autonomous decision making. |
| 3 | 7. | Suresh would inform his parents, because whatever they said or did was for the benefit of Ravi and for his best. |
| 6 | 8. | Suresh would not inform because Ravi had right and freedom which were worth respectively. |
| 6 | 9. | Suresh would not inform his parents because Ravi spent his money as a respect for his property. |
| 2 | 10. | Suresh would inform his parents because the parents fed him, bought clothes for him and spend a lot of money on education. |
| 4A | 11. | Suresh would not inform because the parents authority was regimenting Ravi's life. |
| 1 | 12. | Suresh would not inform his parents about Ravi because he was afraid that his parents might punish him. |

From the 4 best decisions you have just made, rank them of your choice.

| | ITEM NO. |
|---|---|
| Rank I | |
| Rank II | |
| Rank III | |
| Rank IV | |

**Dilemma 3: Kumar's Dilemma**

Kumar's mother was suffering from a severe chest disease. Medicine to cure the disease had to be obtained only from foreign countries. The doctor said that if the medicine was not given within two days, the patient would die.

One druggist in the town had this medicine. He had imported it at a cost of Rs. 400 and selling it for Rs. 2,000. Kumar who knew this collected Rs. 1,000 by raising loans. He went to the druggist and explained his plight and begged him to give the medicine for Rs. 1,000. But, the druggist refused to give for an amount less than Rs. 2,000.

Under these circumstances, Kumar wondered what he should have done (to steal or not to steal the drug).

| Stage No. | Sl.No. | Considerations |
|---|---|---|
| 1 | 1. | Kumar would not steal the drug because he was afraid that if caught, he would be put in jail. |
| 2 | 2. | Kumar would steal the drug because he loved his mother very much and wanted her to live. |
| 3 | 3. | Kumar would not steal the drug because he thought he would plead or beg help from the druggist and get it. |
| 4A | 4. | Kumar would steal the drug because; the law couldn't punish the druggist for selling at an exorbitant rate. |
| 5B | 5. | Kumar would steal the drug because the right to live supersedes the right to property. |

| Stage No. | Sl.No. | Considerations |
|---|---|---|
| 2 | 6. | Kumar would try to steal the drug because he was afraid of the accusation that will be made by his friends and relatives. |
| 5A | 7. | Kumar wouldn't steal the drug because one should obey the law as the law protects the basic rights of the individual. |
| 2 | 8. | Kumar would not steal the drug because the drug belonged to the druggist and he could do what he wanted with it. |
| 6 | 9. | Kumar would steal the drug because the right to live was universal and basic. |
| 4 | 10. | Kumar would steal the drug because the value of human life was more important than property rights. |
| 3 | 11. | Kumar would steal the drug, because the druggist being selfish and greedy. |
| 4 | 12. | Kumar would steal the drug by accepting the responsibility of legal consequences accountable for his actions. |

From the 4 best decisions you have just made, rank them of your choice

| | ITEM NO. |
|---|---|
| Rank I | |
| Rank II | |
| Rank III | |
| Rank IV | |

**Dilemma 4: Policeman's Dilemma**

Kumar determined to steal the drug that night. He went to the druggist's shop and stole the medicine and saved his mother.

A policeman, a neighbor of Kumar was aware of the illness of Kumar's mother, the druggist selling the medicine at an unfairly high price, the refusal of the druggist to give it for Rs. 1000 despite Kumar's earnest appeals and of Kumar's stealing the medicine thereby saving his mother.

In these circumstances, would the police man arrest Kumar or not for stealing. He wondered what he should have done.

| Stage No. | Sl.No. | Considerations |
|---|---|---|
| 4 | 1. | The policeman would arrest Kumar, because he had accepted the responsibility to uphold laws of the society. |
| 1 | 2. | The police man would not arrest Kumar, because he had saved the life of an important person, his mother. |
| 3 | 3. | The policeman would arrest Kumar, to make him realize that he had done wrong. |
| 5A | 4. | The policeman wouldn't arrest Kumar because Kumar recognized that right to life was more basic than property rights. |
| 2 | 5. | Policeman would not arrest Kumar because he liked him and did not want him to be put in jail. |
| 4A | 6. | The policeman would not arrest Kumar because; the law and society couldn't punish the druggist for selling at an exorbitant rate. |
| 1 | 7. | The policeman would arrest Kumar because he was wrong to steal and he didn't obey law. |
| 5B | 8. | Policeman wouldn't arrest Kumar because Kumar's autonomous decision, to save a life was worth respecting. |
| 4 | 9. | The policeman wouldn't arrest Kumar because he was not really a danger to society. |
| 3 | 10. | The policeman would arrest Kumar because it was his duty to uphold law. |
| 6 | 11. | The policeman wouldn't arrest Kumar because he stole the drug to uphold the universal right, the right to live. |
| 2 | 12. | The policeman would arrest Kumar because he had no right to take the druggist's medicine. |

From the 4 best decisions you have just made, rank them of your choice.

| ITEM NO. |
|---|
| Rank I |
| Rank II |
| Rank III |
| Rank IV |

**Dilemma 5: Mohan's Dilemma**

Mohan had planned to go to Mysore to witness the Dasara festival along with his teacher and class-mates for three days during the holidays. He had estimated that the tour would cost him Rs.1,000.

Mohan told his father that his teacher and classmates were planning to go to Mysore to the Dasara festival and that he too would like to go with them. He requested his father to give him Rs.1,000 towards tour expenses.

The father asked Mohan to save money and go to tour, Mohan saved Rs.1,000 during the three months and he was due to go on tour in two days time.

Meanwhile, Mohan's father decided to go on tour to Hyderabad along with his friends. He was short of some money. He called Mohan and explained about his ensue trip to Hyderabad with his friends and about the shortage of some money and asked Mohan to give him his savings.

Under these circumstances, Mohan wondered what he should to do (to give or not to give his savings).

| Stage No. | Sl.No. | Considerations |
|---|---|---|
| 2 | 1. | Mohan would give money to his father because his father had done lot of things to him, fed, bought him cloths, books etc. |
| 4 | 2. | Mohan would give his father the money because out of respect to his position of authority in the family, and to promote family happiness. |

| Stage No. | Sl.No. | Considerations |
|---|---|---|
| 5B | 3. | Mohan would refuse to give, as his father didn't realize his independence of his autonomous decision. |
| 3 | 4. | Mohan would refuse to give his father because his father was being selfish and using it for his own pleasure. |
| 1 | 5. | Mohan would give money to his father because as the head of the family he should obey his father's saying. |
| 5A | 6. | Mohan would refuse to give money to his father, because each person has the right to enjoy his personal property. |
| 1 | 7. | Mohan would give the money because his father might punish him and might never let him go on tour. |
| 4A | 8. | Mohan would refuse because of his aversion towards parental authority and regulations. |
| 3 | 9. | Mohan would give the money to his father to show that how much he loved him and respected him. |
| 6 | 10. | Mohan would refuse to give money because his father was not giving due respect to his individuality and basic rights. |
| 2 | 11. | Mohan would refuse to give because he (Mohan) would feel sad if he did not go on tour. |
| 4 | 12. | Mohan would refuse to give money because father was not using it for the sake of the family welfare. |

From the best 4 decisions you have just made, rank them of your choice.

| | ITEM NO. |
|---|---|
| Rank I | |
| Rank II | |
| Rank III | |
| Rank IV | |

**Dilemma 6: Doctor's Dilemma**

Chandraiah, aged 40, had been suffering from unbearable pain on account of cancer. There was no medicine for the disease. The patient, the doctor and patient's family knew that he would die within three months.

The doctor had been giving some tablets to provide him temporary relief from the pain. The tablets would give him relief for an hour or two. Thereafter, he would continue to suffer from intolerable pain. Again he had to take the tablets and so on.

There was also an injection to give temporary relief from the pain. But an excess dosage of this injection was given, the patient would die. Both the patient and the doctor were aware of this fact.

The patient was experiencing very acute pain, as the days passed. He would not bear the pain any more and requested the doctor to give him an extra dose of the injection and kill him.

Doctor wondered what he should to do (to give or not to give extra dose of the injection).

| Stage No. | Sl.No. | Considerations |
|---|---|---|
| 4 | 1. | The doctor would give the injection if he could arrange for official sanction of his act by legal institution of the state. |
| 1 | 2. | Doctor wouldn't give the injection because it would amount to killing and if get caught he would be sent to jail. |
| 2 | 3. | The doctor would give the injection because he was helping him to get rid of his pain. |
| 3 | 4. | The doctor wouldn't give the injection because doctors were supposed to save the life and not help to die. |
| 4A | 5. | Doctor would give the injection, thinking that people would be much better off with out society regimenting their lives and deaths. |

| Stage No. | Sl.No. | Considerations |
|---|---|---|
| 1 | 6. | Doctor wouldn't give the injection because if get caught he would lose his job. |
| 5A | 7. | The doctor wouldn't give the injection because the right to life (live) supersedes other legal or material rights. |
| 6 | 8. | The doctor wouldn't give his injection because the right to live (life) of an individual is universal. |
| 4 | 9. | The doctor wouldn't give the injection because preserving life was the most responsible aspect of medicinal practice. |
| 2 | 10. | Doctor wouldn't give the injection because his wife and children needed him. |
| 5B | 11. | The doctor would give the injection because, the patient had the right for final decision to choose to live or die his own life. |
| 4 | 12. | The doctor would give the injection if he consulted his relatives, the law and other doctors, and they agreed he should. |

From the 4 best decisions you have just made, rank them of your choice.

| | ITEM NO. |
|---|---|
| Rank I | |
| Rank II | |
| Rank III | |
| Rank IV | |

**Dilemma 7: Ramaiah's Dilemma**

Mr. Chalapati was sentenced for ten years imprisonment for a crime. Two years later he escaped from the prison and reached a remote village. None in the village knew about Chalapati's past life. He worked hard and earned money and did lots of business and became very rich. From his earnings he helped the poor, built temples and schools and earned very good name and respect.

One day Mr. Ramaiah came to the village. Ramaiah completely knew about Chalapati's crime, his punishment, his escape from the prison, the police in search of him and the government reward of Rs. 10,000 who informed the police about his whereabouts.

At the same time, he came to know about Chalapati's goodness, respect in the village.

In these circumstances, Ramaiah wondered what he should do (to inform the police or not).

| Stage No. | Sl.No. | Considerations |
|---|---|---|
| 3 | 1. | He would not inform the police because, the criminal proved himself to be a good man since his escape. |
| 5B | 2. | He would not inform the police because as an individual his freedom and independence are worth regarding. |
| 6 | 3. | Wouldn't inform the police because society would be failing what Mr. Chalapati should fairly accept. |
| 1 | 4. | Ramaiah would inform the police because he did not undergo the punishment as per the law. |
| 2 | 5. | Ramaiah wouldn't inform the police because he was known to him and could be benefited some how in the future. |
| 4 | 6. | Ramaiah would inform about the criminal because it was his duty as a responsible citizen. |
| 4A | 7. | Ramaiah wouldn't inform the police because if reported he was going to hide behind worthless laws, only helped the rich. |
| 5A | 8. | Ramaiah wouldn't inform the police because it was not going to do any good to Chalapati or to any body. |
| 1 | 9. | Ramaiah would not inform the police because he was afraid, if informed the villagers might abuse him. |

| Stage No. | Sl.No. | Considerations |
|---|---|---|
| 4 | 10. | He would inform the police because, if not informed he would be encouraging more crime in the society. |
| 2 | 11. | He would inform about the criminal because he would get the prize money of Rs. 10,000 from the government. |
| 3 | 12. | Ramaiah wouldn't inform the police because it would be cruel and heartless to send a man back to jail who gained good name. |

From the 4 best decisions you have just made, rank them of your choice.

| | ITEM NO. |
|---|---|
| Rank I | |
| Rank II | |
| Rank III | |
| Rank IV | |

### Dilemma 8: Venkat's Dilemma

One night at 11'o clock Mr. Mukund was going to his house, through a secluded street. Suddenly two persons attacked Mukund and threatened him to part with the wrist watch, gold ring and the money he had.

Mr. Mukund escaped from them and ran into nearby friend's house, i.e., Mr. Venkat. He requested to help him as he was being chased by thieves for his gold ring, money etc. Requesting, he just slipped into the adjacent room and locked himself.

In a few seconds, the thieves caught Venkat and threatened him at the knife's point to tell the where bouts of Mukund, whether he was in his house or not, otherwise he would be tortured.

Under these circumstances Venkat wondered what he should do (to rescue him or to inform about him.)

| Stage No. | Sl.No. | Considerations |
|---|---|---|
| 2 | 1. | Venkat would rescue Mukund by lying them because they had right to take away his money and belongings. |
| 3 | 2. | Venkat would rescue Mukund out of love and concern of his friend. |
| 1 | 3. | Venkat wouldn't inform about his presence because he was afraid that they might harm him. |
| 4A | 4. | He would rescue him because he thought it would be worthless to report to the police or court as nothing good would happen. |
| 6 | 5. | Venkat would rescue him because his freedom, individually were worth safeguarding. |
| 3 | 6. | Venkat would not inform them as the thieves were working for their selfish ends and satisfaction. |
| 4 | 7. | Venkat would rescue him because it was the duty of a citizen to fight back stealing, cheating etc., in the society. |
| 5B | 8. | Venkat would rescue him, because his autonomous decision to save a person was worth. |
| 2 | 9. | Venkat would rescue him, because if he helped him now, Mukund might help him in future. |
| 1 | 10. | Venkat would rescue him, if not, his parents' friends might abuse him for his cowardly act. |
| 5A | 11. | Venkat would rescue him because, he thought that it was very important to safeguard Mukund's individuality right and independence. |
| 4 | 12. | Venkat would rescue Mukund because if informed he would be encouraging more crime in the society. |

From the 4 best decisions you have just made, rank them of your choice.

| | ITEM NO. |
|---|---|
| Rank I | |
| Rank II | |
| Rank III | |
| Rank IV | |

## SCORING FOR MORAL JUDGMENT QUESTIONNAIRE

**Step 1:** Data sheet for each sample subject was prepared

Data sheet for each sample subject is given in Table 4.1.

**Step 2:** The best four chosen, out of 12 statements for each dilemma and ranked were taken for calculations.

**Step 3:** For the item marked as first rank, the given chart was consulted to find out at what stage the item examples. For instance, if a subject's first rank on Ramu's dilemma was item No.4, that would be a 'stage 4', the second rank was item No.10, that would be 'stage 5', the third choice, item No.7, would be 'stage 3' and the fourth choice item No.12, would be 'stage 6'.

Item number and its respective stages for each dilemma is given in Table 4.2.

**Step 4:** For each 1st, 2nd, 3rd and 4th ranked statements for 8 stories, appropriate weights were entered in the weights stage column in the subject's data sheet.

For instance in Ramu's dilemma, where the first choice was item No.4, a stage 4 statement, 4 points were entered in the box under stage 4. The second choice was item No.10, a stage 5 statement, 3 points were put under stage 5, the third choice was item No.7, stage 3 statement, 2 points were put under stage 3, and the last choice 4h rank was item No.12, 1 point was put under stage 6. This mode of weighing was done for all the 8 stories on each Ss data sheet.

The completed data sheet would have 4 entries for each dilemma and 32 entries altogether. There could be more than one entry in a box i.e., if first and second choice on a particular

**Table 4.1: Data Sheet for Each Sample Subject**

| Levels | Pre-Conventional | | Conventional | | | Post-Conventional | | |
|---|---|---|---|---|---|---|---|---|
| Stages → Dilemmas ↓ | 1 | 2 | 3 | 4 | 4A | 5A | 5B | 6 |
| Ramu's Dilemma | | | | | | | | |
| Suresh's Dilemma | | | | | | | | |
| Kumar's Dilemma | | | | | | | | |
| Policeman's Dilemma | | | | | | | | |
| Mohan's Dilemma | | | | | | | | |
| Doctor's Dilemma | | | | | | | | |
| Ramaiah's Dilemma | | | | | | | | |
| Venkat's Dilemma | | | | | | | | |
| Raw stage score | | | | | | | | |
| Stage % scores | | | | | | | | |
| Stage % score × stage number | | | | | | | | |
| Total | | | | | | | | |

**Table 4.2: Item No. and its Respective Stages for Each Dilemma**

| Sl. No. | Item No. → Dilemma ↓ | 1 | 2 | 3 | 4 | 5 | 6 | 7 | 8 | 9 | 10 | 11 | 12 |
|---|---|---|---|---|---|---|---|---|---|---|---|---|---|
| 1. | Ramu's Dilemma | 1 | 2 | 3 | 4 | 1 | 2 | 3 | 4 | 4A | 5A | 5B | 6 |
| 2. | Suresh's Dilemma | 3 | 2 | 5A | 1 | 4 | 5B | 3 | 6 | 4 | 2 | 4A | 1 |
| 3. | Kumar's Dilemma | 1 | 2 | 3 | 4A | 5B | 2 | 5A | 2 | 6 | 4 | 3 | 4 |
| 4. | Policeman's Dilemma | 4 | 1 | 3 | 5A | 2 | 4A | 1 | 5B | 4 | 3 | 6 | 2 |
| 5. | Mohan's Dilemma | 2 | 4 | 5B | 3 | 1 | 5A | 1 | 4A | 3 | 6 | 2 | 4 |
| 6. | Doctor's Dilemma | 4 | 1 | 2 | 3 | 4A | 1 | 5A | 6 | 4 | 2 | 5B | 4 |
| 7. | Ramaiah's Dilemma | 3 | 5B | 6 | 1 | 2 | 4 | 4A | 5A | 1 | 6 | 2 | 3 |
| 8. | Venkat's Dilemma | 2 | 3 | 1 | 4A | 6 | 3 | 4 | 5B | 2 | 1 | 5A | 4 |

dilemma might be at the same stage, in such cases both weights 4 and 3 points would be put in the same box.

**Step 5:** On the Ss data sheet each stage column was totaled (i.e., for stage 1, column, the weight on 1) Ramu's dilemma, 2) Suresh's dilemma, 3) Kumar's dilemma, 4) Police's dilemma, 5) Mohan's dilemma 6) Doctor's dilemma, 7) Ramaiah's dilemma, 8) Venkat's dilemma were added and entered in the 9th row of the data sheet. This was done for all the stages 1, 2, 3, 4, 4A, 5A, 5B and 6. These scores were the raw stage scores.

**Step 6:** The raw stage scores were converted into percentage scores by dividing the raw scores by 0.8 as there were 8 stories and entered in the 10th row of the data sheet. The stage percentage scores of stage 1 and stage 2 would yield pre-conventional score. This score was entered in the box, in the 8h column and 10th row.

The stage percentage scores of 'stage 3', 'stage 4' and 'stage 4A' were added and entered in the box, in the 9th column and 10th row. This score was the 'conventional score'.

The stage percentage scores of 'stage 5A', 'stage 5B' and 'stage 6' would yield 'post-conventional scores'. The score was entered in the box in the 10th column and 10th row.

**Step 7:** The stage percentage scores were multiplied by that stage number (i.e., the stage 1 percentage scores was multiplied by I, stage 2 percentage score was multiplied by 2, stage 3 scores by 3, stage 4 and score and stage 4A scores by 4, stahe 5A score by 5, 5B scores by 5 and stage 6 score by 6) and entered in the 11th row of the data sheet.

All the procedure was summed up, which yielded a composite score "the moral judgment score" of that subject.

**Example**: Suppose that a sample subject ranked the statements in the questionnaire the following way:

A sample subject ranked the statements in the questionnaire is given Table 4.3.

## Validity

The moral judgment questionnaire presents 8 moral dilemma stories. Each dilemma has 12 prototypic statements. Each statement represents a moral judgment stage of Kohlberg's stage characteristics. Thus it can be reasonable assumed that the inventory has content validity, Item validity and intrinsic validity. Thus each item of the moral judgment questionnaire was valid.

**Table 4.3: A Sample Subject Ranked the Statements in the Questionnaire**

| Sl. No. | Dilemmas | I Rank Item No. | II Rank Item No. | III Rank Item No. | IV Rank Item No. |
|---|---|---|---|---|---|
| 1 | Ramu's Dilemma | 4 | 10 | 7 | 12 |
| 2 | Suresh's Dilemma | 11 | 7 | 3 | 1 |
| 3 | Kumar's Dilemma | 2 | 10 | 12 | 6 |
| 4 | Policeman's Dilemma | 3 | 8 | 6 | 1 |
| 5 | Mohan's Dilemma | 4 | 9 | 12 | 2 |
| 6 | Doctor's Dilemma | 3 | 2 | 8 | 9 |
| 7 | Ramaiah's Dilemma | 3 | 10 | 5 | 11 |
| 8 | Venkat's Dilemma | 12 | 8 | 4 | 1 |

## Reliability

The reliability of the instrument was established by the authors in split half method. The split half reliability of the test was 0.878.

Similarly, the stability of the test was established by test-retest method and was found to be 0.829. Hence the adopted moral judgment questionnaire was having high reliability.

## STANDARD PROGRESSIVE MATRICES (RPM)

To measure the intelligence of the Ss, the Standard Progressive Matrices prepared and standardized by Raven, J.C. (1950) was adopted.

The Standard Progressive Matrices set, A, B, C, D and E is a test of person's capacity at the time of the test to apprehend meaningless figures presented for his observation, see the relationship between them, conceive the nature of the figure, completing each system of the relation, presented and by doing so developed a systematic method of reasoning.

The scale consists of 60 items, divided into 6 sets. In each set the first problem is as nearly as possible self-evident.

### Scoring

The number of scored responses out of 60 items in the test taken as the index of the subject's Intelligence.

## HIGH SCHOOL PERSONALITY QUESTIONNAIRE (HSPQ)

The investigator searched for the theories of personality and the means of measuring it which account for the totality of behaviour. Cattle's theory, of all the numerous theories, is the only theory based on the principle of totality of behaviour of the individual. According to Cattell (1950) "personality is that which permits of prediction of what a person will do in a given situation". His theory is based on personality sphere concept (Cattell, 1946, 1957, 1964) a design to ensure initial item coverage for all the behaviour that commonly enters rating and the dictionary description of personality. It focuses heavily on "Source traits", Cattell defines source trait as the spring of the human behaviour. Much is becoming known about the nature of these dimensions through studies with ratings, with laboratory measures, with real life situations. According to him, a trait of any variety is a mental structure, which is relatively fixed characteristic of the individual functioning from time to time in behaviour.

### Selection of the Tool

It is obvious that selection of a tool for measuring personality posses serious problems. In this connection it may also be noted the problem of justification of the choice looms large. One may cut a sorry figure in explaining for choice. This situation can be solved if we study the theory behind a particular tool and the rationality with which it was prepared. The selection of Cattell's Junior and Senior High School Personality Questionnaire (HSPQ) test in the present research was also not arbitrary and has been made after a lot of deliberations and the study of theory which has been supported amply by Stern (1921) and Allport (1937) in the following works.

Stern observes, "We have the right and obligation to develop a concept of trait as a definitive doctrine, for in all activity of the person, there besides a variable portion, likewise a constant purposive portion, and this latter we isolate as the concept of trait".

Allport's contention is equally forceful. He asserts, "Traits are discovered not by deductive reasoning, not by faith, not by naming, and are themselves never directly observed. They are discovered only through an inferences made necessary by the demonstrable consistency of the separate observable acts of behaviour".

Vernon (1963) says that a person's behaviour in any situation depends, of course, on specific features of that situation and on his temporary feeling or state of mind, but it depends also on his more enduring characteristics abilities, habits and more general dispositions which may be called traits.

Cattell (1961) says that the source traits, as measure by the HSPQ test, are the spring of human behaviour. He defines personality as "That which permits a prediction of what the person will do in a given situation". (Cattell,1950). This definition is consistent with the contention of Marri and Hillix (1973) that the theory of personality is really identical with general theory of behaviour, for Cattell's definition would fit theories of behaviour.

In view of these theoretical as well as practical considerations, Cattell's High School Personality Questionnaire (HSPQ) was selected.

**Brief Description of the Personality Factors**

The brief description of the each factors is given under:

*Factor A : Reserved Vs Outgoing*

Reserved, detached, critical, cool Vs Outgoing, warm hearted, easy going, participating.

The person who scored low on factor 'A' tends to be stiff, cool, skeptical and alone. He likes things rather than people, working alone, and avoiding class of viewpoints. He is likely to be precise and 'rigid' in his way of doing things and in personal standards, and in many occupations these are desirable traits. Ha may tend, at time, to be critical, obstructive or hard.

The person who scores high on factor 'A' tends to be good-natured, easy going, emotionally expressive, ready to co-operate, attentive to people, soft hearted, kindly adaptable. He likes occupation dealing with people and socially impressive situation. He readily forms active groups. He is generous in personal relations, less afraid of criticism, better able to remember the names of the people.

*Factor B : Less Intelligent Vs More Intelligent*

Less Intelligent, concrete-thinking Vs More intelligent, abstract thinking.

The person scoring low on factor 'B' tends to be slow to learn and grasp, dull, sluggish, he tends to have little capacity for the higher forms of knowledge and to be somewhat boorish. His dullness may be simply a reflection of low intelligence, or it may represent poor functioning due to psychopathology.

The person who scores high factor 'B' tends to be quick to grasp ideas, a fast learner, intelligent. There is some correlation with level of culture, and some with alertness. High score in contrast indicate deterioration of mental functions in pathological conditions.

*Factor C: Emotionally less stable Vs Emotionally stable*

Affected by feeling, emotionally less stable Vs Emotionally stable, calm nature.

The person who scores low on factor 'C' tends to be low in frustration, tolerance for unsatisfactory conditions, changeable, evading necessary reality demands, neurotically fatigued, worrying, easily annoyed, generally dissatisfied, having neurotic symptoms (Phobias, sleep, disturbances, psychosomatic complaints, etc.). Low score on factor 'C' is common to almost all forms of neurotic and mental disorders.

The person who scores high in factor 'C' tends to be emotionally mature, stable, calm, realistic about life, unruffled, possessing ego strength, having an integrated philosophy of life, better able to maintain high group morale. Some times he may be a person making a resigned adjustment to unsolved emotional problems.

*Factor D: Phlegmatic Vs Excitable*

Phlegmatic, deliberates, inactive, stodgy Vs Excitable, impatient, demanding, overactive.

The person who scores low in factor 'D' at first sight be thought the same as 'C' with which it has some behaviour in common. However, it is distinguishable by the more immediate 'temperamental' quality of the excitability, and by an irresponsible, positive, assertive emphasis in the emotionality.

The person who scores high on factor 'D' tends to be a restless sleeper, easily distracted from work by noise or intrinsic difficulty is hurt and angry if not given important positions or whenever he is restrained or punished and so on. This factor has some times failed to appear with adults, but it shows as a really substantial dimension in children and mental hospital populations.

*Factor E: Obedient Vs Assertive*

Obedient, mild, conforming, submissive Vs Assertive, independent, aggressive, stubborn, dominant.

The person who scores low on Factor 'E' tends to be dependent, a follower, and to take action which goes along with the group. He is often soft hearted, expressive and easily upset. This passivity is part of many neurotic syndromes.

The person who scores high on Factor 'E' tends to be assertive, self assumed, independent-minded, bold in his approach to situations. He may at times be hard, a law to himself, hostile, though minded, authoritarian (managing others) and disregards authority.

*Factor F: Sober Vs Happy go lucky*

Sober, prudent, serious, taciturn Vs Happy go lucky, gay enthusiastic, impulsively lively.

The person who scores low on Factor 'F' tends to be restrained, reticent, and introspective. He is sometimes in communicative, pessimistic, anxious and considered to be swung, he tends to be a sober, dependable person.

The person who scores high on this trait tends to be cheerful, active, talkative, frank, expressive, quick, alert, unperturable. He is frequently chosen as an elected leader. He may be impulsive and mercurial.

*Factor G: Moral standards Vs Super ego strength*

Expedient, evades rules i.e., weaker super ego strength Vs Conscientious, preserving, rule bound i.e., stronger super ego strength.

The person who scores low on Factor 'G' tends to be unsteady in purpose. He is often casual and lacking in effort for group undertakings and cultural demands. His freedom from group influence may lead to antisocial acts, but at times make him more effective, while his refusal to be bound by rules causes him to have less somatic upset from stress.

The person who scores high on Factor G' tends to be strong in character, preserving, responsible, determined, consistent, playful, energetic, cautions, well organized. He is usually conscientious or moralistic, and he prefers hard working people to witty companions. The inner 'Categorical imperative' of this essential super ego (in the psycho - analytical sense) should be distinguished from the superficially similar 'social ideal self'

*Factor H: Shy Vs Venture some*

Shy, restrained, diffident, timid Vs Venture some, socially bold, uninhibited, spontaneous.

The person who scores low on this trait tends to be shy, withdrawing, cautious, retiring, cooling, a 'wall flower'. He usually has inferiority feelings. He tends to be slow in speech and expressing himself, dislikes occupations with personal contacts, prefers one or two close friends to large groups, and is not given to keeping in contact with all that is going or around him.

The person who scores high on Factor 'H' tends to be sociable, bold, ready to try new things, spontaneous, and abundant in emotional response. His "thick skinned ness" enables him to face wear and tear in dealing with people and grueling emotional situations without fatigue. However, he can be careful of detail, ignore danger signals and consume much time. He tends to be 'pushy' and actively interested in the opposite sex.

*Factor I: Tough minded Vs Tender minded*

Tough minded, self reliant, realistic, no nonsense Vs Tender minded, dependent, over protected, sensitive.

The person who scores low on Factor 'I' tends to be practical, realistic, masculine, independent, responsible but skeptical of subjective and 'uncultural'. He is some time unmoved, hard, cynical, and smug. He tends to keep a group operating on a practical and realistic 'no nonsense' basic.

The person who scores high on this trait tends to be tender-minded, day-dreaming, and artistically fastidious. He is sometimes demanding of attention and help, impatient, dependent, and impractical. He dislikes crude people and rough occupations. He tends to be slow in group performance and to upset group morals by unrealistic business.

*Factor J: Vigorous Vs Doubting*

Vigorous, goes readily with groups, jestful, given to action Vs Doubting, obstructive, individualistic, reflective, internally restrained, unwilling to act.

The person who scores low on Factor 'J' has so far a difficult pattern to interpret. It has been called variously the Hamlet factor neurasthenia etc.

The person who scores high on Factor 'J' prefers to do things on his own, is physically and intellectually fastidious, thinks over his mistakes and how to avoid them, tends not to forget if he is unfairly treated, has private views differing from the group, but prefers to keep in the background and avoid argument, knows he has fewer friends.

*Factor O: Placed Vs Apprehensive*

Placid, confident, serene, untroubled Vs Apprehensive, worrying depressive, troubled, guilt proneness.

The person who scores low on Factor 'O' tends to be placid, calm, with unshakable nerve. He has a mature, unanxious, confidence in himself and his capacity to deal with things. He is resilient and secure.

The person who scores high on Factor 'O' tends to be depressed, moody, worried, suspicious, brooding, avoiding people. He has a child - like tendency to anxiety in difficulties. He does not feel accepted in groups or free to participate. High factor O score is very common in clinical groups of all types.

*Factor $Q_2$: Group dependent Vs Self-sufficient*

Group dependent – A 'Joiner' and sounds follower Vs Self-sufficient, prefers own decisions, resourceful.

The person who scores low on Factor '$Q_2$'prefers to work and make decisions with other people and depends on social approval and admiration. He tends to go alone with the group and may be lacking in individual resolution. He is not necessarily gregarious by choice, rather he needs group support.

The person who scores high on Factor '$Q_2$' is temperamentally independent, accustomed to go in his own way, making decisions and taking action on his own. He discounts public opinion, but is not necessarily dominant in his relation with other (see Factor E). He does not dislike people but simply does not mind their agreement or support.

*Factor $Q_3$: Undisciplined Vs Controlled*

Undisciplined self conflict, careless of protocol, follows own urges, low integration Vs Controlled socially precise, self disciplined, compulsive, high self-concept control.

The person who scores low on Factor '$Q_3$' will not be bothered with will-control and regard for social demands. He is not over considerate, careful, or painstaking. He may feel maladjusted and may have maladjustment.

The person who scores high on Factor '$Q_3$' tends to have strong control of his emotions and general behaviour in inclined to be socially aware and careful and evidence what is commonly termed 'self-respect' and regard for social reputation. He sometimes tends, however, to be obstinate. Effective leaders and some paranoids are high on $Q_3$.

*Factor $Q_4$: Relaxed Vs Tense*

Relaxed, tranquil, torpid, unfrustrated Vs Tense, driven over wrought, frustrated.

The person who scores low on Factor '$Q_4$' tends to be sedate, relaxed, composed and satisfied (not frustrated). In some situations his over satisfaction can lead to laziness and low performance, in the sense that low motivation produces little trial and error. Conversely high tension level may disrupt school and work performance.

The person who scores high on Factor '$Q_4$' tends to be tense, excitable, restless, fretful impatient. He is often fatigued, but unable to remain inactive. In groups he likes a poor view of the degree or unity, orderliness, and leadership.

After deciding to use the HSPQ, the questionnaire was translated into Telugu, the regional language of the subjects on whom it has to be used. Five judges who were well versed with psychological testing checked the translation. Terms, which were ambiguous, were discussed and resolved. The Telugu version thus prepared was administered. They were asked to answer the items and also check those words, which they could not understood. Such of those terms that the students marked were modified or substituted with simple words.

### Adoption of the Instrument (HSPQ)

Junior-Senior High School Personality Questionnaire (HSPQ) Form A prepared and standardized by Cattell (1950) was adopted for the present study. Telugu version of HSPQ, Form A was used for the present investigation.

### Scoring Procedure for the HSPQ

In the HSPQ, there are totally 142 questions, three alternative answers are given to each question. The students are motivated to give only one answer for each question. A preliminary inspection was made to know whether the students are answering properly or not. Then the answers were scored according to weightage given by the author. The scoring was done for each student and for each factor.

### Validity and Reliability of HSPQ

For calculating validity and reliability, the procedure suggested by Garrett (1973) was followed. Reliability of the two sub tests of each factor (based on raw scores) as obtained by split half technique and validity, which is the square root of reliability, are presented in Table 4.4. The split half reliability was calculated on a sample of 300.

Retest was also conducted on a sample of 300 with a gap of 40 days. The test-retest validity and reliability for each factor are given in Table 4.4.

The result of validity and reliability of HSPQ, Form – A show that all the factors of HSPQ are highly valid and reliable.

## SOCIO-ECONOMIC STATUS SCALE (SES)

Among social factors, Socio-Economic Status (SES) is an important one. The SES influence values, norms of behaviour motivation for improvement social participation etc. The review of related literature revealed that there are number of studies showing the relationship of SES and moral judgment of pupils at school level. But there are limited studies at college level. It is worth studying here whether the SES has got any bearing on the moral judgment of Intermediate students.

**Table 4.4: Reliability and Validity of HSPQ Form A using Split-Half and Test-Retest techniques**

| Sl. No. | Factor | Split-Half technique | | Test-Retest technique | |
|---|---|---|---|---|---|
| | | Reliability | Validity | Reliability | Validity |
| 1. | A | 0.591 | 0.769 | 0.561 | 0.749 |
| 2. | B | 0.732 | 0.844 | 0.750 | 0.866 |
| 3. | C | 0.768 | 0.876 | 0.792 | 0.890 |
| 4. | D | 0.669 | 0.817 | 0.680 | 0.825 |
| 5. | E | 0.811 | 0.900 | 0.851 | 0.922 |
| 6. | F | 0.756 | 0.869 | 0.734 | 0.857 |
| 7. | G | 0.767 | 0.876 | 0.735 | 0.857 |
| 8. | H | 0.727 | 0.852 | 0.709 | 0.842 |
| 9. | I | 0.652 | 0.807 | 0.639 | 0.799 |
| 10. | J | 0.692 | 0.832 | 0.681 | 0.825 |
| 11. | O | 0.593 | 0.770 | 0.610 | 0.781 |
| 12. | $Q_2$ | 0.762 | 0.873 | 0.732 | 0.855 |
| 13. | $Q_3$ | 0.657 | 0.811 | 0.646 | 0.804 |
| 14. | $Q_4$ | 0.647 | 0.804 | 0.635 | 0.797 |

### Selection and Adoption of SES Scale

In India, sociologists have generally utilized multiple criteria in establishing SES scales. A common scale to measure the SES of urban families is the one devised by Kuppuswamy (1962) is of recent origin. A common SES scale for rural and urban areas was constructed by Aaron, P.G., Marihal, V.G. and Malathisha, R.N., published in the year 1970. For the present study, this common SES scale is selected as the Intermediate students hail from rural and urban areas. Following is the brief description about the SES scale.

The authors emphasized three ideas which influenced the construction of SES scale.

- The information elicited should be simple as far as possible and reliable.
- As far as possible, similar rural and urban sources should be tapped to provide information regarding their respective SES.
- The ultimate aim of the scale is to identify and isolate groups of rural and urban people of similar SES.

The variables used in this scale have been tested by other researchers and the combinations of these and other indicators are correlated well with measures of attitude and behaviour. Of the five variables, one refers to father's occupation, another to father's education, and the other three to material possessions. Since children may not have accurate information regarding parent's income, material possession had been introduced in its place. Regarding the weightages given to the various items under five categories, the authors followed trial and error method of revising the weights in a systematic way in order to obtain a normal distribution of the SES scores of rural and urban distributions. By this, they arrived at a stage where the chi - square values obtained for rural as well as urban distribution did not turn out to be significant at 0.05 level.

## Scoring Procedure

There are five categories, viz., occupation of father, father's education, material possession, house, shirts or blouses in the socio-economic survey index. The subject is given a score under each of these categories so that the final SES index is the total of these scores. Only the maximum possible score is considered under each category. The score of course depends upon the weightage of the item. For instance, under category-III, the subject may posses a cycle as well as a radio and no other material. Cycle has a weight age of 2 and radio has a weight age of 5, so the subject's score under this category is 5. Eventually the scores of all the five categories are added and this represents the SES index.

### Validity and Reliability

The validity and reliability for the entire SES scale was established. The concurrent validity of the scale was obtained by finding out to what extent the scores obtained by pupils on the SES scale correspond to an outside criterion i.e, the SES score assigned b the teacher of the class where the pupils were studying. The Pearson's product movement correlation coefficient was computed. The validity and reliability coefficients reported by the authors were as follows:

Concurrent validity (N = 28): 0.61 significant beyond 0.01 level.

Test-Retest Reliability (N = 23): 0.77 Significant beyond 0.01 level.

## ACADEMIC ACHIEVEMENT

The academic achievement of Intermediate students was measured by the investigator. The academic achievement of first year Intermediate students was based on SSC Marks from Board of Secondary Education examinations and for the academic achievement of second year Intermediate students was based on first year Intermediate marks of Board of Intermediate Education examinations. The marks of academic achievement were collected from the records available with the institutions concerned.

## SOCIO-DEMOGRAPHIC SCALE

Socio-Demographic scale regarding the student 1. Name, 2. Age in years, 3. Annual income, 4 Father's education, 5. Mother's education, 6. Father's occupation, 7. Mother's occupation,8. Birth order, 9. Size of the family, 10. Residence 11. Sex, 12. Community, 13. Caste, 14. Locality, 15. Economic position of the family, 16, Medium of the study, 17. Type of the family, 18. Region, 19. Year of study, 20. Course of the study, 21. Management were collected.

## SAMPLE DESIGN

The sample for the investigation consisted of 1080 Intermediate college students. The stratified random sampling was applied in four stages. Geographically Andhra Pradesh state is divided into three regions namely Telangana, Rayalaseema and Coastal. One district in each region was selected at random Ranga Reddy district is taken from Telengana region, Chittoor district is taken from Rayalaseema region and Guntur District is taken from Coastal region. In the next stage 3 colleges in each district were selected (one Government, one Aided, and one Private college). 30 male and 30 female first year students and 30 male and 30 female second year students from each college. In total 540 male and 540 female students included in this study. It is a $2 \times 2 \times 3 \times 3$ factorial design with 1080 sample subjects. The sample design for the study is presented in Table 4.5.

Geographical map showing in Andhra Pradesh, selected districts and Intermediate colleges taken for the investigation is given in Fig. 4.1.

## COLLECTION OF DATA AND ANALYSIS

The investigator personally visited Intermediate colleges with the permission of the principals of the colleges. The students who attended to the college on the day of collection of data are considered for the purpose of the investigation. It was provided to the concerned principals and students of the colleges. The students were given necessary instructions about the various instruments and motivated to respond genuinely to all the items. The moral judgment questionnaire, SES and personal data sheet were administered in the forenoon session. The 14 PF questionnaire and intelligence were administered in the afternoon session.

The information regarding the variable like academic achievement, the Board of Secondary Education examinations marks for the first year Intermediate students. The Board of Intermediate Education first year examinations marks for the second year Intermediate students were collected from the concerned results records of the Board of Secondary Education and Board of Intermediate Education.

The data on each variable in the investigation is properly coded to suit for computer analysis.

The analysis was carried out on the basis of objectives of the investigation and hypotheses formulated by employing appropriate statistical techniques.

Frequency distribution table was prepared for the total sample. Measures of central tendency, measures of dispersion, percentages, skewness, kurtosis and standard error of mean were computed wherever necessary. The inferential statistical techniques such as 't' test (critical ratio) and 'F' test were employed to test different hypotheses. Multiple 'R' was computed by carrying out Step-wise Multiple Regression analysis to find out whether it would be possible to predict moral judgment of Intermediate students. The obtained numerical results are adumbrated by graphical representations. The investigator considered graphical representations for such of those variables, where the mean difference is found to be much larger in moral judgment, moral levels and moral stages.

For statistical formulae, the following books were referred:

- *Statistical Methods for Research Workers*, by Fisher (1950).
- *Fundamental Statistics in Psychology and Education*, by Guilford (1950).
- *Psychometric Methods*, by Guilford (1954).
- Non-Parametric Statistics for the Behavioural Sciences, by Sidney Siegel (1956).
- *Statistics in Education and Psychology*, by Yate (1965).

**Table 4.5: Sample Design**

| Region → | Rayalaseema | | | | Telangana | | | | Coastal | | | | Total |
|---|---|---|---|---|---|---|---|---|---|---|---|---|---|
| Year → | 1st | | 2nd | | 1st | | 2nd | | 1st | | 2nd | | |
| Sex → | Male | Female | Male | Female | Male | Female | Male | Female | Male | Female | Male | Female | |
| Management↓ | | | | | | | | | | | | | |
| **Government** | 30 | 30 | 30 | 30 | 30 | 30 | 30 | 30 | 30 | 30 | 30 | 30 | 360 |
| **Aided** | 30 | 30 | 30 | 30 | 30 | 30 | 30 | 30 | 30 | 30 | 30 | 30 | 360 |
| **Private** | 30 | 30 | 30 | 30 | 30 | 30 | 30 | 30 | 30 | 30 | 30 | 30 | 360 |
| **Total** | 360 | | | | 360 | | | | 360 | | | | **1080** |

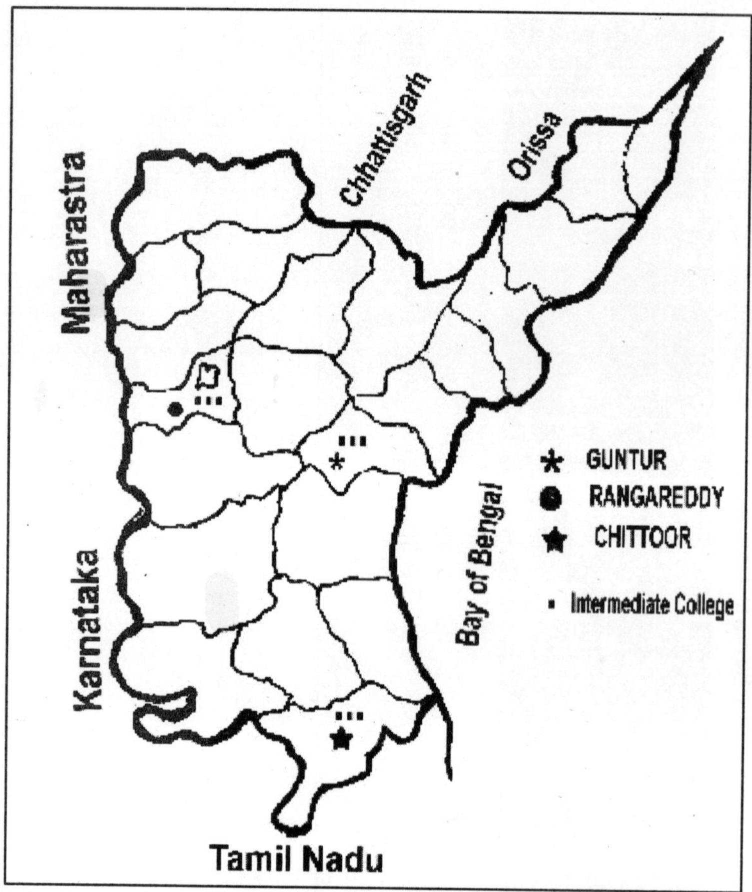


**Fig. 4.1: Geographical map: Andhra Pradesh, Selected Districts and Intermediate Colleges**

- *Experimental Design in Psychological Research*, by Edwards (1971).
- *Statistical Principles in Experimental Design*, by Winer (1971).
- *Statistics in Psychology and Education*, by Garett (1973).
- *Statistical Methods*, by Gupta (1974).

- *Applied Regression Analysis*, by Draper and Smith (1981).
- *Statistics in Psychology and Education*, by Mangal (2002).

The significant levels employed with respective symbols are given below:

** Indicates significant at 0.01 level

* Indicates significant at 0.05 level

@ Indicates not significant at 0.05 level.

# CHAPTER 5

# ANALYSIS AND INTERPRETATION OF THE DATA

This chapter deals with analysis and Interpretation of the data. The data are presented in the form of:

1. Frequency distribution table
2. Factorial designs
3. 't' values and 'F' ratios with respect to the influence of the independent variables on dependent variables and
4. Regression analysis

## FREQUENCY DISTRIBUTION TABLE

Frequency distribution table for the moral judgment scores are presented in the following pages.

### Frequency distribution of Moral Judgment scores

Frequency distribution of moral judgment scores for the whole group and total sample (N = 1080) is presented in Table 5.1.

**Table 5.1: Frequency Distribution of Moral Judgment Scores for Whole Group**

| S. No. | Class Intervals | Mid point | F | cf | cpf |
|---|---|---|---|---|---|
| 1. | 225 - 250 | 237.5 | 5 | 5 | 0.46 |
| 2. | 250 - 275 | 262.5 | 17 | 22 | 2.04 |
| 3. | 275 - 300 | 277.5 | 152 | 174 | 16.11 |
| 4. | 300 - 325 | 312.5 | 290 | 464 | 42.96 |
| 5. | 325 - 350 | 337.5 | 370 | 834 | 77.22 |
| 6. | 350 - 375 | 362.5 | 188 | 1022 | 94.63 |
| 7. | 375 - 400 | 377.5 | 47 | 1069 | 98.98 |
| 8. | 400 - 425 | 412.5 | 6 | 1075 | 99.54 |
| 9. | 425 - 450 | 437.5 | 5 | 1080 | 100.00 |

N = 1080, M = 330.05, Md = 330.00, Mo = 326.25, R = 260.00, SD = 21.18, Sk = 0.191. Ku = 0.980, $SE_M$ = 0.8879.

It is observed from Table 5.1 that the mean moral judgment scores is 330.05, median is 330.00 and mode is 326.25. The gap among mean, median and mode is negligible. Hence, the distribution is very nearer to normal distribution.

The values of skewness and kurtosis are 0.191 and 0.980 respectively. Hence the frequency distribution of moral judgment scores for the whole group is slightly positively skewed and lepto kurtic.

The Bar diagram for the distribution of moral judgment scores for the whole group is given in Fig. 5.1.

The Frequency Polygon for the distribution of moral judgment scores for the whole group is given in Fig. 5.2.

The Ogive for the distribution of moral judgment scores for the whole group is given in Figure 5.3.

The value of N, M, SD, Sk, Ku, R and $SE_M$ for the distribution of moral judgment scores for the different groups of the sample is presented in Table 5.2.

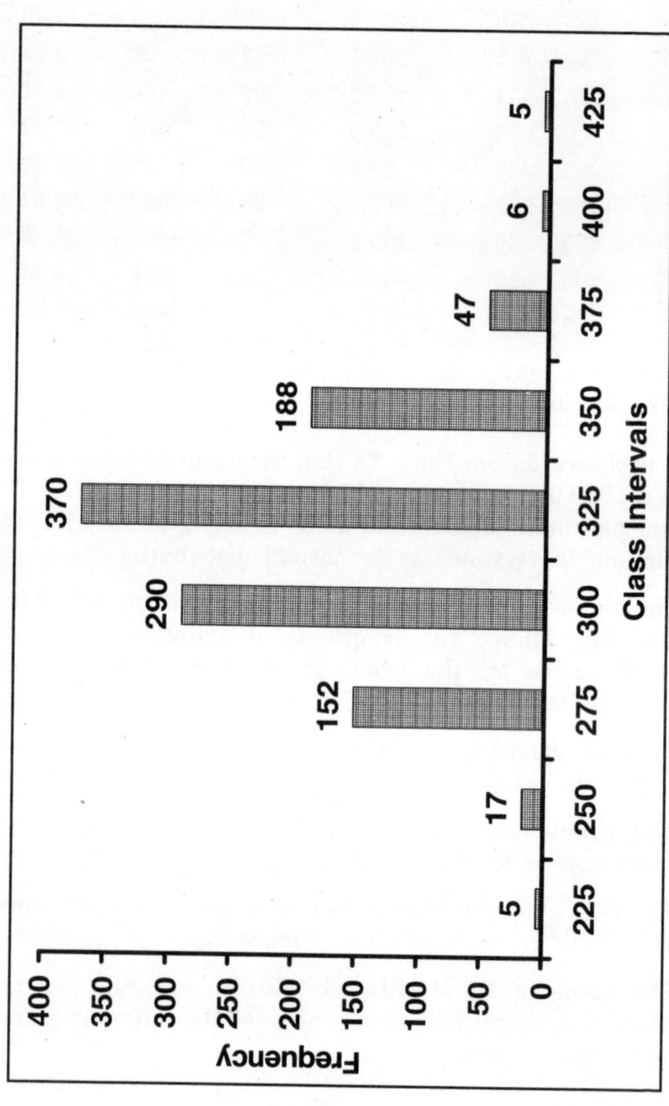


**Fig. 5.1: Bar Diagram for the Distribution of Moral Judgment Scores for the Whole Group**

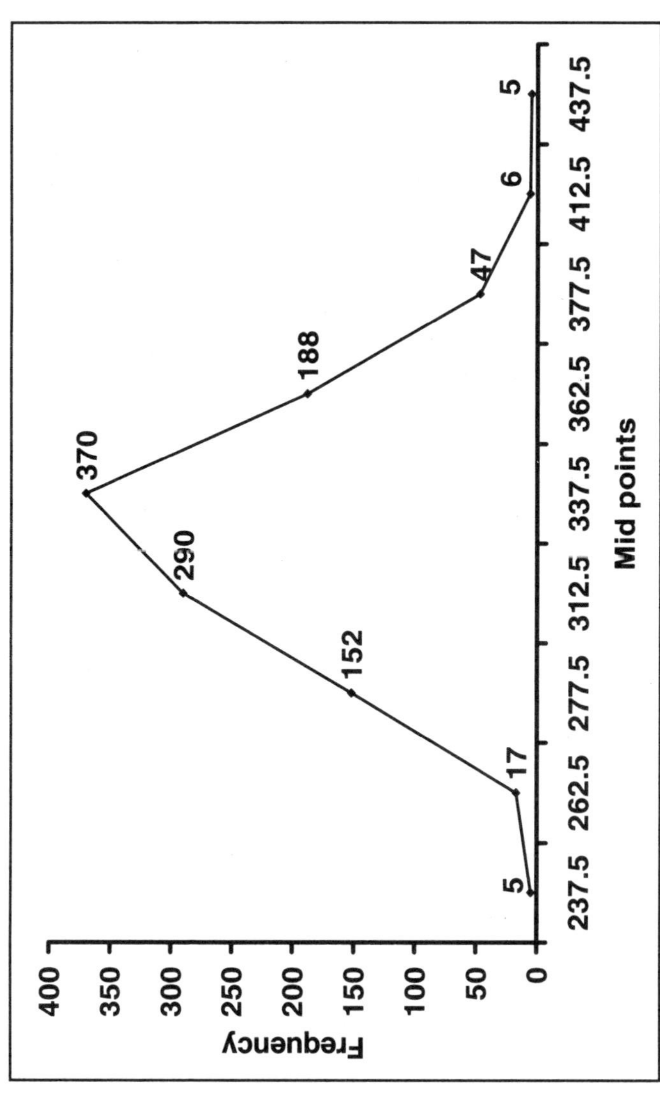


**Fig. 5.2: Frequency Polygon for the Distribution of Moral Judgment Scores for the Whole group**

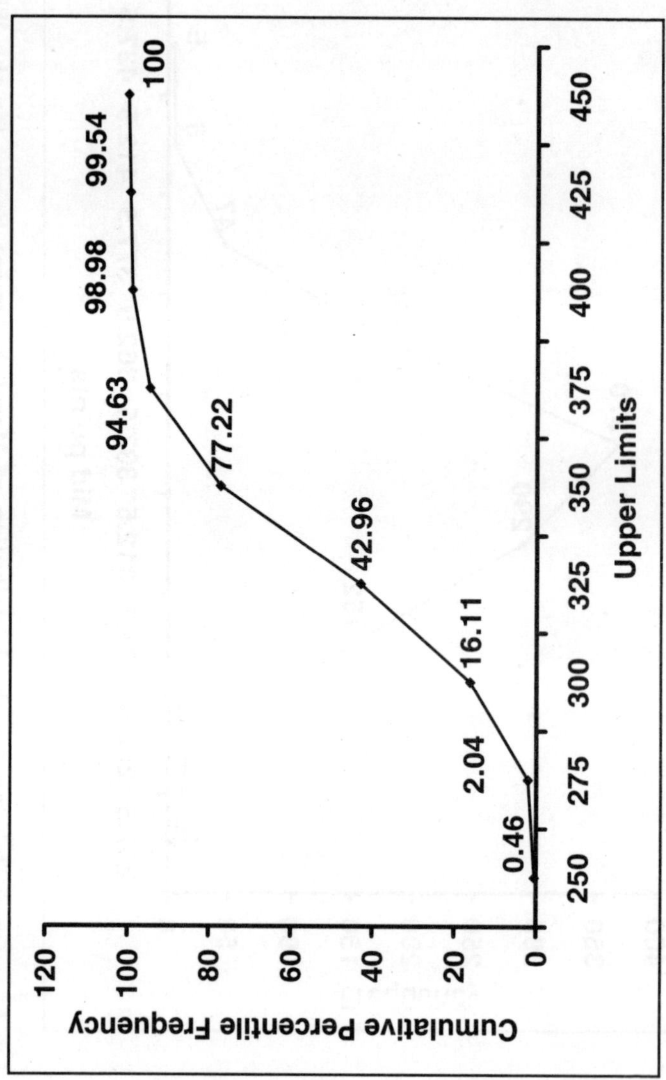


**Fig, 5.3: Ogive for the Distribution of Moral Judgment Scores for the Whole Group**

**Table 5.2: The Value of N , M , SD, Sk , Ku, R and $SE_M$ for the Distribution of Moral Judgment Scores for the Different Groups of the Sample**

| S.No. | Group | N | M | SD | Sk | Ku | R | $SE_M$ |
|---|---|---|---|---|---|---|---|---|
| 1. | Whole | 1080 | 330.05 | 29.18 | 0.191 | 0.980 | 260.00 | 0.8879 |
| 2. | Telangana | 360 | 330.46 | 29.53 | 0.082 | 0.185 | 201.25 | 1.5565 |
| 3. | Rayalaseema | 360 | 329.41 | 29.03 | 0.160 | 0.634 | 211.25 | 1.5301 |
| 4. | Coastal | 360 | 330.28 | 29.04 | 0.336 | 2.234 | 250.00 | 1.5307 |
| 5. | Government | 360 | 324.72 | 27.04 | -0.116 | 0.234 | 173.75 | 1.4249 |
| 6. | Aided | 360 | 334.82 | 31.72 | 0.274 | 1.285 | 260.00 | 1.6716 |
| 7. | Private | 360 | 330.60 | 27.76 | 0.181 | 0.659 | 201.25 | 1.4630 |
| 8. | First Year | 540 | 332.52 | 30.70 | 0.226 | 1.509 | 260.00 | 1.3212 |
| 9. | Second Year | 540 | 327.58 | 27.38 | 0.075 | -0.016 | 190.00 | 1.1782 |
| 10. | Male | 540 | 328.34 | 28.87 | 0.000 | 0.595 | 211.25 | 1.2424 |
| 11. | Female | 540 | 331.76 | 29.41 | 0.367 | 1.281 | 250.00 | 1.2657 |

It is clear from Table 5.2 that the mean moral judgment scores for the students of Aided colleges is the highest (334.82) among all groups and the lowest (327.58) for the students of second year. The SD is the highest (31.72) for the students of Aided colleges and the lowest (27.04) for the students of Government colleges. For Government distribution the value of skewness is negative, hence the distribution is negatively skewed. For male distribution the value of skewness is zero, hence the distribution is normally skewed, for remaining distributions the value of skewness is positive, hence the distributions are positively skewed and kurtosis value is less than 3.00. Hence all the distributions are lepto kurtic.

## Factorial Designs

The influence of sex, year of study, management and region on moral judgment scores of Intermediate students is investigated by employing factorial designs. The influence of above variables is studied under the following heads:

| | |
|---|---|
| 1. Moral Stage 1 | 7. Moral Stage 5B |
| 2. Moral Stage 2 | 8. Moral Stage 6 |
| 3. Moral Stage 3 | 9. Pre-Conventional Level |
| 4. Moral Stage 4 | 10. Conventional Level |
| 5. Moral Stage 4A | 11. Post-Conventional Level |
| 6. Moral Stage 5A | 12. Moral Judgment (MMQ) |

### *Moral Stage 1*

There are two divisions in the sex, two divisions in the year of study, three divisions in the management and three divisions in the region. The influence of sex, year of study, management and region on the reasoning of moral stage 1 scores of Intermediate students is investigated through 2×2×3×3 factorial design. The following hypotheses are framed:

### Hypothesis 1

There would be no significant influence of main effects

namely, sex, year of study, management and region on the reasoning of moral stage 1 of Intermediate students.

**Hypothesis 2**

There would be no significant influence of interaction effects namely, sex, year of study, management and region on the reasoning of moral stage 1 of Intermediate students.

The above hypotheses are tested through 2×2×3×3 factorial design.

The results of Analysis of variance (ANOVA) of 2×2×3×3 factorial design for moral stage 1 scores are presented in Table 5.3.

It is observed from Table 5.3 that the computed value of 'F' for the main effect sex is 9.238 which is significant at 0.01 level. Hence Hypothesis 1 is rejected. It is concluded that sex has significant influence on the reasoning of moral stage 1.

It is observed from Table 5.3 that the computed value of 'F' for the main effect year of study is 17.981 which is significant at 0.01 level. Hence Hypothesis 1 is rejected. It is concluded that year of study has significant influence on the reasoning of moral stage 1. Similar results were reported by Geethanath, (1987) and Rangaswamy, (2006).

It is observed from Table 5.3 that the computed value of 'F' for the main effect management is 17.932 which is significant at 0.01 level. Hence Hypothesis 1 is rejected. It is concluded that management has significant influence on the reasoning of moral stage 1. Similar result was reported by Dayakara Reddy, V. (1987).

To find out which of the management of students differ significantly from one another, the 't' test was employed.

It is observed from Table 5.4 that the computed value of 't' for the students of Government and Aided colleges is 5.57 which is significant at 0.01 level.

It is observed from Table 5.4 that the computed value of 't' for the students of Government and Private colleges is 1.55 which is not significant.

**Table 5.3: Results of ANOVA of 2×2×3×3 Factorial Design for Moral Stage 1 Scores**

Variable A = Sex (2 levels)

Variable B = Year of study (2 levels)

Variable C = Management (3 levels)

Variable D = Region (3 levels)

| Sl. No. | Source of variance | Sum of squares | df | Mean squares | F-value | Level of significance |
|---|---|---|---|---|---|---|
| 1. | A | 355.926 | 1 | 355.926 | 9.238 | ** |
| 2. | B | 692.801 | 1 | 692.801 | 17.981 | ** |
| 3. | C | 1381.826 | 2 | 692.913 | 17.932 | ** |
| 4. | D | 262.433 | 2 | 131.217 | 3.406 | * |
| 5. | AB | 3.061 | 1 | 3.061 | 0.079 | @ |
| 6. | AC | 197.659 | 2 | 98.830 | 2.565 | @ |
| 7. | AD | 143.701 | 2 | 71.85 | 1.865 | @ |
| 8. | BC | 105.489 | 2 | 52.745 | 1.369 | @ |
| 9. | BD | 64.690 | 2 | 32.345 | 0.839 | @ |
| 10. | CD | 868.096 | 4 | 217.024 | 5.633 | ** |
| 11. | ABC | 235.281 | 2 | 117.640 | 3.053 | * |
| 12. | ABD | 155.749 | 2 | 77.875 | 2.021 | @ |
| 13. | ACD | 1199.589 | 4 | 299.897 | 7.784 | ** |
| 14. | BCD | 342.072 | 4 | 85.518 | 2.220 | @ |
| 15. | ABCD | 483.356 | 4 | 120.839 | 3.136 | * |
| 16. | Error | 40225.0 | 1044 | 38.530 | | |
| **17.** | **Total** | **46716.730** | **1079** | | | |

F - Table/critical value for 1 and 1044 df at 0.05 level is 3.84 and at 0.01 level is 6.64.

F - Table/critical value for 2 and 1044 df at 0.05 level is 2.99 and at 0.01 level is 4.60.

F - Table/critical value for 4 and 1044 df at 0.05 level is 2.27 and at 0.01 level is 3.32.

* Indicates significant at 0.05 level;
** Indicates significant at 0.01 level;
@ Indicates not significant at 0.05 level.

Means, SD's and 't' values of management on the reasoning of moral stage 1 scores are presented in Table 5.4.

**Table 5.4: Means, SD's and 't' values of Management on the Reasoning of Moral Stage 1 Scores**

| Sl. No. | Variable | Mean value | SD values | 't' – values | | |
|---|---|---|---|---|---|---|
| | | | | Government | Aided | Private |
| 1. | Government | 17.13 | 6.42 | — | 5.57** | 1.55@ |
| 2. | Aided | 14.45 | 6.50 | — | — | 3.99** |
| 3. | Private | 16.39 | 6.52 | — | — | — |

't' Table / Critical value for 1 and 1078 df at 0.05 level is 1.96 and at 0.01 level is 2.58

** Indicates significant at 0.01 level;

@ Indicates not significant at 0.05 level.

It is observed from Table 5.4 that the computed value oft' for the students of Aided and Private colleges is 3.99 which is significant at 0.01 level.

The Bar diagram showing the mean scores of management on the reasoning of moral stage 1 is given in Figure 5.4.

It is observed from Table 5.3 that the computed value of 'F' for the main effect region is 3.406 which is significant at 0.05 level. Hence Hypothesis 1 is rejected. It is concluded that region has significant influence on the reasoning of moral stage 1.

To find out which of the region of students differ significantly from one another, the 't'-test was employed.

Means, SD's and 't' values of region on the reasoning of moral stage 1 scores are presented in Table 5.5.

It is observed from Table 5.5 that the computed value of 't' for the students of Telangana and Rayalaseema regions is 0.17 which is not significant.

It is observed from Table 5.5 that the computed value of 't' for the students of Telangana and Coastal regions is 2.20 which is significant at 0.05 level.

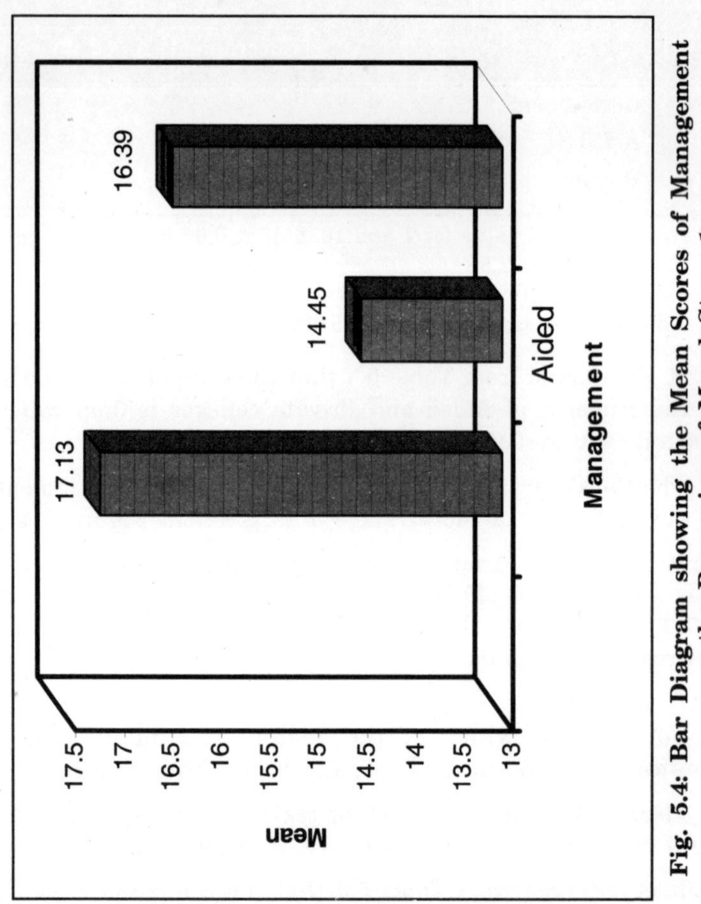


**Fig. 5.4: Bar Diagram showing the Mean Scores of Management on the Reasoning of Moral Stage 1**

**Table 5.5: Means, SD's and 't' Values of Region on the Reasoning of Moral Stage 1 Scores**

| Sl. No. | Variable | Mean value | SD values | 't' – values | | |
|---|---|---|---|---|---|---|
| | | | | Telangana | Rayalaseema | Coastal |
| 1. | Telangana | 15.60 | 6.41 | - | 0.17@ | 2.20* |
| 2. | Rayalaseema | 15.68 | 6.48 | - | - | 2.03* |
| 3. | Coastal | 16.68 | 6.77 | - | - | - |

* Indicates significant at 0.05 level;
@ Indicates not significant at 0.05 level

It is observed from Table 5.5 that the computed value of 't' for the students of Rayalaseema and Coastal regions is 2.03 which is significant at 0.05 level.

It is observed from Table 5.3 that the computed value of 'F' for the two factor interaction effect namely, management Vs region is 5.633 which is significant at 0.01 level. Hence, Hypothesis 2 is rejected. It is concluded that the two factor interaction effect namely, management Vs region has significant influence on the reasoning of moral stage 1.The remaining two factor interaction effects namely, sex Vs year of study, sex Vs management, sex Vs region, year of study Vs management and year of study Vs region do not have significant influence on the reasoning of moral stage 1.

It is observed from Table 5.3 that the computed value of 'F' for the three factor interaction effect namely, sex Vs management Vs region is 7.784 which is significant at 0.01 level. Hence, Hypothesis 2 is rejected. It is concluded that the three factor interaction effect namely, sex Vs management Vs region has significant influence on the reasoning of moral stage 1.

It is observed from Table 5.3 that the computed value of 'F' for the three factor interaction effect namely, sex Vs year of study Vs management is 3.053 which is significant at 0.05 level. Hence Hypothesis 2 is rejected. It is concluded that the three factor interaction effect namely, sex Vs year of study

Vs management has significant influence on the reasoning of moral stage 1. The remaining three factor interaction effects namely, sex Vs year of study Vs region and year of study Vs management Vs region do not have significant influence on the reasoning of moral stage 1.

It is observed from Table 5.3 that the computed value of 'F' for the four factor interaction effect namely, sex Vs year of study Vs management Vs region is 3.136 which is significant at 0.05 level. Hence Hypothesis 2 is rejected. It is concluded that the four factor interaction effects namely, sex Vs year of study Vs management Vs region has significant influence on the reasoning of moral stage 1.

*Moral Stage 2*

There are two divisions in the sex, two divisions in the year of study, three divisions in the management and three divisions in the region. The influence of sex, year of study, management and region on the reasoning of moral stage 2 scores of Intermediate students is investigated through 2×2×3×3 factorial design. The following hypotheses are framed:

**Hypothesis 3**

There would be no significant influence of main effects namely, sex, year of study, management and region on the reasoning of moral stage 2 of Intermediate students.

**Hypothesis 4**

There would be no significant influence of interaction effects namely, sex, year of study, management and region on the reasoning of moral stage 2 of Intermediate students.

The above hypotheses are tested through 2 × 2 × 3 × 3 factorial design.

The results of Analysis of variance (ANOVA) of 2 × 2 × 3 × 3 factorial design for moral stage 2 scores are presented in Table 5.6.

It is observed from Table 5.6 that the computed value of 'F' for the main effect sex is 0.401 which is not significant at 0.05 level. Hence Hypothesis 3 is accepted. It is concluded that sex does not have significant influence on the reasoning of moral stage 2.

It is observed from Table 5.6 that the computed value of 'F' for the main effect year of study is 8.991 which is significant at 0.01 level. Hence Hypothesis 3 is rejected. It is concluded that year of study has significant influence on the reasoning of moral stage 2. Similar results were reported by Geethanath, P.S. (1987) and Rangaswamy, G.(2006).

The Bar diagram showing the mean scores of year of study on the reasoning of moral stage 2 is given in Fig. 5.5.

It is observed from Table 5.6 that the computed value of 'F' for the main effect management is 4.190 which is significant at 0.05 level. Hence Hypothesis 3 is rejected. It is concluded that management has significant influence on the reasoning of moral stage 2.

To find out which of the management of students differ significantly from one another, the 't' test was employed

Means, SD's and 't' values of management on the reasoning of moral stage 2 scores are presented in Table 5.7.

It is observed from Table 5.7 that the computed value of 't' for the students of Government and Aided colleges is 2.51 which is significant at 0.05 level.

It is observed from Table 5.7 that the computed value of 't' for the students of Government and Private colleges is 0.12 which is not significant.

It is observed from Table 5.7 that the computed value of 't' for the students of Aided and Private colleges is 2.43 which is significant at 0.05 level.

It is observed from Table 5.6 that the computed value of 'F' for the main effect region is 2.867 which is not significant. Hence Hypothesis 3 is accepted. It is concluded that region does not have significant influence on the reasoning of moral stage 2.

**Table 5.6: Results of ANOVA of 2×2×3×3 Factorial Design for Moral Stage 2 Scores**

Variable A = Sex (2 levels)
Variable B = Year of study (2 levels)
Variable C = Management (3 levels)
Variable D = Region (3 levels)

| Sl. No. | Source of variance | Sum of squares | df | Mean squares | F-value | Level of significance |
|---|---|---|---|---|---|---|
| 1. | A | 72.593 | 1 | 72.593 | 0.401 | @ |
| 2. | B | 1625.579 | 1 | 1625.579 | 8.991 | ** |
| 3. | C | 1515.035 | 2 | 757.517 | 4.190 | * |
| 4. | D | 1036.701 | 2 | 518.351 | 2.867 | @ |
| 5. | AB | 126.759 | 1 | 126.759 | 0.701 | @ |
| 6. | AC | 1072.650 | 2 | 536.325 | 2.966 | @ |
| 7. | AD | 638.206 | 2 | 319.103 | 1.765 | @ |
| 8. | BC | 95.845 | 2 | 47.922 | 0.265 | @ |
| 9. | BD | 837.928 | 2 | 418.964 | 2.317 | @ |
| 10. | CD | 1217.951 | 4 | 304.488 | 1.684 | @ |
| 11. | ABC | 30.914 | 2 | 15.457 | 0.085 | @ |
| 12. | ABD | 569.803 | 2 | 284.902 | 1.576 | @ |
| 13. | ACD | 2616.655 | 4 | 654.164 | 3.618 | ** |
| 14. | BCD | 431.794 | 4 | 107.948 | 0.597 | @ |
| 15. | ABCD | 1476.794 | 4 | 369.98 | 2.042 | @ |
| 16. | Error | 188762.08 | 1044 | 180.807 | | |
| 17. | **Total** | **202127.29** | **1079** | | | |

* Indicates significant at 0.05 level;
** Indicates significant at 0.01 level;
@ Indicates not significant at 0.05 level.

It is observed from Table 5.6 that the computed values 'F' for the two factor interaction effect namely, sex Vs year of study, sex Vs management, sex Vs region, year of study Vs management, year of study Vs region and management Vs region do not have significant influence on the reasoning of moral stage 2.

**Table 5.7: Means, SD's and 't' values of Management on the Reasoning of Moral Stage 2 Scores**

| Sl. No. | Variable | Mean value | SD values | 't' – values | | |
|---|---|---|---|---|---|---|
| | | | | Government | Aided | Private |
| 1. | Government | 36.55 | 13.77 | - | 2.51* | 0.12@ |
| 2. | Aided | 33.98 | 13.69 | - | - | 2.43* |
| 3. | Private | 36.43 | 13.42 | - | - | - |

** Indicates significant at 0.01 level;
* Indicates significant at 0.05 level;
@ Indicates not significant at 0.05 level.

It is observed from Table 5.6 that the computed value of 'F' for the three factor interaction effect namely, sex Vs management Vs region is 3.618 which is significant at 0.01 level. Hence Hypothesis 4 is rejected. It is concluded that the three factor interaction effect namely, sex Vs management Vs region has significant influence on the reasoning of moral stage 2. The remaining three factor interaction effects namely, sex Vs year of study Vs management, sex Vs year of study Vs region and year of study Vs management Vs region do not have significant influence on the reasoning of moral stage-2.

It is observed from Table 5.6 that the computed value of 'F' for the four factor interaction effect namely, sex Vs year of study Vs management Vs region is 2.042 which is not significant. Hence Hypothesis 4 is accepted. It is concluded that the four factor interaction effects namely, sex Vs year of study Vs management Vs region does not have significant influence on the reasoning of moral stage 2.

*Moral Stage 3*

There are two divisions in the sex, two divisions in the year of study, three divisions in the management and three divisions in the region. The influence of sex, year of study,

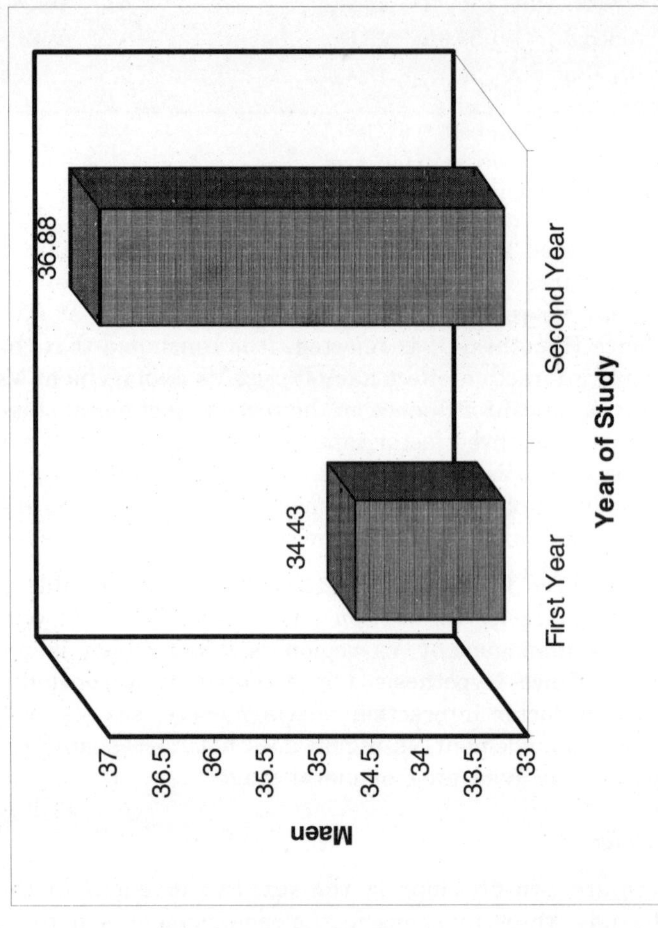


**Fig. 5.5: Bar Diagram showing the Mean Scores of Year of Study on the Reasoning of Moral Stage 2**

management and region on the reasoning of moral stage 3 scores of Intermediate students is investigated through 2×2×3×3 factorial design. The following hypotheses are framed:

**Hypothesis 5**

There would be no significant influence of main effects namely, sex, year of study, management and region on the reasoning of moral stage 3 of Intermediate students.

**Hypothesis 6**

There would be no significant influence of interaction effects namely, sex, year of study, management and region on the reasoning of moral stage 3 of Intermediate students.

The above hypotheses are tested through 2×2×3×3 factorial design.

The results of Analysis of variance (ANOVA) of 2 × 2 × 3 × 3 factorial design for moral stage 3 scores are presented in Table 5.8.

It is observed from Table 5.8 that the computed value of 'F' for the main effect sex is 21.830 which is significant at 0.01 level. Hence Hypothesis 5 is rejected. It is concluded that sex has significant influence on the reasoning of moral stage 3. Similar results were reported by Jennifer (1984), Dayakara Reddy, (1987), Geethanath, (1987) and Rangaswamy, (2006).

It is observed from Table 5.8 that the computed value of 'F' for the main effect year of study is 7.859 which is significant at 0.01 level. Hence Hypothesis 5 is rejected. It is concluded that year of study has significant influence on the reasoning of moral stage 3. Similar results ware reported by Geethanath, (1987) and Rangaswamy, (2006).

It is observed from Table 5.8 that the computed value of 'F' for the main effect management is 8.979 which is significant at 0.01 level. Hence Hypothesis 5 is rejected. It is concluded that management has significant influence on the reasoning of moral stage 3.

**Table 5.8: Results of ANOVA of 2×2×3×3 Factorial Design for Moral Stage 3 Scores**

Variable A = Sex (2 levels)

Variable B = Year of study (2 levels)

Variable C = Management (3 levels)

Variable D = Region (3 levels)

| Sl. No. | Source of variance | Sum of squares | df | Mean squares | F-value | Level of signifi-cance |
|---|---|---|---|---|---|---|
| 1. | A | 8542.969 | 1 | 8542.969 | 21.830 | ** |
| 2. | B | 3075.469 | 1 | 3075.469 | 7.859 | ** |
| 3. | C | 7027.526 | 2 | 3513.763 | 8.979 | ** |
| 4. | D | 245.557 | 2 | 124.779 | 0.319 | @ |
| 5. | AB | 3440.052 | 1 | 3440.052 | 8.790 | ** |
| 6. | AC | 1455.547 | 2 | 727.773 | 1.860 | @ |
| 7. | AD | 319.297 | 2 | 159.648 | 0.408 | @ |
| 8. | BC | 1155.547 | 2 | 577.773 | 1.476 | @ |
| 9. | BD | 2344.297 | 2 | 1172.148 | 2.995 | * |
| 10. | CD | 6180.365 | 4 | 1545.091 | 3.948 | ** |
| 11. | ABC | 4.089 | 2 | 2.044 | 0.005 | @ |
| 12. | ABD | 1161.432 | 2 | 580.716 | 1.484 | @ |
| 13. | ACD | 5776.719 | 4 | 1444.180 | 3.600 | ** |
| 14. | BCD | 2372.187 | 4 | 593.047 | 1.515 | @ |
| 15. | ABCD | 5562.083 | 4 | 1390.521 | 3.553 | ** |
| 16. | Error | 408559.69 | 1044 | 391.341 | | |
| 17. | **Total** | **447226.82** | **1079** | | | |

** Indicates significant at 0.01 level;
* Indicates significant at 0.05 level;
@ Indicates not significant at 0.05 level.

To find out which of the management of students differ significantly from one another, the 't' test was employed. The Bar diagram showing the mean scores of sex on the reasoning of moral stage 3 is given in Fig. 5.6.

Means, SD's and 't' values of management on the reasoning of moral stage 3 scores are presented in Table 5.9.

**Table 5.9: Means, SD's and 't' Values of Management on the Reasoning of Moral Stage 3 Scores**

| Sl. No. | Variable | Mean value | SD values | 't' – values | | |
|---|---|---|---|---|---|---|
| | | | | Government | Aided | Private |
| 1. | Government | 51.46 | 19.44 | - | 5.57** | 0.98@ |
| 2. | Aided | 55.97 | 20.62 | - | - | 3.85** |
| 3. | Private | 49.97 | 21.16 | - | - | - |

** Indicates significant at 0.01 level;
@ Indicates not significant at 0.05 level.

It is observed from Table 5.9 that the computed value of 't' for the students of Government and Aided colleges is 5.57 which is significant at 0.01 level.

It is observed from Table 5.9 that the computed value of't' for the students of Government and Private colleges is 0.98 which is not significant.

It is observed from Table 5.9 that the computed value of't' for the students of Aided and Private colleges is 3.85 which is significant at 0.01 level.

It is observed from Table 5.8 that the computed value of 'F' for the main effect region is 0.319 which is not significant. Hence Hypothesis 5 is accepted. It is concluded that region does not have significant influence on the reasoning of moral stage 3.

It is observed from Table 5.8 that the computed value of 'F' for the two factor interaction effect namely, sex Vs year of study is 8.790 and management Vs region is 3.948 which are significant at 0.01 level. Hence Hypothesis 6 is rejected. It is concluded that the two factor interaction effect namely, sex Vs year of study and management Vs region has significant influence on the reasoning of moral stage 3.

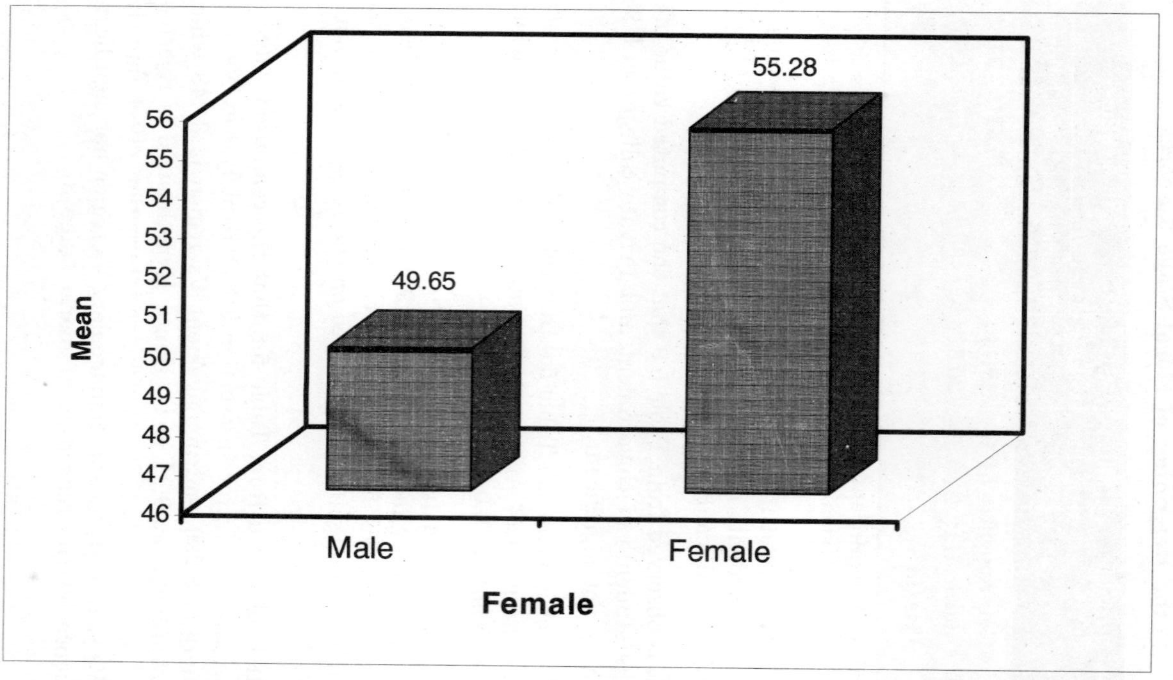


**Figure 5.6: Bar Diagram Showing the Mean Scores of Sex on the Reasoning of Moral Stage 3**

It is observed from Table 5.8 that the computed value of 'F' for the two factor interaction effect namely, year of study Vs region is 2.995 which is significant at 0.05 level. Hence Hypothesis 6 is rejected. It is concluded that the two factor interaction effect namely, year of study Vs region has significant influence on the reasoning of moral stage 3. The remaining two factor interaction effects namely, sex Vs management, sex Vs region and year of study Vs management do not have significant influence on the reasoning of moral stage 3.

It is observed from Table 5.8 that the computed value of 'F' for the three factor interaction effect namely, sex Vs management Vs region is 3.60 which is significant at 0.01 level. Hence Hypothesis 6 is rejected. It is concluded that the three factor interaction effect namely, sex Vs management Vs region has significant influence on the reasoning of moral stage 3. The remaining three factor interaction effects namely, sex Vs year of study Vs management, sex Vs year of study Vs region and year of study Vs management Vs region do not have significant influence on the reasoning of moral stage 3.

It is observed from Table 5.8 that the computed value of 'F' for the four factor interaction effect namely, sex Vs year of study Vs management Vs region is 3.553 which is significant at 0.01 level. Hence Hypothesis 6 is rejected. It is concluded that the four factor interaction effects namely, sex Vs year of study Vs management Vs region has significant influence on the reasoning of moral stage 3.

*Moral Stage 4*

There are two divisions in the sex, two divisions in the year of study, three divisions in the management and three divisions in the region. The influence of sex, year of study, management and region on the reasoning of moral stage 4 scores of Intermediate students is investigated through 2×2×3×3 factorial design. The following hypotheses are framed.

**Hypothesis 7**

There would be no significant influence of main effects namely, sex, year of study, management and region on the reasoning of moral stage 4 of Intermediate students.

**Hypothesis 8**

There would be no significant influence of interaction effects namely, sex, year of study, management and region on the reasoning of moral stage 4 of Intermediate students.

The above hypotheses are tested through 2×2×3×3 factorial design.

The results of Analysis of variance (ANOVA) of 2×2×3×3 factorial design for moral stage 4 scores are presented in Table 5.10.

It is observed from Table 5.10 that the computed value of 'F' for the main effect sex is 4.955 which is significant at 0.05 level. Hence Hypothesis 7 is rejected. It is concluded that sex has significant influence on the reasoning of moral stage 4. Similar results were reported by Geethanath, (1987) and Rangaswamy, (2006).

It is observed from Table 5.10 that the computed value of 'F' for the main effect year of study is 19.161 which is significant at 0.01 level. Hence Hypothesis 7 is rejected. It is concluded that year of study has significant influence on the reasoning of moral stage 4. Similar results were reported by Dayakara Reddy, (1987), Geethanath, (1987) and Rangaswamy, (2006).

The Bar diagram showing the mean scores of year of study on the reasoning of moral stage 4 is given in Fig. 5.7.

It is observed from Table 5.10 that the computed value of 'F' for the main effect management is 1.966 which is not significant. Hence Hypothesis 7 is accepted. It is concluded that management does not have significant influence on the reasoning of moral stage 4.

It is observed from Table 5.10 that the computed value of 'F' for the main effect region is 2.697 which is not significant. Hence Hypothesis 7 is accepted. It is concluded that region does not have significant influence on the reasoning of moral stage 4.

**Table 5.10: Results of ANOVA of 2×2×3×3 Factorial Design for Moral Stage 4 Scores**

Variable A = Sex (2 levels)

Variable B = Year of study (2 levels)

Variable C = Management (3 levels)

Variable D = Region (3 levels)

| Sl. No. | Source of variance | Sum of squares | df | Mean squares | F-value | Level of significance |
|---|---|---|---|---|---|---|
| 1. | A | 3502.801 | 1 | 3502.801 | 4.955 | * |
| 2. | B | 13546.875 | 1 | 13546.875 | 19.161 | ** |
| 3. | C | 2780.185 | 2 | 1390.093 | 1.966 | @ |
| 4. | D | 3813.519 | 2 | 1906.759 | 2.697 | @ |
| 5. | AB | 473.356 | 1 | 473.356 | 0.670 | @ |
| 6. | AC | 7577.963 | 2 | 3788.981 | 5.359 | ** |
| 7. | AD | 10339.074 | 2 | 5169.537 | 7.312 | ** |
| 8. | BC | 2527.222 | 2 | 1263.611 | 1.787 | @ |
| 9. | BD | 4351.667 | 2 | 2175.833 | 3.078 | * |
| 10. | CD | 2514.120 | 4 | 628.530 | 0.889 | @ |
| 11. | ABC | 3353.519 | 2 | 1676.759 | 2.372 | @ |
| 12. | ABD | 36.296 | 2 | 18.148 | 0.026 | @ |
| 13. | ACD | 11231.620 | 4 | 2807.905 | 3.972 | ** |
| 14. | BCD | 4434.861 | 4 | 1108.715 | 1.568 | @ |
| 15. | ABCD | 3936.620 | 4 | 984.155 | 1.392 | @ |
| 16. | Error | 738095.83 | 1044 | 706.988 | | |
| 17. | Total | 812515.53 | 1079 | | | |

** Indicates significant at 0.01 level;
* Indicates significant at 0.05 level;
@ Indicates not significant at 0.05 level.

It is observed from Table 5.10 that the computed value of 'F' for the two factor interaction effect namely, sex Vs management is 5.359 which is significant at 0.01 level. Hence Hypothesis 8 is rejected. It is concluded that the two factor

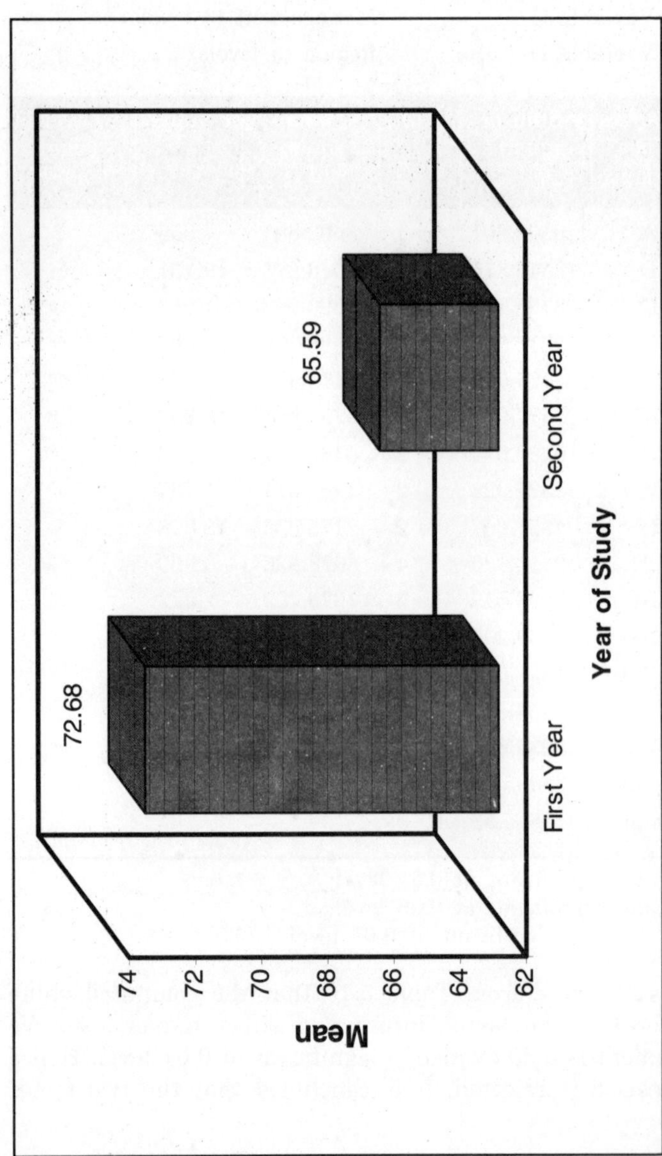


**Fig. 5.7: Bar Diagram Showing the Mean Scores of Year of Study on the Reasoning of Moral Stage- 4**

interaction effect namely, sex Vs management has significant influence on the reasoning of moral stage 4.

It is observed from Table 5.10 that the computed value of 'F' for the two factor interaction effect namely, sex Vs region is 7.312 which is significant at 0.01 level. Hence Hypothesis 8 is rejected. It is concluded that the two factor interaction effect namely, sex Vs region has significant influence on the reasoning of moral stage 4.

It is observed from Table 5.10 that the computed value of 'F' for the two factor interaction effect namely, year of study Vs region is 3.078 which is significant at 0.05 level. Hence Hypothesis 8 is rejected. It is concluded that the two factor interaction effect namely, year of study Vs region has significant influence on the reasoning of moral stage 4. The remaining two factor interaction effects namely, sex Vs year of study, year of study Vs management and management Vs region do not have significant influence on the reasoning of moral stage 4.

It is observed from Table 5.10 that the computed value of 'F' for the three factor interaction effect namely, sex Vs management Vs region is 3.972 which is significant at 0.01 level. Hence Hypothesis 8 is rejected. It is concluded that the three factor interaction effect namely, sex Vs management Vs region has significant influence on the reasoning of moral stage 4. The remaining three factor interaction effects namely, sex Vs year of study Vs management, sex Vs year of study Vs region and year of study Vs management Vs region do not have significant influence on the reasoning of moral stage 4.

It is observed from Table 5.10 that the computed value of 'F' for the four factor interaction effect namely, sex Vs year of study Vs management Vs region is 1.392 which is not significant. Hence Hypothesis 8 is accepted. It is concluded that the four factor interaction effects namely, sex Vs year of study Vs management Vs region does not have significant influence on the reasoning of moral stage 4.

*Moral Stage 4A*

There are two divisions in the sex, two divisions in the year of study, three divisions in the management and three divisions in the region. The influence of sex, year of study, management and region on the moral stage 4A scores of Intermediate students is investigated through 2×2×3×3 factorial design. The following hypotheses are framed.

**Hypothesis 9**

There would be no significant influence of main effects namely, sex, year of study, management and region on the reasoning of moral stage 4A of Intermediate students.

**Hypothesis 10**

There would be no significant influence of interaction effects namely, sex, year of study, management and region on the reasoning of moral stage 4A of Intermediate students.

The above hypotheses are tested through 2×2×3×3 factorial design.

The results of Analysis of variance (ANOVA) of 2×2×3×3 factorial design for moral stage 4A scores are presented in Table 5.11.

It is observed from Table 5.11 that the computed value of 'F' for the main effect sex is 19.680 which is significant at 0.01 level. Hence Hypothesis 9 is rejected. It is concluded that sex has significant influence on the reasoning of moral stage 4A.

It is observed from Table 5.11 that the computed value of 'F' for the main effect year of study is 2.348 which is not significant. Hence Hypothesis 9 is accepted. It is concluded that year of study does not have significant influence on the reasoning of moral stage 4A.

It is observed from Table 5.11 that the computed value of 'F' for the main effect management is 0.078 which is not significant. Hence Hypothesis 9 is accepted. It is concluded that management does not have significant influence on the reasoning of moral stage 4A.

**Table 5.11: Results of ANOVA of 2×2×3×3 Factorial Design for Moral Stage 4A Scores**

Variable A = Sex (2 levels)

Variable B = Year of study (2 levels)

Variable C = Management (3 levels)

Variable D = Region (3 levels)

| Sl. No. | Source of variance | Sum of squares | df | Mean squares | F-value | Level of signifi-cance |
|---|---|---|---|---|---|---|
| 1. | A | 7078.912 | 1 | 7078.912 | 19.680 | ** |
| 2. | B | 844.468 | 1 | 844.468 | 2.348 | @ |
| 3. | C | 56.157 | 2 | 28.079 | 0.078 | @ |
| 4. | D | 1926.435 | 2 | 96.218 | 2.678 | @ |
| 5. | AB | 75.208 | 1 | 75.208 | 0.209 | @ |
| 6. | AC | 372.546 | 2 | 186.273 | 0.518 | @ |
| 7. | AD | 1893.102 | 2 | 946.551 | 2.631 | @ |
| 8. | BC | 799.491 | 2 | 399.745 | 1.111 | @ |
| 9. | BD | 386.991 | 2 | 193.495 | 0.538 | @ |
| 10. | CD | 812.037 | 4 | 203.009 | 0.564 | @ |
| 11. | ABC | 1021.250 | 2 | 510.625 | 1.420 | @ |
| 12. | ABD | 155.139 | 2 | 77.569 | 0.216 | @ |
| 13. | ACD | 6353.148 | 4 | 1588.287 | 4.415 | ** |
| 14. | BCD | 281.759 | 4 | 70.440 | 0.196 | @ |
| 15. | ABCD | 3315.278 | 4 | 828.819 | 2.305 | @ |
| 16. | Error | 375535.83 | 1044 | 359.709 | | |
| **17.** | **Total** | **400907.75** | **1079** | | | |

** Indicates significant at 0.01 level;
@ Indicates not significant at 0.05 level.

It is observed from Table 5.11 that the computed value of 'F' for the main effect region is 2.678 which is not significant. Hence Hypothesis 9 is accepted. It is concluded that region does not have significant influence on the reasoning of moral stage 4A.

The Bar diagram showing the mean scores of sex on the reasoning of moral stage 4A is given in Fig. 5.8.

It is observed from Table 5.11 that the computed value of 'F' for the two factor interaction effect namely, sex Vs year of study, sex Vs management, sex Vs region, year of study Vs management, year of study Vs region and management Vs region do not have significant influence on the reasoning of moral stage 4A.

It is observed from Table 5.11 that the computed value of 'F' for the three factor interaction effect namely, sex Vs management Vs region is 4.415 which is significant at 0.01 level. Hence Hypothesis 10 is rejected. It is concluded that the three factor interaction effect namely, sex Vs management Vs region has significant influence on the reasoning of moral stage 4A. The remaining three factor interaction effects namely, sex Vs year of study Vs management, sex Vs year of study Vs region and year of study Vs management Vs region do not have significant influence on the reasoning of moral stage 4A.

It is observed from Table 5.11 that the computed value of 'F' for the four factor interaction effect namely, sex Vs year of study Vs management Vs region is 2.305 which is not significant. Hence Hypothesis 10 is accepted. It is concluded that the four factor interaction effects namely, sex Vs year of study Vs management Vs region does not have significant influence on the reasoning of moral stage 4A.

*Moral Stage 5A*

There are two divisions in the sex, two divisions in the year of study, three divisions in the management and three divisions in the region. The influence of sex, year of study, management and region on the reasoning of moral stage 5A scores of Intermediate students is investigated through 2×2×3×3 factorial design. The following hypotheses are framed.

**Hypothesis 11**

There would be no significant influence of main effects

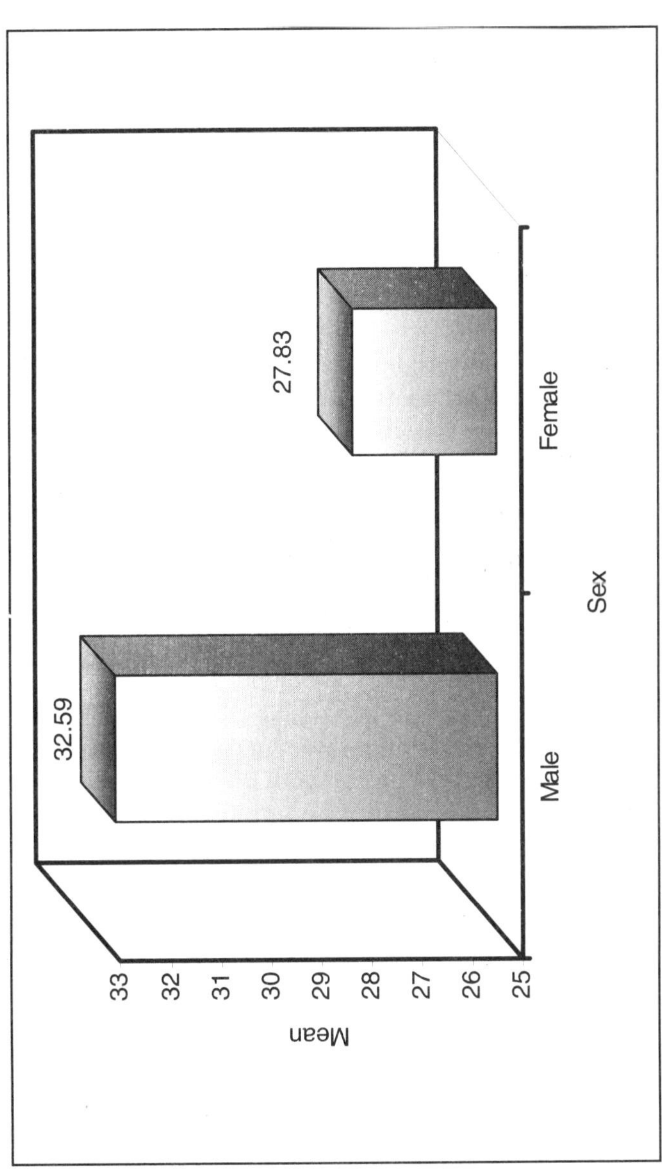


**Figure 5.8: Bar diagram Showing the Mean Scores of Sex on the Reasoning of Moral Stage 4A**

namely, sex, year of study, management and region on the reasoning of moral stage 5A of Intermediate students.

**Hypothesis 12**

There would be no significant influence of interaction effects namely, sex, year of study, management and region on the reasoning of moral stage 5A of Intermediate students.

The above hypotheses are tested through 2×2×3×3 factorial design.

The results of Analysis of variance (ANOVA) of 2×2×3×3 factorial design for moral stage 5A scores are presented in Table 5.12.

It is observed from Table 5.12 that the computed value of 'F' for the main effect sex is 0.073 which is not significant. Hence Hypothesis 11 is accepted. It is concluded that sex does not have significant influence on the reasoning of moral stage 5A.

It is observed from Table 5.12 that the computed value of 'F' for the main effect year of study is 1.519 which is not significant. Hence Hypothesis 11 is accepted. It is concluded that year of study does not have significant influence on the reasoning of moral stage 5A.

It is observed from Table 5.12 that the computed value of 'F' for the main effect management is 3.106 which is significant at 0.05 level. Hence Hypothesis 11 is rejected. It is concluded that management has significant influence on the reasoning of moral stage 5A.

To find out which of the management of students differ significantly from one another, the 't' test was employed.

Means, SD's and 't' values of management on the reasoning of moral stage 5A scores are presented in Table 5.13.

It is observed from Table 5.13 that the computed value of 't' for the students of Government and Aided colleges is 2.17 which is significant at 0.05 level.

It is observed from Table 5.13 that the computed value of 't' for the students of Government and Private colleges is 2.18 which is significant 0.05 level.

**Table 5.12: Results of ANOVA of 2×2×3×3 Factorial Design for Moral Stage 5A Scores**

Variable A = Sex (2 levels)

Variable B = Year of study (2 levels)

Variable C = Management (3 levels)

Variable D = Region (3 levels)

| Sl. No. | Source of variance | Sum of squares | df | Mean squares | F-value | Level of signifi-cance |
|---|---|---|---|---|---|---|
| **1.** | A | 46.875 | 1 | 46.875 | 0.073 | @ |
| **2.** | B | 972.801 | 1 | 972.801 | 1.519 | @ |
| **3.** | C | 3978.371 | 2 | 1989.185 | 3.106 | * |
| **4.** | D | 1157.624 | 2 | 578.812 | 0.904 | @ |
| **5.** | AB | 76.534 | 1 | 76.534 | 0.120 | @ |
| **6.** | AC | 795.790 | 2 | 397.895 | 0.621 | @ |
| **7.** | AD | 5504.123 | 2 | 2752.062 | 4.218 | * |
| **8.** | BC | 133.753 | 2 | 66.876 | 0.104 | @ |
| **9.** | BD | 2613.354 | 2 | 1306.677 | 2.041 | @ |
| **10.** | CD | 1709.346 | 4 | 427.337 | 0.667 | @ |
| **11.** | ABC | 2889.829 | 2 | 1444.915 | 2.256 | @ |
| **12.** | ABD | 1774.378 | 2 | 887.189 | 1.385 | @ |
| **13.** | ACD | 3418.837 | 4 | 854.709 | 1.335 | @ |
| **14.** | BCD | 992.332 | 4 | 248.083 | 0.387 | @ |
| **15.** | ABCD | 2398.582 | 4 | 599.646 | 0.936 | @ |
| **16.** | Error | 668544.27 | 1044 | 640.368 | | |
| **17.** | Total | 697006.80 | 1079 | | | |

* Indicates significant at 0.05 level;

@ Indicates not significant at 0.05 level

It is observed from Table 5.13 that the computed value of 't' for the students of Aided and Private colleges is 0.03 which is not significant.

The Bar diagram showing the means scores of management on the reasoning of moral stage 5A is given in Fig. 5.9.

It is observed from Table 5.12 that the computed value of 'F' for the main effect region is 0.904 which is not significant. Hence Hypothesis 11 is accepted. It is concluded that region does not have significant influence on the reasoning of moral stage 5A.

**Table 5.13: Means, SD's and 't' Values of Management on the Reasoning of Moral Stage 5A Scores**

| Sl. No. | Variable | Mean value | SD values | 't' – values | | |
|---|---|---|---|---|---|---|
| | | | | Government | Aided | Private |
| 1. | Government | 37.14 | 24.62 | - | 2.17* | 2.18* |
| 2. | Aided | 41.18 | 25.49 | - | - | 0.03@ |
| 3. | Private | 41.23 | 25.86 | - | - | - |

* Indicates significant at 0.05 level;
@ Indicates not significant at 0.05 level.

It is observed from Table 5.12 that the computed value of 'F' for the two factor interaction effect namely, sex Vs region is 4.218 which is significant at 0.05 level. Hence Hypothesis 12 is rejected. It is concluded that the two factor interaction effect namely, sex Vs region has significant influence on the reasoning of moral stage 5A. Remaining two factor interaction effects namely, sex Vs year of study, sex Vs management, year of study Vs management, year of study Vs region and management Vs region do not have significant influence on the reasoning of moral stage 5A.

It is observed from Table 5.12 that all the three factor interaction effect namely, sex Vs year of study Vs management, sex Vs year of study Vs region, sex Vs management Vs region and year of study Vs management Vs region do not have significant influence on the reasoning of moral stage 5A.

It is observed from Table 5.12 that the computed value of 'F' for the four factor interaction effect namely, sex Vs year of study Vs management Vs region is 0.936 which is not

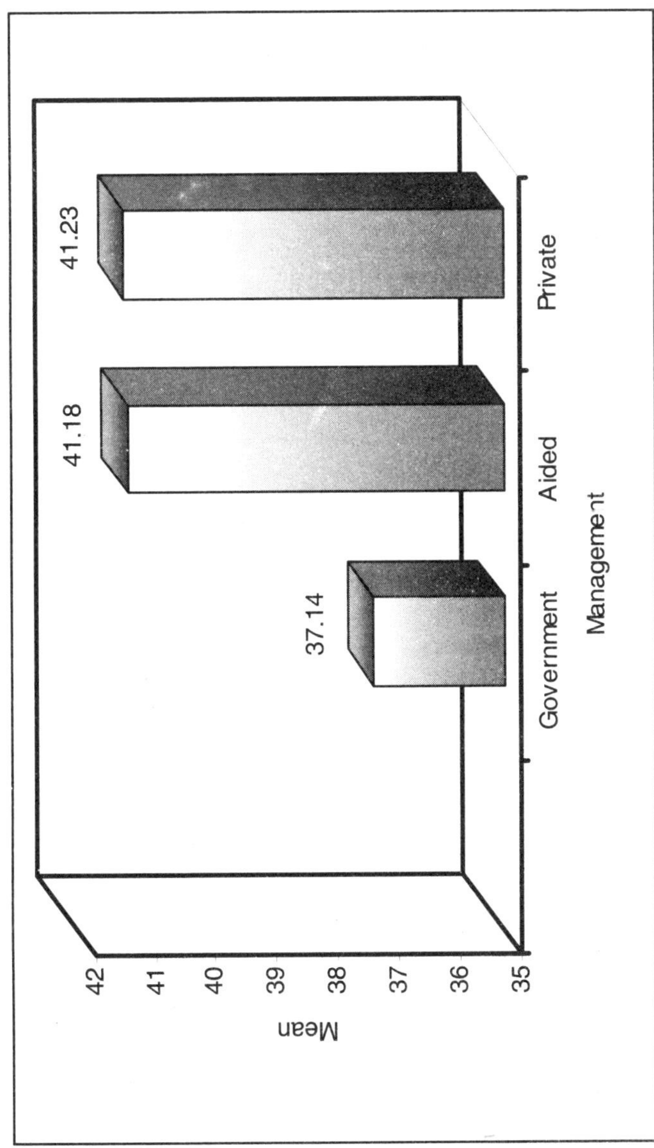


**Fig. 5.9: Bar Diagram Showing the Means Scores of Management on the reasoning of Moral Stage 5A**

significant. Hence Hypothesis 12 is accepted. It is concluded that the four factor interaction effects namely, sex Vs year of study Vs management Vs region does not have significant influence on the reasoning of moral stage 5A.

*Moral Stage 5B*

There are two divisions in the sex, two divisions in the year of study, three divisions in the management and three divisions in the region. The influence of sex, year of study, management and region on the reasoning of moral stage 5B scores of Intermediate students is investigated through 2×2×3×3 factorial design. The following hypotheses are framed:

**Hypothesis 13**

There would be no significant influence of main effects namely, sex, year of study, management and region on the reasoning of moral stage 5B of Intermediate students.

**Hypothesis 14**

There would be no significant influence of interaction effects namely, sex, year of study, management and region on the reasoning of moral stage 5B of Intermediate students.

The above hypotheses are tested through 2×2×3×3 factorial design.

The results of Analysis of variance (ANOVA) of 2×2×3×3 factorial design for moral stage 5B scores are presented in Table 5.14.

It is observed from Table 5.14 that the computed value of 'F' for the main effect sex is 2.055 which is not significant. Hence Hypothesis 13 is accepted. It is concluded that sex does not have significant influence on the reasoning of moral stage 5B.

It is observed from Table 5.14 that the computed value of 'F' for the main effect year of study is 3.143 which is not significant. Hence Hypothesis 13 is accepted. It is concluded that year of study does not have significant influence on the reasoning of moral stage 5B.

It is observed from Table 5.14 that the computed value of 'F' for the main effect management is 0.742 which is not significant. Hence Hypothesis 13 is accepted. It is concluded that management does not have significant influence on the reasoning of moral stage 5B.

**Table 5.14: Results of ANOVA of 2×2×3×3 Factorial Design for Moral Stage 5B Scores**

Variable A = Sex (2 levels)

Variable B = Year of study (2 levels)

Variable C = Management (3 levels)

Variable D = Region (3 levels)

| Sl. No. | Source of variance | Sum of squares | df | Mean squares | F-value | Level of signifi cance |
|---|---|---|---|---|---|---|
| 1. | A | 1033.022 | 1 | 1033.022 | 2.055 | @ |
| 2. | B | 1579.897 | 1 | 1579.897 | 3.143 | @ |
| 3. | C | 745.660 | 2 | 372.830 | 0.742 | @ |
| 4. | D | 3013.889 | 2 | 1506.944 | 2.998 | * |
| 5. | AB | 162.363 | 1 | 162.363 | 0.323 | @ |
| 6. | AC | 271.123 | 2 | 135.561 | 0.270 | @ |
| 7. | AD | 6710.359 | 2 | 3355.179 | 6.675 | ** |
| 8. | BC | 1741.609 | 2 | 870.804 | 1.733 | @ |
| 9. | BD | 3612.269 | 2 | 1806.134 | 3.593 | * |
| 10. | CD | 7576.389 | 4 | 1894.097 | 3.769 | ** |
| 11. | ABC | 574.942 | 2 | 287.471 | 0.572 | @ |
| 12. | ABD | 10272.859 | 2 | 5136.429 | 10.219 | ** |
| 13. | ACD | 6446.759 | 4 | 1611.690 | 3.207 | * |
| 14. | BCD | 1787.905 | 4 | 446.976 | 0.889 | @ |
| 15. | ABCD | 1107.350 | 4 | 276.837 | 0.551 | @ |
| 16. | Error | 524727.86 | 1044 | 502.613 | | |
| 17. | Total | 517364.26 | 1079 | | | |

** Indicates significant at 0.01 level;
* Indicates significant at 0.05 level;
@ Indicates not significant at 0.05 level

It is observed from Table 5.14 that the computed value of 'F' for the main effect region is 2.998 which is significant at 0.05 level. Hence Hypothesis 13 is rejected. It is concluded that region has significant influence on the reasoning of moral stage 5B.

To find out which of the region of students differ significantly from one another, the 't' test was employed.

Means, SD's and 't' values of region on the reasoning of moral stage 5B scores are presented in Table 5.15.

**Table 5.15: Means, SD's and 't' values of Region on the Reasoning of Moral Stage 5B Scores**

| Sl. No. | Variable | Mean value | SD values | 't' – values | | |
|---|---|---|---|---|---|---|
| | | | | Telangana | Rayalaseema | Coastal |
| 1. | Telangana | 39.08 | 24.87 | - | 0.08@ | 1.93@ |
| 2. | Rayalaseema | 39.22 | 20.48 | - | - | 2.21* |
| 3. | Coastal | 35.61 | 23.26 | - | - | - |

* Indicates significant at 0.05 level;
@ Indicates not significant at 0.05 level.

It is observed from Table 5.15 that the computed value of't' for the students of Telangana and Rayalaseema region is 0.08 which is not significant at 0.05 level.

It is observed from Table 5.15 that the computed value of 't' for the students of Telangana and Coastal regions is 1.93 which is not significant.

It is observed from Table 5.15 that the computed value of 't' for the students of Rayalaseema and Coastal regions is 2.21 which is significant at 0.05 level.

It is observed from Table 5.14 that the computed value of 'F' for the two factor interaction effect namely, sex Vs region is 6.675 which is significant at 0.01 level. Hence Hypothesis 14 is rejected. It is concluded that the two factor interaction effect namely, sex Vs region has significant influence on the reasoning of moral stage 5B.

It is observed from Table 5.14 that the computed value of 'F' for the two factor interaction effect namely, management Vs region is 3.769 which is significant at 0.01 level Vs. Hence Hypothesis 14 is rejected. It is concluded that the two factor interaction effect namely, management Vs region has significant influence on the reasoning of moral stage 5B.

The Bar diagram showing the means scores of region on the reasoning of moral stage 5B is given in Fig. 5.10.

It is observed from Table 5.14 that the computed value of 'F' for the two factor interaction effect namely, year of study Vs region is 3.593 which is significant at 0.05 level. Hence Hypothesis 14 is rejected. It is concluded that the two factor interaction effect namely, year of study Vs region has significant influence on the reasoning of moral stage 5B. Remaining two factor interaction effects namely, sex Vs year of study, sex Vs management and year of study Vs management do not have significant influence on the reasoning of moral stage 5B.

It is observed from Table 5.14 that the computed value of 'F' for the three factor interaction effect namely, sex Vs year of study Vs management is 10.219 which is significant at 0.01 level. Hence Hypothesis 14 is rejected. It is concluded that the three factor interaction effect namely, sex Vs year of study Vs management has significant influence on the reasoning of moral stage 5B.

It is observed from Table 5.14 that the computed value of 'F' for the three factor interaction effect namely, sex Vs management Vs region is 3.207 which is significant at 0.05 level. Hence, Hypothesis 14 is rejected. It is concluded that the three factor interaction effect namely, sex Vs management Vs region has significant influence on the reasoning of moral stage 5B. Remaining three factor interaction effects namely, sex Vs year of study Vs management and year of study Vs management Vs region do not have significant influence on the reasoning of moral stage 5B.

It is observed from Table 5.14 that the computed value of 'F' for the four factor interaction effect namely, sex Vs year

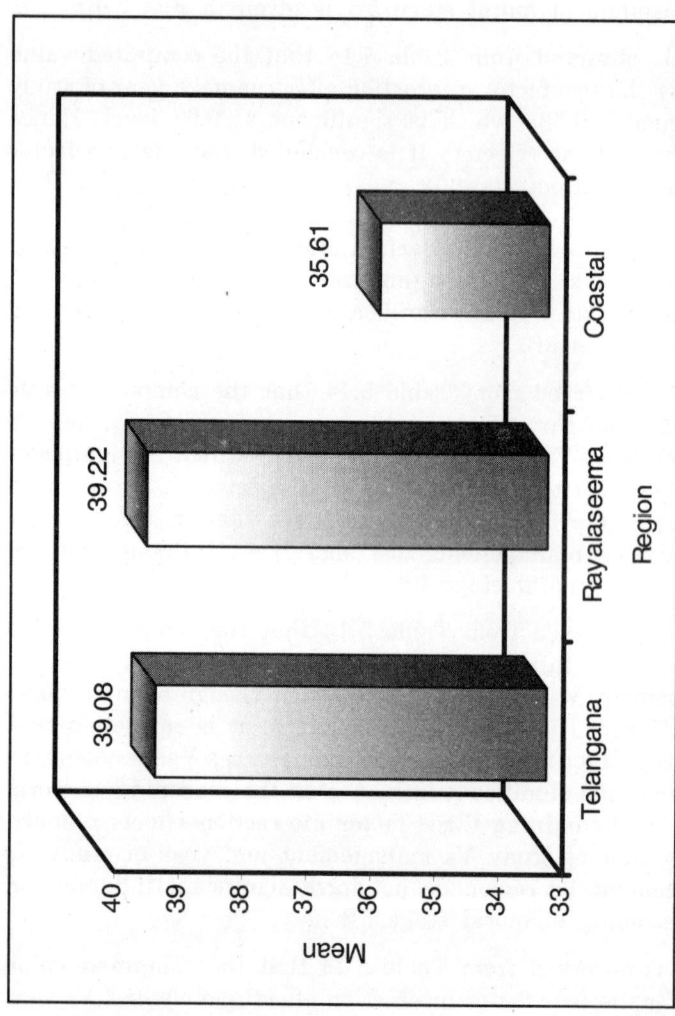


**Fig. 5.10: Bar Diagram Showing the Means Scores of Region on the Reasoning of Moral Stage 5B**

of study Vs management Vs region is 0.551 which is not significant. Hence Hypothesis 14 is accepted. It is concluded that the four factor interaction effects namely, sex Vs year of study Vs management Vs region does not have significant influence on the reasoning of moral stage 5B.

*Moral Stage 6*

There are two divisions in the sex, two divisions in the year of study, three divisions in the management and three divisions in the region. The influence of sex, year of study, management and region on the reasoning of moral stage 6 scores of Intermediate students is investigated through 2×2×3×3 factorial design. The following hypotheses are framed.

**Hypothesis 15**

There would be no significant influence of main effects namely, sex, year of study, management and region on the reasoning of moral stage 6 of Intermediate students.

**Hypothesis 16**

There would be no significant influence of interaction effects namely, sex, year of study, management and region on the reasoning of moral stage 6 of Intermediate students.

The above hypotheses are tested through 2×2×3×3 factorial design.

The results of Analysis of variance (ANOVA) of 2×2×3×3 factorial design for moral stage 6 scores are presented in Table 5.16.

It is observed from Table 5.16 that the computed value of 'F' for the main effect sex is 0.112 which is not significant. Hence Hypothesis 15 is accepted. It is concluded that sex does not have significant influence on the reasoning of moral stage 6.

It is observed from Table 5.16 that the computed value of 'F' for the main effect year of study is 0.018 which is not significant. Hence Hypothesis 15 is accepted. It is concluded that year of study does not have significant influence on the reasoning of moral stage 6.

**Table 5.16: Results of ANOVA of 2×2×3×3 Factorial Design for Moral Stage 6 Scores**

Variable A = Sex (2 levels)
Variable B = Year of study (2 levels)
Variable C = Management (3 levels)
Variable D = Region (3 levels)

| Sl. No. | Source of variance | Sum of squares | df | Mean squares | F-value | Level of significance |
|---|---|---|---|---|---|---|
| 1. | A | 83.333 | 1 | 83.333 | 0.112 | @ |
| 2. | B | 13.333 | 1 | 13.333 | 0.018 | @ |
| 3. | C | 4445.729 | 2 | 2222.865 | 2.989 | @ |
| 4. | D | 4241.979 | 2 | 2120.990 | 2.852 | @ |
| 5. | AB | 385.208 | 1 | 385.208 | 0.518 | @ |
| 6. | AC | 719.479 | 2 | 359.740 | 0.484 | @ |
| 7. | AD | 617.604 | 2 | 308.802 | 0.415 | @ |
| 8. | BC | 4023.854 | 2 | 2011.927 | 2.705 | @ |
| 9. | BD | 1159.479 | 2 | 579.740 | 0.779 | @ |
| 10. | CD | 8615.833 | 4 | 2153.958 | 2.896 | * |
| 11. | ABC | 766.354 | 2 | 383.177 | 0.515 | @ |
| 12. | ABD | 1493.854 | 2 | 746.927 | 1.004 | @ |
| 13. | ACD | 975.833 | 4 | 243.958 | 0.328 | @ |
| 14. | BCD | 1318.958 | 4 | 329.740 | 0.443 | @ |
| 15. | ABCD | 6202.708 | 4 | 1550.677 | 2.085 | @ |
| 16. | Error | 776486.25 | 1044 | 743.861 | | |
| 17. | **Total** | **811549.79** | **1079** | | | |

* Indicates significant at 0.05 level;
@ Indicates not significant at 0.05 level.

It is observed from Table 5.16 that the computed value of 'F' for the main effect management is 2.989 which is not significant. Hence Hypothesis 15 is accepted. It is concluded that management does not have significant influence on the reasoning of moral stage 6.

It is observed from Table 5.16 that the computed value of 'F' for the main effect region is 2.852 which is not significant. Hence Hypothesis 15 is accepted. It is concluded that region does not have significant influence on the reasoning of moral stage 6.

It is observed from Table 5.16 that the computed value of 'F' for the two factor interaction effect namely, management Vs region is 2.896 which is significant at 0.05 level. Hence Hypothesis 16 is rejected. It is concluded that the two factor interaction effect namely, management Vs region has significant influence on the reasoning of moral stage 6. Remaining two factor interaction effects namely, sex Vs year of study, sex Vs management, sex Vs region, year of study Vs management and year of study Vs region does not have significant influence on the reasoning of moral stage 6.

It is observed from Table 5.16 that all the three factor interaction effect namely, sex Vs year of study Vs management, sex Vs year of study Vs region, sex Vs management Vs region and year of study Vs management Vs region do not have significant influence on the reasoning of moral stage 6.

It is observed from Table 5.16 that the computed value of 'F' for the four factor interaction effect namely, sex Vs year of study Vs management Vs region is 2.085 which is not significant. Hence Hypothesis 16 is accepted. It is concluded that the four factor interaction effects namely, sex Vs year of study Vs management Vs region does not have significant influence on the reasoning of moral stage 6.

*Pre-Conventional Level*

There are two divisions in the sex, two divisions in the year of study, three divisions in the management and three divisions in the region. The influence of sex, year of study, management and region on the reasoning of pre-conventional level scores of Intermediate students is investigated through 2 × 2 × 3 × 3 factorial design. The following hypotheses are framed:

**Hypothesis 17**

There would be no significant influence of main effects namely, sex, year of study, management and region on the reasoning of pre-conventional level of Intermediate students.

**Hypothesis 18**

There would be no significant influence of interaction effects namely, sex, year of study, management and region on the reasoning of pre-conventional level of Intermediate students.

The above hypotheses are tested through 2×2×3×3 factorial design.

The results of Analysis of variance (ANOVA) of 2×2×3×3 factorial design for pre-conventional level scores are presented in Table 5.17.

It is observed from Table 5.17 that the computed value of 'F' for the main effect sex is 3.807 which is not significant. Hence Hypothesis 17 is accepted. It is concluded that sex does not have significant influence on the reasoning of pre-conventional level.

It is observed from Table 5.17 that the computed value of 'F' for the main effect year of study is 22.53 which is significant at 0.01 level. Hence Hypothesis 17 is rejected. It is concluded that year of study has significant influence on the reasoning of pre-conventional level.

It is observed from Table 5.17 that the computed value of 'F' for the main effect management is 14.498 which is significant at 0.01 level. Hence Hypothesis 17 is rejected. It is concluded that management has significant influence on the reasoning of pre-conventional level.

To find out which of the management of students differ significantly from one another, the 't' test was employed.

Means, SD's and 't' values of management on the reasoning of pre-conventional level scores are presented in Table 5.18.

**Table 5.17: Results of ANOVA of 2×2×3×3 Factorial Design for Pre-Conventional Level Scores**

Variable A = Sex (2 levels)

Variable B = Year of study (2 levels)

Variable C = Management (3 levels)

Variable D = Region (3 levels)

| Sl. No. | Source of variance | Sum of squares | df | Mean squares | F-value | Level of significance |
|---|---|---|---|---|---|---|
| **1.** | A | 750.0 | 1 | 750.0 | 3.807 | @ |
| **2.** | B | 4440.833 | 1 | 444.833 | 22.53 | ** |
| **3.** | C | 5713.058 | 2 | 2856.529 | 14.498 | ** |
| **4.** | D | 278.701 | 2 | 139.350 | 0.707 | @ |
| **5.** | AB | 90.422 | 1 | 90.422 | 0.459 | @ |
| **6.** | AC | 2191.207 | 2 | 1095.603 | 5.561 | ** |
| **7.** | AD | 565.547 | 2 | 282.773 | 1.435 | @ |
| **8.** | BC | 279.8 | 2 | 139.9 | 0.710 | @ |
| **9.** | BD | 1211.571 | 2 | 605.786 | 3.075 | * |
| **10.** | CD | 2044.155 | 4 | 511.039 | 2.594 | * |
| **11.** | ABC | 266.861 | 2 | 133.430 | 0.677 | @ |
| **12.** | ABD | 130.524 | 2 | 65.262 | 0.331 | @ |
| **13.** | ACD | 6445.486 | 4 | 1611.372 | 8.178 | ** |
| **14.** | BCD | 1154.253 | 4 | 288.563 | 1.465 | @ |
| **15.** | ABCD | 2588.547 | 4 | 647.137 | 3.284 | * |
| **16.** | Error | 205699.38 | 1044 | 197.030 | | |
| **17.** | **Total** | **233850.34** | **1079** | | | |

** Indicates significant at 0.01 level;
* Indicates significant at 0.05 level;
@ Indicates not significant at 0.05 level

It is observed from Table 5.18 that the computed value of 't' for the students of Government and Aided colleges is 4.78 which is significant at 0.01 level.

It is observed from Table 5.18 that the computed value of 't' for the students of Government and Private colleges is 0.82 which is not significant.

**Table 5.18: Means, SD's and 't' values of Management on the Reasoning of Pre-Conventional Level Scores**

| S. No. | Variable | Mean value | SD values | 't' – values | | |
|---|---|---|---|---|---|---|
| | | | | Government | Aided | Private |
| 1. | Government | 53.68 | 14.16 | — | 4.78** | 0.82@ |
| 2. | Aided | 48.43 | 15.31 | — | — | 4.0** |
| 3. | Private | 52.82 | 14.10 | — | — | — |

** Indicates significant at 0.01 level;
* Indicates significant at 0.05 level;
@ Indicates not significant at 0.05 level.

It is observed from Table 5.18 that the computed value of 't' for the students of Aided and Private colleges is 4.00 which is significant at 0.01 level.

The Bar diagram showing the mean scores of management on the reasoning of pre-conventional level is given in Fig. 5.11.

It is observed from Table 5.17 that the computed value of 'F' for the main effect region is 0.707 which is not significant. Hence Hypothesis 17 is accepted. It is concluded that region does not have significant influence on the reasoning of pre-conventional level.

It is observed from Table 5.17 that the computed value of 'F' for the two factor interaction effect namely, sex Vs management is 5.561 which is significant at 0.01 level of significance. Hence Hypothesis 18 is rejected. It is concluded that the two factor interaction effect namely, sex Vs management has significant influence on the reasoning of pre-conventional level.

It is observed from Table 5.17 that the computed value of 'F' for the two factor interaction effect namely, year of study Vs region is 3.075 which is significant at 0.05 level. Hence Hypothesis 18 is rejected. It is concluded that the two factor interaction effect namely, year of study Vs region has significant influence on the reasoning of pre-conventional level.

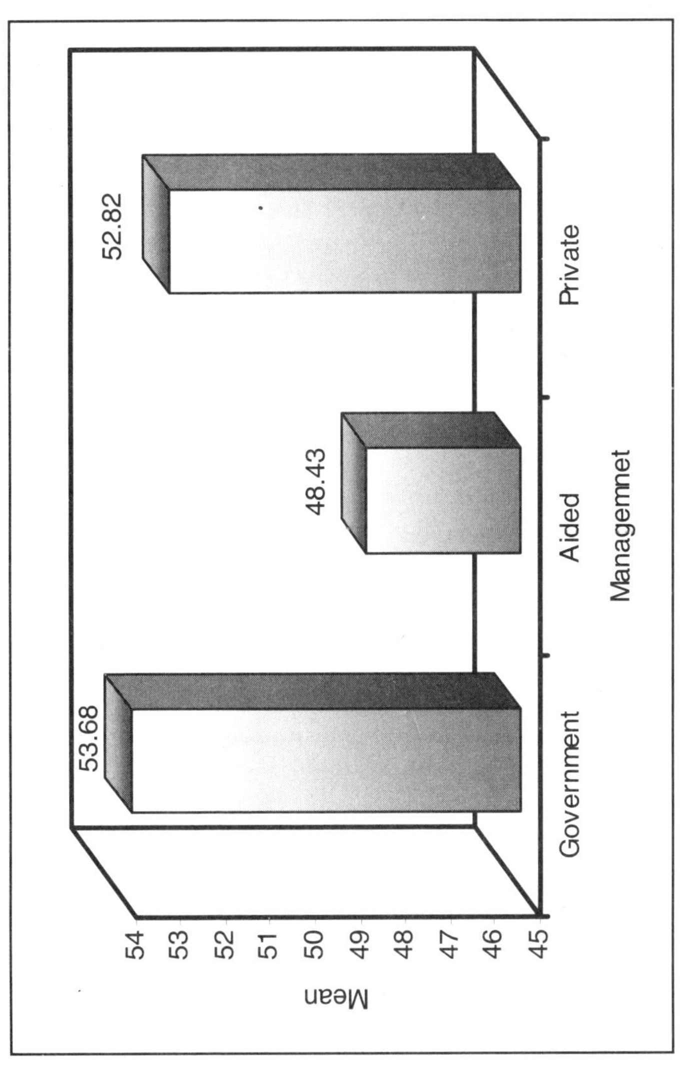


**Fig. 5.11: Bar diagram showing the mean scores of Management on the reasoning of Pre-Conventional Level**

It is observed from Table 5.17 that the computed value of 'F' for the two factor interaction effect namely, management Vs region is 2.594 which is significant at 0.05 level. Hence Hypothesis 18 is rejected. It is concluded that the two factor interaction effect namely, management Vs region has significant influence on the reasoning of pre-conventional level. Remaining two factor interaction effects namely, sex Vs year of study, sex Vs region and year of study Vs management does not have significant influence on the reasoning of pre - conventional level.

It is observed from Table 5.17 that the computed value of 'F' for the three factor interaction effect namely, sex Vs management Vs region is 8.178 which is significant at 0.01 level. Hence Hypothesis 18 is rejected. It is concluded that the three factor interaction effect namely, sex Vs management Vs region has significant influence on the reasoning of pre-conventional level. Remaining three factor interaction effects namely, sex Vs year of study Vs management, sex Vs year of study Vs region and year of study Vs management Vs region do not have significant influence on the reasoning of pre-conventional level.

It is observed from Table 5.17 that the computed value of 'F' for the four factor interaction effect namely, sex Vs year of study Vs management Vs region is 3.284 which is significant at 0.05 level. Hence Hypothesis 18 is rejected. It is concluded that the four factor interaction effects namely, sex Vs year of study Vs management Vs region has significant influence on the reasoning of pre-conventional level.

### *Conventional Level*

There are two divisions in the sex, two divisions in the year of study, three divisions in the management and three divisions in the region. The influence of sex, year of study, management and region on the reasoning of conventional level scores of Intermediate students is investigated through $2 \times 2 \times 3 \times 3$ factorial design. The following hypotheses are framed.

**Hypothesis 19**

There would be no significant influence of main effects namely, sex, year of study, management and region on the reasoning of conventional level of Intermediate students.

**Hypothesis 20**

There would be no significant influence of interaction effects namely, sex, year of study, management and region on the reasoning of conventional level of Intermediate students.

The above hypotheses are tested through 2×2×3×3 factorial design.

The results of Analysis of variance (ANOVA) of 2×2×3×3 factorial design for conventional level scores are presented in Table 5.19.

It is observed from Table 5.19 that the computed value of 'F' for the main effect sex is 4.340 which is significant at 0.05 level. Hence Hypothesis 19 is rejected. It is concluded that sex has significant influence on the reasoning of conventional level.

It is observed from Table 5.19 that the computed value of 'F' for the main effect year of study is 19.436 which is significant at 0.01 level. Hence Hypothesis 19 is rejected. It is concluded that year of study has significant influence on the reasoning of Conventional level. Similar results ware reported by Dayakara Reddy, V. (1987), Geethanath, P.S. (1987) and Rangaswamy, G. (2006).

It is observed from Table 5.19 that the computed value of 'F' for the main effect management is 9.553 which is significant at 0.01 level. Hence Hypothesis 19 is rejected. It is concluded that management has significant influence on the reasoning of conventional level.

To find out which of the management of students differ significantly from one another, the 't' test was employed.

**Table 5.19: Results of ANOVA of 2×2×3×3 Factorial Design for Conventional Level Scores**

Variable A = Sex (2 levels)
Variable B = Year of study (2 levels)
Variable C = Management (3 levels)
Variable D = Region (3 levels)

| Sl. No. | Source of variance | Sum of squares | df | Mean squares | F-value | Level of significance |
|---|---|---|---|---|---|---|
| 1. | A | 4553.061 | 1 | 4553.061 | 4.340 | * |
| 2. | B | 20388.478 | 1 | 20388.478 | 19.436 | ** |
| 3. | C | 20043.561 | 2 | 10021.280 | 9.553 | ** |
| 4. | D | 3086.259 | 2 | 1543.129 | 1.471 | @ |
| 5. | AB | 796.534 | 1 | 796.534 | 0.759 | @ |
| 6. | AC | 10866.531 | 2 | 5433.265 | 5.179 | ** |
| 7. | AD | 3100.697 | 2 | 1550.349 | 1.478 | @ |
| 8. | BC | 5179.170 | 2 | 2589.585 | 2.469 | @ |
| 9. | BD | 1430.211 | 2 | 715.106 | 0.682 | @ |
| 10. | CD | 7819.149 | 4 | 1954.787 | 1.863 | @ |
| 11. | ABC | 6837.781 | 2 | 3418.890 | 3.259 | * |
| 12. | ABD | 1238.388 | 2 | 619.194 | 0.590 | @ |
| 13. | ACD | 22365.388 | 4 | 5591.347 | 5.33 | ** |
| 14. | BCD | 3180.787 | 4 | 795.197 | 0.758 | @ |
| 15. | ABCD | 10077.558 | 4 | 2519.389 | 2.402 | * |
| 16. | Error | 1095150.5 | 1044 | 1048.995 | | |
| 17. | Total | 26166153 | 1079 | | | |

** Indicates significant at 0.01 level;
* Indicates significant at 0.05 level;
@ Indicates not significant at 0.05 level.

Means, SD's and 't' values of management on the reasoning of conventional level scores are presented in Table 5.20.

It is observed from Table 5.20 that the computed value of 't' for the students of Government and Aided colleges is 3.35 which is significant at 0.01 level.

**Table 5.20: Means, SD's and 't' Values of Management on the Reasoning of Conventional Level Scores**

| Sl. No. | Variable | Mean value | SD values | 't' – values | | |
|---|---|---|---|---|---|---|
| | | | | Government | Aided | Private |
| 1. | Government | 149.89 | 31.22 | — | 3.35** | 0.73@ |
| 2. | Aided | 158.00 | 33.62 | — | — | 3.88** |
| 3. | Private | 148.09 | 34.89 | — | — | — |

** Indicates significant at 0.01 level;
@ Indicates not significant at 0.05 level.

It is observed from Table 5.20 that the computed value of 't' for the students of Government and Private colleges is 0.73 which is not significant.

It is observed from Table 5.20 that the computed value of 't' for the students of Aided and Private colleges is 3.88 which is significant at 0.01 level.

It is observed from Table 5.20 that the computed value of 'F' for the main effect region is 1.471 which is not significant. Hence Hypothesis 19 is accepted. It is concluded that region does not have significant influence on the reasoning of conventional level.

It is observed from Table 5.19 that the computed value of 'F' for the two factor interaction effect namely, sex Vs management is 5.179 which is significant at 0.01 level. Hence Hypothesis 20 is rejected. It is concluded that the two factor interaction effect namely, sex Vs management has significant influence on the reasoning of conventional level. Remaining two factor interaction effects namely, sex Vs year of study, sex Vs region, year of study Vs management, year of study Vs region and management Vs region does not have significant influence on the reasoning of conventional level.

The Bar diagram showing the means scores of management on the reasoning of conventional level is given in Fig. 5.12.

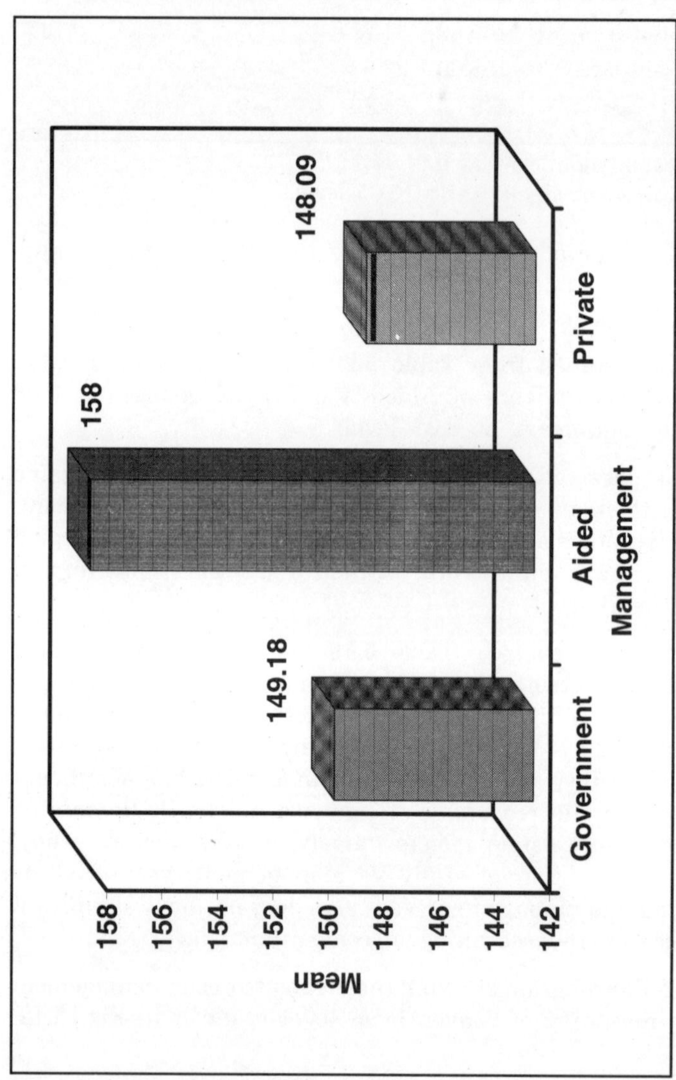


**Fig. 5.12: Bar Siagram Showing the Means Scores of Management on the Reasoning of Conventional Level**

It is observed from Table 5.19 that the computed value of 'F' for the three factor interaction effect namely, sex Vs management Vs region is 5.33 which is significant at 0.01 level. Hence Hypothesis 20 is rejected. It is concluded that the three factor interaction effect namely, sex Vs management Vs region has significant influence on the reasoning of conventional level.

It is observed from Table 5.19 that the computed value of 'F' for the three factor interaction effect namely, sex Vs year of study Vs management is 3.259 which is significant at 0.05 level. Hence Hypothesis 20 is rejected. It is concluded that the three factor interaction effect namely, sex Vs year of study Vs management has significant influence on the reasoning of conventional level. Remaining three factor interaction effects namely, sex Vs year of study Vs region and year of study Vs management Vs region do not have significant influence on the reasoning of conventional level.

It is observed from Table 5.20 that the computed value of 'F' for the four factor interaction effect namely, sex Vs year of study Vs management Vs region is 2.402 which is significant at 0.05 level. Hence Hypothesis 20 is rejected. It is concluded that the four factor interaction effects namely, sex Vs year of study Vs management Vs region has significant influence on the reasoning of conventional level.

*Post-Conventional Level*

There are two divisions in the sex, two divisions in the year of study, three divisions in the management and three divisions in the region. The influence of sex, year of study, management and region on the reasoning of post-conventional level scores of Intermediate students is investigated through 2×2×3×3 factorial design. The following hypotheses are framed

**Hypothesis 21**

There would be no significant influence of main effects namely, sex, year of study, management and region on the reasoning of post-conventional level of Intermediate students.

**Hypothesis 22**

There would be no significant influence of interaction effects namely, sex, year of study, management and region on the reasoning of post-conventional level of Intermediate students.

The above hypotheses are tested through 2×2×3×3 factorial design.

The results of Analysis of variance (ANOVA) of 2×2×3×3 factorial design for post-conventional level scores are presented in Table 5.21.

It is observed from Table 5.21 that the computed value of 'F' for the main effect sex is 0.168 which is not significant. Hence Hypothesis 21 is accepted. It is concluded that sex does not have significant influence on the reasoning of post-conventional level.

It is observed from Table 5.21 that the computed value of 'F' for the main effect year of study is 0.015 which is not significant. Hence Hypothesis 21 is accepted. It is concluded that year of study does not have significant influence on the reasoning of post-conventional level. Similar results ware reported by Dayakara Reddy, (1987), Geethanath, (1987) and Rangaswamy, (2006).

It is observed from Table 5.21 that the computed value of 'F' for the main effect management is 4.900 which is significant at 0.01 level. Hence Hypothesis 21 is rejected. It is concluded that management has significant influence on the reasoning of post-conventional level.

To find out which of the management of students differ significantly from one another, the 't' test was employed

Means, SD's and 't' values of management on the reasoning of post-conventional level scores are presented in Table 5.22.

It is observed from Table 5.22 that the computed value of 't' for the students of Government and Aided colleges is 2.52 which is significant at 0.05 level.

**Table 5.21: Results of ANOVA of 2×2×3×3 Factorial Design for Post-Conventional Level Scores**

Variable A = Sex (2 levels)

Variable B = Year of study (2 levels)

Variable C = Management (3 levels)

Variable D = Region (3 levels)

| Sl. No. | Source of variance | Sum of squares | df | Mean squares | F-value | Level of significance |
|---|---|---|---|---|---|---|
| **1.** | A | 261.321 | 1 | 261.321 | 0.168 | @ |
| **2.** | B | 24.076 | 1 | 24.076 | 0.015 | @ |
| **3.** | C | 15257.954 | 2 | 7628.977 | 4.900 | ** |
| **4.** | D | 2135.888 | 2 | 1067.944 | 0.686 | @ |
| **5.** | AB | 3.474 | 1 | 3.474 | 0.002 | @ |
| **6.** | AC | 511.913 | 2 | 255.956 | 0.164 | @ |
| **7.** | AD | 2160.038 | 2 | 1080.019 | 0.694 | @ |
| **8.** | BC | 483.620 | 2 | 241.810 | 0.155 | @ |
| **9.** | BD | 8110.217 | 2 | 4055.109 | 2.605 | @ |
| **10.** | CD | 20600.83 | 4 | 5150.208 | 3.308 | * |
| **11.** | ABC | 5665.645 | 2 | 2832.823 | 1.819 | @ |
| **12.** | ABD | 2927.260 | 2 | 1463.630 | 0.940 | @ |
| **13.** | ACD | 9413.695 | 4 | 2353.424 | 1.511 | @ |
| **14.** | BCD | 4533.585 | 4 | 1133.396 | 0.728 | @ |
| **15.** | ABCD | 4978.764 | 4 | 1244.691 | 0.799 | @ |
| **16.** | Error | 1625544.3 | 1044 | 1557.035 | | |
| **17.** | **Total** | **1702612.6** | **1079** | | | |

** Indicates significant at 0.01 level;

* Indicates significant at 0.05 level;

@ Indicates not significant at 0.05 level.

It is observed from Table 5.22 that the computed value of 't' for the students of Government and Private colleges is 2.92 which is significant 0.01 level.

It is observed from Table 5.22 that the computed value of 't' for the students of Aided and Private colleges is 0.43 which is not significant.

**Table 5.22: Means, SD's and 't' Values of Management on the Reasoning of Post-Conventional Level Scores**

| Sl. No. | Variable | Mean value | SD values | 't' – values | | |
|---|---|---|---|---|---|---|
| | | | | Government | Aided | Private |
| 1. | Government | 121.15 | 37.28 | - | 2.52* | 2.92** |
| 2. | Aided | 128.40 | 39.99 | - | - | 0.43@ |
| 3. | Private | 129.69 | 41.21 | - | - | - |

** Indicates significant at 0.01 level;
* Indicates significant at 0.05 level;
@ Indicates not significant at 0.05 level.

The Bar diagram showing the means scores of management on the reasoning of post-conventional level is given in Fig. 5.13.

It is observed from Table 5.21 that the computed value of 'F' for the main effect region is 0.686 which is not significant. Hence Hypothesis 21 is accepted. It is concluded that region does not have significant influence on the reasoning of post-conventional level.

It is observed from Table 5.21 the computed value of 'F' for the two factor interaction effect namely, management Vs region is 3.308 which is significant at 0.05 level. Hence Hypothesis 22 is rejected. It is concluded that the two factor interaction effect namely, management Vs region has significant influence on the reasoning of post-conventional level. Remaining two factor interaction effects namely, sex Vs year of study, sex Vs management, sex Vs region, year of study Vs management and year of study Vs region do not have significant influence on the reasoning of post-conventional level.

It is observed from Table 5.21 all the three factor interaction effect namely, sex Vs year of study Vs management, sex Vs year of study Vs region, sex Vs management Vs region

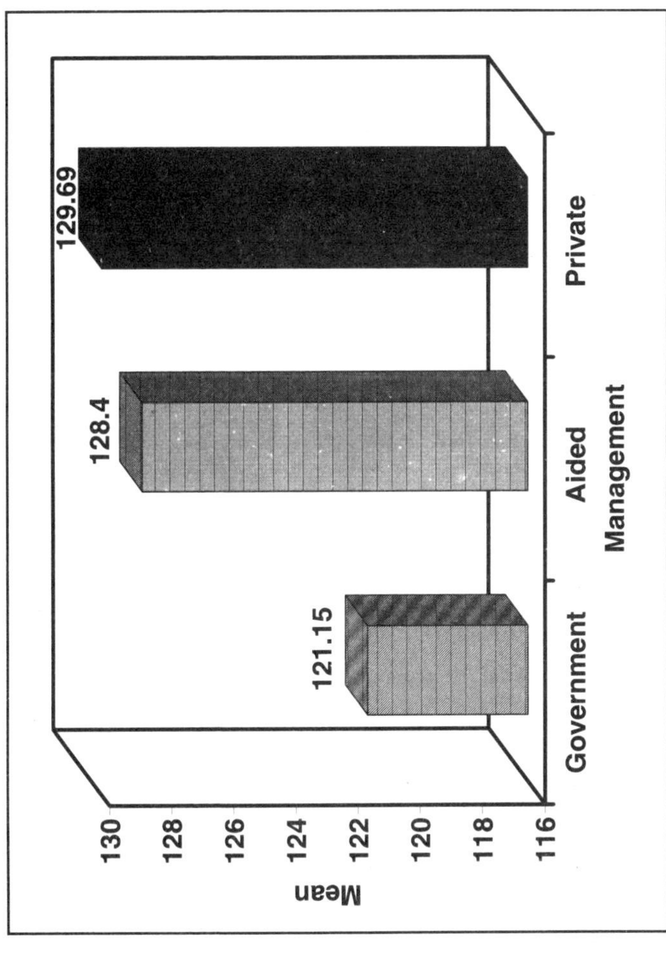


**Fig. 5.13: Bar Diagram Showing the Means Scores of Management on the Reasoning of Post-Conventional Level**

and year of study Vs management Vs region do not have significant influence on the reasoning of post-conventional level.

It is observed from Table 5.21 the computed value of 'F' for the four factor interaction effect namely, sex Vs year of study Vs management Vs region is 0.799 which is not significant. Hence Hypothesis 22 is accepted. It is concluded that the four factor interaction effects namely, sex Vs year of study Vs management Vs region does not significant influence on the reasoning of post-conventional level.

*Moral Judgment*

There are two divisions in the sex, two divisions in the year of study, three divisions in the management and three divisions in the region. The influence of sex, year of study, management and region on the reasoning of moral judgment scores of Intermediate students is investigated through 2×2×3×3 factorial design. The following hypotheses are framed.

**Hypothesis 23**

There would be no significant influence of main effects namely, sex, year of study, management and region on the reasoning of moral judgment of Intermediate students.

**Hypothesis 24**

There would be no significant influence of interaction effects namely, sex, year of study, management and region on the reasoning of moral judgment of Intermediate students.

The above hypotheses are tested through 2×2×3×3 factorial design.

The results of Analysis of variance (ANOVA) of 2×2×3×3 factorial design for moral judgment scores are presented in Table 5.23.

It is observed from Table 5.23 that the computed value of 'F' for the main effect sex is 4.007 which is significant at 0.05 level. Hence Hypothesis 23 is rejected. It is concluded that sex has significant influence on the reasoning of moral judgment. Similar results were reported by Guptha (1977), Dockstander (1979), Bush (1981), Singh (1983), Vanaja (1984), Chaya (1993), Pradhan and Pande (1996), Chaya (2001), Sabitha Reddy (2003), Talwar and Sheela (2006) and Rangaswamy, (2006).

**Table 5.23: Results of ANOVA of 2×2×3×3 Factorial Design for Moral Judgment Scores**

Variable A = Sex (2 levels)

Variable B = Year of study (2 levels)

Variable C = Management (3 levels)

Variable D = Region (3 levels)

| Sl. No. | Source of variance | Sum of squares | df | Mean squares | F-value | Level of significance |
|---|---|---|---|---|---|---|
| 1. | A | 3164.701 | 1 | 3164.701 | 4.007 | * |
| 2. | B | 6569.967 | 1 | 6569.967 | 8.318 | ** |
| 3. | C | 18530.298 | 2 | 9265.149 | 11.730 | ** |
| 4. | D | 229.048 | 2 | 114.524 | 0.145 | @ |
| 5. | AB | 283.925 | 1 | 283.925 | 0.359 | @ |
| 6. | AC | 5923.967 | 2 | 2961.984 | 3.750 | * |
| 7. | AD | 2340.790 | 2 | 1170.395 | 1.482 | @ |
| 8. | BC | 1188.406 | 2 | 594.203 | 0.752 | @ |
| 9. | BD | 922.677 | 2 | 461.338 | 0.584 | @ |
| 10. | CD | 15970.883 | 4 | 3992.721 | 5.055 | ** |
| 11. | ABC | 2347.225 | 2 | 1173.613 | 1.486 | @ |
| 12. | ABD | 511.374 | 2 | 255.687 | 0.324 | @ |
| 13. | ACD | 21084.748 | 4 | 5271.187 | 6.673 | ** |
| 14. | BCD | 6984.667 | 4 | 1746.167 | 2.211 | @ |
| 15. | ABCD | 8037.619 | 4 | 2009.405 | 2.544 | * |
| 16. | Error | 824624.22 | 1044 | 789.870 | | |
| 17. | Total | 918714.51 | 1079 | | | |

** Indicates significant at 0.01 level;
* Indicates significant at 0.05 level;
@ Indicates not significant at 0.05 level.

It is observed from Table 5.23 that the computed value of 'F' for the main effect year of study is 8.318 which is significant at 0.01 level. Hence Hypothesis 23 is rejected. It is concluded that year of study has significant influence on the reasoning of moral judgment. Similar results were reported by Prahallada (1982) and Rangaswamy, (2006).

It is observed from Table 5.24 that the computed value of 'F' for the main effect management is 11.730 which is significant at 0.01 level. Hence Hypothesis 23 is rejected. It is concluded that management has significant influence on the reasoning of moral judgment. Similar results were reported by Bandopadhyay (1981), Prahallada (1982), Singh (1983), Guptha (1984), Singh (1984), Vanaja (1984), Narayanaswamy (1994), Prabhu (1996) and Chaya (2001).

To find out which of the management of students differ significantly from one another. the 't' test was employed.

Means, SD's and 't' values of management on the reasoning of moral judgment scores are presented in Table 5.24.

**Table 5.24: Means, SD's and 't' Values of Management on the Reasoning of Moral Judgment Scores**

| Sl. No. | Variable | Mean value | SD values | 't' – values | | |
|---|---|---|---|---|---|---|
| | | | | Government | Aided | Private |
| 1. | Government | 324.72 | 27.00 | — | 4.60** | 2.88** |
| 2. | Aided | 334.82 | 31.67 | — | — | 1.90@ |
| 3. | Private | 330.60 | 27.72 | — | — | — |

** Indicates significant at 0.01 level;
@ Indicates not significant at 0.05 level.

It is observed from Table 5.24 that the computed value of 't' for the students of Government and Aided colleges is 4.60 which is significant at 0.01 level.

It is observed from Table 5.24 that the computed value of 't' for the students of Government and Private colleges is 2.88 which is significant 0.01 level.

It is observed from Table 5.24 that the computed value of't' for the students of Aided and Private colleges is 1.90 which is not significant.

The Bar diagram showing the means scores of management on the reasoning of moral judgment is given in Fig. 5.14.

It is observed from Table 5.23 that the computed value of 'F' for the main effect region is 0.145 which is not significant. Hence, Hypothesis 23 is accepted. It is concluded that region does not have significant influence on the reasoning of moral judgment.

It is observed from Table 5.23 that the computed value of 'F' for the two-factor interaction effect namely, management Vs region is 5.055 which is significant at 0.01 level. Hence Hypothesis 24 is rejected. It is concluded that the two factor interaction effect namely, management Vs region has significant influence on the reasoning of moral judgment.

It is observed from Table 5.23 that the computed value of 'F' for the two factor interaction effect namely, sex Vs management is 3.750 which is significant at 0.05 level. Hence Hypothesis 24 is rejected. It is concluded that the two factor interaction effect namely, sex Vs management has significant influence on the reasoning of moral judgment. Remaining two factor interaction effects namely, sex Vs year of study, sex Vs region, year of study Vs management and year of study Vs region do not have significant influence on the reasoning of moral judgment.

It is observed from Table 5.23 that the computed value of 'F' for the three-factor interaction effect namely, sex Vs management Vs region is 6.673 which is significant at 0.01 level. Hence Hypothesis 24 is rejected. It is concluded that the three factor interaction effect namely, sex Vs management Vs region has significant influence on the reasoning of moral judgment. Remaining three factor interaction effects namely, sex Vs year of study Vs management, sex Vs year of study Vs region and year of study Vs management Vs region do not have significant influence on the reasoning of moral judgment.

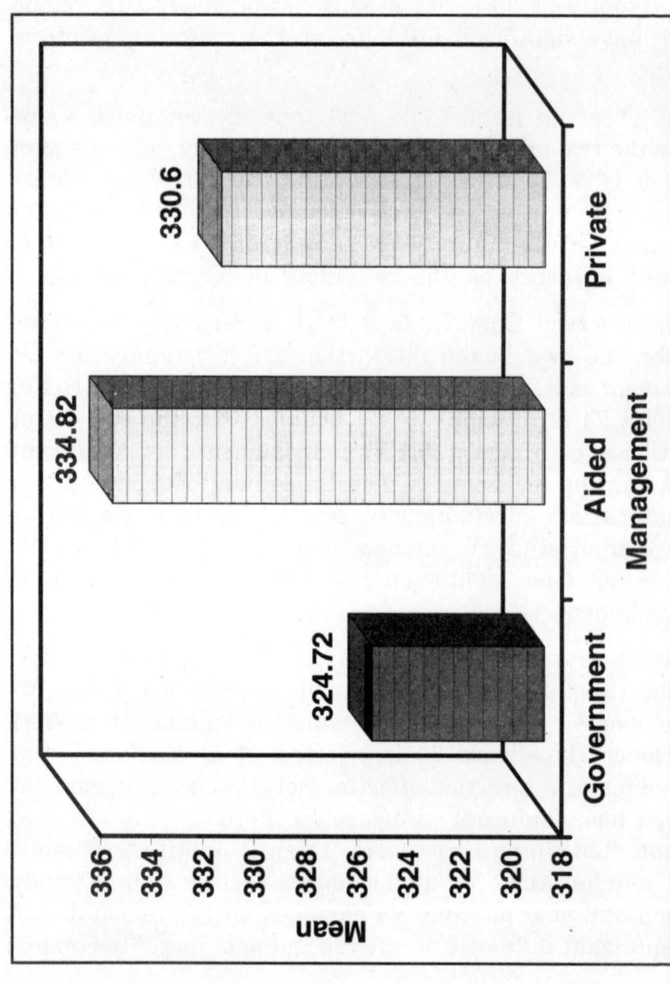


**Fig. 5.14: Bar Diagram Showing the Means Scores of Management on the Reasoning of Moral Judgment**

It is observed from Table 5.23 that the computed value of 'F' for the four-factor interaction effect namely, sex Vs year of study Vs management Vs region is 2.544 which is significant at 0.05 level. Hence Hypothesis 24 is rejected. It is concluded that the four factor interaction effects namely, sex Vs year of study Vs management Vs region has significant influence on the reasoning of moral judgment.

## 't' VALUES AND 'F' RATIO'S WITH RESPECT TO THE INFLUENCE OF THE INDEPENDENT VARIABLES ON DEPENDENT VARIABLES.

Independent variables are divided into four categories. Those are:

1. Academic achievement
2. Psychological variables
3. Socio - Demographic variables
4. Personal variables

### Influence of Academic Achievement

The influence of academic achievement on each moral stage, each moral level and moral judgment score of Intermediate students is investigated.

Academic achievement is divided into three categories that are:

1. Academic achievement in languages
2. Academic achievement in non-languages and
3. Academic achievement in total.

#### *Influence of Academic Achievement in Languages*

On the basis of academic achievement in languages of first year Intermediate students is based on SSC languages marks from Board of Secondary Education examinations and for the academic achievement in languages of second year

Intermediate students is based on first year Intermediate language marks from Board of Intermediate Education examinations. The marks are converted into percentages.

On the basis of academic achievement in languages the students are divided into four groups. Group I is formed with below 50%, Group II is formed with 50%-59% Group III is formed with 60%-69% and Group IV is formed with 70% and above. The impact of academic achievement in languages on the reasoning of each moral stage, moral level and moral judgment is investigated. The corresponding each moral stage, moral level and moral judgment scores of the four groups are analyzed accordingly. The following hypothesis is formulated.

**Hypothesis 25**

There is no significant impact of academic achievement in languages on the reasoning of each moral stage, moral level and moral judgment of Intermediate students.

The above hypothesis is tested by employing one-way ANOVA technique. The results are shown is Table 5.25.

It is clear that Table 5.25 that the computed values of 'F' for moral stage 2, moral stage 4, moral stage 4A, pre-conventional level and moral judgment is greater than table value of 'F' (3.78) for 3 and 1076 df at 0.01 level. Hence, Hypothesis 25 is rejected. It is concluded that achievement in languages has significant impact on the reasoning of moral stage 2, moral stage 4, moral stage 4A, pre-conventional level and moral judgment.

It is clear that Table 5.25 that the computed values of 'F' for moral stage 6 and conventional level is greater than table value of 'F' (2.60) for 3 and 1076 df at 0.05 level. Hence Hypothesis 25 is rejected. It is concluded that achievement in languages has significant impact on the reasoning of moral stage 6 and conventional level.

It is clear that Table 5.25 that the computed values of 'F' for moral stage 1, moral stage 3, moral stage 5A, moral stage 5B and post-conventional level is less than table value of 'F' (2.60) for 3 and 1076 df at 0.05 level. Hence, Hypothesis 25

**Table 5.25: Influence of Academic Achievement in Languages on the Reasoning of Each Moral Stage, Moral Level and Moral Judgment**

| S. No. | Variable | Mean values | | | | SD values | | | | F-value | Level of significance |
|---|---|---|---|---|---|---|---|---|---|---|---|
| | | I | II | III | IV | I | II | III | IV | | |
| 1. | **Moral Stage 1** | 15.66 | 16.27 | 15.69 | 16.53 | 6.91 | 6.64 | 6.31 | 6.47 | 1.098 | @ |
| 2. | **Moral Stage 2** | 33.35 | 37.24 | 34.69 | 38.01 | 14.34 | 13.56 | 13.22 | 13.17 | 6.343 | ** |
| 3. | **Moral Stage 3** | 51.24 | 52.53 | 53.01 | 52.93 | 20.42 | 20.09 | 21.38 | 19.93 | 0.420 | @ |
| 4. | **Moral Stage 4** | 72.52 | 68.76 | 70.37 | 63.61 | 26.40 | 28.05 | 26.99 | 27.72 | 4.492 | ** |
| 5. | **Moral Stage 4A** | 33.73 | 29.36 | 28.43 | 30.95 | 20.33 | 19.25 | 17.82 | 19.74 | 4.082 | ** |
| 6. | **Moral Stage 5A** | 37.08 | 39.72 | 41.91 | 39.87 | 25.35 | 26.65 | 25.42 | 23.54 | 1.777 | @ |
| 7. | **Moral Stage 5B** | 38.59 | 35.50 | 38.97 | 38.57 | 25.14 | 21.16 | 23.13 | 22.08 | 1.331 | @ |
| 8. | **Moral Stage 6** | 51.70 | 47.75 | 49.46 | 44.58 | 28.92 | 24.50 | 27.42 | 28.35 | 2.828 | * |
| 9. | **Pre-Conventional Level** | 49.01 | 53.51 | 50.38 | 54.54 | 15.42 | 14.61 | 14.58 | 13.36 | 7.870 | ** |
| 10. | **Conventional Level** | 157.49 | 150.66 | 151.81 | 147.49 | 32.58 | 36.36 | 31.99 | 32.80 | 3.709 | * |
| 11. | **Post-Conventional Level** | 127.37 | 122.97 | 130.34 | 123.03 | 41.33 | 35.56 | 40.59 | 40.36 | 2.380 | @ |
| 12. | **Moral Judgment** | 333.86 | 327.13 | 332.52 | 325.06 | 30.62 | 27.44 | 30.41 | 26.15 | 5.312 | ** |

** Indicates significant at 0.01 level; * Indicates significant at 0.05 level; @ Indicates not significant at 0.05 level
$N_1$ = 252, $N_2$ = 259, $N_3$ = 353, $N_4$ = 216, df = 3,1076

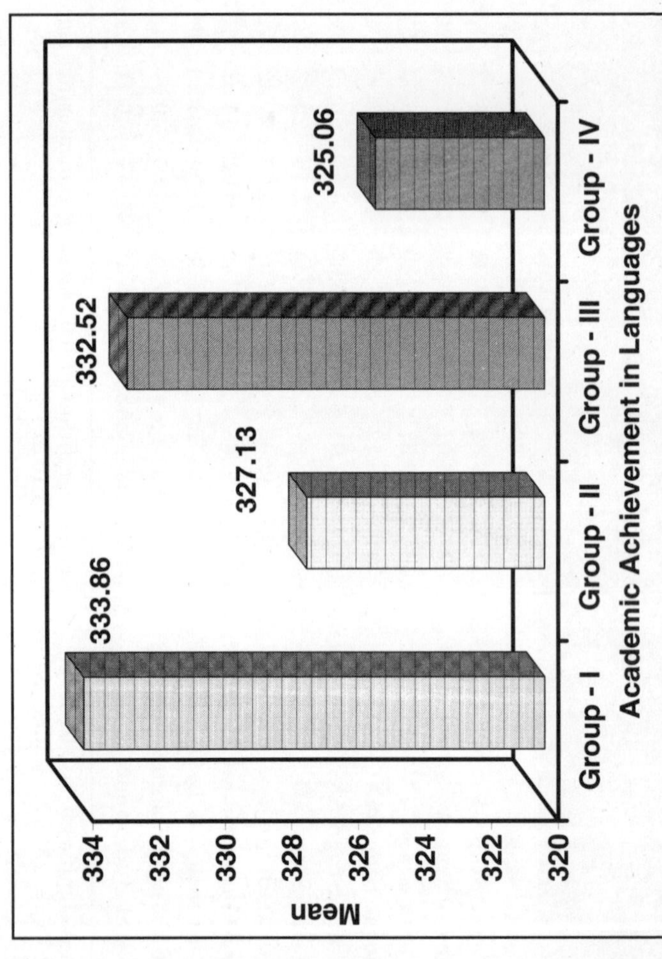


**Figure 5.15: Bar Diagram Showing the Mean Values of Academic Achievement in Languages on the Reasoning of Moral Judgment**

is accepted. It is concluded that achievement in languages do not have significant impact on the reasoning of moral stage 1, moral stage 3, moral stage 5A, moral stage 5B and post-conventional level.

The Bar diagram showing the mean values of academic achievement in languages on the reasoning of moral judgment is given in Fig. 5.15.

*Influence of Academic Achievement in Non-Languages*

On the basis of academic achievement in non-languages of first year Intermediate students is based on SSC non-languages marks from Board of Secondary Education examinations and for the academic achievement in non-languages of second year Intermediate students is based on first year Intermediate non-language marks from Board of Intermediate Education examinations. The marks are converted into percentages.

On the basis of academic achievement in non-languages the students are divided into four groups. Group I is formed with below 50%, Group – II is formed with 50% - 59% Group III is formed with 60%-69% and Group IV is formed with 70% and above. The impact of academic achievement in non-languages on the reasoning of each moral stage, moral level and moral judgment is investigated. The corresponding each moral stage, moral level and moral judgment scores of the four groups are analyzed accordingly. The following hypothesis is formulated.

**Hypothesis 26**

There is no significant impact of academic achievement in non-languages on the reasoning of each moral stage, moral level and moral judgment of Intermediate students.

The above hypothesis is tested by employing one-way ANOVA technique. The results are shown is Table 5.26.

It is clear that Table 5.26 that the computed values of 'F' for moral stage 5B and post-conventional level is greater than table value of 'F' (3.78) for 3 and 1076 df at 0.01 level. Hence

**Table 5.26: Influence of Academic Achievement in Non–Languages on the Reasoning of each Moral Stage, Moral Level and Moral Judgment**

| S. No. | Variable | Mean values | | | | SD values | | | | F-value | Level of significance |
|---|---|---|---|---|---|---|---|---|---|---|---|
| | | I | II | III | IV | I | II | III | IV | | |
| 1. | **Moral Stage 1** | 16.80 | 15.94 | 15.68 | 16.07 | 6.43 | 6.61 | 6.75 | 6.45 | 0.783 | @ |
| 2. | **Moral Stage 2** | 38.83 | 37.07 | 34.71 | 35.20 | 13.46 | 12.88 | 14.08 | 13.54 | 2.938 | * |
| 3. | **Moral Stage 3** | 48.86 | 54.77 | 51.97 | 52.86 | 17.74 | 19.25 | 21.53 | 20.65 | 1.745 | @ |
| 4. | **Moral Stage 4** | 67.91 | 71.02 | 69.23 | 68.74 | 25.20 | 26.53 | 28.50 | 27.31 | 0.331 | @ |
| 5. | **Moral Stage 4A** | 34.34 | 29.80 | 29.43 | 30.48 | 19.48 | 18.99 | 18.83 | 19.52 | 1.713 | @ |
| 6. | **Moral Stage 5A** | 36.16 | 35.59 | 42.70 | 39.82 | 25.02 | 23.10 | 26.86 | 24.77 | 3.563 | * |
| 7. | **Moral Stage 5B** | 33.23 | 33.89 | 38.48 | 39.80 | 22.35 | 22.62 | 22.44 | 23.36 | 4.041 | ** |
| 8. | **Moral Stage 6** | 47.76 | 48.27 | 51.07 | 47.08 | 23.61 | 28.01 | 28.26 | 27.20 | 1.486 | @ |
| 9. | **Pre-Conventional Level** | 55.63 | 53.01 | 50.47 | 51.27 | 13.72 | 12.89 | 15.59 | 14.61 | 3.687 | * |
| 10. | **Conventional Level** | 151.11 | 155.59 | 150.63 | 152.07 | 32.77 | 31.46 | 34.60 | 33.49 | 0.779 | @ |
| 11. | **Post-Conventional Level** | 117.14 | 117.74 | 132.25 | 126.70 | 37.79 | 39.09 | 39.37 | 39.69 | 6.755 | ** |
| 12. | **Moral Judgment** | 323.88 | 326.34 | 333.34 | 330.04 | 26.94 | 27.05 | 30.71 | 28.73 | 3.775 | * |

** Indicates significant at 0.01 level; * Indicates significant at 0.05 level; @ Indicates not significant at 0.05 level

$N_1$ = 98, $N_2$ = 147, $N_3$ = 251, $N_4$ = 484, df = 3,1076

Hypothesis 26 is rejected. It is concluded that achievement in languages has significant impact on the reasoning of moral stage 5B and post-conventional level.

It is clear that Table 5.26 that the computed values of 'F' for moral stage 2 and moral stage 5A, pre-conventional level and moral judgment is greater than table value of 'F' (2.60) for 3 and 1076 df at 0.05 level. Hence, Hypothesis 26 is rejected. It is concluded that achievement in non-languages has significant impact on the reasoning of moral stage 2, moral stage 5A, post-conventional level and moral judgment.

It is clear that Table 5.26 that the computed values of 'F' for moral stage 1, moral stage 3, moral stage 4, moral stage 4A, moral stage 6 and conventional level is less than table value of 'F' (2.60) for 3 and 1076 df at 0.05 level. Hence, Hypothesis 26 is accepted. It is concluded that achievement in non-languages do not have significant impact on the reasoning of moral stage 1, moral stage 3, moral stage 4, moral stage 4A, moral stage 6 and conventional level.

The Bar diagram showing the mean values of academic achievement in non-languages on the reasoning of moral judgment is given in Fig. 5.16.

*Influence of Academic Achievement in Total*

On the basis of academic achievement in total of first year Intermediate students is based on SSC Total marks from Board of Secondary Education examinations and for the academic achievement in total of second year Intermediate students is based on first year Intermediate total marks from Board of Intermediate Education examinations. The marks are converted into percentages.

On the basis of academic achievement in total the students are divided into four groups. Group I is formed with below 50%, Group II is formed with 50%-59% Group III is formed with 60% - 69% and Group IV is formed with 70% and above. The impact of academic achievement in total on the reasoning of each moral stage, moral level and moral judgment is investigated. The corresponding each moral stage, moral level

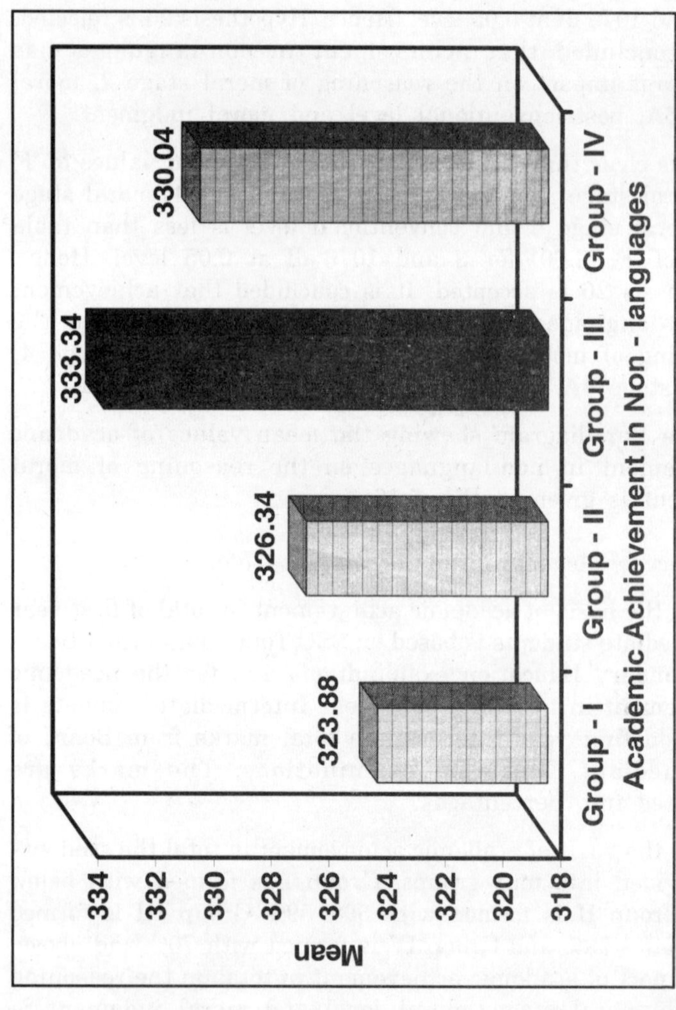


**Fig. 5.16: Bar Diagram Showing the Mean Values of Academic Achievement in Non-Languages on the Reasoning of Moral Judgment**

and moral judgment scores of the four groups are analyzed accordingly. The following hypothesis is formulated.

**Hypothesis 27**

There is no significant impact of academic achievement in total on the reasoning of each moral stage, moral level and moral judgment of Intermediate students.

The above hypothesis is tested by employing one-way ANOVA technique. The results are shown is Table 5.27.

It is clear that Table 5.27 that the computed values of 'F' for moral stage 3, moral stage 4A and moral stage 5B is greater than table value of 'F' (3.78) for 3 and 1076 df at 0.05 level. Hence, Hypothesis 27 is rejected. It is concluded that academic achievement in total has significant impact on the reasoning of moral stage 3, moral stage 4A and moral stage 5B.

It is clear that Table 5.27 that the computed values of 'F' for moral stage 1, moral stage 2, moral stage 4, moral stage 5A, moral stage 6, pre-conventional level, conventional level, post-conventional level and moral judgment and moral stage 5A is less than table value of 'F' (2.60) for 3 and 1076 df at 0.05 level. Hence, Hypothesis 27 is accepted. It is concluded that academic achievement in total do not have significant impact on the reasoning of moral stage 1, moral stage 2, moral stage 4, moral stage 5A,moral stage 6, pre-conventional level, conventional level, post-conventional level and moral judgment.

The Bar diagram showing the mean values of academic achievement in total on the reasoning of moral stage 4A is given in Fig. 5.17.

**Influence of Psychological Variables**

The influence of psychological variables on the reasoning of moral judgment of Intermediate students is investigated. The following psychological variables are considered in the present investigation.

1. The Cattell's 14 Personality Factors (HSPQ)
2. Raven's Progressive Matrices test (RPM)

**Table 5.27: Influence of Academic Achievement in Total on the Reasoning of Each Moral Stage, Moral Level and Moral Judgment**

| S. No. | Variable | Mean values | | | | SD values | | | | F-value | Level of significance |
|---|---|---|---|---|---|---|---|---|---|---|---|
| | | I | II | III | IV | I | II | III | IV | | |
| 1. | **Moral Stage 1** | 16.09 | 16.23 | 16.04 | 15.71 | 6.25 | 7.02 | 6.53 | 6.38 | 0.320 | @ |
| 2. | **Moral Stage 2** | 37.63 | 34.90 | 35.42 | 35.94 | 13.91 | 13.94 | 13.61 | 13.45 | 0.971 | @ |
| 3. | **Moral Stage 3** | 49.60 | 52.60 | 51.13 | 55.01 | 17.31 | 20.81 | 21.03 | 20.38 | 2.854 | * |
| 4. | **Moral Stage 4** | 68.82 | 72.02 | 69.49 | 66.63 | 24.46 | 28.01 | 29.27 | 26.41 | 1.791 | @ |
| 5. | **Moral Stage 4A** | 35.86 | 30.06 | 30.19 | 29.33 | 19.41 | 18.68 | 19.80 | 18.66 | 2.874 | * |
| 6. | **Moral Stage 5A** | 36.22 | 36.91 | 40.94 | 41.58 | 25.90 | 25.29 | 25.94 | 24.30 | 2.448 | @ |
| 7. | **Moral Stage 5B** | 33.27 | 35.77 | 39.12 | 39.39 | 22.34 | 22.91 | 22.89 | 23.11 | 2.793 | * |
| 8. | **Moral Stage 6** | 49.52 | 50.49 | 48.82 | 46.64 | 24.84 | 28.22 | 26.90 | 28.08 | 0.960 | @ |
| 9. | **Pre-Conventional Level** | 53.72 | 51.14 | 51.46 | 51.64 | 13.99 | 14.86 | 14.93 | 14.47 | 0.732 | @ |
| 10. | **Conventional Level** | 154.27 | 154.68 | 150.80 | 150.97 | 32.87 | 33.45 | 34.96 | 31.69 | 0.927 | @ |
| 11. | **Post-Conventional Level** | 119.01 | 123.18 | 128.80 | 127.63 | 36.60 | 40.36 | 38.46 | 41.30 | 2.261 | @ |
| 12. | **Moral Judgment** | 327.00 | 328.99 | 331.15 | 330.22 | 26.22 | 30.81 | 29.18 | 28.63 | 0.648 | @ |

* Indicates significant at 0.05 level; @ Indicates not significant at 0.05 level

$N_1$ = 93, $N_2$ = 235, $N_3$ = 432, $N_4$ = 320, df = 3,1076.

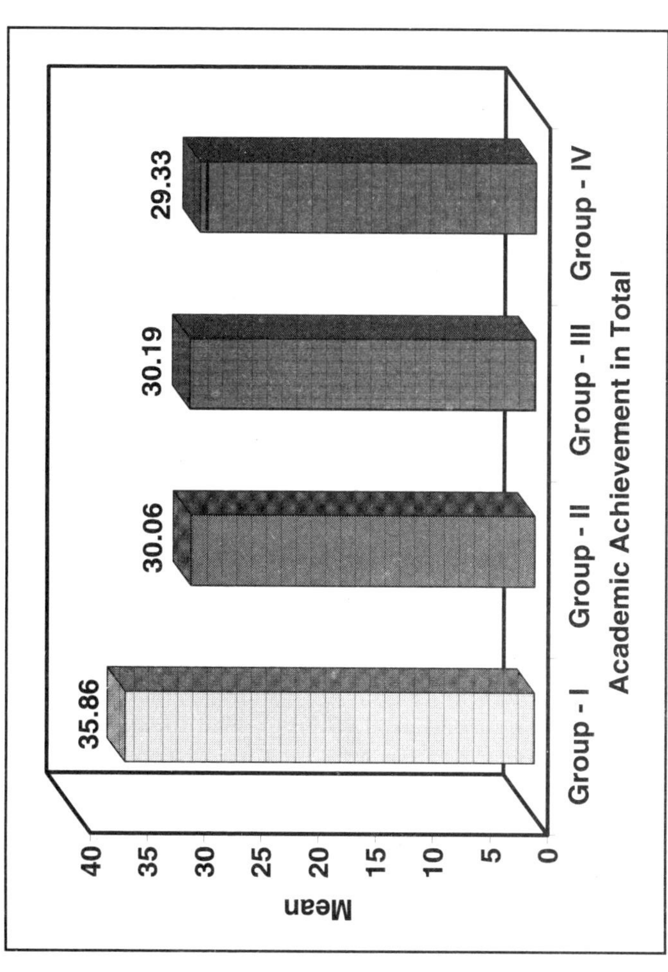


**Figure 5.17: Bar Diagram Showing the Mean Values of Academic Achievement in Total on the Reasoning of Moral Stage 4A**

*The Cattell's 14 Personality Factors (HSPQ)*

The Cattell's 14 PF questionnaire form A was adopted as a tool to access the personality of Intermediate students.

To identify the influence of 14 PF on the reasoning of moral judgment of Intermediate students. As recommended by Cattell (1970), The criterion in the division of the groups based on the stenvalues, was used the stenvalues 1 to 4 were grouped as low scorers (Group I), 5 and 6 as average scorers (Group II) and 7 to 10 as high scorers (Group III).

*Moral Stage 1*

The corresponding moral stage 1 scores of the three groups were analyzed accordingly. The mean values of moral stage 1 scores for the three groups for the each personality factors ware tested for significance by employing one-way ANOVA technique. The following hypothesis is framed.

**Hypothesis 28**

There would be no significant influence of '14 Personality Factors' on the reasoning of moral stage 1 of Intermediate students.

The above hypothesis is tested by employing one-way ANOVA. The results are presented in Table 5.28.

It is clear from the Table 5.29 that the calculated values of 'F' for B and C factors is greater than table value of 'F' (2.99) 2 and 1077 df at 0.05 level of significance. Hence Hypothesis 28 is rejected. For the remaining personality factors Hypothesis 28 is accepted at 0.05 level. The mean values of moral stage 1 in favour of Group I for the personality factors B and C. It is inferred that the students who are having personality characteristics of (1) More intelligent, abstract thinking and (2) Emotionally stable, calm nature have significant influence on the reasoning of moral stage 1 than the students who are having the personality characteristics of (1) Less intelligent, concrete thinking and (2) Affected by feeling, emotionally less stable.

Table 5.28: Impact of 14 PF (HSPQ) on the reasoning of Moral Stage 1

| Sl. No. | Personality Factor | No of observations | | | Mean values | | | SD values | | | F-value | Level of significance |
|---|---|---|---|---|---|---|---|---|---|---|---|---|
| | | I | II | III | I | II | III | I | II | III | | |
| 1. | A | 122 | 404 | 554 | 15.75 | 15.84 | 16.15 | 7.07 | 6.21 | 6.72 | 0.354 | @ |
| 2. | B | 785 | 152 | 143 | 16.33 | 14.65 | 15.55 | 6.40 | 7.01 | 6.83 | 4.553 | * |
| 3. | C | 274 | 402 | 404 | 16.72 | 15.36 | 16.12 | 6.32 | 6.86 | 6.40 | 3.621 | * |
| 4. | D | 397 | 484 | 199 | 15.43 | 16.44 | 15.99 | 6.49 | 6.84 | 5.99 | 2.581 | @ |
| 5. | E | 268 | 438 | 374 | 15.17 | 16.33 | 16.18 | 6.52 | 6.65 | 6.48 | 2.836 | @ |
| 6. | F | 356 | 372 | 352 | 16.07 | 15.74 | 16.17 | 6.56 | 6.51 | 6.65 | 0.435 | @ |
| 7. | G | 402 | 407 | 271 | 15.87 | 16.37 | 15.58 | 6.57 | 6.49 | 6.69 | 1.275 | @ |
| 8. | H | 312 | 381 | 387 | 16.25 | 15.53 | 16.23 | 7.18 | 6.15 | 6.45 | 1.441 | @ |
| 9. | I | 106 | 314 | 660 | 17.22 | 16.05 | 15.76 | 6.69 | 6.42 | 6.61 | 2.268 | @ |
| 10. | J | 189 | 376 | 515 | 16.01 | 15.86 | 16.08 | 6.44 | 6.79 | 6.46 | 0.122 | @ |
| 11. | O | 424 | 381 | 275 | 16.42 | 15.77 | 15.62 | 6.54 | 6.78 | 6.30 | 1.550 | @ |
| 12. | $Q_2$ | 463 | 365 | 252 | 15.87 | 16.27 | 15.80 | 6.67 | 6.74 | 6.13 | 0.502 | @ |
| 13. | $Q_3$ | 418 | 422 | 240 | 16.37 | 15.87 | 15.54 | 6.62 | 6.60 | 6.44 | 1.339 | @ |
| 14. | $Q_4$ | 261 | 428 | 391 | 15.85 | 15.72 | 16.37 | 6.35 | 6.73 | 6.54 | 1.052 | @ |

* Indicates significant at 0.05 level; @ Indicates not significant at 0.05 level.

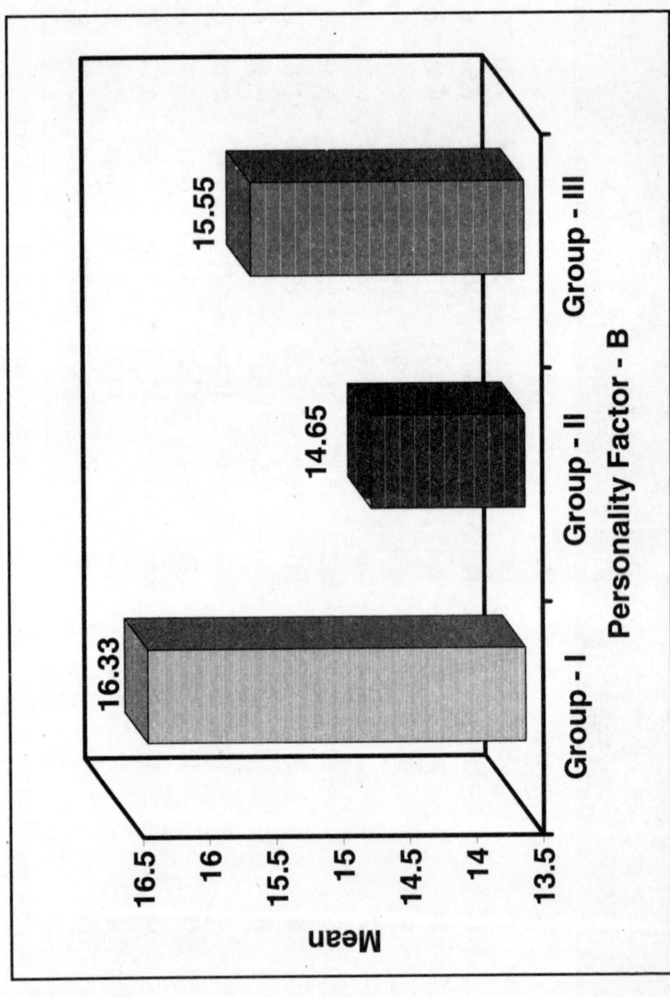


**Fig. 5.18: Bar Diagram Showing the Mean Values of Personality Factor B on the Reasoning of Moral Stage 1**

The Bar diagram showing the mean values of personality factor B on the reasoning of moral stage 1 is given in Fig. 5.18.

*Moral Stage 2*

The corresponding moral stage 2 scores of the three groups were analyzed accordingly. The mean values of moral stage 2 scores for the three groups for the each personality factor were tested for significance by employing one-way ANOVA technique. The following hypothesis is framed.

**Hypothesis 29**

There would be no significant influence of '14 Personality Factors' on the reasoning of moral stage 2 of Intermediate students.

The above hypothesis is tested by employing one-way ANOVA. The results are presented in Table 5.29.

It is clear from the Table 5.29 that the calculated values of 'F' for B, F and $Q_3$ factors is greater than Table value of 'F' (2.99) 2 and 1077 df at 0.05 level. Hence Hypothesis 29 is rejected. For the remaining personality factors Hypothesis 29 is accepted at 0.05 level. The mean values of moral stage 2 in favour of Group I for the personality factors B and $Q_3$. In favour of Group III for the personality factor F. It is inferred that the students who are having personality characteristics of (1) More intelligent, abstract thinking (2) Happy go lucky, gay enthusiastic, impulsively lively and (3) Controlled socially precise, self disciplined, compulsive, high self-concept control have significant influence on the reasoning of moral stage 2 than the students who are having the personality characteristics of (1) Less intelligent, concrete thinking, (2) Sober, prudent, serious, taciturn and (3) Undisciplined self-conflict, careless of protocol, follows own urges, low integration.

The Bar diagram showing the mean values of personality factor B on the reasoning of moral stage 2 is given in Fig. 5.19.

**Table 5.29: Impact of 14 PF (HSPQ) on the Reasoning of Moral Stage 2**

| Sl. No. | Personality Factor | No of observations | | | Mean values | | | SD values | | | F-value | Level of significance |
|---|---|---|---|---|---|---|---|---|---|---|---|---|
| | | I | II | III | I | II | III | I | II | III | | |
| 1. | A | 122 | 404 | 554 | 35.92 | 36.39 | 35.06 | 14.38 | 13.20 | 13.83 | 1.126 | @ |
| 2. | B | 785 | 152 | 143 | 36.40 | 33.78 | 33.55 | 13.50 | 13.67 | 14.25 | 4.298 | * |
| 3. | C | 274 | 402 | 404 | 36.18 | 35.52 | 35.42 | 13.50 | 13.87 | 13.60 | 0.275 | @ |
| 4. | D | 397 | 484 | 199 | 35.73 | 35.83 | 35.06 | 14.04 | 13.46 | 13.48 | 0.232 | @ |
| 5. | E | 268 | 438 | 374 | 35.86 | 35.03 | 36.24 | 13.34 | 13.85 | 13.69 | 0.826 | @ |
| 6. | F | 356 | 372 | 352 | 35.65 | 34.26 | 37.12 | 13.58 | 13.31 | 14.0 | 3.978 | * |
| 7. | G | 402 | 407 | 271 | 36.01 | 35.43 | 35.46 | 14.24 | 13.70 | 12.76 | 0.215 | @ |
| 8. | H | 312 | 381 | 387 | 35.84 | 36.23 | 34.93 | 13.97 | 13.38 | 13.71 | 0.913 | @ |
| 9. | I | 106 | 314 | 660 | 34.67 | 35.53 | 35.87 | 12.90 | 13.87 | 13.71 | 0.366 | @ |
| 10. | J | 189 | 376 | 515 | 35.54 | 34.64 | 36.43 | 13.73 | 13.71 | 13.53 | 1.871 | @ |
| 11. | O | 424 | 381 | 275 | 35.75 | 35.43 | 35.81 | 14.12 | 13.38 | 13.40 | 0.077 | @ |
| 12. | $Q_2$ | 463 | 365 | 252 | 35.52 | 35.78 | 35.70 | 13.30 | 13.72 | 14.29 | 0.038 | @ |
| 13. | $Q_3$ | 418 | 422 | 240 | 36.56 | 35.83 | 33.76 | 13.62 | 13.70 | 13.56 | 3.263 | * |
| 14. | $Q_4$ | 261 | 428 | 391 | 35.28 | 34.97 | 36.65 | 13.17 | 13.46 | 14.19 | 1.668 | @ |

* Indicates significant at 0.05 level; @ Indicates not significant at 0.05 level

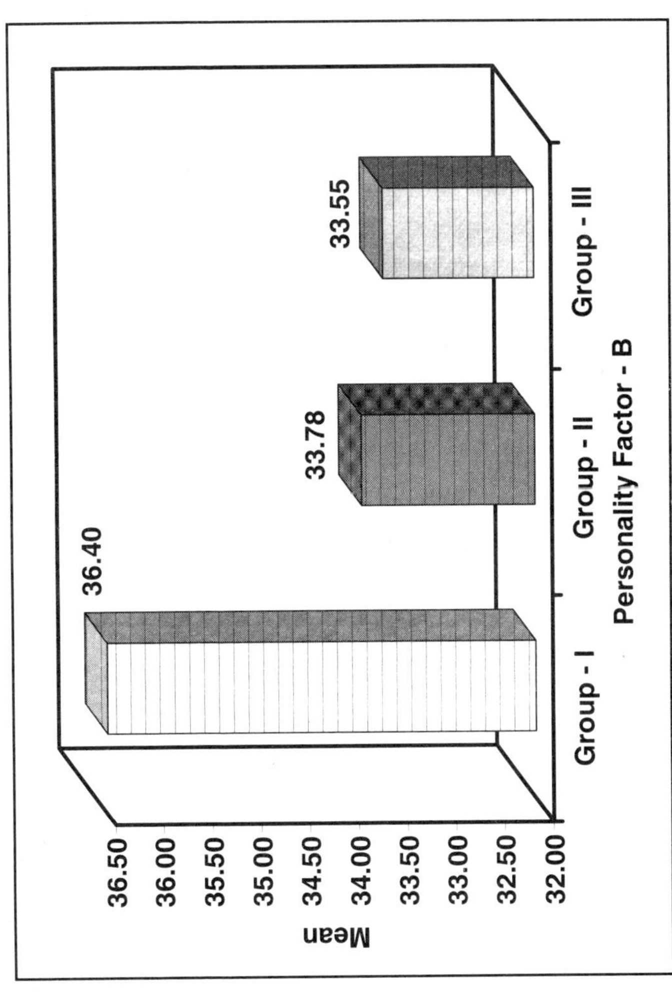


**Fig. 5.19: Bar Diagram Showing the Mean Values of Personality Factor B on the Reasoning of Moral Stage 2**

*Moral Stage 3*

The corresponding moral stage 3 scores of the three groups were analyzed accordingly. The mean values of moral stage 3 scores for the three groups for the each personality factor were tested for significance by employing one-way ANOVA technique. The following hypothesis is framed.

**Hypothesis 30**

There would be no significant influence of '14 Personality Factors' on the reasoning of moral stage 3 of Intermediate students.

The above hypothesis is tested by employing one-way ANOVA. The results are presented in Table 5.30.

It is clear from the Table 5.30 that the calculated value of 'F' for factor C is greater than table value of 'F' (4.60) for 2 and 1077 df at 0.01 level. Hence Hypothesis 30 is rejected.

It is clear from the Table 5.30 that the calculated value of 'F' for factor J is greater than table value of 'F' (2.99) for 2 and 1077 df at 0.05 level. Hence, Hypothesis 30 is rejected. For the remaining personality factors Hypothesis 30 is accepted at 0.05 level. The mean values of moral stage 3 in favour of Group II for the personality factors B and $Q_3$. In favour of Group III for the personality factors C and J. It is inferred that the students who are having personality characteristics of (1) Emotionally stable, calm nature and (2) Doubting, obstructive individualistic, reflective, internally restrained, unwilling to act, have significant influence on the reasoning of moral stage 3 than the students who are having the personality characteristics of (1)Affected by feeling, emotionally less stable, (2) Vigorous, goes readily with groups, jestful, given to action.

The Bar diagram showing the mean values of personality factor C on the reasoning of moral stage 3 is given in Fig. 5.20.

*Moral Stage 4*

The corresponding moral stage 4 scores of the three groups were analyzed accordingly. The mean values of moral stage

**Table 5.30: Impact of 14 PF (HSPQ) on the Reasoning of Moral Stage 3**

| Sl. No. | Personality Factor | No of observations | | | Mean values | | | SD values | | | F-value | Level of significance |
|---|---|---|---|---|---|---|---|---|---|---|---|---|
| | | I | II | III | I | II | III | I | II | III | | |
| 1. | A | 122 | 404 | 554 | 54.71 | 50.63 | 53.31 | 21.24 | 19.60 | 21.02 | 2.797 | @ |
| 2. | B | 785 | 152 | 143 | 51.77 | 54.42 | 54.20 | 20.20 | 21.38 | 21.47 | 1.650 | @ |
| 3. | C | 274 | 402 | 404 | 48.63 | 55.10 | 52.44 | 18.80 | 21.74 | 22.12 | 8.170 | ** |
| 4. | D | 397 | 484 | 199 | 52.34 | 52.72 | 52.10 | 21.23 | 19.80 | 21.08 | 0.074 | @ |
| 5. | E | 268 | 438 | 374 | 51.27 | 54.24 | 51.25 | 20.36 | 21.33 | 19.66 | 2.741 | @ |
| 6. | F | 356 | 372 | 352 | 54.04 | 51.86 | 51.51 | 21.53 | 21.21 | 18.73 | 1.578 | @ |
| 7. | G | 402 | 407 | 271 | 51.38 | 52.75 | 53.65 | 21.35 | 19.24 | 21.25 | 1.045 | @ |
| 8. | H | 312 | 381 | 387 | 53.40 | 51.77 | 52.39 | 20.46 | 19.83 | 21.35 | 0.541 | @ |
| 9. | I | 106 | 314 | 660 | 53.0 | 51.25 | 52.96 | 20.42 | 20.32 | 20.69 | 0.776 | @ |
| 10. | J | 189 | 376 | 515 | 49.52 | 54.29 | 52.22 | 19.44 | 22.06 | 19.70 | 3.453 | * |
| 11. | O | 424 | 381 | 275 | 51.77 | 52.62 | 53.33 | 20.65 | 21.18 | 19.54 | 0.499 | @ |
| 12. | $Q_2$ | 463 | 365 | 252 | 52.88 | 52.83 | 51.18 | 20.03 | 20.92 | 21.00 | 0.646 | @ |
| 13. | $Q_3$ | 418 | 422 | 240 | 51.29 | 52.41 | 54.61 | 19.71 | 20.51 | 21.88 | 1.990 | @ |
| 14. | $Q_4$ | 261 | 428 | 391 | 53.43 | 52.89 | 51.35 | 20.51 | 20.02 | 21.16 | 0.957 | @ |

** Indicates significant at 0.01 level; * Indicates significant at 0.05 level; @ Indicates not significant at 0.05 level.

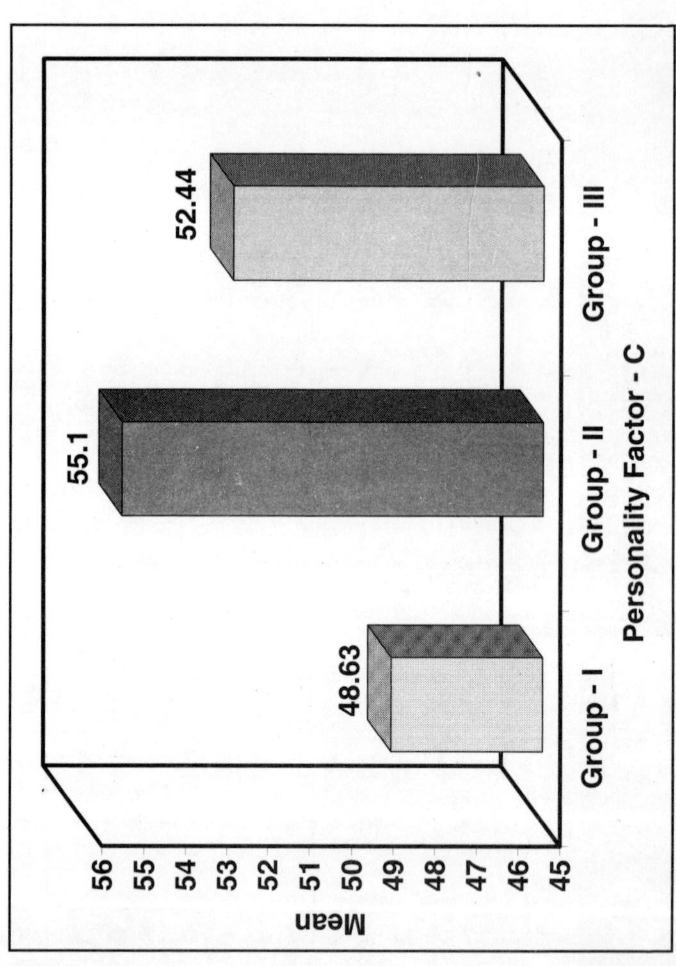


**Fig. 5.20: Bar Diagram showing the Mean Values of Personality Factor C on the Reasoning of Moral Stage 3**

4 scores for the three groups for the each personality factor were tested for significance by employing one-way ANOVA technique. The following hypothesis is framed.

**Hypothesis 31**

There would be no significant influence of '14 Personality Factors' on the reasoning of moral stage 4 of Intermediate students.

The above hypothesis is tested by employing one-way ANOVA. The results are presented in Table 5.31.

It is clear from the Table 5.31 that the calculated value of 'F' for factor $Q_4$ is greater than table value of 'F' (2.91) for 2 and 1077 df at 0.05 level of significance. Hence Hypothesis 31 is rejected. For the remaining personality factors Hypothesis 31 is accepted at 0.05 level. The mean values of moral stage 4 in favour of Group II for the personality factor $Q_4$. It is inferred that the students who are having personality characteristic of (1) Tense, driven over wrought, frustrated have significant influence on the reasoning of moral stage 4 than the students who are having the personality characteristic of (1) Relaxed, tranquil, torpid, unfrustrated.

The Bar diagram showing the mean values of personality factor $Q_4$ on the reasoning of moral stage 4 is given in Fig. 5.21.

*Moral Stage 4A*

The corresponding moral stage 4A scores of the three groups were analyzed accordingly. The mean values of moral stage 4A scores for the three groups for the each personality factor were tested for significance by employing one-way ANOVA technique. The following hypothesis is framed.

**Hypothesis 32**

There would be no significant influence of '14 Personality Factors' on the reasoning of moral stage 4A of Intermediate students.

**Table 5.31: Impact of 14 PF (HSPQ) on the Reasoning of Moral Stage 4**

| Sl. No. | Personality Factor | No of observations | | | Mean values | | | SD values | | | F-value | Level of significance |
|---|---|---|---|---|---|---|---|---|---|---|---|---|
| | | I | II | III | I | II | III | I | II | III | | |
| 1. | A | 122 | 404 | 554 | 72.54 | 63.03 | 68.46 | 26.98 | 26.21 | 28.33 | 1.112 | @ |
| 2. | B | 785 | 152 | 143 | 69.50 | 70.82 | 65.31 | 27.73 | 27.80 | 24.89 | 1.746 | @ |
| 3. | C | 274 | 402 | 404 | 67.55 | 69.59 | 69.75 | 28.69 | 27.27 | 26.66 | 0.611 | @ |
| 4. | D | 397 | 484 | 199 | 70.88 | 68.34 | 67.59 | 26.49 | 26.88 | 30.27 | 1.326 | @ |
| 5. | E | 268 | 438 | 374 | 68.71 | 67.40 | 71.47 | 25.78 | 26.03 | 29.89 | 2.270 | @ |
| 6. | F | 356 | 372 | 352 | 68.13 | 69.73 | 69.52 | 27.13 | 27.94 | 27.16 | 0.359 | @ |
| 7. | G | 402 | 407 | 271 | 69.64 | 69.24 | 68.23 | 28.39 | 25.64 | 28.53 | 0.218 | @ |
| 8. | H | 312 | 381 | 387 | 67.44 | 68.45 | 71.18 | 28.05 | 27.66 | 26.55 | 1.789 | @ |
| 9. | I | 106 | 314 | 660 | 69.67 | 68.18 | 69.50 | 28.01 | 27.88 | 27.11 | 0.266 | @ |
| 10. | J | 189 | 376 | 515 | 66.24 | 70.53 | 69.17 | 25.83 | 27.18 | 28.09 | 1.538 | @ |
| 11. | O | 424 | 381 | 275 | 67.74 | 70.46 | 69.45 | 27.65 | 26.71 | 27.97 | 1.014 | @ |
| 12. | $Q_2$ | 463 | 365 | 252 | 69.42 | 67.96 | 70.32 | 28.22 | 26.48 | 27.24 | 0.593 | @ |
| 13. | $Q_3$ | 418 | 422 | 240 | 67.56 | 70.05 | 70.27 | 25.79 | 27.56 | 29.74 | 1.128 | @ |
| 14. | $Q_4$ | 261 | 428 | 391 | 69.98 | 71.07 | 66.45 | 27.83 | 27.61 | 26.73 | 3.084 | * |

* Indicates significant at 0.05 level; @ Indicates not significant at 0.05 level.

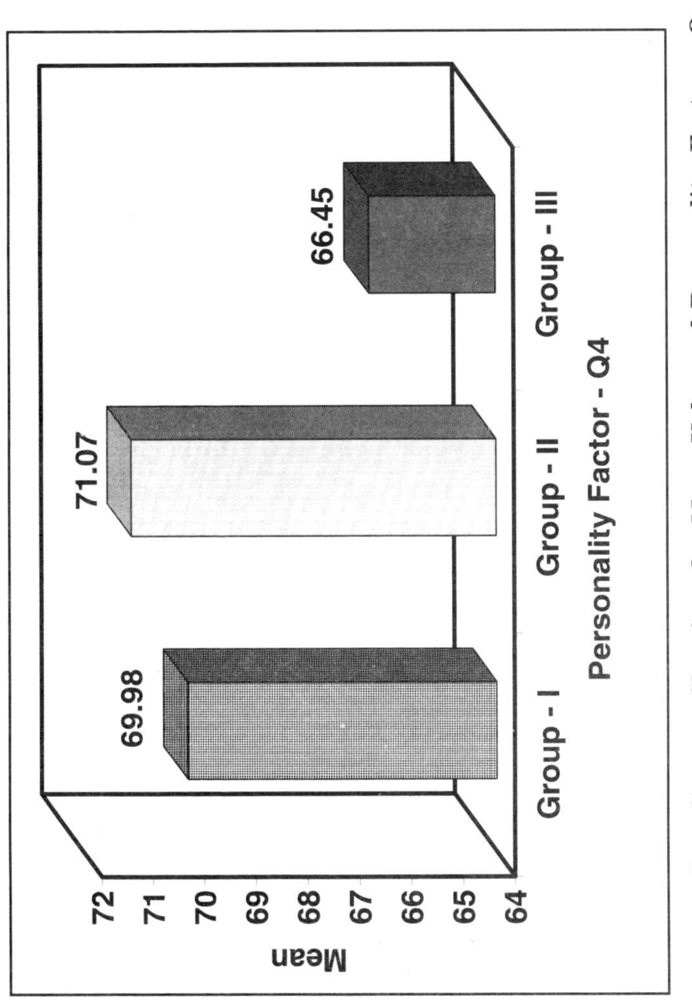


**Fig. 5.21: Bar diagram Showing the Mean Values of Personality Factor - $Q_4$ on the Reasoning of Moral Stage 4**

The above hypothesis is tested by employing one-way ANOVA. The results are presented in Table 5.32.

It is clear from the Table 5.32 that the calculated values of 'F' for factors C, H and J is greater than table value of 'F' (2.91) for 2 and 1077 df at 0.05 level of significance. Hence, Hypothesis 32 is rejected. For the remaining personality factors Hypothesis 32 is accepted at 0.05 level. The mean values of moral stage 4A in favour of Group I for the Personality Factor C. In favour of Group II for the Personality Factors H and J. It is inferred that the students who are having personality characteristics of (1) Emotionally stable, calm nature (2) Venturesome, socially bold, uninhibited, spontaneous and (3) Doubting, obstructive, individualistic, reflective, internally restrained, unwilling to act have significant influence on the reasoning of moral stage 4A than the students who are having the personality characteristics of (1) Affected by feeling Emotionally less stable, (2) Shy, restrained, diffident, timid and (3) Vigorous, goes readily with groups, jestful, given to action.

The Bar diagram showing the mean values of personality factor J on the reasoning of moral stage 4A is given in Fig. 5.22.

*Moral Stage 5A*

The corresponding moral stage 5A scores of the three groups were analyzed accordingly. The mean values of moral stage 5A scores for the three groups for the each personality factor were tested for significance by employing one-way ANOVA technique. The following hypothesis is framed.

**Hypothesis 33**

There would be no significant influence of '14 Personality Factors' on the reasoning of moral stage 5A of Intermediate students.

The above hypothesis is tested by employing one-way ANOVA. The results are presented in Table 5.33.

**Table 5.32: Impact of 14 PF (HSPQ) on the reasoning of Moral Stage 4A**

| Sl. No. | Personality Factor | No. of observations | | | Mean values | | | SD values | | | F-value | Level of significance |
|---|---|---|---|---|---|---|---|---|---|---|---|---|
| | | I | II | III | I | II | III | I | II | III | | |
| 1. | A | 122 | 404 | 554 | 28.93 | 30.98 | 30.29 | 18.83 | 20.54 | 18.36 | 0.543 | @ |
| 2. | B | 785 | 152 | 143 | 29.87 | 30.10 | 33.57 | 19.62 | 17.42 | 18.87 | 2.247 | @ |
| 3. | C | 274 | 402 | 404 | 32.39 | 28.63 | 30.79 | 18.23 | 18.94 | 20.10 | 3.249 | * |
| 4. | D | 397 | 484 | 199 | 30.64 | 29.79 | 31.36 | 19.91 | 18.29 | 20.19 | 0.516 | @ |
| 5. | E | 268 | 438 | 374 | 31.94 | 30.34 | 29.34 | 19.32 | 19.25 | 19.17 | 1.419 | @ |
| 6. | F | 356 | 372 | 352 | 29.55 | 31.25 | 30.34 | 18.74 | 19.90 | 19.08 | 0.709 | @ |
| 7. | G | 402 | 407 | 271 | 30.76 | 30.10 | 30.30 | 19.63 | 18.98 | 19.14 | 0.123 | @ |
| 8. | H | 312 | 381 | 387 | 28.59 | 32.43 | 29.84 | 19.08 | 20.05 | 18.44 | 3.663 | * |
| 9. | I | 106 | 314 | 660 | 31.70 | 31.91 | 29.46 | 20.10 | 19.80 | 18.81 | 1.990 | @ |
| 10. | J | 189 | 376 | 515 | 33.54 | 28.68 | 30.49 | 20.37 | 18.28 | 19.40 | 4.034 | * |
| 11. | O | 424 | 381 | 275 | 30.91 | 30.79 | 29.05 | 18.52 | 20.24 | 18.95 | 0.894 | @ |
| 12. | $Q_2$ | 463 | 365 | 252 | 30.33 | 30.75 | 29.98 | 18.53 | 20.15 | 19.28 | 0.124 | @ |
| 13. | $Q_3$ | 418 | 422 | 240 | 31.88 | 29.32 | 29.69 | 19.31 | 19.51 | 18.59 | 2.053 | @ |
| 14. | $Q_4$ | 261 | 428 | 391 | 31.13 | 29.45 | 30.93 | 17.51 | 19.57 | 20.00 | 0.856 | @ |

* Indicates significant at 0.05 level; @ Indicates not significant at 0.05 level.

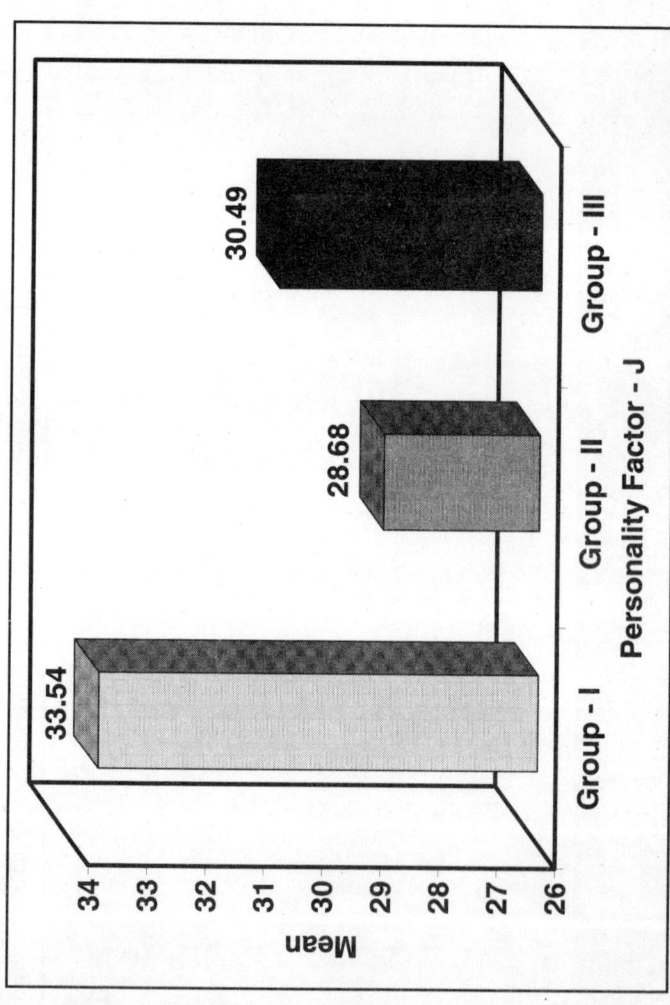


**Figure 5.22: Bar Diagram Showing the Mean Values of Personality Factor J on the Reasoning of Moral Stage 4A**

It is clear from the Table 5.33 that the calculated value of 'F' for factor H is greater than table value of 'F' (2.91) for 2 and 1077 df at 0.05 level of significance. Hence, Hypothesis 33 is rejected. For the remaining personality factors Hypothesis 33 is accepted at 0.05 level. The mean values of moral stage 5A in favour of Group I for the personality factor H. It is inferred that the students who are having personality characteristic of (1) Venturesome, socially bold, uninhibited, spontaneous have significant influence on the reasoning of moral stage 5A than the students who are having the personality characteristics of (1) Shy, restrained, diffident, timid.

The Bar diagram showing the mean values of personality factor H on the reasoning of moral stage 5A is given in Fig. 5.23.

*Moral Stage 5B*

The corresponding moral stage 5B scores of the three groups were analyzed accordingly. The mean values of moral stage 5B scores for the three groups for the each personality factor were tested for significance by employing one-way ANOVA technique. The following hypothesis is framed.

**Hypothesis 34**

There would be no significant influence of '14 Personality Factors' on the reasoning of moral stage 5B of Intermediate students.

The above hypothesis is tested by employing one-way ANOVA. The results are presented in Table 5.34.

It is clear from the Table 5.34 that the calculated values of 'F' for factors F and J is greater than table value of 'F' (2.91) for 2 and 1077 df at 0.05 level of significance. Hence, Hypothesis 34 is rejected. For the remaining personality factors Hypothesis 34 is accepted at 0.05 level. The mean values of moral stage 5B in favour of Group I and II for the personality factor F. In favour Group II for the personality factor J. It is inferred that the students who are having personality characteristics

**Table 5.33: Impact of 14 PF (HSPQ) on the Reasoning of Moral Stage 5A**

| Sl. No. | Personality Factor | No. of observations | | | Mean values | | | SD values | | | F-value | Level of significance |
|---|---|---|---|---|---|---|---|---|---|---|---|---|
| | | I | II | III | I | II | III | I | II | III | | |
| 1. | A | 122 | 404 | 554 | 39.34 | 40.18 | 39.72 | 28.63 | 26.02 | 24.16 | 0.064 | @ |
| 2. | B | 785 | 152 | 143 | 39.63 | 41.37 | 39.42 | 26.04 | 23.68 | 23.52 | 0.318 | @ |
| 3. | C | 274 | 402 | 404 | 39.10 | 40.39 | 39.82 | 25.42 | 25.63 | 25.16 | 0.212 | @ |
| 4. | D | 397 | 484 | 199 | 40.65 | 38.62 | 41.24 | 24.78 | 26.39 | 24.01 | 1.056 | @ |
| 5. | E | 268 | 438 | 374 | 39.69 | 40.38 | 39.34 | 23.49 | 26.04 | 25.94 | 0.177 | @ |
| 6. | F | 356 | 372 | 352 | 38.64 | 41.60 | 39.22 | 23.48 | 28.12 | 24.13 | 1.392 | @ |
| 7. | G | 402 | 407 | 271 | 41.06 | 37.70 | 41.28 | 26.89 | 23.46 | 25.72 | 2.349 | @ |
| 8. | H | 312 | 381 | 387 | 42.89 | 38.32 | 38.91 | 26.34 | 24.63 | 25.18 | 3.200 | * |
| 9. | I | 106 | 314 | 660 | 35.20 | 40.23 | 40.42 | 27.42 | 25.06 | 25.15 | 1.976 | @ |
| 10. | J | 189 | 376 | 515 | 42.33 | 37.73 | 40.50 | 25.60 | 25.00 | 25.51 | 2.397 | @ |
| 11. | O | 424 | 381 | 275 | 39.80 | 40.44 | 39.11 | 27.04 | 23.99 | 24.68 | 0.217 | @ |
| 12. | $Q_2$ | 463 | 365 | 252 | 40.05 | 39.54 | 39.93 | 26.52 | 24.84 | 24.08 | 0.043 | @ |
| 13. | $Q_3$ | 418 | 422 | 240 | 39.50 | 40.61 | 39.11 | 25.23 | 25.86 | 24.86 | 0.328 | @ |
| 14. | $Q_4$ | 261 | 428 | 391 | 36.85 | 41.03 | 40.55 | 25.10 | 25.88 | 24.92 | 2.434 | @ |

* Indicates significant at 0.05 level; @ Indicates not significant at 0.05 level.

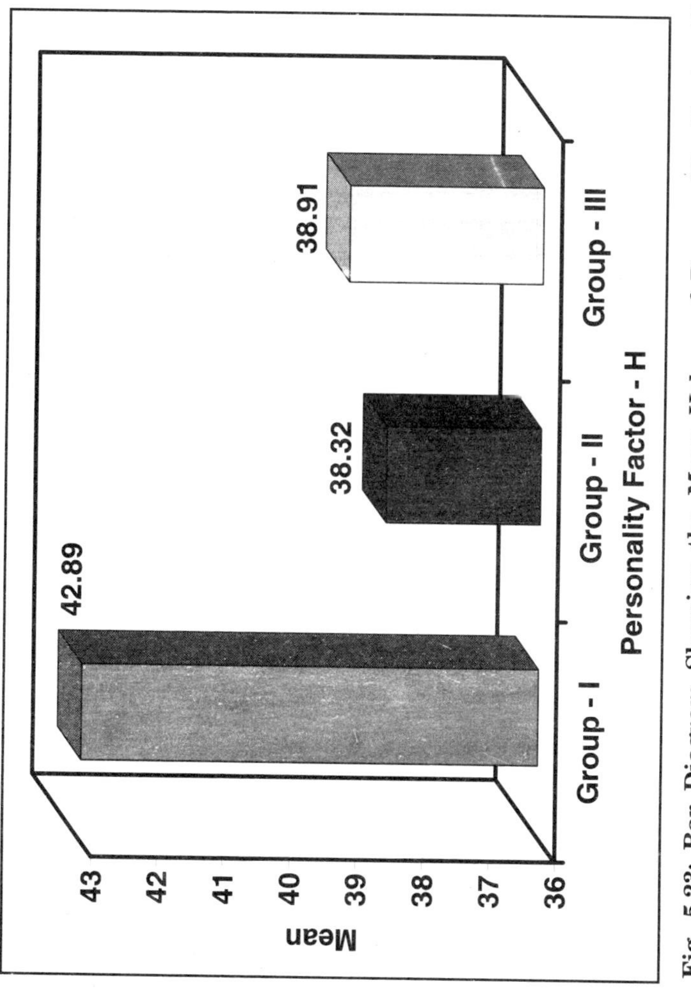


**Fig. 5.23: Bar Diagram Showing the Mean Values of Personality Factor H on the Reasoning of Moral Stage 5A**

**Table 5.34: Impact of 14 PF (HSPQ) on the reasoning of Moral Stage 5B**

| Sl. No. | Personality Factor | No. of observations | | | Mean values | | | SD values | | | F-value | Level of significance |
|---|---|---|---|---|---|---|---|---|---|---|---|---|
| | | I | II | III | I | II | III | I | II | III | | |
| 1. | A | 122 | 404 | 554 | 35.50 | 38.58 | 38.06 | 21.21 | 24.23 | 22.42 | 0.849 | @ |
| 2. | B | 785 | 152 | 143 | 37.34 | 39.88 | 39.38 | 22.48 | 24.54 | 23.93 | 1.088 | @ |
| 3. | C | 274 | 402 | 404 | 38.05 | 38.96 | 36.93 | 23.24 | 23.03 | 22.76 | 0.789 | @ |
| 4. | D | 397 | 484 | 199 | 37.45 | 39.22 | 35.96 | 22.97 | 22.89 | 23.50 | 1.571 | @ |
| 5. | E | 268 | 438 | 374 | 39.27 | 37.01 | 38.15 | 23.07 | 22.08 | 23.94 | 0.818 | @ |
| 6. | F | 356 | 372 | 352 | 39.33 | 39.33 | 35.16 | 22.69 | 23.89 | 22.07 | 3.921 | * |
| 7. | G | 402 | 407 | 271 | 38.68 | 37.36 | 37.82 | 21.74 | 22.20 | 25.79 | 0.339 | @ |
| 8. | H | 312 | 381 | 387 | 36.66 | 38.27 | 38.73 | 20.81 | 23.44 | 24.17 | 0.748 | @ |
| 9. | I | 106 | 314 | 660 | 36.32 | 38.54 | 37.96 | 18.73 | 23.72 | 23.26 | 0.366 | @ |
| 10. | J | 189 | 376 | 515 | 37.73 | 40.23 | 36.41 | 21.14 | 23.72 | 22.99 | 3.015 | * |
| 11. | O | 424 | 381 | 275 | 37.51 | 36.83 | 40.25 | 23.36 | 22.42 | 23.07 | 1.906 | @ |
| 12. | $Q_2$ | 463 | 365 | 252 | 37.80 | 37.79 | 38.54 | 22.85 | 22.76 | 23.60 | 0.102 | @ |
| 13. | $Q_3$ | 418 | 422 | 240 | 37.01 | 38.27 | 39.11 | 23.49 | 21.70 | 24.26 | 0.699 | @ |
| 14. | $Q_4$ | 261 | 428 | 391 | 38.10 | 37.75 | 38.12 | 23.79 | 23.04 | 22.42 | 0.033 | @ |

* Indicates significant at 0.05 level; @ Indicates not significant at 0.05 level.

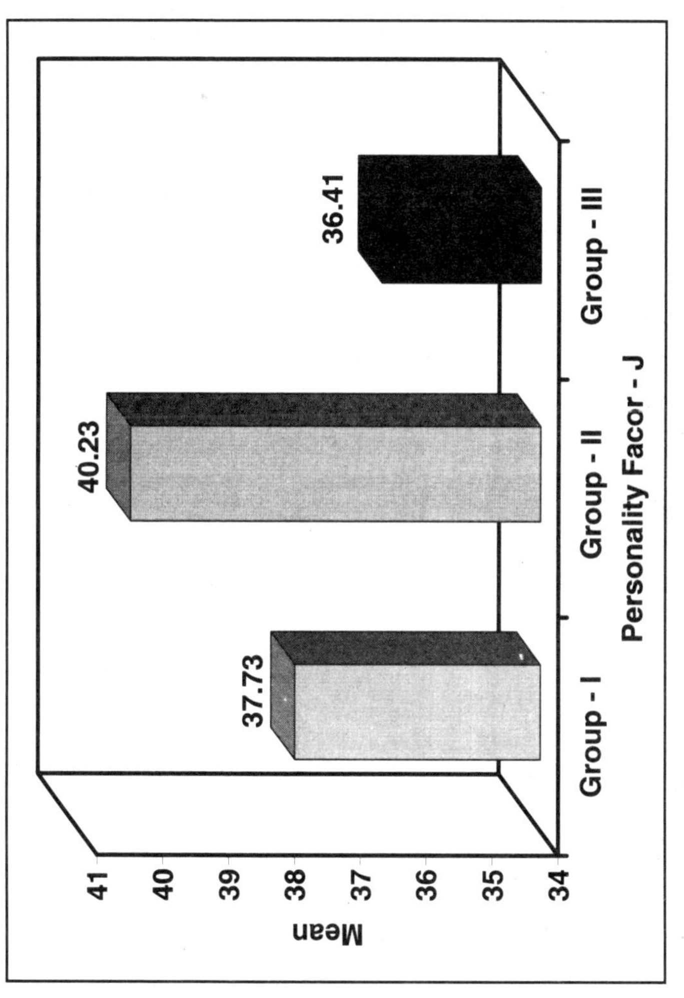


**Fig. 5.24: Bar Diagram Showing the Mean Values of Personality Factor J on the Reasoning of Moral Stage 5B**

of (1) Happy go lucky, gay enthusiastic, impulsively lively and (2) Doubting, obstructive, individualistic, reflective, internally restrained, unwilling to act have significant influence on the reasoning of moral stage 5B than the students who are having the personality characteristics of (1) Sober, prudent, serious, taciturn and (2) Vigorous, goes readily groups, jestful, given to action.

The Bar diagram showing the mean values of personality factor J on the reasoning of moral stage 5B is given in Fig. 5.24.

*Moral Stage 6*

The corresponding moral stage 6 scores of the three groups were analyzed accordingly. The mean values of moral stage 6 scores for the three groups for the each Personality Factor were tested for significance by employing one-way ANOVA technique. The following hypothesis is framed.

**Hypothesis 35**

There would be no significant influence of '14 Personality Factors' on the reasoning of moral stage 6 of Intermediate students.

The above hypothesis is tested by employing one-way ANOVA. The results are presented in Table 5.35.

It is clear from the Table 5.35 that the calculated value of 'F' for factor G is greater than table value of 'F' (2.91) for 2 and 1077 df at 0.05 level. Hence, Hypothesis 35 is rejected. For the remaining personality factors Hypothesis 35 is accepted at 0.05 level. The mean values of moral stage 6 in favour of Group III for factor G. It is inferred that the students who are having personality characteristic of (1) Conscientious, preserving, rule bound i.e., stronger super ego strength have significant influence on the reasoning of moral stage 6 than the students who are having the personality characteristics of (1) Expedient, evades rules i.e., weaker super ego strength

The Bar diagram showing the mean values of personality factor G on the reasoning of moral stage 6 is given in Fig. 5.25.

**Table 5.35: Impact of 14 PF (HSPQ) on the Reasoning of Moral Stage 6**

| Sl. No. | Personality Factor | No. of observations | | | Mean values | | | SD values | | | F-value | Level of significance |
|---|---|---|---|---|---|---|---|---|---|---|---|---|
| | | I | II | III | I | II | III | I | II | III | | |
| 1. | A | 122 | 404 | 554 | 48.63 | 48.04 | 48.99 | 28.08 | 27.41 | 27.26 | 0.140 | @ |
| 2. | B | 785 | 152 | 143 | 48.21 | 49.59 | 49.67 | 27.32 | 26.28 | 29.01 | 0.286 | @ |
| 3. | C | 274 | 402 | 404 | 49.35 | 48.12 | 48.56 | 26.75 | 28.19 | 27.05 | 0.166 | @ |
| 4. | D | 397 | 484 | 199 | 48.97 | 47.42 | 50.73 | 26.50 | 27.93 | 27.79 | 1.085 | @ |
| 5. | E | 268 | 438 | 374 | 51.41 | 48.27 | 46.97 | 27.58 | 27.26 | 27.32 | 2.106 | @ |
| 6. | F | 356 | 372 | 352 | 47.00 | 49.13 | 49.64 | 26.36 | 28.11 | 27.63 | 0.930 | @ |
| 7. | G | 402 | 407 | 271 | 42.95 | 49.16 | 51.67 | 27.50 | 27.51 | 26.76 | 3.677 | * |
| 8. | H | 312 | 381 | 387 | 47.52 | 50.22 | 47.87 | 27.17 | 27.29 | 27.67 | 1.040 | @ |
| 9. | I | 106 | 314 | 660 | 49.46 | 50.18 | 47.70 | 28.10 | 27.96 | 27.00 | 0.927 | @ |
| 10. | J | 189 | 376 | 515 | 50.99 | 48.91 | 47.49 | 28.16 | 27.50 | 27.00 | 1.165 | @ |
| 11. | O | 424 | 381 | 275 | 48.66 | 48.74 | 48.30 | 27.46 | 28.02 | 26.46 | 0.022 | @ |
| 12. | $Q_2$ | 463 | 365 | 252 | 49.11 | 47.34 | 49.46 | 28.30 | 26.60 | 26.85 | 0.590 | @ |
| 13. | $Q_3$ | 418 | 422 | 240 | 48.07 | 47.99 | 50.59 | 28.29 | 26.37 | 27.55 | 0.818 | @ |
| 14. | $Q_4$ | 261 | 428 | 391 | 50.34 | 48.17 | 47.90 | 27.13 | 27.63 | 27.31 | 0.709 | @ |

* Indicates significant at 0.05 level; @ Indicates not significant at 0.05 level.

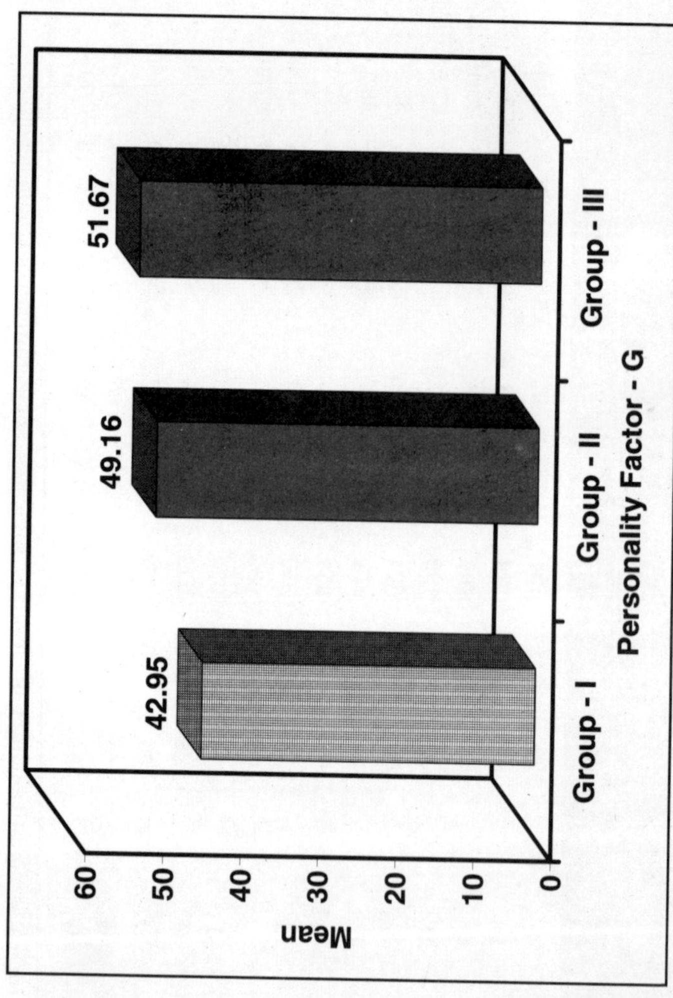


**Fig. 5.25: Bar Diagram Showing the Mean Values of Personality Factor G on the Reasoning of Moral Stage 6**

*Pre-Conventional Level*

The corresponding pre-conventional level scores of the three groups were analyzed accordingly. The mean values of pre-conventional level scores for the three groups for the each personality factor were tested for significance by employing one-way ANOVA technique. The following hypothesis is framed.

### Hypothesis 36

There would be no significant influence of '14 Personality Factors' on the reasoning of pre-conventional level of Intermediate students.

The above hypothesis is tested by employing one-way ANOVA. The results are presented in Table 5.36.

It is clear from the Table 5.36 that the calculated values of 'F' for factor B and $Q_3$ is greater than table value of 'F' (4.60) for 2 and 1077 df at 0.01 level. Hence Hypothesis 36 is rejected.

It is clear from the Table 5.36 that the calculated value of 'F' for factor F is greater than table value of 'F' (2.99) for 2 and 1077 df at 0.01 level. Hence Hypothesis 36 is rejected. For the remaining personality factors Hypothesis 36 is accepted at 0.05 level. The mean values of pre-conventional level in favour of Group I for factor B and $Q_3$. In favour of Group III for factor F. It is inferred that the students who are having personality characteristics of (1) More intelligent, abstract thinking (2) Happy go lucky, gay enthusiastic, impulsively lively and (3) Controlled socially precise, self disciplined, compulsive, high self-concept control have significant influence on the reasoning of moral level - 1 than the students who are having the personality characteristics of (1) Less intelligent, concrete thinking (2) Sober, prudent, series, taciturn and (3) Un disciplined self-conflict, careless of protocol, follows own urges, low integration.

The Bar diagram showing the mean values of personality factor B on the reasoning of pre-conventional level is given in Fig. 5.26.

**Table 5.36: Impact of 14 PF (HSPQ) on the Reasoning of Pre-Conventional Level**

| Sl. No. | Personality Factor | No. of observations | | | Mean values | | | SD values | | | F-value | Level of significance |
|---|---|---|---|---|---|---|---|---|---|---|---|---|
| | | I | II | III | I | II | III | I | II | III | | |
| 1. | A | 122 | 404 | 554 | 51.67 | 52.22 | 51.21 | 15.94 | 13.96 | 14.96 | 0.556 | @ |
| 2. | B | 785 | 152 | 143 | 52.73 | 48.43 | 49.10 | 14.27 | 15.97 | 14.89 | 7.983 | ** |
| 3. | C | 274 | 402 | 404 | 52.89 | 50.89 | 51.54 | 13.16 | 15.46 | 14.90 | 1.529 | @ |
| 4. | D | 397 | 484 | 199 | 51.16 | 52.28 | 51.06 | 15.32 | 14.19 | 14.66 | 0.817 | @ |
| 5. | E | 268 | 438 | 374 | 51.03 | 51.36 | 52.41 | 14.24 | 14.90 | 14.79 | 0.829 | @ |
| 6. | F | 356 | 372 | 352 | 51.73 | 50.00 | 53.29 | 14.26 | 14.92 | 14.76 | 4.570 | * |
| 7. | G | 402 | 407 | 271 | 51.88 | 51.80 | 51.04 | 15.40 | 13.98 | 14.74 | 0.302 | @ |
| 8. | H | 312 | 381 | 387 | 52.09 | 51.76 | 51.16 | 15.08 | 13.69 | 15.36 | 0.365 | @ |
| 9. | I | 106 | 314 | 660 | 51.89 | 51.59 | 51.63 | 13.50 | 14.25 | 15.11 | 0.017 | @ |
| 10. | J | 189 | 376 | 515 | 51.55 | 50.50 | 52.51 | 14.44 | 15.13 | 14.45 | 2.036 | @ |
| 11. | O | 424 | 381 | 275 | 52.17 | 51.20 | 51.42 | 15.03 | 14.46 | 14.55 | 0.468 | @ |
| 12. | $Q_2$ | 463 | 365 | 252 | 51.39 | 52.03 | 51.51 | 14.67 | 14.60 | 14.95 | 0.215 | @ |
| 13. | $Q_3$ | 418 | 422 | 240 | 52.93 | 51.70 | 49.30 | 14.28 | 14.99 | 14.69 | 4.681 | ** |
| 14. | $Q_4$ | 261 | 428 | 391 | 51.13 | 50.70 | 53.02 | 14.87 | 14.29 | 14.97 | 2.760 | @ |

** Indicates significant at 0.01 level; * Indicates significant at 0.05 level; @ Indicates not significant at 0.05 level.

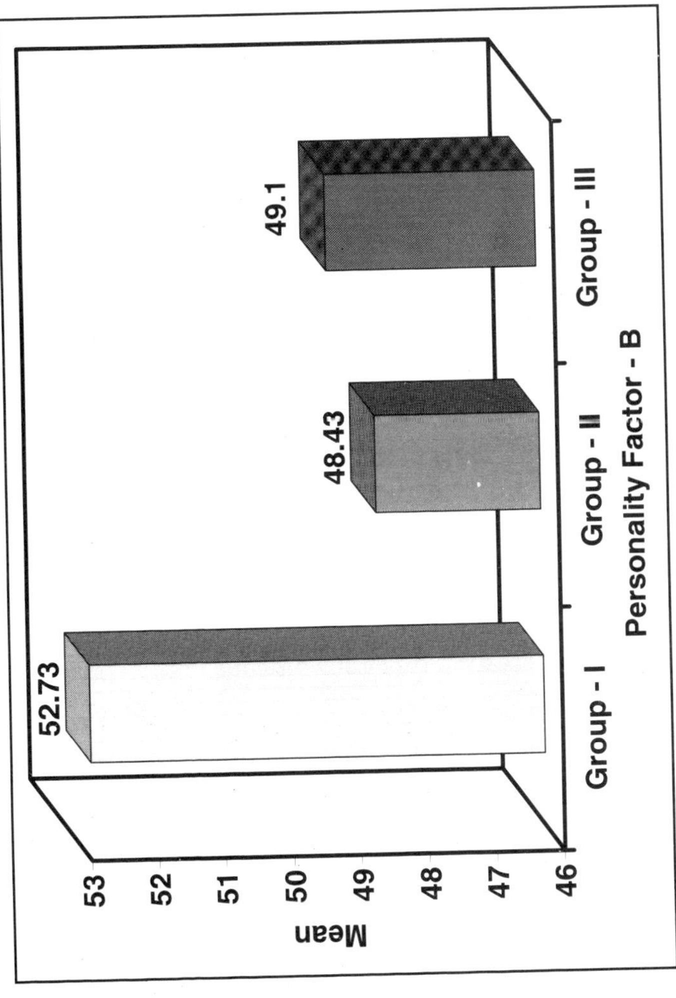


**Fig. 5.26: Bar Diagram Showing the Mean Values of Personality Factor - B on the Reasoning of Pre-Conventional Level**

*Conventional Level*

The corresponding conventional level scores of the three groups were analyzed accordingly. The mean values of conventional level scores for the three groups for the each personality factor were tested for significance by employing one-way ANOVA technique. The following hypothesis is framed.

**Hypothesis 37**

There would be no significant influence of '14 Personality Factors' on the reasoning of conventional level of Intermediate students.

The above hypothesis is tested by employing one-way ANOVA. The results are presented in Table 5.37.

It is clear from the Table 5.37 that the calculated value of 'F' for factor $Q_4$ is greater than table value of 'F' (2.99) for 2 and 1077 df at 0.05 level of significance. Hence, Hypothesis 37 is rejected. For the remaining personality factors Hypothesis 37 is accepted at 0.05 level. The mean values of conventional level in favour of Group I for factor $Q_4$. It is inferred that the students who are having personality characteristic of (1) Tense, driven over wrought, frustrated have significant influence on the reasoning of conventional level than the students who are having the personality characteristic of (1) Relaxed, tranquil, torpid, unfrustrated.

The Bar diagram showing the mean values of personality factor $Q_4$ on the reasoning of conventional level is given in Fig. 5.27.

*Post-Conventional Level*

The corresponding post-conventional level scores of the three groups were analyzed accordingly. The mean values of post-conventional level scores for the three groups for the each personality factor were tested for significance by employing one-way ANOVA technique. The following hypothesis is framed.

**Table 5.37: Impact of 14 PF (HSPQ) on the reasoning of Conventional Level**

| Sl. No. | Personality Factor | No. of observations | | | Mean values | | | SD values | | | F-value | Level of significance |
|---|---|---|---|---|---|---|---|---|---|---|---|---|
| | | I | II | III | I | II | III | I | II | III | | |
| 1. | A | 122 | 404 | 554 | 156.19 | 150.65 | 152.05 | 36.50 | 32.95 | 33.24 | 1.279 | @ |
| 2. | B | 785 | 152 | 143 | 151.14 | 155.35 | 153.09 | 34.06 | 34.41 | 29.31 | 1.084 | @ |
| 3. | C | 274 | 402 | 404 | 148.57 | 153.32 | 152.99 | 33.69 | 33.59 | 33.27 | 1.920 | @ |
| 4. | D | 397 | 484 | 199 | 153.86 | 150.85 | 151.05 | 33.78 | 33.41 | 33.29 | 0.977 | @ |
| 5. | E | 268 | 438 | 374 | 151.92 | 151.98 | 152.06 | 30.07 | 33.62 | 35.78 | 0.002 | @ |
| 6. | F | 356 | 372 | 352 | 151.72 | 152.85 | 151.37 | 33.40 | 33.93 | 33.29 | 0.192 | @ |
| 7. | G | 402 | 407 | 271 | 151.78 | 152.09 | 152.17 | 33.82 | 33.05 | 35.32 | 0.014 | @ |
| 8. | H | 312 | 381 | 387 | 149.43 | 152.65 | 153.41 | 34.81 | 32.72 | 33.22 | 1.332 | @ |
| 9. | I | 106 | 314 | 660 | 154.36 | 151.34 | 151.92 | 34.76 | 33.95 | 33.15 | 0.324 | @ |
| 10. | J | 189 | 376 | 515 | 149.31 | 153.50 | 151.88 | 31.60 | 32.82 | 34.70 | 0.985 | @ |
| 11. | O | 424 | 381 | 275 | 150.41 | 153.86 | 151.84 | 33.91 | 33.13 | 33.46 | 1.067 | @ |
| 12. | $Q_2$ | 463 | 365 | 252 | 152.63 | 151.54 | 151.47 | 33.91 | 33.20 | 33.40 | 0.147 | @ |
| 13. | $Q_3$ | 418 | 422 | 240 | 150.73 | 151.78 | 154.57 | 33.65 | 33.74 | 33.93 | 1.012 | @ |
| 14. | $Q_4$ | 261 | 428 | 391 | 154.55 | 153.42 | 148.73 | 33.06 | 33.72 | 33.45 | 3.001 | * |

* Indicates significant at 0.05 level; @ Indicates not significant at 0.05 level.

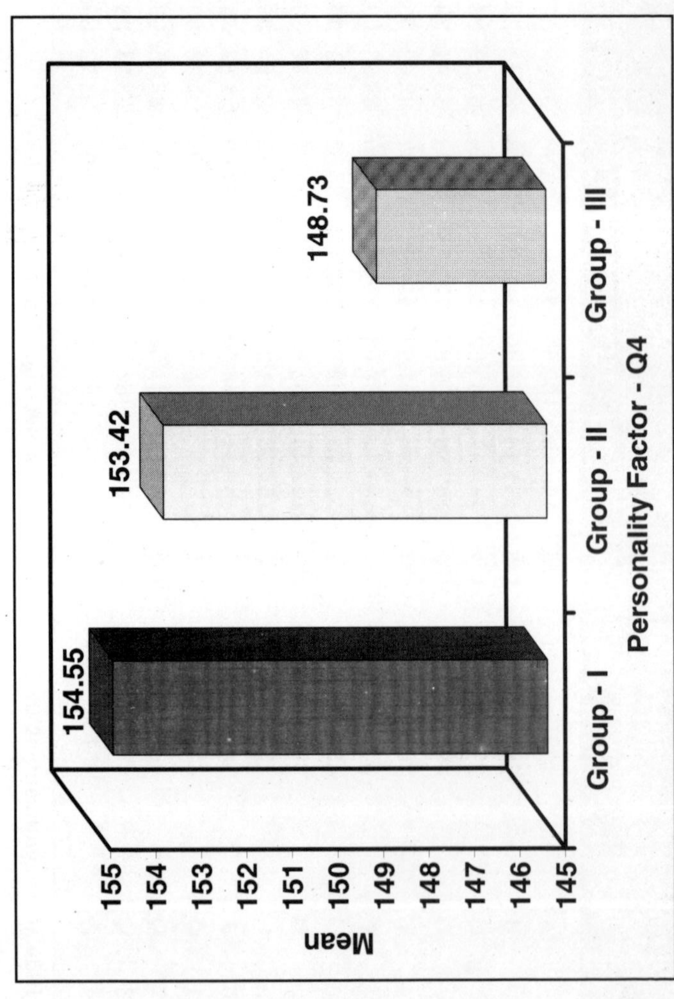


**Fig. 5.27: Bar Diagram Showing the Mean Values of Personality Factor $Q_4$ on the Reasoning of Conventional Level**

**Hypothesis 38**

There would be no significant influence of '14 Personality Factors' on the reasoning of post-conventional level of Intermediate students.

The above hypothesis is tested by employing one-way ANOVA. The results are presented in Table 5.38.

It is clear from the Table 5.38 that the calculated values of 'F' for all factors is less than table value of 'F' (2.99) for 2 and 1077 df at 0.05 level. Hence, Hypothesis 38 is accepted. It is concluded that 14 personality factors do not have significant impact on the reasoning of post-conventional level.

*Moral Judgment*

The corresponding moral judgment scores of the three groups were analyzed accordingly. The mean values of moral judgment scores for the three groups for the each personality factor were tested for significance by employing one-way ANOVA technique. The following hypothesis is framed.

**Hypothesis 39**

There would be no significant influence of '14 Personality Factors' on the reasoning of moral judgment of Intermediate students.

The above hypothesis is tested by employing one-way ANOVA. The results are presented in Table 5.39.

It is clear from the Table 5.39 that the calculated value of 'F' for factor G is greater than table value of 'F' (2.99) for 2 and 1077 df at 0.05 level of significance. Hence, Hypothesis 39 is rejected. For the remaining personality factors Hypothesis 39 is accepted at 0.05 level. The mean values of moral judgment in favour of Group III for factor G. It is inferred that the students who are having personality characteristic of (1) Conscientious, preserving, rule bound i.e., stronger super ego strength have significant influence on the reasoning of moral judgment than the students who are having the personality characteristic of (1) Expedient, evades rules i.e.,

**Table 5.39: Impact of 14 PF (HSPQ) on the reasoning of Moral Judgment**

| Sl. No. | Personality Factor | No of observations | | | Mean values | | | SD values | | | F-value | Level of significance |
|---|---|---|---|---|---|---|---|---|---|---|---|---|
| | | I | II | III | I | II | III | I | II | III | | |
| 1. | A | 122 | 404 | 554 | 331.33 | 329.68 | 330.04 | 31.26 | 28.74 | 28.99 | 0.155 | @ |
| 2. | B | 785 | 152 | 143 | 329.06 | 334.61 | 330.66 | 27.96 | 33.08 | 30.70 | 2.350 | @ |
| 3. | C | 274 | 402 | 404 | 327.96 | 331.68 | 329.85 | 27.60 | 31.70 | 27.41 | 1.340 | @ |
| 4. | D | 397 | 484 | 199 | 332.09 | 328.38 | 330.03 | 28.94 | 29.18 | 29.34 | 1.769 | @ |
| 5. | E | 268 | 438 | 374 | 333.32 | 329.00 | 328.93 | 30.29 | 28.63 | 28.78 | 2.246 | @ |
| 6. | F | 356 | 372 | 352 | 328.42 | 332.91 | 328.68 | 28.17 | 31.25 | 27.61 | 2.733 | @ |
| 7. | G | 402 | 407 | 271 | 329.35 | 328.11 | 333.99 | 30.70 | 26.83 | 29.82 | 3.497 | * |
| 8. | H | 312 | 381 | 387 | 328.59 | 331.22 | 330.07 | 29.87 | 26.99 | 30.57 | 0.700 | @ |
| 9. | I | 106 | 314 | 660 | 327.23 | 331.88 | 329.63 | 26.78 | 30.23 | 28.97 | 1.179 | @ |
| 10. | J | 189 | 376 | 515 | 331.91 | 330.85 | 328.78 | 30.18 | 29.57 | 28.43 | 1.010 | @ |
| 11. | O | 424 | 381 | 275 | 328.56 | 331.07 | 330.94 | 29.62 | 29.95 | 27.20 | 0.916 | @ |
| 12. | $Q_2$ | 463 | 365 | 252 | 330.99 | 328.26 | 330.93 | 28.53 | 31.18 | 27.12 | 1.038 | @ |
| 13. | $Q_3$ | 418 | 422 | 240 | 328.24 | 330.35 | 332.69 | 27.24 | 30.85 | 29.15 | 1.811 | @ |
| 14. | $Q_4$ | 261 | 428 | 391 | 330.97 | 331.07 | 328.32 | 27.70 | 30.50 | 28.55 | 1.081 | @ |

* Indicates significant at 0.05 level; @ Indicates not significant at 0.05 level.

weaker super ego strength. Similar results were reported by Dayakara Reddy, V. (1987) and Rangaswamy, G. (2006).

The Bar diagram showing the mean values of personality factor G of moral judgment is given in Fig. 5.28.

*Influence of Intelligence on the reasoning of each Moral Stage, Moral Level and Moral Judgment*

To identify the influence of intelligence on the reasoning of each moral stage, each moral level and moral judgment of Intermediate student is investigated. The criterion in the division of the groups based on the RPM score was used. The RPM scores up to 243 grouped as low scorers (Group I), 244-262 grouped as average scorers (Groups II), above 262 grouped as high scorers (Group III). The impact of intelligence on the reasoning of each moral stage, moral level and moral judgment is investigated. The corresponding each moral stage, moral level and moral judgment scores of the three groups are analyzed accordingly. The following hypothesis is formulated.

**Hypothesis 40**

There would be no significant influence of 'Intelligence' on the reasoning of each moral stage, moral level and moral judgment of Intermediate students.

The above hypothesis is tested by employing one-way ANOVA technique; the results are presented in Table 5.40.

It is clear from the Table 5.40 that the calculated value of 'F' for the moral stage 1 is greater than table value of 'F' (4.60) for 2 and 1077 df at 0.01 level. Hence, Hypothesis 40 is rejected. It is concluded that intelligence has significant impact on the reasoning of moral stage 1.

The Bar diagram showing the mean values of intelligence on the reasoning of moral stage 1 is given in Fig. 5.29.

It is clear from the Table 5.40 that the calculated value of 'F' for the moral stage 2, moral stage 3, moral stage 4, moral stage 4A, moral stage 5A, moral stage 5B, moral stage 6, pre-conventional level, conventional level, post conventional

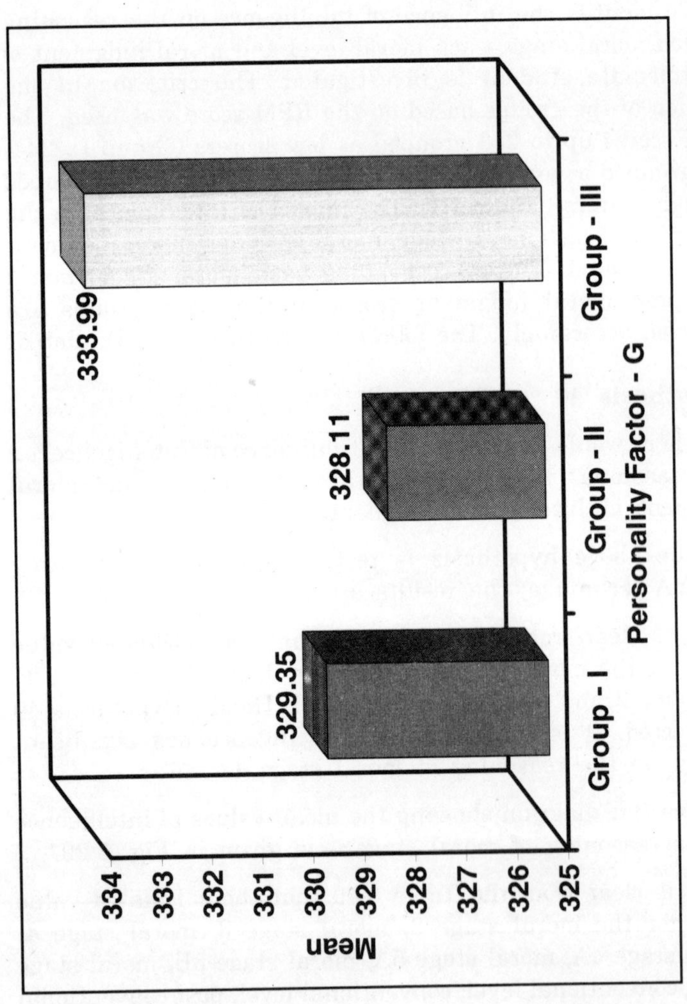


**Fig. 5.28: Bar Diagram Showing the Mean Values of Personality Factor G on the Reasoning of Moral Judgment**

**Table 5.40: Impact of Intelligence on the Reasoning of Each Moral Stage, Moral Level and Moral Judgment**

| Sl. No. | Variable | Mean values | | | SD values | | | F-value | Level of significance |
|---|---|---|---|---|---|---|---|---|---|
| | | I | II | III | I | II | III | | |
| 1. | **Moral Stage 1** | 16.67 | 15.38 | 16.55 | 6.54 | 6.65 | 6.35 | 4.781 | ** |
| 2. | **Moral Stage 2** | 35.39 | 35.80 | 35.62 | 13.55 | 13.41 | 14.34 | 0.080 | @ |
| 3. | **Moral Stage 3** | 51.14 | 52.96 | 52.81 | 19.78 | 20.61 | 21.24 | 0.761 | @ |
| 4. | **Moral Stage 4** | 70.26 | 69.01 | 68.23 | 27.72 | 27.80 | 26.27 | 0.377 | @ |
| 5. | **Moral Stage 4A** | 31.67 | 30.26 | 29.77 | 19.93 | 18.93 | 19.19 | 0.816 | @ |
| 6. | **Moral Stage 5A** | 40.64 | 39.79 | 39.15 | 24.27 | 26.17 | 24.92 | 0.232 | @ |
| 7. | **Moral Stage 5B** | 35.67 | 39.47 | 37.24 | 21.22 | 23.23 | 24.04 | 2.668 | @ |
| 8. | **Moral Stage 6** | 46.24 | 48.98 | 50.27 | 29.35 | 26.75 | 26.51 | 1.551 | @ |
| 9. | **Pre-Conventional Level** | 52.06 | 51.18 | 52.17 | 14.41 | 14.69 | 15.04 | 0.551 | @ |
| 10. | **Conventional Level** | 153.06 | 152.03 | 150.81 | 33.74 | 33.27 | 33.91 | 0.300 | @ |
| 11. | **Post-Conventional Level** | 122.54 | 128.24 | 126.65 | 40.28 | 40.86 | 36.22 | 1.883 | @ |
| 12. | **Moral Judgment** | 327.66 | 331.44 | 329.63 | 29.74 | 29.89 | 26.78 | 1.561 | @ |

** Indicates significant at 0.01 level; @ Indicates not significant at 0.05 level; $N_1$ = 273; $N_2$ = 545; $N_3$ = 262; df = 2,1077.

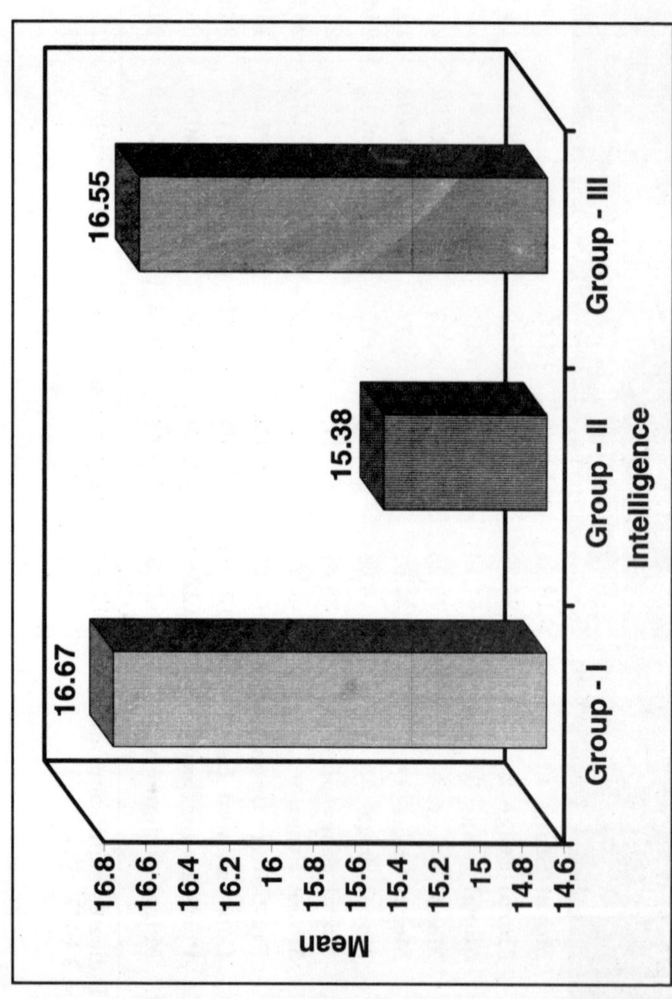


**Fig. 5.29: Bar Diagram Showing the Mean Values of Intelligence on the Reasoning of Moral Stage 1**

level and moral judgment is less than table value of 'F' (2.99) for 2 and 1077 df at 0.05 level. Hence, Hypothesis 40 is accepted. It is concluded that intelligence does not have significant impact on the reasoning of moral stage 2, moral stage 3, moral stage 4, moral stage 4A, moral stage 5A, moral stage 5B, moral stage 6, pre-conventional level, conventional level, post-conventional level and moral judgment.

## Influence of Socio-Demographic Variables

The influence of socio-demographic variables on the reasoning of each moral stage, each moral level and moral judgment of Intermediate students is investigated. The following socio-demographic variables are considered in the present investigation.

1. Caste,
2. Community,
3. Locality,
4. Socio-Economic Status (SES) and
5. Residence.

*Caste*

On the basis of caste, the students are divided into three groups. Group I is formed with Open Category (OC) students Groups II is formed with Backward Caste (BC) students Group III is formed with Scheduled Caste (SC) and Scheduled Tribe (ST) students. The impact of caste on the reasoning of moral judgment of the Intermediate students is studied in this investigation. The corresponding each moral stage, moral level and moral judgment scores of the three groups were analyzed accordingly. The following hypothesis is framed.

## Hypothesis 41

There would be no significant influence of 'Caste' on the reasoning of each moral stage, moral level and moral judgment of Intermediate students.

The above hypothesis is tested by employing one-way ANOVA technique. The results are presented in Table 5.41.

The Bar diagram showing the mean values of caste on the reasoning of moral stage 1 is given in Fig. 5.30.

It is clear from Table 5.41 that the computed values of 'F' for the moral stage 1 is greater than table value of 'F' (2.99) for 2 and 1077 df at 0.05 level. Hence, Hypothesis 41 is rejected. It is concluded that caste has significant influence on the reasoning of moral stage 1.

It is clear from Table 5.41 that the computed value of 'F' for the moral stage 2, moral stage 3, moral stage 4, moral stage 4A, moral stage 5A, moral stage 5B, moral stage 6, pre-conventional level, conventional level, post-conventional level and moral judgment is less than table value of 'F' (2.99) for 2 and 1077 df at 0.01 level. Hence, Hypothesis 41 is accepted. It is concluded that caste does not have significant influence on the reasoning of moral stage 2, moral stage 3, moral stage 4, moral stage 4A, moral stage 5A, moral stage 5B, moral stage 6, pre-conventional level, conventional level, post-conventional level and moral judgment.

*Community*

On the basis of community, there are three community students in Intermediate course. Among the sample subjects, there are 912 Hindus 147 Muslims and 21 Christians. On the basis of community the students are divided into two groups. Group I is formed with Hindus and Group II is formed with Muslims and Christians because the number of students in Muslim and Christian communities are very low. The corresponding each moral stage, moral level and moral judgment scores of the two groups were analyzed accordingly. The following hypothesis is formulated.

**Hypothesis 42**

There would be no significant influence of 'Community' on the reasoning of each moral stage, moral level and moral judgment of Intermediate students.

**Table 5.41: Influence of Caste on the reasoning of each Moral Stage, Moral Level and Moral Judgment**

| Sl. No. | Variable | Mean values | | | SD values | | | F-value | Level of significance |
|---|---|---|---|---|---|---|---|---|---|
| | | I | II | III | I | II | III | | |
| 1. | **Moral Stage 1** | 16.80 | 15.37 | 16.55 | 6.33 | 6.87 | 6.15 | 4.065 | * |
| 2. | **Moral Stage 2** | 35.16 | 36.26 | 35.07 | 13.72 | 13.84 | 13.04 | 0.916 | @ |
| 3. | **Moral Stage 3** | 51.16 | 53.74 | 51.89 | 20.43 | 20.56 | 20.73 | 1.837 | @ |
| 4. | **Moral Stage 4** | 69.43 | 68.85 | 69.24 | 27.81 | 27.11 | 27.45 | 0.051 | @ |
| 5. | **Moral Stage 4A** | 31.34 | 29.38 | 31.07 | 20.73 | 17.81 | 19.59 | 1.295 | @ |
| 6. | **Moral Stage 5A** | 39.44 | 40.83 | 38.03 | 25.07 | 25.61 | 25.46 | 0.878 | @ |
| 7. | **Moral Stage 5B** | 36.44 | 38.95 | 38.70 | 21.54 | 23.58 | 24.36 | 1.449 | @ |
| 8. | **Moral Stage 6** | 50.54 | 46.95 | 48.77 | 29.11 | 26.17 | 26.49 | 1.928 | @ |
| 9. | **Pre-Conventional Level** | 51.66 | 51.63 | 51.62 | 14.73 | 14.88 | 14.30 | 0.001 | @ |
| 10. | **Conventional Level** | 151.94 | 151.97 | 152.20 | 34.28 | 32.61 | 34.24 | 0.004 | @ |
| 11. | **Post-Conventional Level** | 126.42 | 126.74 | 125.50 | 39.40 | 39.80 | 40.13 | 0.063 | @ |
| 12. | **Moral Judgment** | 230.01 | 330.34 | 329.32 | 27.15 | 30.50 | 29.78 | 0.080 | @ |

* Indicates significant at 0.05 level; @ Indicates not significant at 0.05 level.

$N_1$ = 406; $N_2$ = 497; $N_3$ = 177; df = 2,1077.

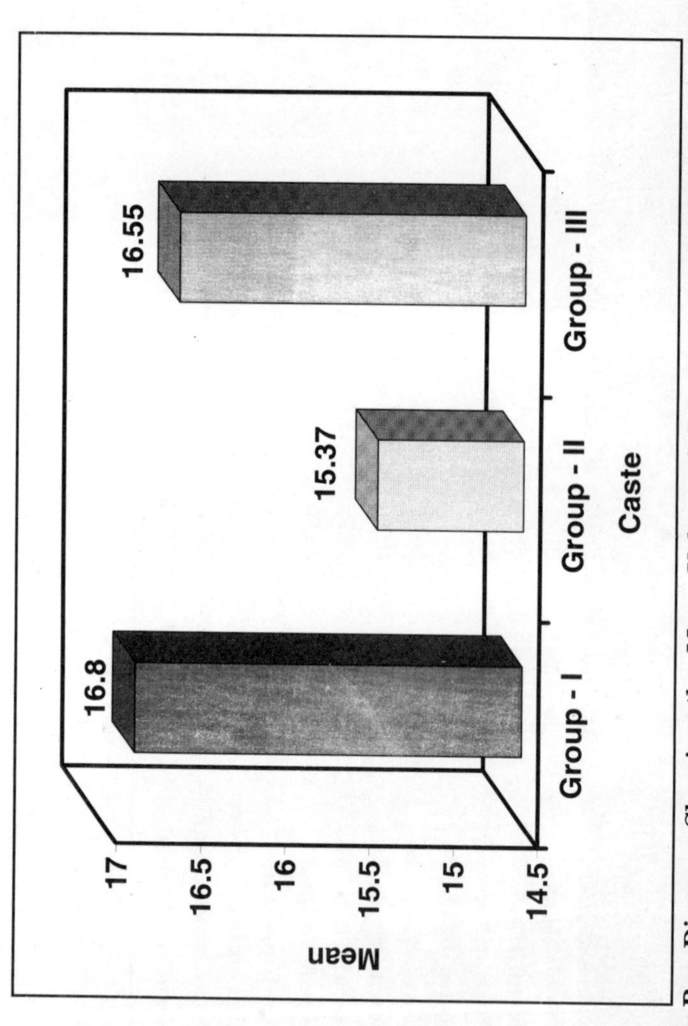


**Fig. 5.30: Bar Diagram Showing the Mean Values of Caste on the Reasoning of Moral Stage 1**

The above hypothesis is tested by employing'ť'- test. The results are presented in Table 5.42.

It is clear from the Table 5.42 that the computed values of 't' for the moral stage 1, moral stage 2, moral stage 3, moral stage 4, moral stage 4A, moral stage 5A, moral stage 5B, moral stage 6, pre-conventional level, conventional level, post-conventional level and moral judgment is less than table value of 'F' (1.96) for 1 and 1078 df at 0.05 level. Hence, Hypothesis 42 is accepted. It is concluded that community do not have significant influence on the reasoning of moral stage 1, moral stage 2, moral stage 3, moral stage 4, moral stage 4A, moral stage 5A, moral stage 5B, moral stage 6, pre-conventional level, conventional level, post-conventional level and moral judgment.

*Locality*

On the basis of locality, the students are divided into two groups. The students of rural area come under Group I the students of urban area come under Group II. The impact of locality on the reasoning of moral judgment of the Intermediate students is investigated. The corresponding each moral stage, moral level and moral judgment scores of the two groups were analyzed accordingly. The following hypothesis is framed.

**Hypothesis 43**

There would be no significant influence of 'Locality' on the reasoning of each moral stage, each moral level and moral judgment of Intermediate students.

The above hypothesis is tested by employing't' - test. The results are presented in Table 5.43.

It is clear from Table 5.43 that the computed values of 't' for the moral stage 1, moral stage 2, moral stage 3, moral stage 4, moral stage 4A, moral stage 5A, moral stage 5B, moral stage 6, pre-conventional level, conventional level, post-conventional level and moral judgment is less than table value of 'F' (1.96) for 1 and 1078 df at 0.05 level. Hence, Hypothesis 43 is accepted. It is concluded that locality do not have

**Table 5.42: Influence of Community on the Reasoning of each Moral Stage, Moral Level and Moral Judgment**

| Sl. No. | Variable | Mean values | | SD values | | 't'-value | Level of significance |
|---|---|---|---|---|---|---|---|
| | | I | II | I | II | | |
| **1.** | **Moral Stage 1** | 15.90 | 16.45 | 6.65 | 6.17 | 1.04 | @ |
| **2.** | **Moral Stage 2** | 35.70 | 35.39 | 13.85 | 12.73 | 0.29 | @ |
| **3.** | **Moral Stage 3** | 52.53 | 52.10 | 20.61 | 20.39 | 0.25 | @ |
| **4.** | **Moral Stage 4** | 68.99 | 69.94 | 27.42 | 27.45 | 0.41 | @ |
| **5.** | **Moral Stage 4A** | 30.68 | 28.84 | 19.34 | 18.77 | 1.16 | @ |
| **6.** | **Moral Stage 5A** | 40.19 | 37.98 | 25.47 | 24.97 | 1.05 | @ |
| **7.** | **Moral Stage 5B** | 38.10 | 37.24 | 22.92 | 23.41 | 0.44 | @ |
| **8.** | **Moral Stage 6** | 47.98 | 51.96 | 26.78 | 30.41 | 1.59 | @ |
| **9.** | **Pre-Conventional Level** | 51.60 | 51.84 | 14.97 | 39.27 | 0.20 | @ |
| **10.** | **Conventional Level** | 152.20 | 150.88 | 33.90 | 31.62 | 0.49 | @ |
| **11.** | **Post-Conventional Level** | 126.27 | 127.19 | 39.00 | 43.35 | 0.26 | @ |
| **12.** | **Moral Judgment** | 330.08 | 329.90 | 28.83 | 30.95 | 0.07 | @ |

@ Indicates not significant at 0.05 level.

$N_1$ = 912; $N_2$ = 168; df = 1,1078.

**Table 5.43: Influence of Locality on the Reasoning of Each Moral Stage, Moral Level and Moral Judgment**

| Sl. No. | Variable | Mean values | | SD values | | 't'-value | Level of significance |
|---|---|---|---|---|---|---|---|
| | | I | II | I | II | | |
| 1. | **Moral Stage 1** | 15.96 | 16.01 | 6.98 | 6.10 | 0.13 | @ |
| 2. | **Moral Stage 2** | 35.30 | 36.05 | 14.01 | 13.29 | 0.90 | @ |
| 3. | **Moral Stage 3** | 53.24 | 51.60 | 20.78 | 20.31 | 1.32 | @ |
| 4. | **Moral Stage 4** | 69.34 | 68.90 | 27.12 | 27.77 | 0.26 | @ |
| 5. | **Moral Stage 4A** | 29.97 | 30.86 | 19.42 | 19.08 | 0.76 | @ |
| 6. | **Moral Stage 5A** | 38.96 | 40.85 | 23.96 | 26.89 | 1.21 | @ |
| 7. | **Moral Stage 5B** | 38.89 | 36.94 | 23.36 | 22.90 | 1.40 | @ |
| 8. | **Moral Stage 6** | 48.91 | 48.25 | 26.79 | 28.08 | 0.39 | @ |
| 9. | **Pre-Conventional Level** | 51.26 | 52.06 | 15.28 | 14.04 | 0.90 | @ |
| 10. | **Conventional Level** | 152.56 | 151.36 | 33.36 | 33.77 | 0.59 | @ |
| 11. | **Post-Conventional Level** | 126.76 | 126.03 | 39.21 | 40.25 | 0.30 | @ |
| 12. | **Moral Judgment** | 330.58 | 329.46 | 29.66 | 28.59 | 0.63 | @ |

@ Indicates not significant at 0.05 level

$N_1$ = 570; $N_2$ = 510; df = 1,1078.

significant influence on the reasoning of moral stage 1, moral stage 2, moral stage 3, moral stage-4, moral stage 4A, moral stage 5A, moral stage 5B, moral stage 6, pre-conventional level, conventional level, post-conventional level and moral judgment.

*Socio-Economic Status (SES)*

A common Socio-Economic Status (SES) scale for rural and urban areas constructed by Aaron, P.G., Marihal, V.G. and Malathisha, R.N. was adopted for the present investigation the distribution characteristics of socio-economic status score for the whole group are N = 1080, $Q_1$ = 25, $Q_2$ = 40 and $Q_3$ = 55.

The relationship of moral judgment of Intermediate students with their socio-economic status is studied in the present investigation. On the basis of socio-economic status scores, the Intermediate students are divided into three groups using quartile values. The students whose socio-economic status score is up to $Q_1$value forms the Group I, Group II forms with above $Q_1$ and up to $Q_3$ value and Group III forms with above $Q_3$ value. The corresponding each moral stage, moral level and moral judgment of the three groups were analyzed accordingly. The mean values of moral judgment scores for the three groups were tested for significance by employing one-way ANOVA technique. The following hypothesis is framed.

**Hypothesis 44**

There would be no significant impact of 'Socio-Economic Status' on the reasoning of each moral stage, moral level and moral judgment of Intermediate students.

The above hypothesis is tested by employing one-way ANOVA technique. The results are presented in Table 5.44.

It is clear from Table 5.44 that the computed value of 'F' for moral stage 3 is greater than table value of 'F' (4.60) for 2 and 1077 df at 0.01 level. Hence, Hypothesis 44 is rejected. It is concluded that the socio-economic status has significant influence on the reasoning of moral stage 3.

**Table 5.44: Influence of Socio-Economic Status on the Reasoning of Each Moral Stage, Moral Level and Moral Judgment**

| Sl. No. | Variable | Mean values | | | SD values | | | F-value | Level of signifi-cance |
|---|---|---|---|---|---|---|---|---|---|
| | | I | II | III | I | II | III | | |
| **1.** | **Moral Stage 1** | 16.88 | 15.66 | 15.74 | 6.69 | 6.59 | 6.31 | 3.460 | * |
| **2.** | **Moral Stage 2** | 36.61 | 35.16 | 35.70 | 14.06 | 13.70 | 13.11 | 1.047 | @ |
| **3.** | **Moral Stage 3** | 48.26 | 55.26 | 50.75 | 19.53 | 20.63 | 20.60 | 12.052 | ** |
| **4.** | **Moral Stage 4** | 67.54 | 68.61 | 72.25 | 28.20 | 26.01 | 29.36 | 2.112 | @ |
| **5.** | **Moral Stage 4A** | 31.49 | 29.50 | 31.22 | 18.68 | 18.61 | 21.27 | 1.272 | @ |
| **6.** | **Moral Stage 5A** | 41.70 | 38.31 | 41.33 | 25.71 | 26.15 | 22.90 | 2.187 | @ |
| **7.** | **Moral Stage 5B** | 36.71 | 38.90 | 37.24 | 23.13 | 23.58 | 21.29 | 0.992 | @ |
| **8.** | **Moral Stage 6** | 48.97 | 48.63 | 48.09 | 28.23 | 27.32 | 26.65 | 0.067 | @ |
| **9.** | **Pre-Conventional Level** | 53.49 | 50.82 | 51.44 | 14.25 | 15.06 | 14.22 | 3.112 | * |
| **10.** | **Conventional Level** | 147.29 | 153.37 | 154.22 | 33.79 | 32.64 | 34.88 | 3.741 | * |
| **11.** | **Post-Conventional Level** | 127.38 | 125.84 | 126.66 | 39.84 | 40.10 | 38.57 | 0.147 | @ |
| **12.** | **Moral Judgment** | 328.17 | 330.02 | 332.32 | 28.72 | 30.06 | 27.32 | 1.297 | @ |

** Indicates significant at 0.01 level; * Indicates significant at 0.05 level; @ Indicates not significant at 0.05 level

$N_1$ = 278; $N_2$ = 564; $N_3$ = 238; df = 2,1077.

It is clear from Table 5.44 that the computed value of 'F' for moral stage 1, pre-conventional level and conventional level is greater than table value of 'F' (2.99) for 2 and 1077 df at 0.05 level. Hence Hypothesis 44 is rejected. It is concluded that the socio-economic Status has significant influence on the reasoning of moral stage 1, pre-conventional level and conventional level.

It is clear from Table 5.44 that the computed value of 'F' for moral stage 2, moral stage 4, moral stage 4A, moral stage 5A, moral stage 5B, moral stage 6, post-conventional level and moral judgment is less than table value of 'F' (2.99) for 2 and 1077 df at 0.05 level. Hence Hypothesis 44 is accepted. It is concluded that the Social Economics Status do not have significant influence on the reasoning of moral stage 2, moral stage 4, moral stage 4A, moral stage 5A, moral stage 5B, moral stage 6, post-conventional level and moral judgment.

The Bar diagram showing the mean values of socio-economic status on the reasoning of moral stage 3 is given in Figure 5.31.

*Residence*

On the basis of residence, the students are divided into two groups that are hostlers come under Group I and day scholars come under Group II. The impact of residence on the reasoning of moral judgment of the Intermediate students is investigated. The corresponding each moral stage, moral level and moral judgment scores of the two groups were analyzed accordingly. The following hypothesis is framed.

**Hypothesis 45**

There would be no significant impact of 'Residence'on the reasoning of each moral stage, each moral level and moral judgment of Intermediate students.

The above hypothesis is tested by employing't'-test. The results are presented in Table 5.45.

It is clear from Table 5.45 that the computed value of 't' for moral stage 1, pre-conventional level and moral judgment

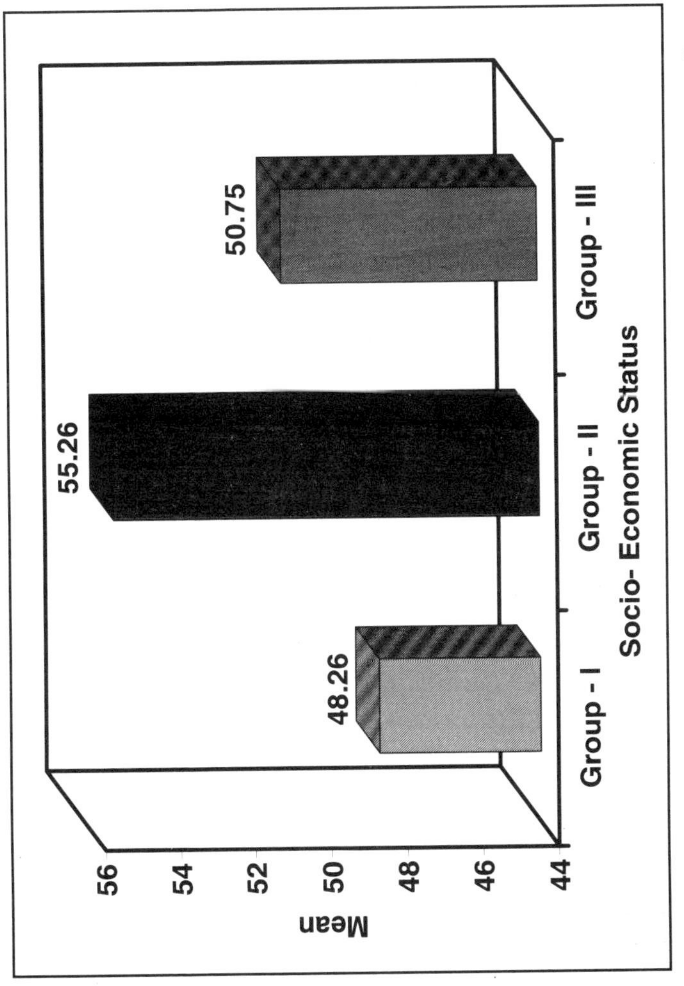


**Fig. 5.31: Bar Diagram Showing the Mean Values of Socio-Economic Status on the Reasoning of Moral Stage 3**

**Table 5.45: Influence of Residence on Each Moral Stage, Moral Level and Moral Judgment**

| Sl. No. | Variable | Mean values | | SD values | | 't'-value | Level of significance |
|---|---|---|---|---|---|---|---|
| | | I | II | I | II | | |
| 1. | **Moral Stage 1** | 15.06 | 16.46 | 6.60 | 6.52 | 3.30 | ** |
| 2. | **Moral Stage 2** | 34.42 | 36.28 | 14.00 | 13.47 | 2.10 | * |
| 3. | **Moral Stage 3** | 53.45 | 51.97 | 21.01 | 20.34 | 1.11 | @ |
| 4. | **Moral Stage 4** | 70.34 | 68.52 | 27.32 | 27.46 | 1.04 | @ |
| 5. | **Moral Stage 4A** | 30.98 | 30.10 | 19.76 | 19.00 | 0.70 | @ |
| 6. | **Moral Stage 5A** | 41.79 | 38.86 | 24.31 | 25.89 | 1.83 | @ |
| 7. | **Moral Stage 5B** | 40.11 | 36.88 | 22.73 | 23.06 | 2.20 | * |
| 8. | **Moral Stage 6** | 48.71 | 48.54 | 29.13 | 26.49 | 0.09 | @ |
| 9. | **Pre-Conventional Level** | 49.48 | 52.74 | 15.46 | 14.19 | 3.37 | ** |
| 10. | **Conventional Level** | 154.77 | 150.78 | 34.84 | 32.79 | 1.90 | @ |
| 11. | **Post-Conventional Level** | 130.69 | 124.28 | 39.33 | 39.72 | 2.49 | * |
| 12. | **Moral Judgment** | 334.86 | 327.61 | 30.47 | 28.17 | 3.79 | ** |

** Indicates significant at 0.01 level;
* Indicates significant at 0.05 level;
@ Indicates not significant at 0.05 level
$N_1$ = 364; $N_2$ = 716; df = 1,1078.

is greater than table value of 't' (2.58) for 1 and 1078 df at 0.01 level. Hence, Hypothesis 45 is rejected. It is concluded that the residence has significant influence on the reasoning of moral stage 1, pre-conventional level and moral judgment.

The Bar diagram showing the mean values of residence on the reasoning of moral judgment is given in Fig. 5.32.

It is clear from Table 5.45 that the computed value of 't' for moral stage 2, moral stage 5B and post-conventional level is greater than table value of 't' (1.96) for 1 and 1078 df at 0.05 level. Hence, Hypothesis 45 is rejected. It is concluded that the residence has significant influence on the reasoning of for moral stage 2, moral stage 5B and post-conventional level.

It is clear from Table 5.45 that the computed value of 'F' for moral stage 3, moral stage 4, moral stage 4A, moral stage 5A, moral stage 6 and conventional level is less than table value of 't' (1.96) for 1 and 1078 df at 0.05 level. Hence Hypothesis 45 is accepted. It is concluded that the residence do not have significant influence on the reasoning of moral stage 3, moral stage 4, moral stage 4A, moral stage 5A, moral stage 6 and conventional level.

## Influence of Personal Variables

The influence of personal variables on the reasoning of each moral stage, moral level and moral judgment of Intermediate students is investigated. The following personal variables are considered in the present investigation:

1. Age,
2. Birth order,
3. Annual income,
4. Father's education,
5. Mother's education,
6. Father's occupation,
7. Mother's occupation,

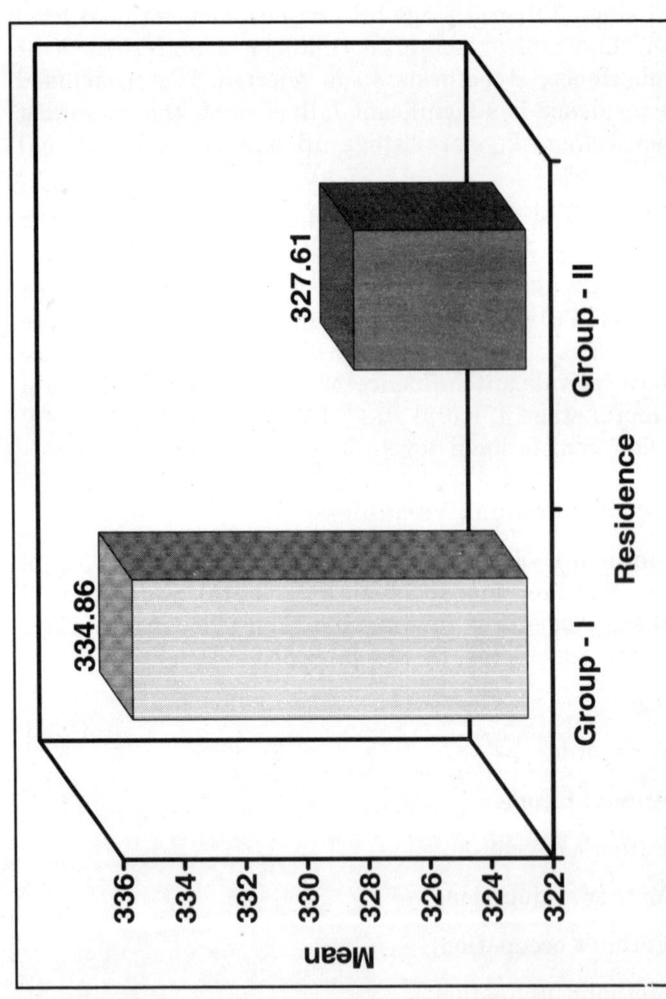


**Figure 5.32: Bar Diagram Showing the Mean Values of Residence on the Reasoning of Moral Judgment**

8. Size of the family,
9. Economic position of the family,
10. Type of the family,
11. Medium of the study,
12. Course of the study.

*Age*

On the basis of age, the distribution characteristics of Age for the whole group are N = 1080, $Q_1$ = 16, $Q_2$ = 17, $Q_3$ = 18.

The relationship of moral judgment of Intermediate students with their age is studied in the present investigation. On the basis of age, the students are divided into three groups using quartile values. The student whose age is up to $Q_1$ value forms the Group I, Group II forms with above $Q_1$ and up to $Q_3$ value and Group III forms with above $Q_3$ value. The corresponding each moral stage, each moral level and moral judgment of the three groups were analyzed accordingly. The mean values of moral judgment scores for the three groups were tested for significance by employing one-way ANOVA technique. The following hypothesis is framed.

**Hypothesis 46**

There would be no significant impact of 'Age' on the reasoning of each moral stage, moral level and moral judgment of Intermediate students.

The above hypothesis is tested by employing one-way ANOVA technique. The results are presented in Table 5.46.

It is clear from Table 5.46 that the computed value of 'F' for moral stage 5B, is greater than table value of 'F' (2.99) for 2 and 1077 df at 0.05 level. Hence, Hypothesis 46 is rejected. It is concluded that the age has significant influence on the reasoning of moral stage 5B.

The Bar diagram showing the mean values of age on the reasoning of moral stage 5B is given in Fig. 5.33.

**Table 5.46: Influence of Age on the Reasoning of Each Moral Stage, Moral Level and Moral Judgment**

| Sl. No. | Variable | Mean values | | | SD values | | | F-value | Level of significance |
|---|---|---|---|---|---|---|---|---|---|
| | | I | II | III | I | II | III | | |
| 1. | **Moral Stage 1** | 15.76 | 16.04 | 16.52 | 6.54 | 6.52 | 6.81 | 0.828 | @ |
| 2. | **Moral Stage 2** | 36.11 | 35.61 | 34.47 | 13.11 | 13.56 | 13.25 | 0.880 | @ |
| 3. | **Moral Stage 3** | 52.11 | 53.34 | 51.13 | 20.18 | 20.88 | 20.77 | 0.814 | @ |
| 4. | **Moral Stage 4** | 71.14 | 67.88 | 66.71 | 28.13 | 26.81 | 26.62 | 2.371 | @ |
| 5. | **Moral Stage 4A** | 29.88 | 30.20 | 32.38 | 19.63 | 19.10 | 18.52 | 1.056 | @ |
| 6. | **Moral Stage 5A** | 40.28 | 39.55 | 39.41 | 27.21 | 23.76 | 24.25 | 0.124 | @ |
| 7. | **Moral Stage 5B** | 36.08 | 38.84 | 41.08 | 22.84 | 23.15 | 22.56 | 3.439 | * |
| 8. | **Moral Stage 6** | 49.10 | 47.26 | 50.76 | 27.40 | 27.40 | 27.29 | 1.118 | @ |
| 9. | **Pre-Conventional Level** | 51.87 | 51.64 | 50.98 | 14.56 | 15.05 | 14.22 | 0.219 | @ |
| 10. | **Conventional Level** | 153.14 | 151.43 | 150.21 | 34.27 | 33.11 | 32.54 | 0.567 | @ |
| 11. | **Post-Conventional Level** | 125.46 | 125.65 | 131.25 | 39.80 | 38.10 | 43.17 | 1.436 | @ |
| 12. | **Moral Judgment** | 330.46 | 328.72 | 332.45 | 28.83 | 29.01 | 30.35 | 1.057 | @ |

* Indicates significant at 0.05 level; @ Indicates not significant at 0.05 level

$N_1$ = 474; $N_2$ = 442; $N_3$ = 164; df = 2,1077.

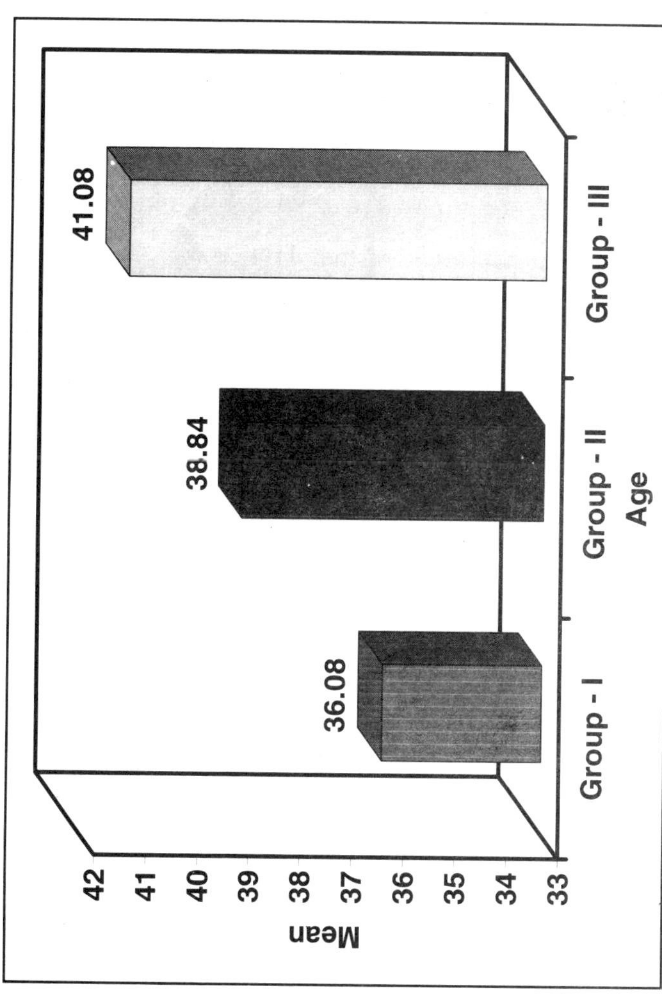


**Fig. 5.33: Bar Diagram Showing the Mean values of Age on the Reasoning of Moral Stage 5B**

It is clear from Table 5.46 that the computed value of 'F' for moral stage 1, moral stage 2, moral stage 3, moral stage 4, moral stage 4A, moral stage 5A, moral stage 6, pre-conventional level, conventional level, post-conventional level and moral judgment is and less than table value of 'F' (2.99) for 2 and 1077 df at 0.05 level. Hence, Hypothesis 46 is accepted. It is concluded that the age do not have significant influence on the reasoning of moral stage 1, moral stage 2, moral stage 3, moral stage 4, moral stage 4A, moral stage 5A, moral stage 6, pre-conventional level, conventional level, post-conventional level and moral judgment.

*Birth Order*

Birth order means order of the child to the parents like first child, second child. On the basis of birth order, the students are divided into four groups. Group I is formed with birth order one. Group II is formed with birth order two. Group III formed with birth order three and Group IV is formed with birth order four and above. The impact of birth order on the reasoning of moral judgment of Intermediate students is investigated. The corresponding moral judgment of the four groups was analyzed accordingly. The mean values of moral judgment scores for the four groups were tested for significance by employing one-way ANOVA technique. The following hypothesis is framed.

**Hypothesis 47**

There would be no significant impact of 'Birth Order' on the reasoning of each moral stage, moral level and moral judgment of Intermediate students.

The above hypothesis is tested by employing one-way ANOVA technique. The results are presented in Table 5.47.

It is clear from Table 5.47 that the computed values of 'F' for moral stage 1 , moral stage 2, moral stage 3, moral stage 4, moral stage 4A, moral stage 5A, moral stage 5B, moral stage 6, pre-conventional level, conventional level, post-conventional level and moral judgment is less than table value of 'F' (2.60) for 3 and 1076 df at 0.05 level. Hence, Hypothesis

**Table 4.47: Influence of Birth Order on the Reasoning of Each Moral Stage, Moral Level and Moral Judgment**

| Sl. No. | Variable | Mean values | | | | SD values | | | | F-value | Level of significance |
|---|---|---|---|---|---|---|---|---|---|---|---|
| | | I | II | III | IV | I | II | III | IV | | |
| 1. | **Moral Stage 1** | 16.19 | 15.91 | 15.67 | 16.33 | 6.61 | 6.55 | 6.42 | 6.86 | 0.392 | @ |
| 2. | **Moral Stage 2** | 35.30 | 35.97 | 36.13 | 34.57 | 13.81 | 13.67 | 13.50 | 13.61 | 0.470 | @ |
| 3. | **Moral Stage 3** | 51.99 | 53.40 | 51.30 | 52.84 | 19.90 | 20.40 | 20.59 | 22.95 | 0.592 | @ |
| 4. | **Moral Stage 4** | 67.81 | 69.85 | 70.91 | 66.86 | 25.99 | 27.64 | 28.22 | 28.89 | 0.921 | @ |
| 5. | **Moral Stage 4A** | 32.42 | 29.49 | 29.67 | 29.09 | 20.56 | 18.90 | 17.42 | 19.67 | 1.812 | @ |
| 6. | **Moral Stage 5A** | 38.88 | 39.44 | 40.97 | 42.05 | 23.58 | 25.73 | 25.00 | 29.76 | 0.618 | @ |
| 7. | **Moral Stage 5B** | 39.25 | 36.72 | 38.19 | 38.24 | 23.03 | 21.55 | 24.10 | 25.47 | 0.761 | @ |
| 8. | **Moral Stage 6** | 47.91 | 48.79 | 47.73 | 51.75 | 27.51 | 28.10 | 26.44 | 26.20 | 0.635 | @ |
| 9. | **Pre-Conventional Level** | 51.49 | 51.88 | 51.81 | 50.90 | 14.50 | 14.94 | 14.61 | 14.68 | 0.151 | @ |
| 10. | **Conventional Level** | 152.21 | 152.74 | 151.88 | 148.80 | 30.24 | 35.22 | 35.15 | 33.28 | 0.405 | @ |
| 11. | **Post-Conventional Level** | 126.04 | 124.95 | 126.90 | 132.03 | 40.33 | 40.08 | 36.38 | 42.32 | 0.942 | @ |
| 12. | **Moral Judgment** | 329.74 | 329.56 | 330.58 | 331.73 | 28.74 | 29.26 | 27.79 | 32.56 | 0.194 | @ |

@ Indicates not significant at 0.05 level

$N_1$ = 335; $N_2$ = 410; $N_3$ = 225; $N_4$=110; df = 3,1076.

47 is accepted. It is concluded that the birth order do not have significant influence on the reasoning of moral stage 1, moral stage 2, moral stage 3, moral stage 4, moral stage 4A, moral stage 5A, moral stage 5B, moral stage 6, pre-conventional level, conventional level, post-conventional level and moral judgment.

*Annual Income*

On the basis of annual income, the students are divided into three groups. Group I is formed with annual income up to Rs. 12,000, Group II formed with annual income from Rs. 12,000 to Rs. 36,000 Group III is formed with annual income above Rs.36,000. The impact of annual income on the reasoning of moral judgment of Intermediate students is investigated. The corresponding moral judgment of the three groups was analyzed accordingly. The mean values of moral judgment scores for the three groups were tested for significance by employing one-way ANOVA technique. The following hypothesis is framed.

**Hypothesis 48**

There would be no significant impact of 'Annual Income' on the reasoning of each moral stage, moral level and moral judgment of Intermediate students.

The above hypothesis is tested by employing one-way ANOVA technique. The results are presented in Table 5.48.

It is clear from Table 5.48 that the computed value of 'F' for moral stage 1 is greater than table value of 'F' (4.60) for 2 and 1077 df at 0.01 level. Hence Hypothesis 48 is rejected. It is concluded that the annual income has significant influence on the reasoning of moral stage 1.

It is clear from Table 5.48 that the computed value of 'F' for moral stage 3 and conventional level is greater than table value of 'F' (2.99) for 2 and 1077 df at 0.05 level. Hence Hypothesis 48 is rejected. It is concluded that the annual income has significant influence on the reasoning of moral stage 3 and conventional level.

**Table 5.48: Influence of Annual Income on the Reasoning of Each Moral Stage, Moral Level and Moral Judgment**

| Sl. No. | Variable | Mean values | | | SD values | | | F-value | Level of signifi-cance |
|---|---|---|---|---|---|---|---|---|---|
| | | I | II | III | I | II | III | | |
| 1. | **Moral Stage 1** | 16.95 | 15.67 | 14.19 | 6.42 | 6.61 | 6.36 | 7.688 | ** |
| 2. | **Moral Stage 2** | 34.69 | 36.41 | 33.88 | 13.90 | 13.49 | 13.72 | 2.549 | @ |
| 3. | **Moral Stage 3** | 51.16 | 52.44 | 58.50 | 19.21 | 20.62 | 24.66 | 4.181 | * |
| 4. | **Moral Stage 4** | 68.80 | 68.96 | 72.00 | 27.83 | 27.32 | 26.27 | 0.475 | @ |
| 5. | **Moral Stage 4A** | 31.04 | 29.91 | 31.38 | 18.57 | 19.62 | 19.40 | 0.513 | @ |
| 6. | **Moral Stage 5A** | 40.58 | 39.41 | 40.08 | 25.56 | 25.46 | 24.16 | 0.247 | @ |
| 7. | **Moral Stage 5B** | 36.14 | 38.90 | 38.67 | 23.40 | 23.06 | 20.06 | 1.700 | @ |
| 8. | **Moral Stage 6** | 49.99 | 48.30 | 44.72 | 27.39 | 27.39 | 27.23 | 1.303 | @ |
| 9. | **Pre-Conventional level** | 51.65 | 52.08 | 48.06 | 14.34 | 14.66 | 16.21 | 2.663 | @ |
| 10. | **Conventional Level** | 151.01 | 151.31 | 161.88 | 32.97 | 33.56 | 34.50 | 3.772 | * |
| 11. | **Post-Conventional Level** | 126.72 | 126.61 | 123.47 | 40.58 | 38.95 | 41.56 | 0.238 | @ |
| 12. | **Moral Judgment** | 329.37 | 330.01 | 333.41 | 27.00 | 29.99 | 31.52 | 0.620 | @ |

** Indicates significant at 0.01 level; * Indicates significant at 0.05 level;
@ Indicates not significant at 0.05 level
$N_1$ = 359; $N_2$ = 641; $N_3$ = 80; df = 2,1077.

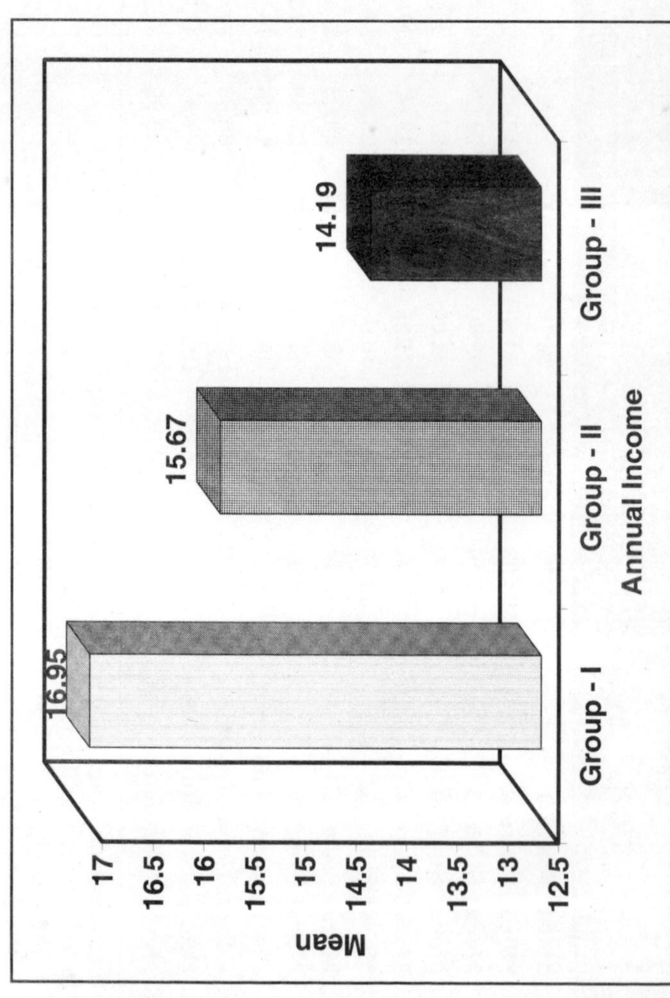


**Fig. 5.34: Bar Diagram Showing the Mean Values of Annual Income on the Reasoning of Moral Stage 1**

It is clear from Table 5.48 that the computed value of 'F' for moral stage 2, moral stage 4, moral stage 4A, moral stage 5A, moral stage 5B, moral stage 6, pre-conventional level, post-conventional level and moral judgment is less than table value of 'F' (2.99) for 2 and 1077 df at 0.05 level. Hence Hypothesis 48 is accepted. It is concluded that the annual income do not have significant influence on the reasoning of moral stage 2, moral stage 4, moral stage 4A, moral stage 5A, moral stage 5B, moral stage 6, pre-conventional level, post-conventional level and moral judgment.

The bar diagram showing the mean values of annual income on the reasoning of moral stage 1 is given Fig. 5.34.

*Father's Education*

On the basis of father's education, the students are divided into four groups. Group I is formed with illiterate fathers Group II formed with up to high educational fathers. Group III is formed with graduate fathers and Group IV is formed with post graduation and above and professional educational fathers. The impact of father's education on the reasoning of moral judgment of Intermediate students is investigated. The corresponding each moral stage, moral level and moral judgment of the four groups were analyzed accordingly. The mean values of moral judgment scores for the four groups were tested for significance by employing one-way ANOVA technique. The following hypothesis is framed.

**Hypothesis 49**

There would be no significant impact of 'Father's Education' on the reasoning of each moral stage, moral level and moral judgment of Intermediate students.

The above hypothesis is tested by employing one-way ANOVA technique. The results are presented in Table 5.49.

It is clear from Table 5.49 that the computed value of 'F' for moral stage 1, moral stage 2, moral stage 3, moral stage 4, moral stage 4A, moral stage 5A, moral stage 5B, moral stage 6, pre-conventional level, conventional level, post-

**Table 5.49: Influence of Father's Education on the Reasoning of Each Moral Stage, Moral Level and Moral Judgment**

| Sl. No. | Variable | Mean values | | | | SD values | | | | F-value | Level of significance |
|---|---|---|---|---|---|---|---|---|---|---|---|
| | | I | II | III | IV | I | II | III | IV | | |
| 1. | **Moral Stage 1** | 16.11 | 16.02 | 15.15 | 17.55 | 6.61 | 6.60 | 6.48 | 5.98 | 1.797 | @ |
| 2. | **Moral Stage 2** | 35.61 | 36.50 | 34.25 | 32.50 | 14.08 | 13.15 | 13.66 | 14.39 | 1.984 | @ |
| 3. | **Moral Stage 3** | 51.23 | 53.35 | 53.79 | 49.97 | 20.27 | 20.40 | 21.96 | 19.11 | 1.224 | @ |
| 4. | **Moral Stage 4** | 68.79 | 68.11 | 73.31 | 67.61 | 27.74 | 26.19 | 29.11 | 29.21 | 1.544 | @ |
| 5. | **Moral Stage 4A** | 31.62 | 29.66 | 28.16 | 34.67 | 18.71 | 18.53 | 21.59 | 21.17 | 2.269 | @ |
| 6. | **Moral Stage 5A** | 39.56 | 39.91 | 41.64 | 35.46 | 25.72 | 74.98 | 26.33 | 21.89 | 0.745 | @ |
| 7. | **Moral Stage 5B** | 38.28 | 37.28 | 39.72 | 35.87 | 24.79 | 21.93 | 21.55 | 21.39 | 0.604 | @ |
| 8. | **Moral Stage 6** | 49.87 | 46.95 | 47.81 | 56.58 | 27.37 | 26.78 | 27.64 | 31.03 | 2.195 | @ |
| 9. | **Pre-Conventional Level** | 51.72 | 52.52 | 49.40 | 5.05 | 15.26 | 13.68 | 15.44 | 16.08 | 1.995 | @ |
| 10. | **Conventional Level** | 151.64 | 151.12 | 155.26 | 152.26 | 34.20 | 32.46 | 35.14 | 32.08 | 0.633 | @ |
| 11. | **Post-Conventional Level** | 127.70 | 124.15 | 129.17 | 127.91 | 41.70 | 37.38 | 38.74 | 45.73 | 0.927 | @ |
| 12. | **Moral Judgment** | 331.06 | 327.79 | 333.83 | 330.22 | 30.14 | 27.11 | 30.12 | 34.13 | 2.007 | @ |

@ Indicates not significant at 0.05 level

$N_1$ = 410; $N_2$ = 461; $N_3$ = 163; $N_4$ = 46; df = 3,1076.

conventional level and moral judgment is less than table value of 'F' (2.60) for 3 and 1076 df at 0.05 level. Hence, Hypothesis 49 is accepted. It is concluded that the father's education do not have significant influence on the reasoning of moral stage 1, moral stage 2, moral stage 3, moral stage 4, moral stage 4A, moral stage 5A, moral stage 5B, moral stage 6, pre-conventional level, conventional level, post-conventional level and moral judgment.

*Mother's Education*

On the basis of mother's education, the students are divided into two groups. Group I is formed with illiterate mothers Group II formed with literate mothers. The impact of mother's education on the reasoning of moral judgment of Intermediate students is investigated. The corresponding each moral stage, moral level and moral judgment of the two groups were analyzed accordingly. The mean values of moral judgment scores for the two groups were tested for significance by employing't' test the following hypothesis is framed.

**Hypothesis 50**

There would be no significant impact of 'Mother's Education' on the reasoning of each moral stage, moral level and moral judgment of Intermediate students.

The above hypothesis is tested by employing 't'-test. The results are presented in Table 5.50.

It is clear from Table 5.50 that the computed value of 't' for moral stage 1, moral stage 2, moral stage 3, moral stage 4, moral stage 4A, moral stage 5A, moral stage 5B, moral stage 6, pre-conventional level, conventional level, post-conventional level and moral judgment is less than table value of 't' (1.96) for 1 and 1078 df at 0.05 level. Hence, Hypothesis 50 is accepted. It is concluded that the mother's education do not have significant influence on the reasoning of moral stage 1, moral stage 2, moral stage 3, moral stage 4, moral stage 4A, moral stage 5A, moral stage 5B, moral stage 6, pre-conventional level, conventional level, post-conventional level and moral judgment.

**Table 5.50: Influence of Mother's Education on the Reasoning of Each Moral Stage, Moral Level and Moral Judgment**

| Sl. No. | Variable | Mean values | | SD values | | 't'-value | Level of signifi-cance |
|---|---|---|---|---|---|---|---|
| | | I | II | I | II | | |
| 1. | **Moral Stage 1** | 16.10 | 15.84 | 6.73 | 6.37 | 0.63 | @ |
| 2. | **Moral Stage 2** | 36.08 | 35.09 | 13.69 | 13.64 | 1.17 | @ |
| 3. | **Moral Stage 3** | 51.95 | 53.15 | 20.12 | 21.14 | 0.95 | @ |
| 4. | **Moral Stage 4** | 67.88 | 70.80 | 27.62 | 27.09 | 1.74 | @ |
| 5. | **Moral Stage 4A** | 30.69 | 30.00 | 18.61 | 20.10 | 0.58 | @ |
| 6. | **Moral Stage 5A** | 40.06 | 39.57 | 25.75 | 24.94 | 0.31 | @ |
| 7. | **Moral Stage 5B** | 37.34 | 38.81 | 23.27 | 22.61 | 1.04 | @ |
| 8. | **Moral Stage 6** | 49.94 | 46.81 | 27.26 | 27.51 | 1.86 | @ |
| 9. | **Pre-Conventional Level** | 52.17 | 50.93 | 14.46 | 15.02 | 1.36 | @ |
| 10. | **Conventional Level** | 150.52 | 153.95 | 33.55 | 33.47 | 1.67 | @ |
| 11. | **Post-Conventional Level** | 127.34 | 125.19 | 39.86 | 39.47 | 0.88 | @ |
| 12. | **Moral Judgment** | 330.03 | 330.08 | 29.03 | 29.35 | 0.03 | @ |

@ Indicates not significant at 0.05 level

$N_1$ = 616; $N_2$ = 464; df = 1,1078.

*Father's Occupation*

On the basis of father's occupation, the students are divided into three groups. Group I is formed with students of unemployed and labour fathers. Group II formed with fathers of caste occupation/small business/cultivation/clerk/elementary teacher. Group III is formed with fathers of high school teacher/ technician/equal cadre employees and fathers of high Government official/land lord/professor. The impact of father's occupation on the reasoning of moral judgment of Intermediate students is investigated. The corresponding moral judgment of the three groups were analyzed accordingly. The mean values of moral judgment scores for the three groups were tested for significance by employing one-way ANOVA technique. The following hypothesis is framed.

**Hypothesis 51**

There would be no significant impact of 'Father's Occupation' on the reasoning of each moral stage, moral level and moral judgment of Intermediate students.

The above hypothesis is tested by employing one-way ANOVA technique. The results are presented in Table 5.51.

It is clear from Table 5.51 that the computed values of 'F' for moral stage 3 and post-conventional level is greater than table value of 'F' (2.99) for 2 and 1077 at 0.05 level. Hence Hypothesis 51 is rejected. It is concluded that the father occupation has significant influence on the reasoning of moral stage 3 and post-conventional level.

It is clear from Table 5.52 that the computed value of 'F' for moral stage 1, moral stage 2, moral stage 4, moral stage 4A, moral stage 5A, moral stage 5B, moral stage 6, pre-conventional level, conventional level and moral judgment is less than table value of 'F' (2.99) for 2 and 1077 df at 0.05 level. Hence Hypothesis 51 is accepted. It is concluded that the father occupation do not have significant influence on the reasoning of moral stage 1, moral stage 2, moral stage 4, moral stage 4A, moral stage 5A, moral stage 5B, moral stage 6, pre-conventional level, conventional level and moral judgment.

**Table 5.51: Influence of Father's Occupation on the Reasoning of each Moral Stage, Moral Level and Moral Judgment**

| Sl. No. | Variable | Mean values | | | SD values | | | F-value | Level of significance |
|---|---|---|---|---|---|---|---|---|---|
| | | I | II | III | I | II | III | | |
| 1. | **Moral Stage 1** | 15.68 | 16.18 | 16.38 | 6.56 | 6.71 | 5.99 | 0.927 | @ |
| 2. | **Moral Stage 2** | 35.89 | 35.48 | 35.43 | 13.43 | 13.70 | 14.56 | 0.127 | @ |
| 3. | **Moral Stage 3** | 51.89 | 53.95 | 49.29 | 20.03 | 21.25 | 18.99 | 3.868 | * |
| 4. | **Moral Stage 4** | 68.34 | 69.98 | 68.65 | 27.09 | 27.78 | 27.13 | 0.449 | @ |
| 5. | **Moral Stage 4A** | 31.83 | 29.22 | 29.70 | 18.90 | 19.72 | 18.35 | 2.299 | @ |
| 6. | **Moral Stage 5A** | 39.79 | 39.11 | 43.32 | 25.16 | 24.92 | 28.04 | 1.284 | @ |
| 7. | **Moral Stage 5B** | 38.04 | 37.33 | 40.49 | 23.86 | 20.16 | 22.91 | 0.888 | @ |
| 8. | **Moral Stage 6** | 49.36 | 47.49 | 50.35 | 28.21 | 26.25 | 28.87 | 0.828 | @ |
| 9. | **Pre-Conventional Level** | 51.58 | 51.66 | 51.82 | 14.48 | 14.90 | 14.85 | 0.013 | @ |
| 10. | **Conventional Level** | 152.07 | 153.15 | 146.64 | 33.24 | 33.82 | 33.13 | 1.764 | @ |
| 11. | **Post-Conventional Level** | 127.19 | 123.92 | 134.15 | 41.24 | 37.96 | 39.72 | 3.272 | * |
| 12. | **Moral Judgment** | 330.84 | 328.74 | 332.61 | 30.18 | 28.60 | 27.08 | 1.118 | @ |

* Indicates significant at 0.05 level;
@ Indicates not significant at 0.05 level
$N_1$ = 464; $N_2$ = 501; $N_3$ =115; df = 2,1077.

**Table 5.52: Influence of Mother's Occupation on the Reasoning of each Moral Stage, Moral Level and Moral Judgment**

| Sl. No. | Variable | Mean values | | SD values | | 't'-value | Level of significance |
|---|---|---|---|---|---|---|---|
| | | I | II | I | II | | |
| 1. | **Moral Stage 1** | 15.92 | 16.90 | 6.58 | 6.41 | 1.26 | @ |
| 2. | **Moral Stage 2** | 35.63 | 36.03 | 13.75 | 12.65 | 0.26 | @ |
| 3. | **Moral Stage 3** | 52.58 | 50.86 | 20.87 | 15.92 | 0.87 | @ |
| 4. | **Moral Stage 4** | 69.31 | 66.64 | 27.57 | 25.23 | 0.87 | @ |
| 5. | **Moral Stage 4A** | 30.27 | 32.05 | 19.12 | 21.11 | 0.70 | @ |
| 6. | **Moral Stage 5A** | 40.21 | 34.93 | 25.67 | 20.74 | 2.06 | * |
| 7. | **Moral Stage 5B** | 37.79 | 40.41 | 22.88 | 24.42 | 0.89 | @ |
| 8. | **Moral Stage 6** | 48.40 | 51.27 | 27.21 | 29.92 | 0.79 | @ |
| 9. | **Pre-Conventional Level** | 51.55 | 52.93 | 14.80 | 13.43 | 0.84 | @ |
| 10. | **Conventional Level** | 152.17 | 149.55 | 33.55 | 33.61 | 0.64 | @ |
| 11. | **Post-Conventional Level** | 126.40 | 126.61 | 39.79 | 38.58 | 0.04 | @ |
| 12. | **Moral Judgment** | 330.12 | 329.09 | 28.48 | 37.37 | 0.23 | @ |

* Indicates significant at 0.05 level;
@ Indicates not significant at 0.05 level
$N_1$ = 1007; $N_2$ = 73; df = 1,1008.

The Bar diagram showing the mean values of father's occupation on the reasoning of moral stage 3 is given in Fig. 5.35.

*Mother's Occupation*

On the basis of mother's occupation, the students are divided into two groups. Group I is formed with unemployed and labourers mothers. Group II formed with mothers of employed. The impact of mother's occupation on the reasoning of moral judgment of Intermediate students is investigated. The corresponding moral judgment of the two groups were analyzed accordingly. The mean values of moral judgment scores for the two groups were tested for significance by employing 't' test. The following hypothesis is framed.

**Hypothesis 52**

There would be no significant impact of 'Mother's Occupation' on the reasoning of each moral stage, moral level and moral judgment of Intermediate students.

The above hypothesis is tested by employing 't' test. The results are presented in Table 5.52.

It is clear from Table 5.52 that the computed value of 't' for moral stage 5A is greater than table value of 't' (1.96) for 1 and 1078 at 0.05 level. Hence Hypothesis 52 is rejected. It is concluded that the mother's occupation has significant influence on the reasoning of moral stage 5A.

It is clear from Table 5.52 that the computed value of 't' for moral stage 1, moral stage 2, moral stage 3, moral stage 4, moral stage 4A, moral stage 5B, moral stage 6, pre-conventional level, conventional level, post-conventional level and moral judgment is less than table value of 't' (1.96) for 1 and 1078 df at 0.05 level. Hence Hypothesis 52 is accepted. It is concluded that the mother occupation do not have significant influence on the reasoning of moral stage 1, moral stage 2, moral stage 3, moral stage 4, moral stage 4A, moral stage 5B, moral stage 6, pre-conventional level, conventional level, post-conventional level and moral judgment.

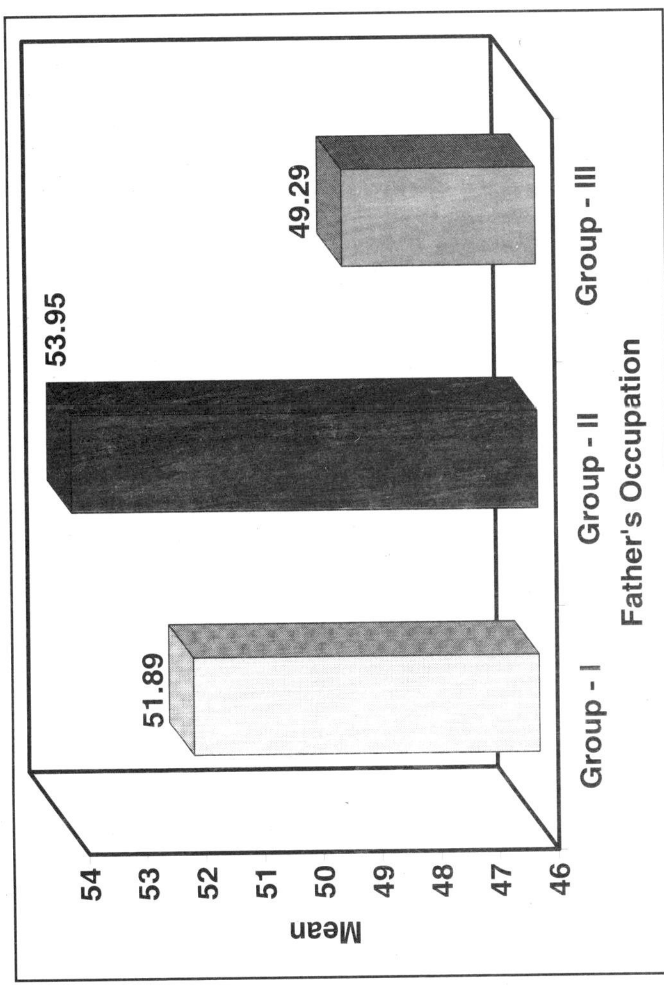


**Fig. 5.35: Bar Diagram Showing the Mean values of Father's Occupation on the Reasoning of Moral Stage 3**

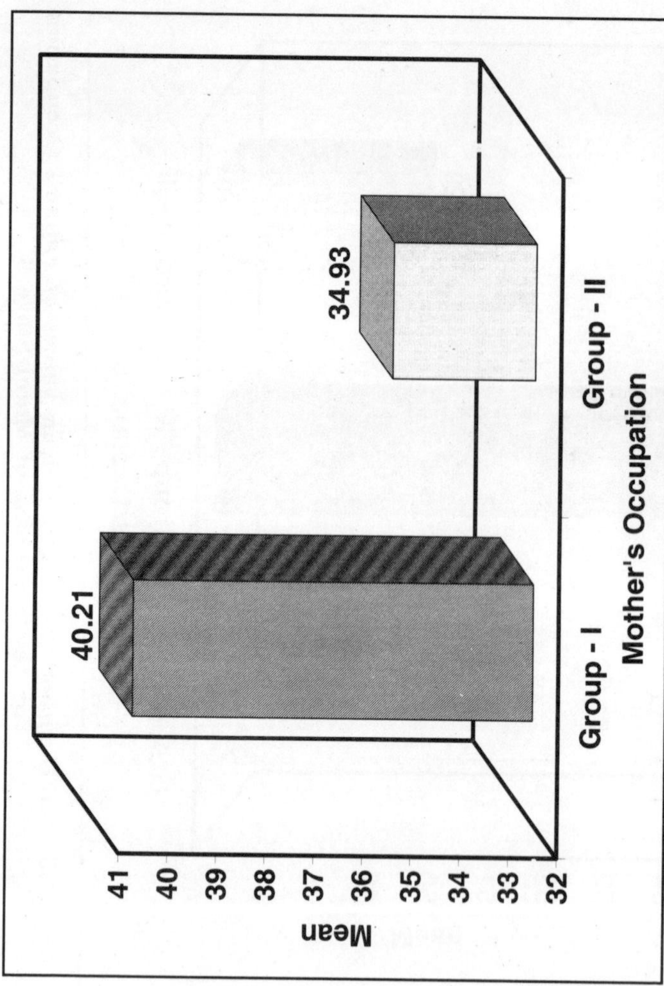


**Fig. 5.36: Bar Diagram Showing the Mean Values of Mother's Occupation on the Reasoning of Moral Stage 5A**

The Bar diagram showing the mean values of mother's occupation on the reasoning of moral stage 5A is given in Fig. 5.36.

*Size of the Family*

Size of the family means total members of the family. On the basis of size of the family, the students are divided into four groups. Group I is formed with three members of the family. Group II formed with four members of the family. Group III is formed with five members of the family and Group IV is formed with above five members of the family. The impact of size of the family on the reasoning of moral judgment of Intermediate students is investigated. The corresponding moral judgment of the four groups were analyzed accordingly. The mean values of moral judgment scores for the four groups were tested for significance by employing one-way ANOVA technique. The following hypothesis is framed.

**Hypothesis 53**

There would be no significant impact of 'Size of the Family' on the reasoning of each moral stage, moral level and moral judgment of Intermediate students.

The above hypothesis is tested by employing one-way ANOVA technique. The results are presented in Table 5.53.

It is clear from Table 5.53 that the computed values of 'F' for moral stage 1, moral stage 2, moral stage 3, moral stage 4, moral stage 4A, moral stage 5A, moral stage 5B, moral stage 6, pre-conventional level, conventional level, post-conventional level and moral judgment is less than table value of 'F' (2.60) for 3 and 1076 df at 0.05 level. Hence Hypothesis 53 is accepted. It is concluded that the size of the family do not have significant influence on the reasoning of moral stage 1, moral stage 2, moral stage 3, moral stage 4, moral stage 4A, moral stage 5A, moral stage 5B, moral stage 6, pre-conventional level, conventional level, post-conventional level and moral judgment.

**Table 5.53: Influence of Size of the Family on the Reasoning of Each Moral Stage, Moral Level and Moral Judgment**

| Sl. No. | Variable | Mean values | | | | SD values | | | | F-value | Level of significance |
|---|---|---|---|---|---|---|---|---|---|---|---|
| | | I | II | III | IV | I | II | III | IV | | |
| 1. | **Moral Stage 1** | 17.19 | 15.80 | 16.32 | 15.51 | 6.62 | 6.13 | 7.05 | 6.49 | 1.779 | @ |
| 2. | **Moral Stage 2** | 32.25 | 36.16 | 35.27 | 36.40 | 13.17 | 13.65 | 13.93 | 13.39 | 2.201 | @ |
| 3. | **Moral Stage 3** | 52.03 | 52.99 | 52.22 | 52.17 | 18.36 | 19.80 | 21.45 | 21.10 | 0.130 | @ |
| 4. | **Moral Stage 4** | 72.38 | 68.02 | 69.35 | 69.45 | 25.82 | 27.30 | 27.64 | 27.69 | 0.599 | @ |
| 5. | **Moral Stage 4A** | 31.25 | 30.37 | 31.25 | 29.15 | 17.86 | 19.68 | 19.63 | 18.57 | 0.669 | @ |
| 6. | **Moral Stage 5A** | 39.06 | 41.14 | 39.07 | 39.17 | 22.22 | 27.35 | 22.64 | 26.59 | 0.508 | @ |
| 7. | **Moral Stage 5B** | 36.95 | 36.48 | 37.22 | 41.16 | 22.63 | 22.20 | 22.03 | 24.91 | 2.516 | @ |
| 8. | **Moral Stage 6** | 47.34 | 48.09 | 49.07 | 49.07 | 28.43 | 27.03 | 27.99 | 26.89 | 0.161 | @ |
| 9. | **Pre-Conventional Level** | 49.44 | 51.96 | 51.58 | 51.91 | 13.26 | 14.29 | 15.57 | 14.56 | 0.689 | @ |
| 10. | **Conventional Level** | 155.66 | 151.39 | 152.83 | 150.77 | 29.85 | 31.82 | 35.69 | 34.08 | 0.553 | @ |
| 11. | **Post-Conventional Level** | 123.36 | 125.71 | 125.36 | 129.50 | 35.34 | 39.98 | 39.65 | 40.39 | 0.843 | @ |
| 12. | **Moral Judgment** | 328.45 | 329.06 | 329.77 | 332.17 | 29.36 | 28.45 | 31.26 | 27.28 | 0.729 | @ |

@ Indicates not significant at 0.05 level

$N_1$ = 80; $N_2$ = 379; $N_3$ =339; $N_4$ =282; df = 3,1076.

*Economic Position of the Family*

On the basis of economic position of the family, the students are divided into three groups. Group I is formed rich economic position. Group II formed with medium economic position and Group III is formed with poor economic position of the family. The impact of economic position of the family on the reasoning of moral judgment of Intermediate students is investigated. The corresponding each moral stage, each moral level and moral judgment of the three groups were analyzed accordingly. The mean values of moral judgment scores for the three groups were tested for significance by employing one-way ANOVA technique. The following hypothesis is framed.

**Hypothesis 54**

There would be no significant impact of 'Economic Position of the Family' on the reasoning of each moral stage, moral level and moral judgment of Intermediate students.

The above hypothesis is tested by employing one-way ANOVA technique. The results are presented in Table 5.54.

It is clear from Table 5.54 that the computed values of 'F' for moral stage 3, moral stage 4 and conventional level is greater than table value of 'F' (2.99) for 2 and 1077 at 0.05 level. Hence Hypothesis 54 is rejected. It is concluded that the economic position of the family has significant influence on the reasoning of moral stage 3 and moral stage 4 and conventional level.

It is clear from Table 5.54 that the computed values of 'F' for moral stage 1, moral stage 2, moral stage 4A,moral stage 5A, moral stage 5B, moral stage 6, pre-conventional level, post-conventional level and moral judgment is less than table value of 'F' (2.99) for 2 and 1077 df at 0.05 level. Hence Hypothesis 54 is accepted. It is concluded that the economic position of the family do not have significant influence on the reasoning of moral stage 1, moral stage 2, moral stage 4A, moral stage 5A, moral stage 5B, moral stage 6, pre-conventional level, post-conventional level and moral judgment.

**Table 5.54: Influence of Economic Position of the Family on the Reasoning of Each Moral Stage, Moral Level and Moral Judgment**

| S. No. | Variable | Mean values | | | SD values | | | F-value | Level of significance |
|---|---|---|---|---|---|---|---|---|---|
| | | I | II | III | I | II | III | | |
| 1. | **Moral Stage 1** | 15.19 | 15.86 | 16.70 | 6.16 | 6.58 | 6.64 | 1.874 | @ |
| 2. | **Moral Stage 2** | 34.96 | 35.36 | 36.95 | 12.98 | 13.63 | 14.01 | 1.238 | @ |
| 3. | **Moral Stage 3** | 51.87 | 53.34 | 49.38 | 20.13 | 20.64 | 20.15 | 3.187 | * |
| 4. | **Moral Stage 4** | 74.77 | 69.59 | 65.75 | 27.31 | 28.14 | 24.18 | 3.132 | * |
| 5. | **Moral Stage 4A** | 31.38 | 29.74 | 32.53 | 16.72 | 19.43 | 19.20 | 1.879 | @ |
| 6. | **Moral Stage 5A** | 40.77 | 39.92 | 39.30 | 22.20 | 25.81 | 24.76 | 0.095 | @ |
| 7. | **Moral Stage 5B** | 35.87 | 38.14 | 37.97 | 24.52 | 23.50 | 20.47 | 0.293 | @ |
| 8. | **Moral Stage 6** | 50.42 | 48.51 | 48.38 | 29.11 | 27.78 | 26.22 | 0.155 | @ |
| 9. | **Pre-Conventional Level** | 50.15 | 51.22 | 53.65 | 14.82 | 14.87 | 13.90 | 2.668 | @ |
| 10. | **Conventional Level** | 158.03 | 152.67 | 147.66 | 32.83 | 34.25 | 30.55 | 3.014 | * |
| 11. | **Post-Conventional Level** | 127.06 | 126.47 | 125.65 | 41.46 | 40.10 | 37.61 | 0.054 | @ |
| 12. | **Moral Judgment** | 335.23 | 330.46 | 326.96 | 33.47 | 29.36 | 26.63 | 2.317 | @ |

* Indicates significant at 0.05 level; @ Indicates not significant at 0.05 level

$N_1$ = 65; $N_2$ = 800; $N_3$ =215; df = 2,1077.

The Bar diagram showing the mean values of economic position of the family on the reasoning of conventional level is given in Fig. 5.37.

*Type of the Family*

On the basis of type of the family, the students are divided into two groups. Group I is formed nuclear family and Group II formed with joint family. The impact of type of the family on the reasoning of moral judgment of Intermediate students is investigated. The corresponding moral judgment of the two groups were analyzed accordingly. The mean values of moral judgment scores for the two groups were tested for significance by employing 't' test. The following hypothesis is framed.

**Hypothesis 55**

There would be no significant impact of 'Type of the Family' on the reasoning of each moral stage, moral level and moral judgment of Intermediate students.

The above hypothesis is tested by employing 't' test. The results are presented in Table 5.55.

It is clear from Table 5.55 that the computed values of 't' for moral stage 4, conventional level and moral judgment is greater than table value of 't' (1.96) for 1 and 1078 at 0.05 level. Hence Hypothesis 55 is rejected. It is concluded that the type of the family has significant influence on the reasoning of moral stage 4, conventional level and moral judgment.

The Bar diagram showing the mean values of type of the family on the reasoning of moral judgment is given in Fig. 5.38.

It is clear from Table 5.55 that the computed values of 't' for moral stage 1, moral stage 2, moral stage 3, moral stage 4A, moral stage 5A, moral stage 5B, moral stage 6, pre-conventional level and post-conventional level is less than table value of 't' (1.96) for 1 and 1078 df at 0.05 level. Hence Hypothesis 55 is accepted. It is concluded that the type of the family do not have significant influence on the reasoning of moral stage 1, moral stage 2, moral stage 3, moral stage 4A,

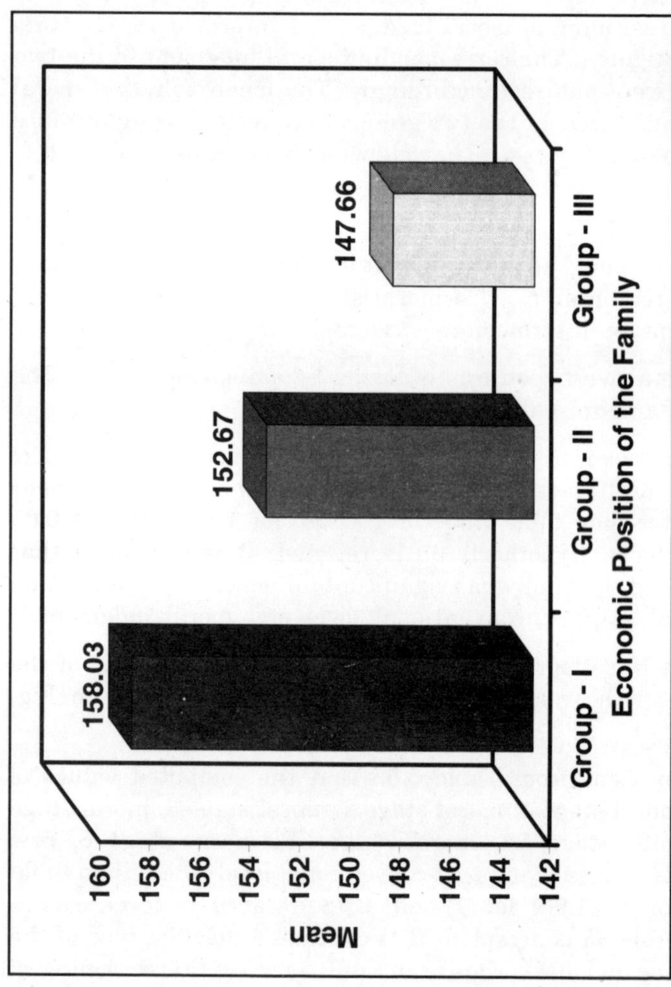


**Fig. 5.37: Bar Diagram Showing the Mean Values of Economic Position of the Family on the Reasoning of Conventional Level**

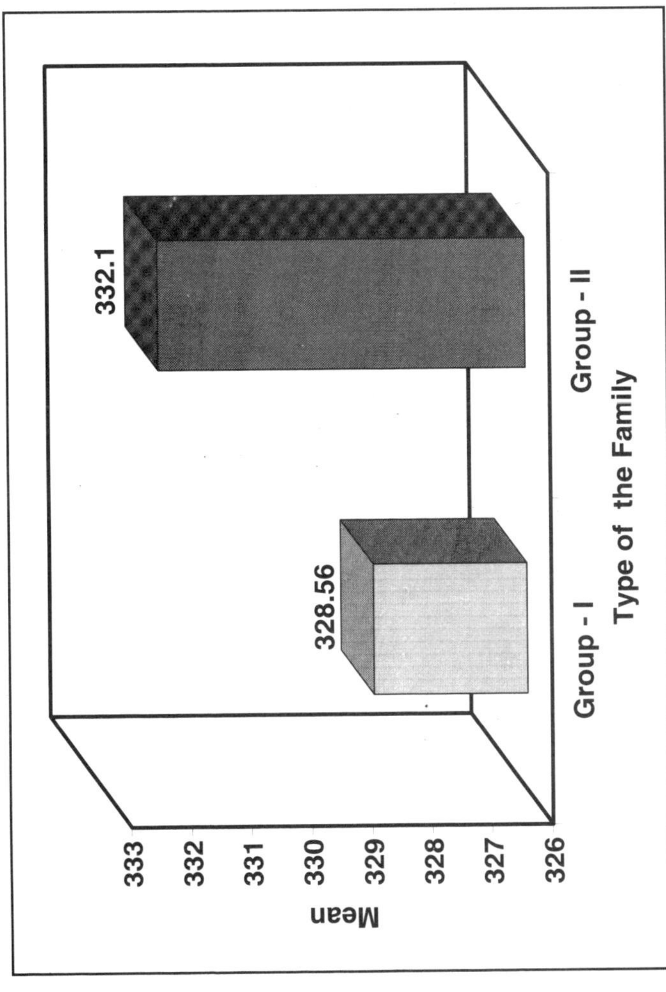


**Fig. 5.38: Bar Diagram showing the Mean Values of Type of the Family on the Reasoning of Moral Judgment**

**Table 5.55: Influence of Type of the Family on the Reasoning of Each Moral Stage, Moral Level and Moral Judgment**

| Sl. No. | Variable | Mean values | | SD values | | 't'-value | Level of significance |
|---|---|---|---|---|---|---|---|
| | | I | II | I | II | | |
| 1. | **Moral Stage 1** | 16.30 | 15.56 | 6.65 | 6.45 | 1.83 | @ |
| 2. | **Moral Stage 2** | 35.44 | 35.95 | 13.97 | 13.27 | 0.62 | @ |
| 3. | **Moral Stage 3** | 52.40 | 52.56 | 21.13 | 19.79 | 0.13 | @ |
| 4. | **Moral Stage 4** | 67.32 | 71.63 | 26.96 | 27.87 | 2.54 | * |
| 5. | **Moral Stage 4A** | 30.38 | 30.41 | 19.03 | 19.59 | 0.02 | @ |
| 6. | **Moral Stage 5A** | 41.03 | 38.22 | 26.00 | 24.47 | 1.82 | @ |
| 7. | **Moral Stage 5B** | 38.04 | 37.87 | 22.34 | 23.88 | 0.12 | @ |
| 8. | **Moral Stage 6** | 47.65 | 49.91 | 28.00 | 26.52 | 1.35 | @ |
| 9. | **Pre-Conventional Level** | 51.73 | 51.51 | 15.31 | 13.84 | 0.25 | @ |
| 10. | **Conventional Level** | 150.11 | 154.60 | 33.72 | 33.15 | 2.18 | * |
| 11. | **Post-Conventional Level** | 126.72 | 125.99 | 40.07 | 39.18 | 0.30 | @ |
| 12. | **Moral Judgment** | 328.56 | 332.10 | 28.91 | 29.40 | 1.97 | * |

* Indicates significant at 0.05 level; @ Indicates not significant at 0.05 level

$N_1$ = 626; $N_2$ = 442; df = 1,1078.

moral stage 5A, moral stage 5B, moral stage 6, pre-conventional level and post-conventional level.

*Medium of the Study*

On the basis of medium of the study, the students are divided into two groups. Group I is formed with Telugu medium and Group II formed with English medium. The impact of medium of the study on the reasoning of moral judgment of Intermediate students is investigated. The corresponding moral judgment of the two groups were analyzed accordingly. The mean values of moral judgment scores for the two groups were tested for significance by employing 't' test. The following hypothesis is framed.

**Hypothesis 56**

There would be no significant impact of 'Medium of the Study' on the reasoning of each moral stage, moral level and moral judgment of Intermediate students.

The above hypothesis is tested by employing 't' test. The results are presented in Table 5.56.

It is clear from Table 5.56 that the computed values of 't' for moral stage 5B and moral judgment is greater than table value of 't' (2.58) for 1 and 1078 at 0.01 level. Hence Hypothesis 56 is rejected. It is concluded that the medium of the study has significant influence on the reasoning of moral stage 5B and moral judgment. Similar result was reported by Prabhu (1996).

It is clear from Table 5.56 that the computed values of 't' for moral stage 1, moral stage 3 and post-conventional level is greater than table value of 't' (1.96) for 1 and 1078 at 0.05 level. Hence Hypothesis 56 is rejected. It is concluded that the medium of the study has significant influence on the reasoning of moral stage 1, moral stage 3 and post-conventional level.

It is clear from Table 5.56 that the computed values of 't' for, moral stage 2, moral stage 4, moral stage 4A, moral stage 5A, moral stage 6, pre-conventional level and

**Table 5.56: Influence of Medium of the Study on the Reasoning of each Moral Stage, Moral Level and Moral Judgment**

| Sl. No. | Variable | Mean values | | SD values | | 't'-value | Level of significance |
|---|---|---|---|---|---|---|---|
| | | I | II | I | II | | |
| 1. | **Moral Stage 1** | 15.63 | 16.51 | 6.63 | 6.47 | 2.18 | * |
| 2. | **Moral Stage 2** | 35.52 | 35.85 | 13.39 | 14.08 | 0.39 | @ |
| 3. | **Moral Stage 3** | 53.64 | 50.77 | 20.14 | 21.07 | 2.24 | * |
| 4. | **Moral Stage 4** | 68.06 | 70.69 | 26.05 | 29.23 | 1.52 | @ |
| 5. | **Moral Stage 4A** | 30.52 | 30.21 | 18.52 | 22.29 | 0.24 | @ |
| 6. | **Moral Stage 5A** | 39.63 | 40.17 | 25.56 | 25.17 | 0.34 | @ |
| 7. | **Moral Stage 5B** | 39.54 | 35.70 | 23.52 | 22.04 | 2.73 | ** |
| 8. | **Moral Stage 6** | 49.54 | 47.24 | 26.98 | 27.96 | 1.35 | @ |
| 9. | **Pre-Conventional Level** | 51.14 | 52.36 | 14.55 | 14.92 | 1.33 | @ |
| 10. | **Conventional Level** | 152.21 | 151.67 | 32.18 | 35.45 | 0.26 | @ |
| 11. | **Post-Conventional Level** | 128.70 | 123.12 | 39.41 | 39.90 | 2.27 | * |
| 12. | **Moral Judgment** | 332.06 | 327.15 | 29.22 | 28.84 | 2.74 | ** |

** Indicates significant at 0.01 level;
* Indicates significant at 0.05 level;
@ Indicates not significant at 0.05 level
$N_1$ = 638; $N_2$ = 442; df = 1,1078.

conventional level is less than table value of 't' (1.96) for 1 and 1078 df at 0.05 level. Hence Hypothesis 56 is accepted. It is concluded that medium of the study do not have significant influence on the reasoning of moral stage 2, moral stage 4, moral stage 4A, moral stage 5A, moral stage 6, pre-conventional level and conventional level.

The Bar diagram showing the mean values of medium of the study on the reasoning of moral judgment is given in Fig. 5.39.

*Course of the Study*

Course of the study means Intermediate students are taken some specializations for example M.P.C., Bi.P.C., C.E.C., and H.E.C. etc., On the basis of course of the study, the students are divided into four groups. Group I is formed with M.P.C. students Group II formed with Bi.P.C. students, Groups III is formed with C.E.C. students and Group IV is formed with H.E.C. students. The impact of course of the study on the reasoning of moral judgment of Intermediate students is investigated. The corresponding moral judgment of the four groups were analyzed accordingly. The mean values of moral judgment scores for the four groups were tested for significance by employing one-way ANOVA technique. The following hypothesis is framed.

**Hypothesis 57**

There would be no significant impact of 'Course of the Study' on the reasoning of each moral stage, moral level and moral judgment of Intermediate students.

The above hypothesis is tested by employing one-way ANOVA Technique. The results are presented in Table 5.57.

It is clear from Table 5.57 that the computed values of 'F' for moral stage 1, moral stage 3, moral stage 4, pre-conventional level and conventional level is greater than table value of 'F' (3.78) for 3 and 1076 at 0.01 level. Hence Hypothesis 57 is rejected. It is concluded that the course of the study has significant influence on the reasoning of moral stage 1, moral

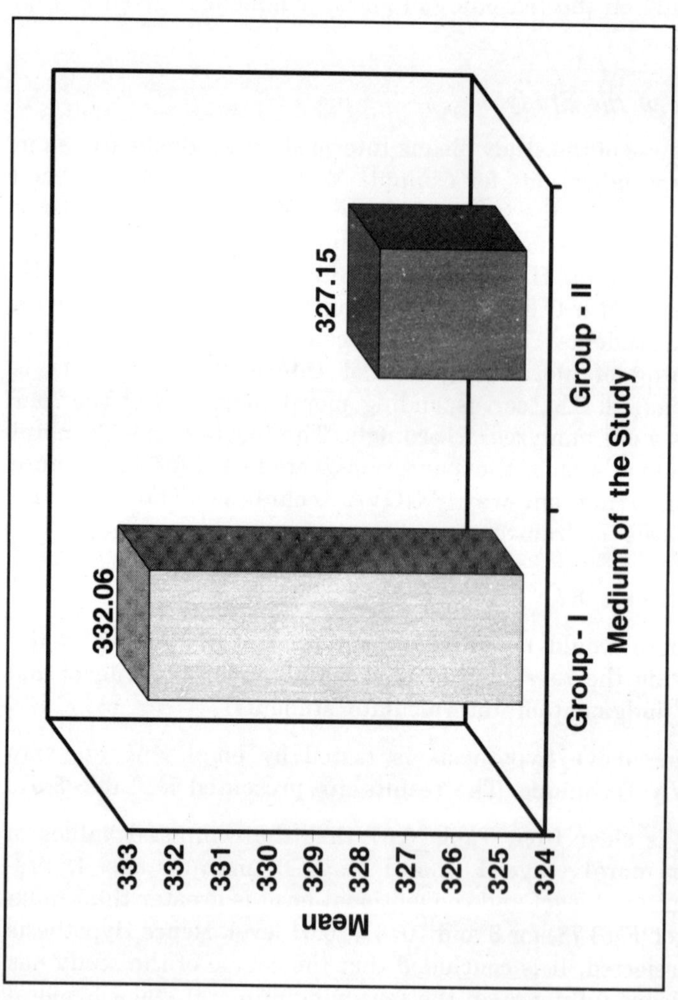


**Fig. 5.39: Bar Diagram Showing the Mean Values of Medium of the Study on the Reasoning of Moral Judgment**

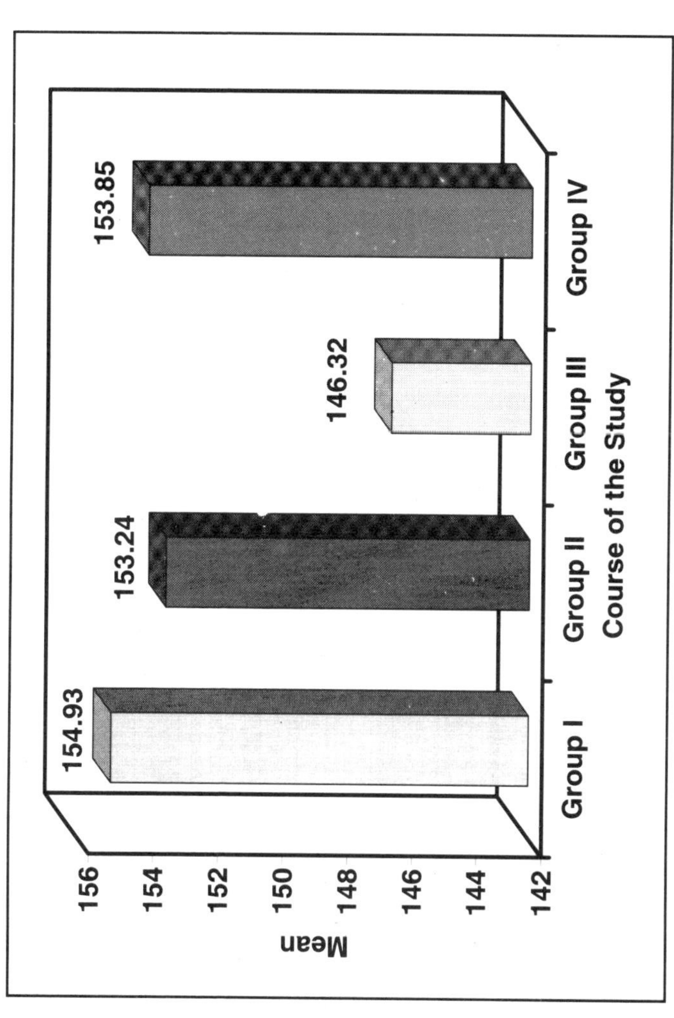


**Figure 5.40: Bar Diagram Showing the Mean Values of Course of the Study on the Reasoning of Conventional Level**

**Table 5.57: Influence of Course of the Study on the Reasoning of Each Moral Stage, Moral Level and Moral Judgment**

| Sl. No. | Variable | Mean values | | | | SD values | | | | F-value | Level of significance |
|---|---|---|---|---|---|---|---|---|---|---|---|
| | | I | II | III | IV | I | II | III | IV | | |
| 1. | **Moral Stage 1** | 15.44 | 15.39 | 16.99 | 16.40 | 6.63 | 6.73 | 6.28 | 6.57 | 4.260 | ** |
| 2. | **Moral Stage 2** | 35.58 | 33.87 | 36.71 | 35.67 | 13.87 | 14.59 | 13.02 | 12.86 | 1.638 | @ |
| 3. | **Moral Stage 3** | 53.91 | 54.06 | 48.83 | 54.32 | 21.46 | 22.12 | 18.68 | 17.70 | 4.806 | ** |
| 4. | **Moral Stage 4** | 72.60 | 68.49 | 64.66 | 68.10 | 28.29 | 27.80 | 25.63 | 25.97 | 5.546 | ** |
| 5. | **Moral Stage 4A** | 28.42 | 30.69 | 32.83 | 31.43 | 19.53 | 19.66 | 19.20 | 16.43 | 3.523 | * |
| 6. | **Moral Stage 5A** | 38.18 | 41.75 | 41.90 | 38.04 | 24.62 | 24.94 | 26.66 | 25.09 | 1.896 | @ |
| 7. | **Moral Stage 5B** | 37.76 | 42.07 | 36.80 | 35.65 | 23.61 | 22.97 | 22.25 | 21.61 | 2.508 | @ |
| 8. | **Moral Stage 6** | 48.82 | 48.00 | 49.28 | 46.50 | 28.18 | 27.95 | 25.77 | 27.72 | 0.308 | @ |
| 9. | **Pre-Conventional Level** | 51.03 | 49.26 | 53.71 | 52.10 | 14.86 | 16.07 | 13.68 | 13.87 | 3.980 | ** |
| 10. | **Conventional Level** | 154.93 | 153.24 | 146.32 | 153.85 | 34.22 | 33.80 | 32.32 | 31.58 | 4.505 | ** |
| 11. | **Post-Conventional Level** | 124.76 | 131.82 | 127.98 | 120.19 | 39.98 | 40.60 | 39.40 | 36.38 | 2.391 | @ |
| 12. | **Moral Judgment** | 330.72 | 334.31 | 328.01 | 326.13 | 28.83 | 31.18 | 27.85 | 30.09 | 2.494 | @ |

** Indicates significant at 0.01 level; * Indicates significant at 0.05 level;
@ Indicates not significant at 0.05 level
$N_1$ = 479; $N_2$ = 175; $N_3$=321; $N_4$ = 105; df = 3,1076.

stage 3, moral stage 4, pre-conventional level and conventional level.

The Bar diagram showing the mean values of course of the study on the reasoning of conventional level is given in Fig. 5.40.

It is clear from Table 5.57 that the computed value of 'F' for moral stage 4A is greater than table value of 'F' (2.60) for 3 and 1076 at 0.05 level. Hence Hypothesis 57 is rejected. It is concluded that the course of the study has significant influence on the reasoning of moral stage 4A.

It is clear from Table 5.57 that the computed values of 'F' for moral stage 2, moral stage 5A, moral stage 5B, moral stage 6, post-conventional level and moral judgment is less than table value of 'F' (2.60) for 3 and 1076 df at 0.05 level. Hence Hypothesis 57 is accepted. It is concluded that course of the study do not have significant influence on the reasoning of moral stage 2, moral stage 5A, moral stage 5B, moral stage 6, post-conventional level and moral judgment.

## STEP-WISE MULTIPLE REGRESSION ANALYSIS

This section deals with the analysis of the relative contribution or magnitude of the effect of each of the different independent variables to the dependent variable. The reasoning of moral judgment of Intermediate students is predicted with the help of independent variables.

It is appropriate to know the meaning and nature of regression analysis. Regression means to estimate or predict one variable with the help of other variable/variables. According to dictionary the term 'regression' means act of returning or 'going back'. In $19^{th}$ century, Francis Galton for the first time used the word 'regression' while studying the relationship between the height of father and sons. Galton found that the off spring of abnormally tall or short parents tend to 'regress' or 'step back' to the average population height. But the term 'regression' as now used in statistics is only a convenient term without having any reference to biometry. In regression analysis there are two types of variables. The variable whose value is influenced or is to be predicted is called dependent variable and the variable which influences values or is used for prediction, is called independent variables. The independent variable is also called regressor or predictor.

Now-a-days regression analysis is employed widely in all scientific disciplines, such as physical, natural and social sciences.

Correlation is a tool of ascertaining the degree of relationship between two variables. The objective of regression analysis is to study nature of relationship, between the variables the cause and effect relation is clearly indicated through regression analysis than by correlation. The step-wise multiple regression analysis is employed in the present investigation to predict the dependent variables with the help of independent variables.

As already mentioned, there are 40 variables in this investigation for the purpose of step-wise multiple regression analysis the variable number, description of the variable and symbol used are presented in Table 5.58.

**Table 5.58: Variable Number, Description of the Variable and Symbol Used**

| Variable No. (VN) | Description of the Variable | Symbol Used |
|---|---|---|
| 1. | Sex | S |
| 2. | Year of Study | YOS |
| 3. | Management | M |
| 4. | Region | R |
| 5. | Age | A |
| 6. | Annual Income | AI |
| 7. | Father's Education | FE |
| 8. | Mother's Education | ME |
| 9. | Father Occupation | FO |
| 10. | Mother Occupation | MO |
| 11. | Birth Order | BO |
| 12. | Size of the Family | SF |

| Variable No. (VN) | Description of the Variable | Symbol Used |
|---|---|---|
| 13. | Residence | RE |
| 14. | Community | C |
| 15. | Caste | CA |
| 16. | Locality | L |
| 17. | Economic Position of the Family | EPF |
| 18. | Medium of Study | MOS |
| 19. | Type of Family | TOF |
| 20. | Groups of Study | G |
| 21. | Academic Achievement in Languages | AAL |
| 22. | Academic Achievement in Non-Languages | AANL |
| 23. | Academic Achievement in Total | AAT |
| 24. | Socio-Economic Status | SES |
| 25. | 14 PF Factor A | FA |
| 26. | 14 PF Factor B | FB |
| 27. | 14 PF Factor C | FC |
| 28. | 14 PF Factor D | FD |
| 29. | 14 PF Factor E | FE |
| 30. | 14 PF Factor F | FF |
| 31. | 14 PF Factor G | FG |
| 32. | 14 PF Factor H | FH |
| 33. | 14 PF Factor I | FI |
| 34. | 14 PF Factor J | FJ |
| 35. | 14 PF Factor O | FO |
| 36. | 14 PF Factor $Q_2$ | $FQ_2$ |
| 37. | 14 PF Factor $Q_3$ | $FQ_3$ |
| 38. | 14 PF Factor $Q_4$ | $FQ_4$ |
| 39. | Intelligence | I |
| 40. | Moral Judgment | MMQ |

Variable number 40 is the dependent variable in the present investigation.

## Prediction of the Reasoning of Moral Judgment with the Help of Independent Variables

The relative contribution all the 39 independent variables (VN 1 to 39 in Table 85) to the moral judgment is dependent variable (VN 40) in Table 85 is investigated with the help of step-wise multiple regression analysis. The results of regression analysis are presented in Table 5.59.

It is observed from Table 5.59 where the results of Step-wise Multiple Regression Analysis carried out on the criterion variable namely, Moral Judgment ($X_1$) with the host of independent variables represented by $X_2$ to $X_7$. From the Table - 86 the multiple R in step 1 for the $X_2$ [RE (13)] is 0.115 it can explain about 1.3% of variance in $X_1$ that is criterion variable. Which is evident from the $R^2$ value (0.013 x 100). The F – Value for R is 14.39 with (1,1078) df which is significant at 0.01 level. The standard error of multiple estimate is 29.005 which represents that 68% of the obtained $X_1$ scores will lie with in the range of ± 29.005 points of predicted scores through $X_2$ [RE (13)]. The b-coefficient or partial regression coefficient is -6.66 which indicates that $X_1$ increases by -6.66 units for every unit increase in $X_2$ [RE (13)]. The 't'-value for b-coefficient is 3.79 which is significant at 0.01 level.

The general form of the multiple regression equation may be given as

$$X_1^1 = A + b_2 X_2 + b_3 X_3 + b_4 X_4 + \ldots + b_n X_n$$

where A = Constant

$b_2, b_3, b_4 \ldots b_n$ are partial regression coefficients.

$X_2, X_3, X_4 \ldots X_n$ are the scores on different independent variables.

$X_1^1$ = Predicted $X_1$ value.

With $X_2$ alone as a predictor variable the regression equation can be formed as follows the variable explained by $X_2$ [RE (13)]. Is about 1.317%. The constant A is 341.20, $b_1$ = -6.66.

The regression equation is 1st step written as

$X_1^1 = 341.20 + (-6.66)\ X_2$

$MMQ = 341.20 + (-6.66)\ RE.$

In the second step the next predictor variable include in the step wise analysis in $X_3$ [MOS(18)]. In this step the multiple R is 0.153 it indicates the strength of relationship between the dependent variable $X_1$ [MMQ (40)] and two independent variables viz; $X_2$ [RE(13)] and $X_3$ [MOS(18)] combined with optiomal weights the 'F' – value to test the significance of multiple R is 12.97(2,1077) df at 0.01 level. The $R^2$ value is in the step is 0.024 which explained 2.4% of the variance in $X_1$ [MMQ (40)] association with $X_2$ [RE(13)] and $X_3$ [MOS(18)] out of this variance 1.514 and 0.838 are employed by these two predictor variables respectively. The standard error of multiple estimate is 28.865 which shows that obtained $X_1$ [MMQ (40)] values to lie with in the range of ± 28.865 points of predictor scores of $X_1$ [MMQ (40)] with the help of $X_2$ [RE(13)] and $X_3$ [MOS(18)]. The partial regression coefficients for $X_2$ and $X_3$ are -7.65 and -6.02 respectively. It explains the $X_1$ increases by -7.65 and -6.02 units due to one unit increase in $X_2$ and $X_3$ respectively. The 't'-values for b-coefficients are 4.32 and 3.38 which are significant at 0.01 level.

The prediction equation is given:

$X_1^1 = A + b_2\ X_2 + b_3\ X_3$

where $A = 351.38$

$b_2 = -7.65,\ b_3 = -\ 6.02$

regression equation 2nd step can be shows.

$X_1^1 = 351.38 + (-7.65)\ X_2 + (-\ 6.02)\ X_3$

$MMQ = 351.38 + (-7.65)\ RE + (-\ 6.02)\ MOS.$

In the third step the next predictor variable include in the step wise analysis in $X_4$ [M (3)]. In this step the multiple R is 0.184 it indicates the strength of relationship between the dependent variable $X_1$ [MMQ (40)] and three independent variables viz.; $X_2$ [RE (13)], $X_3$ [MOS (18)] and $X_4$ [M (3)] combined with optional weights the 'F'-value to test the significance of multiple R is 12.51 (3,1076) df at 0.01 level.

**Table 5.59: Prediction of Moral Judgment scores with the help of Independent variables**

| Step No. | Independent Variable entered in each step (VN) | Multiple R | $R^2$ | Standard error of multiple estimate (SER) | F-value for R (df) | Partial Regression Co-efficient b(VN) | 't'-value for b | Constant | B-beta co-efficient (B) | Simple correlation with dependent variable (r) | Percentage of variance explained by each independent variable |
|---|---|---|---|---|---|---|---|---|---|---|---|
| 1 | 2 | 3 | 4 | 5 | 6 | 7 | 8 | 9 | 10 | 11 | 12 |
| 1 | **RE (13), $X_2$** | 0.115 | 0.013 | 29.005 | 14.39**<br>-11,078 | -6.66 (13) | 3.79** | 341.2 | -0.112 | -0.115 | 1.317 |
| 2 | **MOS (18), $X_3$** | 0.153 | 0.024 | 28.865 | 12.97**<br>-21,077 | -7.65 (13)<br>-6.02 (18) | 4.32**<br>3.38** | 351.38 | -0.132<br>-0.103 | -0.072 | 1.514<br>0.838 |
| 3 | **M (3), $X_4$** | 0.184 | 0.034 | 28.728 | 12.51**<br>-31,076 | -7.68 (13)<br>-7.07 (18)<br>-5.98(3) | 4.36**<br>3.93**<br>3.37** | 361.87 | -0.132<br>-0.121<br>-0.103 | -0.085 | 1.52<br>0.984<br>0.866 |

| | | | | | | | | | | | |
|---|---|---|---|---|---|---|---|---|---|---|---|
| 4 | **YOS (2), $X_5$** | 0.2 | 0.04 | 28.652 | 11.10** | -6.93 (13) | 3.89** | 355.92 | -0.12 | 0.082 | 1.371 |
| | | | | | -41,075 | -7.62 (18) | 4.21** | | -0.131 | | 1.061 |
| | | | | | | -6.93 (3) | 3.44** | | -0.104 | | 0.883 |
| | | | | | | 2.83 (2) | 2.59** | | 0.079 | | 0.652 |
| 5 | **I (39), $X_6$** | 0.211 | 0.045 | 28.594 | 9.98** | -8.11 (13) | 4.38** | 336.6 | -0.14 | 0.036 | 1.604 |
| | | | | | -51,074 | -7.52 (18) | 4.17** | | -0.129 | | 1.048 |
| | | | | | | -6.25 (3) | 3.53** | | -0.107 | | 0.906 |
| | | | | | | 2.73 (2) | 2.52* | | 0.077 | | 0.633 |
| | | | | | | 8.54 (39) | 2.32@ | | 0.072 | | 0.257 |
| 6 | **FG (31), $X_7$** | 0.22 | 0.048 | 28.55 | 9.07** | -8.11(13) | 4.39** | 331.45 | -0.14 | 0.066 | 1.604 |
| | | | | | -61,073 | -7.33 (18) | 4.06** | | -0.126 | | 1.021 |
| | | | | | | -6.20 (3) | 3.51** | | -0.106 | | 0.899 |
| | | | | | | 2.76 (2) | 2.53* | | 0.08 | | 0.636 |
| | | | | | | 8.58 (39) | 2.34* | | 0.073 | | 0.258 |
| | | | | | | 0.88(31) | 2.07@ | | 0.062 | | 0.41 |

The $R^2$ value is in the step is 0.034 which explained 3.4% of the variance in $X_1$ [MMQ (40)] association with $X_2$ [RE (13)], $X_3$ [MOS (18)] and $X_4$ [M (3)] out of this variance 1.520,0.984 and 0.866 are employed by these three predictor variables respectively. The standard error of multiple estimate is 28.728 which shows that obtained $X_1$ [MMQ (40)] values to lie with in the range of ± 28.728 points of predictor scores of $X_1$ [MMQ (40)] with the help of $X_2$ [RE (13)], $X_3$ [MOS (18)] and $X_4$ [M (3)]. The partial regression coefficients for $X_2$, $X_3$ and $X_4$ are -7.68, -7.07 and -5.98 respectively. It explains the $X_1$ increases by -7.68, -7.07 and -5.98 units due to one unit increase in $X_2$, $X_3$ and $X_4$ respectively. The 't'-values for b-coefficients are 4.36,3.93 and 3.37 which are significant at 0.01 level.

The prediction equation is given as:

$X_1^1 = A + b_2 X_2 + b_3 X_3 + b_4 X_4$

where $A = 361.87$

$b_2 = -7.68,$

$b_3 = -7.07,$

$b_4 = -5.98$

regression equation 3[d] step can be shows.

$X_1^1 = 361.87 + (-7.68)\ X_2 + (-7.07)\ X_3 + (-5.98)\ X_4$

MMQ = 361.87 + (-7.68) RE+ (-7.07) MOS + (-5.98) M

In the fourth step the next predictor variable include in the step wise analysis in $X_5$ [YOS (2)]. In this step the multiple R is 0.200 it indicates the strength of relationship between the dependent variable $X_1$ [MMQ (40)] and four independent variables viz; $X_2$ [RE (13)], $X_3$ [MOS (18)], $X_4$ [M (3)] and $X_5$[YOS (2)] combined with optimal weights the 'F'-value to test the significance of multiple R is 11.10 (4,1075) df at 0.01 level of significance. The $R^2$ value is in the step is 0.040 which explained 4.0% of the variance in $X_1$ [MMQ (40)] association with $X_2$ [RE (13)], $X_3$ [MOS (18)], $X_4$ [M (3)] and $X_5$[YOS (2)] out of this variance 1.371,1.061, 0.883 and 0.652 are employed by these four predictor variables respectively. The standard error of multiple estimate is 28.652 which shows that obtained $X_1$ [MMQ

(40)] values to lie with in the range of ± 28.652 points of predictor scores of $X_1$ [MMQ (40)] with the help of $X_2$ [RE (13)], $X_3$ [MOS (18)], $X_4$ [M(3)] and $X_5$[YOS (2)]. The partial regression coefficients for $X_2$, $X_3$, $X_4$ and $X_5$ are -6.93, -7.62, -6.93 and 2.83 respectively. It explains the $X_1$ increases by -6.93, -7.62, -6.93 and 2.83 units due to one unit increase in $X_2$, $X_3$, $X_4$ and $X_5$ respectively. The 't'-values for b-coefficients are 3.89, 4.21, 3.44 and 2.59 which are significant at 0.01 level.

The prediction equation is given as:

$$X_1' = A + b_2 X_2 + b_3 X_3 + b_4 X_4$$

where A = 355.92,

$b_2$ = - 6.93,

$b_3$ = -7.62,

$b_4$ = - 6.93,

$b_5$ = 2.83

regression equation $4^{h}$ step can be shows.

$$X_1' = 355.92 + (-6.93)\ X_2 + (-7.62)\ X_3 + (-6.93)\ X_4 + (2.83)\ X_5$$

MMQ = 355.92 + (- 6.93)RE + (-7.62) MOS + (- 6.93) M +(2.83) YOS

In the fifth step the next predictor variable include in the step wise analysis in $X_6$ [I (39)]. In this step the multiple R is 0.211 it indicates the strength of relationship between the dependent variable $X_1$ [MMQ (40)] and five independent variables viz; $X_2$ [RE (13)], $X_3$ [MOS (18)], $X_4$ [M(3)], $X_5$ [(YOS (2)] and $X_6$[I (39)] combined with optimal weights the 'F'-value to test the significance of multiple R is 9.98 (5,1074) df at 0.01 level. The $R^2$ value is in the step is 0.045 which explained 4.5% of the variance in $X_1$ [MMQ (40)] association with $X_2$ [RE (13)], $X_3$ [MOS (18)], $X_4$ [M (3)], $X_5$[YOS (2)] and X6 [I (39)] out of this variance 1.604, 1.048, 0.906, 0.633 and 0.257 are employed by these five predictor variables respectively. The standard error of multiple estimate is 28.594 which shows that obtained $X_1$ [MMQ (40)] values to lie with in the range of ± 28.594 points of predictor scores of $X_1$ [MMQ (40)] with the help of $X_2$ [RE (13)], $X_3$ [MOS (18)], $X_4$ [M (3)], $X_5$[YOS (2)] and X6[I(39)]. The partial regression coefficients for $X_2$, $X_3$, $X_4$, $X_5$ and $X_6$ are -8.11, -7.52, -6.25, 2.73 and 8.54 respectively. It explains the $X_1$ increases by -8.11, -7.52, -6.25, 2.73 and 8.54 units due to one unit increase in $X_2$, $X_3$, $X_4$, $X_5$ and $X_6$ respectively. The 't'-values for b-coefficients are 4.38, 4.17 and 3.53 which are significant at 0.01 level. The 't'- value of $X_5$ for b-coefficient is 2.52, which is significant at 0.05 level. The 't'-value of $X_6$ for b-coefficient is 2.32, which is not significant at 0.05 level.

The prediction equation is given as:

$$X_1^1 = A + b_2 X_2 + b_3 X_3 + b_4 X_4 + b_5 X_5 + b_6 X_6$$

where A = 336.60

$b_2 = -8.11$,

$b_3 = -7.52$,

$b_4 = -6.25$,

$b_5 = 2.73$,

$b_6 = 8.54$

regression equation 5th step can be shows

$$X_1^1 = 336.60 + (-8.11)\ X_2 + (-7.52)\ X_3 + (-6.25)\ X_4 + (2.73)\ X_5 + (8.54)\ X_6$$

MMQ = 336.60 + (- 8.11) RE + (- 7.52) MOS + (- 6.25) M +(2.73) YOS+(8.54) I

In the sixth step the next predictor variable include in the step wise analysis in $X_7$ [FG (31)]. In this step the multiple R is 0.220 it indicates the strength of relationship between the dependent variable $X_1$ [MMQ (40)] and six independent variables viz; $X_2$ [RE (13)], $X_3$ [MOS (18)], $X_4$ [M (3)], $X_5$ [(YOS (2)], $X_6$[I (39)] and $X_7$[FG (31)] combined with optimal weights the 'F'-value to test the significance of multiple R is 0.220 (6,1073) df at 0.01 level. The $R^2$ value is in the step is 0.048 which explained 4.8% of the variance in $X_1$ [MMQ (40)] association with $X_2$ [RE (13)], $X_3$ [MOS (18)], $X_4$ [M (3)], $X_5$[YOS (2)], $X_6$ [I (39)] and $X_7$[FG (31)] out of this variance 1.604,1.021, 0.899, 0.636,0.258 and 0.410 are employed by these six predictor variables respectively. The standard error of multiple estimate is 28.550 which shows that obtained $X_1$ [MMQ (40)] values to lie with in the range of ± 28.550 points of predictor scores of $X_1$ [MMQ (40)] with the help of $X_2$ [RE (13)], $X_3$ [MOS (18)], $X_4$ [M (3)], $X_5$[YOS (2)], X6[I(39)] and $X_7$[FG (31)]. The partial regression coefficients for $X_2$, $X_3$, $X_4$, $X_5$, $X_6$ and $X_7$ are -8.1, -7.33, -6.20, 2.76, 8.58 and 0.88 respectively. It explains the $X_1$ increases by -8.11, -7.33, -6.20, 2.76, 8.58 and 0.88 units due to one unit increase in $X_2$, $X_3$, $X_4$, $X_5$, $X_6$ and $X_7$ respectively. The 't'-values of $X_2$, $X_3$ and $X_4$, b-coefficients are 4.39, 4.06 and 3.51 which are significant at 0.01 level. The 't'-value of $X_5$ and $X_6$ for b-coefficients is 2.53 and 2.34, which are significant at 0.05 level. The 't'-value of $X_7$ for b-coefficients is 2.07, which is not significant at 0.05 level.

The prediction equation is given as:

$$X_1^1 = A + b_2 X_2 + b_3 X_3 + b_4 X_4 + b_5 X_5 + b_6 X_6 + b_7 X_7$$

where $A = 331.45$

$b_2 = -8.11$,

$b_3 = -7.33$,

$b_4 = -6.20$,

$b_5 = 2.76$,

$b_6 = 8.58$

$b_7 = 0.88$

regression equation 5[h] step can be shows.

$$X_1^1 = 331.45 + (-8.11)X_2 + (-7.33)X_3 + (-6.20)X_4 + (2.76)X_5 + (8.58)X_6 + (0.88)X_7$$

$$MMQ = 331.45 + (-8.11)RE + (-7.33)MOS + (-6.20)M + (2.76)YOS + (8.58)I + (0.88)FG$$

With the help of above six variables namely: (1) Residence, (2) Medium of study, (3) Management, (4) Year of study, (5) Intelligence and (6) Personality Factor G.

It could be possible to explain 4.8% of variable in the dependent variable i.e., moral judgment.

CHAPTER 6

# SUMMARY, MAJOR FINDINGS, CONCLUSIONS, EDUCATIONAL IMPLICATIONS AND SUGGESTIONS FOR FURTHER RESEARCH

This chapter deals with the summary, major findings, conclusions, educational implications and suggestions for further research.

## SUMMARY

The goal of education, broadly conceived, includes not only the intellectual development of students but also their moral and social development. The development of cognitive abilities may be considered to be affecting the development of moral reasoning capabilities. According to Kohlberg (1975), cognitive development is a necessary, but not a sufficient condition for moral development. Therefore, school-related experiences, to the extent that they have an influence on cognitive development, can also have an influence on the development of moral reasoning capabilities.

Moral judgment plays an important role in the moral development. Moral judgment involves a cognitive capacity to define situations in terms of rights and duties. It requires the knowledge of standards in terms or rights and duties and abilities to perceive the situations in which to apply. It was the insight to see the relationship between the abstract principles and concrete cases. At the same time it requires moral insights on the ability to look for the common features of apparently different situations and the capacity to judge them as right or wrong.

## INTRODUCTION

Lawrence Kohlberg's (1969), "Theory of Moral Development" is one of the most widely used approaches to the examines of moral reasoning. This stage theory is based on various responses to scenarios, which involved a moral dilemma. Kohlberg recognized three levels of moral development, which encompassed six stages. A brief description of the levels and stages are as follows:

### Level 1, The Pre-Conventional Level

Children at this level respond to moral cues from their social reference group, most commonly parents. At this level children are extremely self-involved and moral behaviour is only in response to sanctions and reward based on behaviour.

#### *Stage 1, Obedience and Punishment Orientation*

Avoidance of punishments and unquestioning deference to power are valued in their own right.

#### *Stage 2, Obedience Relativism Orientation*

That which instrumentally satisfied one's own needs and occasionally the needs of others is considered right.

### Level 2, The Conventional Level

Moral reasoning is now based on existing social norms as well as the rights of others. Kohlberg asserts that most adolescents and some adults operate at this level of reasoning.

*Stage 3, Interpersonal Concordance Orientation*

This stage indicates that the individual has developed the ability to empathize and is no longer selfish in their moral reasoning.

*Stage 4, Law and Order Orientation*

At this stage moral activity becomes a function of following rules and has no association with the need for personal approval.

*Stage 4A, Anti-Establishment Orientation*

This stage involves rejection of conventional morality by late adolescents.

**Level 3, The Post-Conventional level**

This is the most advanced level of moral reasoning which relies on universal principles in approaching moral problems.

*Stage 5A, Social Contract Legalistic Orientation*

This stage identifies right action as that which is defined in terms of general individual rights and in terms of standards which have been critically examined and agreed upon by the society.

*Stage 5B, Morality of Intuitive Humanism Orientation*

At this stage obligations stem from "certain ideals".

*Stage 6, Universal Ethical Principles Orientation*

This stage is rarely reached. The orientation relies on principles that are self-generated and universally applicable.

According to Kohlberg (1969) Education plays a major role in moral development. His strongest statement to this effect is that moral reasoning stops at the same point that formal education stops. Although this assertion has stimulated much needed discussion above moral education, there has been a great deal of resistance.

## MAJOR FINDINGS OF THE STUDY

The statistical treatment of the data reveals the following major findings of the study:

### Distribution Characteristics of Moral Judgment Scores.

1. The mean moral judgment scores is 330.05, median is 330.00 and mode is 326.25. The gap among mean, median and mode is negligible. Hence, the distribution is very nearer to normal distribution.
2. The values of skewness and kurtosis are 0.191 and 0.980 respectively. Hence the frequency distribution of moral judgment scores for the whole group is slightly positively skewed and lepto kurtic.
3. The frequency distribution of moral judgment is very nearer to normal distribution.
4. The mean moral judgment scores for the students of aided colleges is the highest (334.82) among all groups and the lowest (327.58) for the students of second year. The SD is the highest (31.72) for the students of Aided colleges and the lowest (27.04) for the students of Government colleges. For Government distribution, the value of skewness is negative, hence the distribution is negatively skewed. For male distribution the value of skew ness is zero, hence the distribution is normally skewed, for remaining distributions the value of skewness is positive, hence the distributions is positively skewed and kurtosis value is less than 3.00. Hence all the distributions are lepto kurtic

### Factorial Designs

5. There is significant influence of sex at 0.01 level on the reasoning of moral stage 1, moral stage 3 and moral stage 4A and has significant influence at 0.05 level on the reasoning of moral stage 4, conventional level and moral judgment of Intermediate students.

6. There is significant influence of year of study at 0.01 level on the reasoning of moral stage 1, moral stage 2, moral stage 3, moral stage 4, pre-conventional level, conventional level and moral judgment of Intermediate students.
7. There is significant influence of management at 0.01 level on the reasoning of moral stage 1, moral stage 3, pre-conventional level, conventional level, post-conventional level and moral judgment and has significant influence at 0.05 level on the reasoning of moral stage 2 and moral stage 5A of Intermediate students.
8. There is significant influence of region at 0.05 level on the reasoning of moral stage 1 and moral stage 5B of Intermediate students.
9. There is significant interaction effect of sex Vs year of study at 0.01 level on reasoning of moral stage 3 of Intermediate students.
10. There is significant interaction effect of sex Vs management at 0.01 level on reasoning of moral stage 4, pre-conventional level and conventional and has interaction effect of sex Vs management at 0.05 level on the reasoning moral judgment of Intermediate students.
11. There is significant interaction effect of sex Vs region at 0.01 level on the reasoning of moral stage 4 and moral stage 5B and has interaction effect of sex Vs management at 0.05 level on the reasoning of moral stage 5A of Intermediate students.
12. There is significant interaction effect of year of study Vs region at 0.05 level on reasoning of moral stage 3, moral stage 4, moral stage 5B and pre-conventional level of Intermediate students
13. There is significant interaction effect of management Vs region at 0.01 level on reasoning of moral stage 1, moral stage 3, moral stage 5B and moral judgment and has interaction effect of management Vs region at 0.05 level

on the reasoning of moral stage 6, pre-conventional level and post-conventional level of Intermediate students.

14. There is significant interaction effect of sex Vs year of study Vs management at 0.05 level on reasoning of moral stage 1 and conventional level of Intermediate students

15. There is significant interaction effect of sex Vs year of study Vs region at 0.01 level on reasoning of moral stage 5B of Intermediate students

16. There is significant interaction effect of sex Vs management Vs region at 0.01 level on reasoning of moral stage 1, moral stage 2, moral stage 3, moral stage 4, moral stage 4A, pre-conventional level, conventional level and moral judgment and has interaction effect of sex Vs management Vs region at 0.05 level on the reasoning of moral stage 5B of Intermediate students.

17. There is significant interaction effect of sex Vs year of study Vs management Vs region at 0.01 level on reasoning of moral stage 3 and has interaction effect of sex Vs year of study Vs management Vs region at 0.05 level on the reasoning of moral stage 1, pre- conventional level, conventional level and moral judgment of Intermediate students.

**Influence of Academic Achievement**

18. There is significant influence of academic achievement in languages at 0.01 level on the reasoning of moral stage 2, moral stage 4, moral stage 4A, pre-conventional level, and moral judgment and has significant influence at 0.05 level on the reasoning of moral stage 6 and conventional level of Intermediate students.

19. There is significant influence of achievement in non-languages at 0.01 level on the reasoning of moral stage 5B and post-conventional level and has significant influence at 0.05 level on the reasoning of moral stage 2 moral stage 5A pre-conventional level and moral judgment of Intermediate students.

20. There is significant influence of achievement in total at 0.05 level on the reasoning of moral stage 3, moral stage 4A and moral stage 5B of Intermediate students.

**Influence of Psychological variables**

21. It is found that the students who are having personality characteristics of (1) More intelligent, abstract thinking (2) Emotionally stable, calm nature have significantly better on the reasoning of moral stage 1 then the students who are having the personality characteristics of (1) Less intelligent, concrete thinking (2)Affected by feeling, emotionally less stable.

22. It is found that the students who are having personality characteristics of (1) More intelligent, abstract thinking (2) Happy go lucky, gay enthusiastic, impulsively lively and (3) Controlled socially precise, self-disciplined, compulsive, high self-concept control have significant influence on the reasoning of moral stage 2 than the students who are having the personality characteristics of (1) Less intelligent, concrete thinking, (2) Sober, prudent, serious, taciturn and (3) Un disciplined self concept, careless of protocol, follows own urges, low integration.

23. It is found that the students who are having personality characteristics of (1) Emotionally stable, calm nature and (2) Doubting, obstructive individualistic, reflective, internally restrained, unwilling to act have significant influence on the reasoning of moral stage 3 than the students who are having the personality characteristics of (1) Affected by feeling, emotionally less stable and (2) Vigorous, goes readily with groups, jestful, given to action.

24. It is inferred that the students who are having personality characteristic of (1) Tense, driven over wrought, frustrated have significant influence on the reasoning of moral stage 4 than the students who are having the personality characteristic of (1) Relaxed, tranquil, torpid, unfrustrated.

25. It is inferred that the students who are having personality characteristics of (1) Emotionally stable, calm nature (2) Venturesome, socially bold, uninhibited, spontaneous and (3) Doubting, obstructive, individualistic, reflective, internally restrained, unwilling to act have significant influence on the reasoning of moral stage – 4A than the students who are having the personality characteristics of (1) Affected by feeling, emotionally less stable, (2) Shy, restrained, diffident, timid and (3) Vigorous goes readily with groups, jestful, given to action.

26. It is inferred that the students who are having personality characteristic of (1) Venturesome, socially bold, uninhibited, spontaneous have significant influence on the reasoning of moral stage 5A than the students who are having the personality characteristics of (1) Shy, restrained, diffident, timid.

27. It is inferred that the students who are having personality characteristics of (1) Happy go lucky, gay, enthusiastic, impulsively lively and (2) Doubting, obstructive, individualistic, reflective, internally restrained, unwilling to act have significant influence on the reasoning of moral stage 5B than the students who are having the personality characteristics of (1) Sober, prudent, serious, taciturn and (2) Vigorous, goes readily with groups, jestful, given to action.

28. It is inferred that the students who are having personality characteristic of (1) Conscientious, preserving, rule bound i.e., stronger ego strength have significant influence on the reasoning of moral stage 6 than the students who are having the personality characteristics of (1) Expedient, evades rules i.e., weaker super ego strength.

29. It is inferred that the students who are having personality characteristics of (1) More intelligent, abstract thinking(2) Happy go lucky, gay, enthusiastic, impulsively lively and (3) Controlled socially precise, self disciplined, compulsive, high self-concept control have

significant influence on the reasoning of pre-conventional level than the students who are having the personality characteristics of (1) Less intelligent, concrete thinking (2) Sober, prudent, serious, taciturn and (3) Un disciplined self concept, careless of protocol, follows own urges, low integration.

30. It is inferred that the students who are having personality characteristic of (1) Tense, driven over wrought, frustrated have significant influence on the reasoning of conventional level than the students who are having the personality characteristic of (1) Relaxed, tranquil, torpid, unfrustrated.

31. It is inferred that the students who are having personality Characteristic of (1) Conscientious, preserving, rule bound i.e., stronger super ego strength have significant influence on the reasoning of moral judgment than the students who are having the personality characteristic of (1) Expedient, evades rules i.e., weaker super ego strength.

32. There is significant influence of intelligence at 0.01 level on the reasoning of moral stage 1 of Intermediate students.

## Socio-Demographic variables

33. There is significant influence of caste at 0.05 level on the reasoning of moral stage 1 of Intermediate students

34. There is significant influence of socio-economic status at 0.01 level on the reasoning of moral stage 3, and has significant influence at 0.05 level on the reasoning of moral stage 1, pre-conventional level and conventional level of Intermediate students

35. There is significant influence of residence at 0.01 level on the reasoning of moral stage 1, pre-conventional level and moral judgment and has significant influence at 0.05 level on the reasoning of moral stage 2, and moral stage 5B and post conventional level of Intermediate students.

### Influence of Personal variables

36. There is significant influence of age at 0.05 level on the reasoning of moral stage 5B of Intermediate students.
37. There is significant influence of annual income at 0.01 level on the reasoning of moral stage 1 and has significant influence at 0.05 level on the reasoning of moral stage 3 and conventional level of Intermediate students.
38. There is significant influence of father's occupation at 0.05 level on the reasoning of moral stage 3 and post-conventional level of Intermediate students
39. There is significant influence of mother's occupation at 0.05 level on the reasoning of moral stage 5A and of Intermediate students.
40. There is significant influence of economic position of the family at 0.05 level on the reasoning of moral stage 3, moral stage 4 and conventional level of Intermediate students.
41. There is significant influence of type of the family at 0.05 level on the reasoning of moral stage 4, conventional level and moral judgment of Intermediate students.
42. There is significant influence of medium of the study at 0.01 level on the reasoning of moral stage 5B and moral judgment and has significant influence at 0.05 level on the reasoning of moral stage 1, moral stage 3 and post-conventional level of Intermediate students.
43. There is significant influence of course of the study at 0.01 level on the reasoning of moral stage 1, moral stage 3, moral stage 4, pre-conventional level and conventional level and has significant influence at 0.05 level on the reasoning of moral stage 4A of Intermediate students.

### Step-wise Multiple Regression Analysis

44. It is found that the best regression equations for predicting moral judgment of Intermediate students are with the help of all the 39 Independent variables.

MMQ = 331.45 + (-8.11) RE + (-7.33) MOS + (-6.20) M +(2.76) YOS+(8.58) I +(0.88) FG

With the help of above six variables namely (1) Residence, (2) Medium of study, (3) Management, (4) Year of study, (5) Intelligence and (6) Personality Factor G. It could be possible to explain 4.8% of variable in the dependent variable i.e., moral judgment.

## CONCLUSIONS

In the light of the findings presented in preceding pages, the following conclusions are drawn.

1. The Frequency distribution of moral judgment of Intermediate students is very nearer to normal distribution.
2. All the Intermediate students do not have same reasoning of moral judgment.
3. Sex has significant influence on the reasoning of moral stage 1, moral stage 3, moral stage 4, moral stage 4A, conventional level and moral judgment of Intermediate students.
4. Year of study has significant influence on the reasoning of moral stage 1, moral stage 2, moral stage 3, moral stage 4, pre-conventional level, conventional level and moral judgment of Intermediate students.
5. Management has significant influence on the reasoning of moral stage 1, moral stage 2, moral stage 3, moral stage 5A, pre-conventional level, conventional level post-conventional level and moral judgment of Intermediate students.
6. Region has significant influence on the reasoning of moral stage 1, moral stage 5B of Intermediate students.
7. There is significant interaction effects of sex Vs year of study on the reasoning of moral stage 3 of Intermediate students.

8. There are significant interaction effects of sex Vs management on the reasoning of moral stage 4, pre-conventional level, conventional level and moral judgment of Intermediate students.
9. There is significant interaction effects of sex Vs region on the reasoning of moral stage 4, moral stage 5A and moral stage 5B of Intermediate students.
10. There is significant interaction effects of year of study Vs region on the reasoning of moral stage 3, moral stage 4, moral stage 5B and pre-conventional level of Intermediate students.
11. There is significant interaction effects of management Vs region on the reasoning of moral stage 1, moral stage 3, moral stage 5B, moral stage 6, pre-conventional level, post-conventional level and moral judgment of Intermediate students.
12. There is significant interaction effects of sex Vs year of study Vs management on the reasoning of moral stage 1 and conventional level of Intermediate students.
13. There is significant interaction effects of sex Vs year of study Vs region on the reasoning of moral stage 5B of Intermediate students.
14. There is significant interaction effects of sex Vs management Vs region on the reasoning of moral stage 1, moral stage 2 , moral stage 3, moral stage 4, moral stage 4A and moral stage 5B, pre-conventional level, conventional level and moral judgment of Intermediate students.
15. There is significant interaction effects of sex Vs year of study Vs management Vs region on the reasoning of moral stage 1, moral stage 3, pre-conventional level, conventional level, moral judgment of Intermediate students.
16. Academic achievement in languages has significant influence on the reasoning of moral stage 2, moral stage

4, moral stage 4A, moral stage 6, pre-conventional level, conventional level and moral judgment of Intermediate students.

17. Academic achievement in non-languages has significant influence on the reasoning of moral stage 2, moral stage 5A, moral stage 5B, pre-conventional level, post-conventional level and moral judgment of Intermediate students.
18. Academic achievement in total has significant influence on the reasoning of moral stage 3, moral stage 4A and moral stage 5B of Intermediate students.
19. Personality factors B and C have significant influence on the reasoning of moral stage 1.
20. Personality factors B, G and $Q_3$ have significant influence on the reasoning of moral stage 2.
21. Personality factors C and J have significant influence on the reasoning of moral stage 3.
22. Personality factor $Q_3$ has significant influence on the reasoning of moral stage 4.
23. Personality factors C, H and J have significant influence on the reasoning of moral stage 4A.
24. Personality factor H has significant influence on the reasoning of moral stage 5A.
25. Personality factors F and J have significant influence on the reasoning of moral stage 5B.
26. Personality factor G has significant influence on the reasoning of moral stage 6.
27. Personality factors B, F and $Q_3$ have significant influence on the reasoning of pre-conventional level.
28. Personality factor $Q_4$ has significant influence on the reasoning of conventional level.
29. Personality factor G has significant influence on the reasoning of moral judgment.

30. Intelligence has significant influence on the reasoning of moral stage 1 of Intermediate students.
31. Caste has significant influence on the reasoning of moral stage 1 of Intermediate students.
32. Socio-Economic Status has significant influence on the reasoning of moral stage 1, moral stage 3, pre-conventional level and conventional level of Intermediate students.
33. Residence has significant influence on the reasoning of moral stage 1, moral stage 2, moral stage 5B, pre-conventional level, post-conventional level and moral judgment of Intermediate students.
34. Age has significant influence on the reasoning of moral stage 5B of Intermediate students.
35. Annual income has significant influence on the reasoning of moral stage 1, moral stage 3 and conventional level and moral judgment of Intermediate students.
36. Father's occupation has significant influence on the reasoning of moral stage 3 and post-conventional level of Intermediate students.
37. Mother's occupation has significant influence on the reasoning of moral stage 5A of Intermediate students.
38. Economic position of the family has significant influence on the reasoning of moral stage 3, moral stage 4 and conventional level of Intermediate students.
39. Type of the family has significant influence on the reasoning of moral stage 4, conventional level and moral judgment of Intermediate students.
40. Course of the study has significant influence on the reasoning of moral stage 1, moral stage 3, moral stage 4, moral stage 4A, pre-conventional level, conventional level of Intermediate students.

41. It is possible to predict the moral judgment of Intermediate students in moral judgment with the help of different sets of Independent variables

## EDUCATIONAL IMPLICATIONS

A number of psychologists like Piaget, Kohlberg and others have studied extensively the problem of moral judgment among children and hence the student's potential upholders are already available to the teachers. But what is to be done is that the teachers have to take up the responsibility of providing moral instructions to the children, so that they can sharpen their sense of discrimination.

The findings of the present research have raised some important questions related to the educational needs of the students with special reference to their moral development.

1. The children have certain amount of moral stages namely Good and Bad, and Obedient and Punishment before entering to the school age. If seems to be an immediate need to develop other stages of Kohlberg's moral development.
2. There is a need to develop specific curriculum for inculcation of values for different grades of schooling.
3. Certain specific theme training programmes were conducted to teachers at both levels (Elementary and Higher). So that the teachers are providing moral education to their students.
4. The present study has shown that, there is significant difference in moral judgment of male and female students. This appears to be a positive sign for the development of the society. The moral education in colleges not showed any gender difference.
5. The present study has shown that year of study in which the student is studying appears to be the significant factor that determine the capacity of moral judgment. Hence it is an essential to change the moral atmosphere where the students have exhibited moral sense and

discrimination. Even the NPE-1986 also emphasis the importance of moral education as an integral part of the general educational system.

6. Necessary infra-structural facilities and physical facilities may be created in Intermediate colleges. Congenial atmosphere may be developed in Intermediate colleges.

7. Higher authorities of Board of Intermediate Education have to organize a series of workshops, seminars, orientation programmes, symposia etc. on moral education for re orienting Intermediate education in A.P.

8. Academic achievement is positively correlated with moral judgment, special care and extra coaching may be provided to the Intermediate students, where the academic achievement is moderately low.

9. At present the system of education forget its main task in fostering the development of whole sum personality among students because of a sense of insecurity among the students. Hence in every school the guidance and counseling centers are opened to mould the student's personality within the current techniques show that they can have a stable mind. The following personality characteristic may be developed in Intermediate students through guidance and counseling for better reasoning of moral judgment (1) More intelligent, abstract thinking, (2) Emotionally stable, calm nature, (3) Happy go lucky, gay, enthusiastic, impulsively lively (4) Conscientious, preserving, rule bound i.e., stronger super ego strength (5) Venture some, socially bold, uninhibited, spontaneous, (6) Doubting, obstructive individualistic, reflective, internally restrained, unwilling to act, (7) Controlled socially precise, self disciplined, compulsive, high self-concept control and (8) Tense, driven over wrought, frustrated

10. The quality of the society is determine by the persons those who are having quality of intellectual and social values. In the present investigation intelligence was

significant relation with moral judgment. Hence the teachers are transmit the moral values among the individuals the same may be preserve, conserve an transmit for the future generation on these lines the curriculum and teaching learning process may be implemented in the schools.

11. The reasoning of moral judgment of OC students is better than BC, SC and ST students. Special programmes may be provided for BC, SC and ST students. Common hostel facility may be provided for OC, BC, SC and ST students.

12. It was found that Hindus, Muslims and Christian students do not differ significantly in their moral judgment. Traditionally religion has been the basis of morality. Hence it is essential that students should be made to understand these core principles of every religion. This helps in developing secular values and this would contribute to global peace.

13. The administrators have to take necessary steps for better hostel facilities

14. SES, economic position of the family and annual income are positively correlated with moral judgment. Government has to take necessary steps for give scholarships and hostel facilities may be provided to the poor students on the basis of SES, economic position and annual income of the family of the students.

15. To provide relevant programmes for lower age Intermediate students for better reasoning of moral judgment.

16. Education and occupation status of the parents are positively correlated with moral judgment of students. Government has to take necessary steps for better amenities for the parents.

17. Joint family is positively related to the reasoning of moral judgment, the Government should take necessary steps and to give some concessions to joint families

18. Medium of the study is positively correlated with moral judgment. Additional motivation may be provided to the English medium students for better reasoning of moral judgment.
19. Course of the study is positively related with moral judgment. Relevant programmes may be provided to the C.E.C. students for better reasoning of moral judgment.
20. In addition to above teachers should try to create interest among the students through their method of teaching and co-curricular activities.

## SUGGETIONS FOR FURTHER RESEARCH

The following suggestion are considered for the research

1. Taking subjects from other states can carry out a similar study.
2. The study is confined only to Intermediate first year and second year students. A similar investigation may be conducted by taking students from higher classes also, namely under-graduate, post-graduate courses and teacher training like D.Ed., B.Ed., M.Ed., Pandit training courses, B.P.Ed., M.P.Ed. etc.
3. The study may be undertaken to cover the other age groups.
4. An analytical study of moral judgment can be undertaken as related to the moral of their parents and teachers.
5. Many social factors like modernization, atavism and so on may be examined for their effect on moral judgment.
6. Many psychological factors like self-esteem, self-concept, religiosity, study habits, emotional maturity and cognitive development and so on may be examined for their effect on moral judgment.
7. Other significant factors like parental attitude towards morality, emotional maturity, parental commitment, parental behavior, child rearing practice may be studied

for their effect on moral judgment.

8. Experimental designs may be planned to examine the effective methods of developing programmes and techniques of giving moral instructions to children at various levels of schooling.

9. Experimental designs may be developed in order to test different methods of teaching morality and their effect on moral judgment and moral behavior of students.

10. Some projects related to moral judgment for enhancing competency among the teachers in the educational system.

11. A cross cultural study may be conducted for the tribal and non-tribal groups; Indians and abroad like American, Tibetans etc., for comparing their moral behavior and moral judgment.

12. The present study is confined to 1080 Intermediate students it is suggested that future researchers may under take studies with larger sample.

13. Similar studies may be conducted in other professional courses like engineering and medicine etc.

14. This is a presage – product study in the area of moral judgment presage – process, process – product and presage – process – product studies may be undertaken in the area of moral judgment.

# BIBLIOGRAPHY


Aaron, P.G., Marihal, V.G. and Malathisa, R.N. (1970), "Socio-economic status scale for rural and urban areas".

Agarwal (1985), "A study of feeling of security in moral development and under developed adolescence as related to their self-concept and personality", *Dissertation Abstract International, November*, Vol.40, No.5, p.1882 - A.

Al-Deen, Hala, F. (1991), "Moral judgment in mentally retarded children", *Derasat-Nafsevah*, Vol.1(14), pp.553 - 570.

Aleixo-Paulo, A. and Norris Claire, E. (2000), "Personality and moral reasoning in young offenders", *Personality and Individual Differences*, March, Vol.28 (3), pp.609 - 623.

Allport, et al., (1964), "Study of values", A Scale for Measuring Dominant Interests in Personality, 3rd Edition, Boston, Houghton, Miffin.

Allport, G.W. (1937), "Personality – A psychological interpretation", Hort, New York.

Anastaci (1966), as quoted by Vanaja (1984), "A study of moral judgment among 9th and 10th standard students in relation to their self confidence, sex, socio-economic status and the type of school", An unpublished M.Phil. Dissertation, Bangalore University, Bangalore, p. 32.

Aristotle, as quoted in Rangaswamy, G.(2006), "A study of moral judgment of high school pupils in relations to certain factors", Ph.D. in Education, SVU, Tirupati, p.8.

Aronfreed, J. (1968), "Aversive control of internalization", Nebraska Symposium on Motivation, Vol.16, Lincoln, University of Nebraska Press, pp.271-320.

Aronfreed, J. (1968), "Conduct and conscience", New York and London: Academic Press.

Arsenio William Frank (1986), "Affective components of social cognitive and their relation to behaviour", *Dissertation Abstract International*, August, Vol.47(2), p.266-A.

Ayesha Noor (2001), "A comparative study of the effect of personality traits on the moral judgment of tenth standard students in Bangalore urban secondary schools", Unpublished M.Ed. Dissertation, Bangalore University, Bangalore.

Baldwin, J.M. (1906), "Social and ethical interpretations in mental development", New York, Macmillan.

Bandopadhyay, R.(1981), "Growth and development of moral judgment in children" as quoted in Buch, M.B. (Ed.), "The second survey of research in education", Vol.2, CASE, Baroda.

Bandura (1963), as quoted in Vanaja (1984), "A study of moral judgment among 9th and 10th standard students in relation to their self confidence, sex, socio-economic status and the type of school", An unpublished M.Phil. Dissertation, Bangalore University, Bangalore, p.11.

Bandura (1971) , as quoted in Rangaswamy, G.(2006), "A study of moral judgment of high school pupils in relations to certain factors", Ph.D. in Education, SVU, Tirupati, p.27.

Bandura and Walters (1963), as quoted in Vanaja (1984), "A study of moral judgment among 9th and 10th standard students in relation to their self confidence, sex, socio-economic status and the type of school", An unpublished M.Phil. Dissertation, Bangalore University, Bangalore, p.11.

Bandura, A. and Walters, R.H. (1959), "Adolescent aggression", New York, Ronald.

Bandura, Albert., and Mc Donald, F.J.(1963), "Influence of social reinforcement and the behavior of models in shaping children's moral judgments", *Journal of Abnormal and Social Psychology*, Vol.67, pp. 274-281.

Bannon, S. (1982), as quoted in Chaya, C.V.(2001), "A study of moral judgment of 10th standard students in relation to their parental behaviour, child rearing practices, emotional maturity and personality traits", Ph.D. In Education, Bangalore University, Bangalore, pp. 117-118.

Bartar Dalceil, et al. (1985), "Relationship between the development of helping behaviour and of social perspective and moral judgment", *Psychology Monograph*, February, Vol. II (1), pp. 23-40.

Bartels, Daniel, M. (2008), *Cognition*, Vol.108, N. 2, pp. 381-417.

Batson, C. Daniel et al. (1999), "Moral hypocrisy: appearing moral to oneself without being so", *Journal of Personality Social Psychology*, September Vol.77 (3), pp. 525-537.

Begum Shahina, R. B.(1983), "The effect of personality traits on the moral judgment of X standard students", Unpublished M.Ed., Dissertation, Bangalore University, Bangalore.

Belanky (1975), as quoted in Rangaswamy, G.(2006), "A study of moral judgment of high school pupils in relations to certain factors", Ph.D. in Education, SVU, Tirupati, p. 104.

Benninga Jacques (1976), "The relationship of self concept, sex and intelligence to moral judgment in young children", *Dissertation Abstract International*, April, 1977, Vol.37, No.10, p. 6357-A.

Bhargava (1986), "A study of moral judgment among children at a concrete and formal operational stages and its relationship with variables of home and educational environment", *Dissertation Abstract International*, May, Vol.51, No.10, p. 6231-A.

Bhattacharya, S and Mukhopadhyay (2002), "Social life adjustment pattern and moral behaviour : a study with reference to students studying in Bengali medium at secondary and higher secondary level of education", *Behavioural Scientist*, Vol..3(2), pp. 117-120.

Bhushan, L.I. (1970), "Religiosity scale", *Indian Journal of Psychology*, Vol.45 (4), pp. 335-342.

Bhushan, L. I. (1971), "Religiosity as a function of age, education, and sex", *Indian Psychological Review*, Vol.8(1), pp. 1-4.

Bhushan, L. I. (1972), "Manual of religiosity scale (In Hindi)", National Psychological Corporation, Labh Chand Market, Raja Mandi, Agra - 2.

Biaggio, Angela, M. (1976), "A developmental study of moral judgment of brilliant children and adolescents", *Revista Inteamericansa de psicologia*, Vol.10 (1-2), pp. 71-78, *Psychological Abstracts*, (1977), Vol.58, p. 884.

Blasi, A. (2004), "Moral functioning : moral understanding and personality", In: Lapsley, D. K. and Narvaez, D. (Eds.), *Morality, Self, and Identity*, Mahwah, NJ: Erlbaum.

Blatt and Kohlberg (1975), as quoted in Rangaswamy, G. (2006), "A study of moral judgment of high school pupils in relations to certain factors", Ph.D. in Education, SVU, Tirupati, p. 104.

Boehm, L. (1957), "The development of independence: a comparative study", *Child Development*, Vol. 28, pp. 85-92.

Boehm, L. and Nass, M.L. (1962), "Social class difference in conscience development", *Child Development*, Vol. 33, pp. 565-575.

Boehm, L.(1962), "The development of conscience: A comparison of American children", *Child Development*, Vol. 29, pp. 85-87.

Boom, Jan; Wouters, Hans and Keller, Monika (2007), *Cognitive Development*, Vol. 22, N. 2, pp. 213-229.

Brain, Brunham (1976), as quoted in Rangaswamy, G.(2006), "A study of moral judgment of high school pupils in relations to certain factors", Ph.D. in Education, SVU, Tirupati, p. 99.

Brain, Burnham and Joseph Murphy (1976), "Measuring the moral reasoning power of elementary school students", A report of the two-year study, The York Counter Board of Education, Box 40, Aurova, Ontario.

Brimi, Hunter (2009), *Clearing house: A journal of educational stratages, issues and ideas*, Vol. 82, N.3, pp.125-130.

Bronfenbrenner (1962), as quoted in Suma Rani, R. (2001), "Moral judgment among students of IX standard in relation to their gender, type of school, urban and rural background and social maturity", Unpublished M.Ed. Dissertation, Bangalore University, Bangalore, p. 506.

Bronfenbrenner, U. (1976), as quoted in Vanaja (1984), "A study of moral judgment among 9th and 10th standard students in relation to their self confidence, sex, socio-economic status and the type of school", An unpublished M.Phil. Dissertation, Bangalore University, Bangalore, p.12.

Bruggman, Elizebeth Leistler (1996), "Cheating, lying and moral reasoning by religious and secular high school students", *Journal of Educational Research*, July-August, Vol. 89(6), pp. 340-344.

Bull, J. Norman (1969), *Moral judgment from childhood to Adolescence: A text-book*, Routledge and Keganpaul Ltd., London.

Bull, N.J.(1969), *Moral education: A text-book*, Routledge and Keganpaul Ltd., London.

Bunch, Wilton, H. (2005), *Journal Moral Education*, Vol. 34, N. 3, pp. 363-370.

Burke (1998), "The effects of a school based sociomoral mentoring program on pre -adolescents' cognitive, emotional and behavioural development", *Dissertation Abstracts International* - Section B: *The Science and Engineering*, July, Vol. 59(1-12), p. 411.

Burton (1963), as quoted in Rangaswamy, G.(2006), "A study of moral judgment of high school pupils in relations to certain factors", Ph.D. in Education, SVU, Tirupati, p. 102.

Bush (1981), "A comparison of the effect of Kohlberg's dilemmas Vs Alerato dilemma in the moral stages of adolescents", *Dissertation Absrtract International*, June,1982, Vol. 42, N. 12, p. 5010-A.

Cattell (1935, 1940, 1949, 1961, 1971), as quoted by Lakshmi, N.(1996), "Problems of scheduled caste, scheduled tribe and non-scheduled caste girls of secondary schools in relation to a few social and psychological factors", Ph.D. in Education, Bangalore University, Bangalore, p.158.

Cattell, R.B. (1946, 1965), "The description and measurement of personality", World, New York.

Cattell, R.B. (1950), "The main personality factors in a questionnaire, self estimated material", *Journal of Social Psychology*, Vol. 31, pp. 3-38.

Cattell, R.B. (1957), "Personality and motivation structure and measurement", World, New York.

Cattell, R.B. (1964), "Beyond validity and reliability some further concepts and coefficients for evaluating tests", *Journal of Extension Education*, Vol. 33, pp. 133-144.

Central Ministry of Eduction (1981), as quoted in Sapru Alka (1982), "A study of a few socio-psychological factors in relation to moral judgment of IX standard students of a few high schools of Bangalore city", An unpublished M.Ed. Dissertation, Bangalore Univeristy, Bangalore, p.19.

Chambers 20th Century Dictionary, as quoted in Sapru Alka (1982), "A study of a few socio-psychological factors in relation to moral judgment of IX standard students of a few high schools of Bangalore city", An Unpublished M.Ed. Dissertation, Bangalore University, Bangalore, p. 11.

Chaya, A. Heblikar (2001), "A study of moral judgment of 10th standard students in relation to their parental behaviour: child rearing practices, emotional maturity and personality traits", Ph.D. In Education, Bangalore University, Bangalore.

Chaya, C.V. (1993), "Moral judgment among students of eighth standard in relation to their sex, intelligence, religiosity and socio-economic status", Unpublished M.Ed. Dissertation, Bangalore University, Bangalore, p. 56.

Chaya, C.V. (1996), "A study of moral judgment of ninth standard students in relation to their parental behaviour and values", Un published M.Ed. Dissertation, Bangalore University, Bangalore.

Colby, A., Kohlberg, L., Speicher - Dubin, B, Hewer, A., Candee, D., Gibbs and Power, C. (1987), *The measurement of moral judgment: A text-book*, Routledge and Keganpaul Ltd., London.

Commons, Michael Lamport; Galaz-Fonters, Jesus Francisco; Morse, Stanley Jay (2006), *Journal of Moral Education*, Vol. 35, N. 2, pp. 247-267.

Comunia, Anna, L.; Glelen, UWe, P.(2006), *Journal of Moral Education*, Vol. 35, N. 1, pp. 51-69.

Cooper, Merryl, Schwartz, Robert (2007), *Journal of College Student Development.*

Crowne, D.P. (1979), *The Experimental Study of Personality*, Erlbavm Press, Hillsdale, New Jersey.

Crownes (1979), *Educational Psychology*, Eurasia Publishing House, New Delhi.

Cummings, Rhoda; Harlow,Steve; Maddux, Cleborne, D. (2007), *Journal of Moral Education*, Vol. 36(1), pp. 67-78.

Daman, W. (1971), "The child's conception of justice. M.A. in Education, University of California.

Damon, W. (1973), "The development of the children's conception of justice", Paper presented at the annual meeting of the society for research in child development, Philadelphia.

Damon, W. (1974), "Studying early moral development : some techniques for interviewing young children and for analyzing the results", Unpublished manuscript, Clerk University.

Daniel, M. Bartels (2008), *Cognition*, Vol. 108, I-2, pp. 381-413.

Danielle, E. Warren, Kristin Smith-Crown (2008), *Research in Organizational Behaviour*, Vol. 28, pp. 81-103.

Das, R.C. (1990), "Existing programmes for moral development in selected secondary schools in India", *Dissertation Abstract International*, May, Vol. 46.

Davidson, G.W., Seaton, M.A. and Simpson, J. (1988) (Eds), *Chambers concise 20$^{th}$ century dictionary*, Allied publishers, Pvt. Ltd., pp. 346, 889.

Dawson (2002), "New tools, new insights : Kohlberg's moral judgment stages revisited", *International Journal of Behavioural Development*, March, Vol. 26(2), pp. 154-166.

Dayakara Reddy, V. (1987), "A study of moral judgment in relation to intelligence, personality and other variables", Ph.D. in Education, SVU, Tirupati.

Debruin Ellun, N.M. and Van Large Paul, A.M. (1999), "Impression formation and co-operative behaviour",

*European Journal of Social Psychology*, March, Vol. 29(2-3), pp. 305-328.

Dectionary of Education (1973), as quoted in Apsar Pasha, S.A. (1986), "Insecurity among scheduled caste, scheduled tribe and non-scheduled caste students of high primary schools in relation to their social maturity", Unpublished M.Ed. Dissertation, Bangalore University, Bangalore, p. 136.

Deguchi, Yasuyuki and Ohkawa Chilkara (2000), "A study on the empathy of juvenile delinquents : relationship between empathy + offense type and empathy + moral judgment", *Japanese Journal of Criminal Psychology*, Vol. 38(2), pp. 17-36.

Denitici, Ornella-Andream and Pagnin-Adriano (1992), "Moral reasoning in gifted adolescents : cognitive level and social values", *European Journal for High Ability*, Vol. 3(1), pp. 105-114.

Derr Alice, M. (1986), "How learning disabled adolescent boys make moral Judgment", *Journal of Learning Disabilities*, March, Vol. 79(3), pp. 106-164.

Derryberry, W. Pitt; Barger, Brian (2008), *Gifted Child Quarterly*, Vol. 52, N. 4, pp. 340-352.

Derryberry, W. Pitt; Thoma, Stephen, J. (2005), *Journal of Moral Education*, Vol. 34, N. 1, pp. 89-106.

Derryberry, W. Pitt; Thoma, Stephen, J. (2005), *Merrill Palmer Quarterly Journal of Developmental Psychology*, Vol. 51, N. 1, pp. 67-92.

Devendra and Mishra (1981), "Moral judgment patterns significantly changes with sex differences", as quoted in Chaya, C.V. (1996), "A study of moral judgment of ninth standard students in relation to their parental behaviour and values", An Unpublished M.Phil. Dissertation, Bangalore University, Bangalore.

Dewey, John (1959), *Moral principles in education*, New York Philosophical Library.

Dewey, John (1967), *Theory of moral life*, Wiley Eastern Private Ltd., New Delhi.

Dewey, J. and Tufts, J.H. (1932), *Ethics* (Revised edition), Holt, New York.

Diener, et al. (1975), as quoted in Rangaswamy, G.(2006), "A study of moral judgment of high school pupils in relations to certain factors", Ph.D. in Education, SVU, Tirupati, p. 27.

Dockstander (1979), "Comparative study of development sex differences in moral reasoning", *Dissertation Abstract International*, September, Vol. 40, N. 3, p. 1239-A.

Dolers (1977), "A study of two methods of training upon the development of moral judgment in young children", *Dissertation Abstract International*, Vol. 3, N. 7, February, p. 4828-A.

Draper, N.R. and Smith, H. (1981), *Applied regression analysis, A text-book*, second edition, John Wiley and sons New York.

Durkheim, Emile (1961), *Moral education*, The Free Press of Glencoe, Illinois, New York.

Durkheim, E. (1925), *Education Morale*, translated by Everett, K.Wilson and Herman Schnurer (1973), New York, The Free Press.

Durkheim, E. (1953), *Sociology and Philosophy*, Free Press of Glencoe, Illinois, New York.

Durkin, D. (1959 c), "Children's Concept of Justice : a further comparison with the Piaget data", *Journal of Educational Research*, Vol. 52, pp. 252-257.

Durkin, D. (1961), "The specificity of children's moral judgments", *Journal of Genetic Psychology*, Vol. 98, pp. 3-14.

Dutt (1971), as quoted in Rama Sachindran (1987), "Value orientation of college entrants in relation to parental authority, personality, academic achievement and social class", Unpublished M.Phil. Dissertation, Bangalore University, Bangalore, p. 34.

Dutt, N.K. (1970), "A study of anxiety and some correlates", *Journal of Psychological Research*, Vol. 14(2),pp. 50-52.

Earnest Hemingway (1955), as quoted in Sapru Alka (1982), "A study of a few socio-psychological factors in relation to moral judgment of IX standard students of a few high schools of Bangalore city", An Unpublished M.Ed. Dissertation, Bangalore University, Bangalore, p. 13.

Edward, J.B. (1965), "Some moral attitude of boys in a secondary modern school - part 1", *Educational Review*, Vol. 17, pp. 114-127.

Edwards, A.L. (1971), Experimental design in psychological research, A Text Book, Amerind Publishing Co. Pvt. Ltd., New Delhi.

Edwards, J.B. (1974), "A developmental study of the acquisition of some moral concepts in children aged 7 to 15", *Educational Research*, Vol. 16(2), pp. 83-93.

Eisenberg, Nancy; Cumberiand, Amanda; Guthrie, Ivanna, k; Murphy, Brindget, C.; Shepard, Stephanie, A. (2005), *Journal of Research on Adolescence*, Vol. 15(3), pp. 235-260.

Elbedour Salman, et ai. (1997), "The impact of political violence on moral reasoning in children", *Child Abuse and Neglect*, Vol. 21(11), pp.1053-066.

Encyclopedia of Social Sciences, as quoted in Rangaswamy, G. (2006), "A study of moral judgment of high school pupils in relations to certain factors", Ph.D. in Education, SVU, Tirupati, p. 6.

Evans (1980), As quoted in Rangaswamy, G. (2006), "A study of moral judgment of high school pupils in relation to certain factors", Ph.D. in Education, SVU Tirupati. p. 56.

Eysenck (1960, 1964), as quoted in Vanaja (1984), "A study of moral judgment among 9th and 10th standard students in relation to their self confidence, sex, socio-economic status and the type of school", An Unpublished M.Phil. Dissertation, Bangalore University, Bangalore, p. 11.

Feather, N.T. (1988), "Moral judgment and human values", British *Journal of Social Psychology*, Vol. 27(3), pp. 239-246.

Feffer and Gourevitch (1960), as quoted in Sandhya, G.K. (1988), "A study of moral judgment among children of primary schools in relation to their social maturity", An Unpublished M.Ed., Dissertation, Bangalore University, Bangalore, p. 29.

Fifis, Daniel Francis (1978), "The relationship of predictive ability, empathy, intelligence and sex to moral judgment in adolescents", *Dissertation Abstract International*, Vol. 39, No.12, p. 7162-A.

Fisher, R.A. (1950), *Statistical methods for research workers: A text book*, Hafner Publishing Co., New York.

Fowler, J. (1981), *Stages of Faith*, San Francisco: Harper and Row.

Fowler, Samantha, R.; Zeidler, Dana, L. and Sadler, Troy, D.(2009), *International Journal of Science Education*, Vol.31, N. 2, pp. 279-296.

Frankena (1962), as quoted in Rangaswamy, G.(2006), "A study of moral judgment of high school pupils in relations to certain factors", Ph.D. in Education, SVU, Tirupati, p. 25.

Freeman (1974), "Individual differences in moral judgment in relation to age and sex" as quoted in Ayesha Noor (2001), "A comparative study of the effect of personality traits on the moral judgment of tenth standard students in Bangalore urban secondary schools", Unpublished M.Phil. Dissertation, Bangalore University, Bangalore, p. 29.

Freud (1914), as quoted in Vanaja (1984), "A study of moral judgment among 9th and 10th standard students in relation to their self confidence, sex, socio economic status and the type of school". An Unpublished M.Phil. Dissertation, Bangalore University, Bangalore, p. 11.

Freud (1935), as quoted in as quoted by Prabhu, K.H. (1996), "A study on the moral judgment of IX standard students in relation to their parent-child interaction, modernization and their level of anxiety", An Unpublished M.Phil. Dissertation, Bangalore University, Bangalore, p. 34.

Frisancho, Susana (1996), "Moral judgment and cognitive complexity development through an instructional design", *Revista-de-Psicologia*, Vol. 14(1), pp. 81-106.

Gage, N.Y. (1983) (Ed.), *Handbook of research of teaching*, Rand and McNally Company, Chicago.

Garg (1983), "A study of children's perception of parental disciplinary practice and its relation to development of personality needs, moral judgment, and problem-solving ability as quoted in Buch, M.B.(Ed.), *Research in Education*, Vol. 4, 4th Edition, p. 457.

Garrett, H.E. (1973), *Statistics in psychology and education, A text book*, Vakills, Faffer and Simons Pvt. Ltd., Bombay, India. pp. 213-215 and 337-370.

Geethanath, P.S.(1987), "A study of moral judgment in relation to some selected variables" Ph.D. in Education, SVU, Tirupati.

Gibbs, et al.,(1986), "Construction and validation of a multiple choice measure of moral reasoning", *Child Development.*

Gillian Wark (2006), "Personality, gender, and the ways people perceive moral dilemmas in everyday life", Journal of College and Character, Vol. 2, 2006.

Gilligan, C. (1977), "In a different voice : women's conception of self and morality", *Harvard Educational Review*, Vol. 47, N. 4, pp. 418-517.

Gilligan, C. (1982), "In a Different Voice", Harvard University Press, Cambridge.

Gilligen, Kohlberg, Lerner and Belanky (1975), as quoted in Rangaswamy, G. (2006), "A study of moral judgment of high school pupils in relations to certain factors", Ph.D. in Education, SVU, Tirupati, p. 104.

Gilliland ( 1971), as quoted in Rangaswamy, G.(2006), "A study of moral judgment of high school pupils in relations to certain factors", Ph.D. in Education, SVU, Tirupati, p. 104.

Glover (1991), as quoted in Aysha Noor (2001), "A comparative study of the effect of personality traits on the moral judgment of tenth standard students in Bangalore urban secondary schools", Unpublished M.Phil. Dissertation, Bangalore University, Bangalore, p. 45.

Good and Cartwright (1998), "The development of moral judgment among undergraduate university students", *College-Student Journal*, June, Vol. 32(2), pp. 270-276.

Good, C.V. (1973) (Ed.), *Dictionary of Education*, McGraw-Hill Book Company, New Delhi, p. 49.

Gopalaiah (1981), "A study of moral judgment in children: experiments in education", *Indian Psychological Abstracts*, Vol. 30, N. 11, March, p. 297.

Gorgre (1981), "A study of moral judgment using the defining issues test for 3 ethnic groups at Bacon college", *Dissertation Abstract International, November*, Vol. 42, N. 5, p. 1986-A.

Gorgre (1981), as quoted in Sandhya, G.K. (1988), "A study of moral judgment among children of primary schools in relation to their social maturity", An Unpublished M.Ed. Dissertation, Bangalore University, Bangalore.

Green, H.A., Jorgensen and Kelly (1927-43), "IOWA silent reading tests", New York, Brace and World Inc.

Greene, Joshua, D.; Morelli, Sylvia, A.; Lowenberg, Kelly; Nystrom, Leigh, E.; Cohen, Jonathan, D. (2008), *Cognition*, Vol. 107, N. 3, pp. 1144-1154.

Grunwald, Heidi, E.; Mayhew, Matthew, J. (2008), *Research in Higher Education*, Vol. 49, N. 8, pp. 758-775.

Guilford (1964), "Field of psychology (3rd Ed.)", Princeton, N.J., Van Nostand.

Guilford, J.P. (1954), "Psychometric methods", A text book, McGraw-Hill publishing company, New York.

Guilford, J.P. (1950), "Fundamental statistics in psychology and education", A text book, International Student Edition Mc Graw Hill Book Co., Inc., New York.

Gupta (1977), as quoted by Narayanaswamy (1994), "Moral judgment among students of higher primary school in relation to their sex, type of school, standard and self-concept", Unpublished M.Ed. Dissertation, Bangalore University, Bangalore, p. 77.

Gupta (1984), as quoted by Chaya, C.V. (1993), "Moral judgment among students of eighth standard in relation to their sex, intelligence, religiosity and socio-economic status", Unpublished M.Ed. Dissertation, Bangalore University, Bangalore, p. 46.

Gupta, S.P. (1974); "Statistical methods", A text book, Sultan Chand and sons, New Delhi.

Hagelskamp, Jeanette-Louse (2001), "The effect of teaching critical thinking by infusion with focus on transfer of skills on the moral judgment and critical thinking of secondary school students", *Dissertation Abstract International*, Section - A Humanities and Social Sciences, May, Vol. 61(10-A), p. 3875.

Haidt, Jonathan, et al. (1993), "Affect, culture and morality or is it wrong to eat your Dog?", *Journal of Personality and Social Psychology*, October, Vol. 65(4), pp. 613-628.

Hare (1952), as quoted in Rangaswamy, G.(2006), "A study of moral judgment of high school pupils in relations to certain factors", Ph.D. in Education, SVU, Tirupati, pp. 25-26.

Hartshorne, H. and May, M.A. (1928), "Studies in the nature of character, Vol. 1, *Studies in Deceit*, Macmillan, New York.

Hartshorne, H., May, M.A., and Maller, J.B. (1929). "Studies in the nature of character", Vol. 2, *Studies in Self-Control*, Macmillan, New York.

Hartshorne, H., May, M.A., and Shuttle worth, F.K. (1930), Studies in the nature of character, Vol. 3, Studies in the organization of the character, Macmillan, New York.

Havighurst, R.J.and Taba Hilda (1949, 1966), *Adolescent Character and Personality*, New York, John Wiley and sons Inc.

Helen Mane Heishman (1973), "The effect of age, SES and IQ on moral judgment", *Dissertation Abstract International*, January, 1974, Vol. 34, N. 7, p. 4404-A.

Helwig, Charles, C., Arnold, Mary, Louise Tan, Dingliang Boyd, Dwight (2007), *Cognitive Development*, Vol. 22, N. 1, pp. 96-109.

Henry (1989), as quoted in Ayesha Noor (2001), "A comparative study of the effect of personality traits on the moral judgment of tenth standard students in Bangalore urban secondary schools", Unpublished M.Ed. Dissertation, Bangalore University, Bangalore, p. 43.

Herington, Carmel; Weaven, Scott (2007), *Journal of Marketing Education*, Vol. 29(2), pp. 154-163.

Hill, Kenneth Edwin (1996), "Critical thinking and its relation to academic, personal and moral development in the college years", *Dissertation Abstract International*: Section B – *The Science and Engineering*, February, Vol. 56(8-B), p. 4603.

Hilton (1978), "The relationship between the level of moral judgment of high school students and their levels of interpersonal trust, socio-economic status and intelligence", *Dissertation Abstract International*, Vol. 39, No. 6, p. 3375 - A.

Hobhouse, L.T. (1906), *Moral in Evolution*, London: Chapman and Hall.

Holstein (1973), "Irreversible stepwise sequence in the development of moral judgment : a longitudinal study of males and females", *Child Development*, pp. 51-60.

Horner (1972), as quoted in Vanaja (1984), "A study of moral judgment among 9th and 10th standard students in relation to their self confidence, sex, socio-economic status and the type of school", An Unpublished M.Phill. Dissertation, Bangalore University, Bangalore, p. 32.

Humphries, et al. (2000), "Predictors of moral reasoning among African American children : preliminary study", *Journal of Black Psychology*, February, Vol. 26(1), pp. 51-64.

Hunn (1971), as quoted in Vanaja (1984), "A study of moral judgment among 9th and 10th standard students in relation to their self confidence, sex, socio-economic status and the type of school", An Unpublished M.Ed. Dissertation, Bangalore University, Bangalore, p. 33.

James, R. Rest (1979), as quoted in Rangaswamy, G.(2006), "A study of moral judgment of high school pupils in relations to certain factors", Ph.D. in Education, SVU, Tirupati, p. 99.

Jennifer (1984), as quoted b Prabhu, K.H. (1996), "A study on the moral judgment of IX standard students in relation to their parent-child interaction, modernization and their level of anxiety", An Unpublished M.Phil. Dissertation, Bangalore University, Bangalore, p. 66.

John Belligham (2004), *Academic's Dictionary of Education*, Academic (India) Publishers, New Delhi, pp. 20-21.

John, C. Gibbs (2006), *Psychological Review*, Vol. 113, I. 3, pp. 666-672.

Johnson (1979, 1981), "A Study of determine the effect of moral judgment among VII grade students utilizing the Kohlberg's theory of moral judgment on selected children's stories", *Dissertation Abstract International*, December, 1971, Vol. 42(6), p. 2471-A.

Johnson (1981), as quoted in Chaya, C.V. (1993), "Moral judgment among students of eighth standard in relation to their sex, intelligence, religiosity and socio-economic status", Unpublished M.Ed. Dissertation, Bangalore University, Bangalore, Vol. 56, p. 120.

Johnson Dale Allen (1978), "An experimental study in developing moral Judgment using different instructional patterns with laws of control and religious attitudes and learner characteristics", *Dissertation Abstract International*, Vol. 39, p. 2724-A.

Johnson, R.C. (1962), "A study of children's moral judgment", *Child Development*, Vol. 33, pp. 327-354.

Johnston (1981), "Relationship between moral judgment and moral behaviour studies of 5th grade students in dissimilar settings", *Dissertation Abstract International*, June, 1980, Vol. 40, N. 12, p. 6202 - A.

Kaileen (1968), as quoted in Ayesha Noor (2001), "A comparative study of the effect of personality traits on the moral judgment of tenth standard students in Bangalore urban secondary schools", Unpublished M.Ed. Dissertation, Bangalore University, Bangalore, p. 36.

Kalra (1978), "A relationship between intelligence and moral development", as quoted by Chaya, C.V. (1993), "Moral judgment among students of eighth standard in relation to their sex, intelligence, religiosity and socio-economic status", Unpublished M.Ed. Dissertation, Bangalore University, Bangalore, p. 56.

Kapur (1986), as quoted in Chaya, C.V. (2001), "A study of moral judgment of 10th standard students in relation to their parental behaviour, child rearing practices, emotional maturity and personality traits", Ph.D. in Education, Bangalore University, Bangalore, p. 85.

Kaul (1974), as quoted in Rangaswamy, G.(2006), "A study of moral judgment of high school pupils in relations to certain factors", Ph.D. in Education, SVU, Tirupati, p. 32.

Kay (1968), "Moral Development", A text book, George, Allen and Unwin Ltd., London.

Kennedy-May, G., et al. (1988), "Social problem solving and adjustment in adolescence: the influence of moral reasoning level, scoring alternatives and family climate", Journal of Clinical Child Psychology, March, Vol. 17(1), pp. 73-83.

Kenney James, Francis (1980), as quoted in Ayesha Noor (2001), "A comparative study of the effect of personality traits on the moral judgment of tenth standard students in Bangalore urban secondary schools", Unpublished M.Ed. Dissertation, Bangalore University, Bangalore, p. 26-33.

Kenvin (1981), "A study of the effect of systematic value instruction on the level of moral judgment", *Dissertation Abstract International*, Vol. 42(4), p. 1582-A.

Kitchener Karen, S., et al. (1984), "A longitudinal study of moral and ego development in young adults", Journal of Youth and Adolescents, January, Vol. 13(3), pp. 197-211.

Koexnig Amy Lynn (2001), "Moral development - the effects of childhood maltreatment on prosocial behaviours and transgressions", Dissertation Abstract Internal - Section B: *The Sciences and Engineering*, April, Vol. 61(9-B), p. 4990.

Kohlberg (1958), as quoted in Vanaja, "A study of moral judgment among 9th and 10th standard students in relation to their self confidence, sex, socio-economic status and the type of school", An Unpublished M.Phill. Dissertation, Bangalore University, Bangalore, p. 15.

Kohlberg (1964), as quoted in Chaya (1993), "Moral judgment among students of eighth standard in relation to their sex, intelligence, religiosity and socio - economic status", Unpublished M.Ed. Dissertation, Bangalore University, Bangalore, p. 52.

Kohlberg (1966), *Social psychology, A text book*, Holt Rinehart and Winston, New York.

Kohlberg (1975), as quoted in Rangaswamy, G. (2006), "A study of moral judgment of high school pupils in relations to certain factors", Ph.D. in Education, SVU, Tirupati, pp. 99-104.

Kohlberg (1984), as quoted in Piaget, Kathleen and Wright Lois (1998), "The moral reasoning abilities of neglected children", Paper presented at the International conference on research for social work practice, Orlando, Florida, January 26, 1998, p. 1.

Kohlberg (1986), as quoted in Rangaswamy, G. (2006), "A study of moral judgment of high school pupils in relations to certain factors", Ph.D. in Education, SVU, Tirupati, p. 98.

Kohlberg and Turiel (1971), "From is to ought", *Cognitive Development and Epistemology*, New York Academic Press.

Kohlberg Lawrence (1981, 1984), as cited in Bear and Gubbs (1997) p. 3 as quoted in Piaget, Kathleen and Wright Lois, "Moral reasoning abilities of neglected children", paper presented at the International Conference on Research for social work practice, Orlando, Florida, January 26, 1998, p. 1.

Kohlberg, L. (1963), "Moral development and identification", in Stevenson, H.W. (Ed.), *Child Psychology: Yearbook of the National Society for the Study of Education*, Part-I, Chicago University.

Kohlberg, L. (1966), "A cognitive development analysis of children's Sex role concepts and attitudes", pp. 82 - 173 in Eleanor, E. Maccoby (Ed.), *The Development of Sex Differences*, Stanford, California, Stanford University Press.

Kohlberg, L. (1969), "Stage and sequence: the cognitive developmental approach to socialization, pp. 347-480 in Gostin, D.A. (Ed.), *Handbook of Socialization Theory and Research*, Chicago, Rand-McNally.

Kohlberg, L. (1971), "Stages of moral development as a basis for moral education", in Beek, C.M., Crittenden, B.S. and Sullivan, E.V., *Moral Education: Interdisciplinary*

*Approaches*, Toronto, University of Toronto Press, pp. 23-92.

Kothari Commission (1964-66), as quoted in Sapru Alka (1982), "A study of a few socio-psychological factors in relation to moral judgment of IX standard students of a few high schools of Bangalore city", An Unpublished M.Ed. Dissertation, Bangalore University, Bangalore, p. 18.

Kuhlen Raymond, G. (1952), *The Psychology of Adolescent Development*, Harper and Brothers, New York.

Kuppuswamy (1962), "Socio-economic status scale for urban areas".

Lagerspetz (1998), "Moral approval of aggression and sex role identity in officers, trainees, conscientious objectors of military service and in a female reference group", *Aggressive Behaviour*, Vol. 14(5), pp. 303-313.

Landis (1952), as quoted in Chaya, C.V. (2001), "A study of moral judgment of 10th standard students in relation to their parental behaviour, child rearing practices, emotional maturity and personality traits", Ph.D. in Education, Bangalore University, Bangalore, p. 6.

Larner (1975), as quoted in Rangaswamy, G. (2006), "A study of moral judgment of high school pupils in relations to certain factors", Ph.D. in Education, SVU, Tirupati, p. 112.

Laura Day (2000), "Pulling yourself in other peoples' shoes: the use of forum theatre to explore refugee and homeless issues in schools", pp. 13-14.

Lee, Seon - Young; Olszewski - Kubillus, Paula (2006), *Journal for the Education of the Gifted*, Vol. 30 N. 1 pp. 29-67.

Leming, J. "Moral reasoning, sense of control and social-political activism among adolescents", *Adolescence*, Vol. 9, N. 36, pp. 507-528.

Lerner, E.(1937), "Constraint areas and the moral judgment of children", Menasha, Wrist George Banta Publication Co.

Lewis (1982), "The relationship of moral development and cognitive development within gifted students examined in the light of variables of sex, SES and age, *Dissertation*

*Abstract International*, June, 1982, Vol. 42, N. 12, Part I, p. 5088-A.

Lickona, Thomas (1976), "Research on Piaget's theory of moral development, moral development and behaviour, theory, research, and social issues", Editor: Thomas lickona, Holt, Rinehart and Winston, New York.

Lock wood (1974), as quoted in Rangaswamy, G.(2006), "A study of moral judgment of high school pupils in relations to certain factors", Ph.D. in Education, SVU, Tirupati, p. 104.

Locke, as quoted in Dayakara Reddy, V. (1987) , "A study of moral judgment in relation to intelligence, personality and other variables, Ph.D. in Education, SVU, Tirupati, p. 36.

Loos-Helga, *et al.* (1999), "Moral judgment: a comparison of guilt feeling between children of orphanage and low income background", *Psychologia-Refflexao-e-Cfritica*, Vol. 12(1), pp. 47-69.

Maccoby (1966), as quoted by Prabhu, K.H. (1966), "A study on the moral judgment of IX standard students in relation to their parent-child interaction, modernization and their level of anxiety", An Unpublished M.Phil. Dissertation, Bangalore University, Bangalore, p. 19.

Macek and Osecka (1990), as quoted in Rangaswamy, G.(2006), "A study of moral judgment of high school pupils in relations to certain factors", Ph.D. in Education, SVU, Tirupati, p. 83.

Madhu Raj (1996) (Ed.), "Encyclopedic dictionary of psychology and education", Anmol Publications Pvt. Ltd., New Delhi, Vol. 1, p. 18.

Manchala, C.(2005), "Influence of certain psycho-sociological factors on scholastic Achievement of B.Ed. students" Ph.D. in Education, SVU, Tirupati.

Mangal, S.K.(2002), "Statistics in psychology and education", A text book, second edition, Prentice-Hall of India Pvt. Ltd., New Delhi.

Marrie and Elliot (1984), "Children's conception of moral and prudential rules", Child development, Vol. 55.

Marrie and Hillx (1973), as quoted in Rangaswamy, G. (2006), "A study of moral judgment of high school pupils in relations to certain factors", Ph.D. in Education, SVU, Tirupati, p. 128.

Marx, Benjamin, R.; Job, R.F. Soames; White, Fiona, A.; Wilson, J.Clare (2007), *Journal of Moral Education*, Vol. 36(2), pp. 199-219.

Mayhew, Matthew, J.; King, Patricia (2008), *Journal of Moral Education*, Vol. 37, N. 1, pp. 17-40.

Mc Dougall, W, (1908,1960), "An introduction to social psychology", 23rd Edition, Methuen, London.

Mc Pherson, Michael, S.; Schapiro, Morton Owen (2007), *Chronicle of Higher Education*, Vol. 54, N. 2, p. 10.

Mead (1934), as quoted in Narayanaswamy (1994), "Moral judgment among students of higher primary schools in relation to their sex, type of school, standard and self-concept", An Unpublished M.Ed.. Dissertation, Bangalore University, Bangalore, p. 44.

Mead, G.H. (1934), "Mind, Self and Society", University of Chicago Press. Chicago.

Meera Varma (1976), " Moral development in children", Chugh Publications, Vol. 2, Strochey Road, Allahabad, India.

Meera Verma (1976), as quoted in Ayesha Noor (2001), "A comparative study of the effect of personality traits on the moral judgment of tenth standard students in Bangalore urban secondary schools" An Unpublished M.Ed.. Dissertation, Bangalore University, Bangalore, p. 29.

Mestre Escriva, V., *et al.* (1998), "A field interval in moral development and self concept", *Revista-de-Psicologia-General-Y-Applicada*, Vol. 51(2), pp.184-200.

Mifsud (1985), as quoted in Rangaswamy, G.(2006), "A study of moral judgment of high school pupils in relations to certain factors", Ph.D. in Education, SVU, Tirupati, p. 25.

Milgram (1974), "The experience of living in cities", *Science*, p. 167.

Millis Lori, A. (1999), "Contextual effects on the development of children's socio moral judgment: A comparison of public school and non-school dilemma contexts", Dissertation abstract international - Section A: *Humanities and Social Sciences*, December, Vol. 60(6-A), p. 1923.

Ministry of Education (1966), "Education and national development", NCERT, New Delhi.

Mischel and Mischel (1962), as quoted in Rangaswamy, G.(2006), "A study of moral judgment of high school pupils in relations to certain factors", Ph.D. in Education, SVU, Tirupati, p. 33.

Mischel, W. and Metzner, R. (1962), "Preference for delayed reward as a function of age, intelligence and length of delay interval", *Journal of Abnormal Social Psychology*, N. 64, pp. 425-431.

Mohundro (1976), "Stages of moral reasoning and value hierarchies of sixth grade students", *Dissertation Abstract International*, February, 1978, Vol. 37, N. 8, p. 5026-A.

Moran, et al. (1963), a quoted in Sandhya, G.K. (1988), A study of moral judgment among children of primary schools in relation to their social maturity", An Unpublished M.Ed. Dissertation, Bangalore University, Bangalore, p. 33.

Morris, J.F. (1958), "The development of adolescent value judgments", *British Journal of Educational Psychology*, Vol. 28, Part I, pp. 1-14.

Morton, Kelly, Worthley, Joanna, S.; Testerman, John, k.; Mahoney, Marita, L. (2006), *Journal of Moral Education*, Vol. 35, N. 3, pp. 387-406.

Mynatt and Herman (1975), as quoted in Rangaswamy, G.(2006), "A study of moral judgment of high school pupils in relations to certain factors", Ph.D. in Education, SVU, Tirupati, p. 28.

Myyry Liisa and Helkamma Kalaus (1998), "The role of value priorities and professional ethics training in moral sensitivity", pp. 24-25.

Naga Raju, M.T.V. (2001), "Study habits of high school pupils in relation to certain psycho sociological factors, Ph.D. in Education, SVU, Tirupati.

Narayanaswamy (1994),"Moral judgment among students of higher primary schools in relation to their sex, type of school, standard and self-concept", An Unpublished M.Ed. Dissertation, Bangalore University, Bangalore.

Nash (1958), as quoted in Vanaja (1984), "A study of moral judgment among 9th and 10th standard students in relation to their self-confidence, sex, socio-economic status and the type of school", An Unpublished M.Ed. Dissertation, Bangalore University, Bangalore, p. 12.

National Policy of Education (NPE) (1986), "A report of ministry of human resource development", New Delhi, India.

NCERT Seminar (1981), as quoted in Sapru Alka (1982), "A study of a few socio-psychological factors in relation to moral judgment of IX standard students of a few high schools of Bangalore City", An Unpublished M.Ed. Dissertation, Bangalore University, Bangalore, p. 19.

O'Connor Navy, O'Rovree (1982), "Sex, and leadership differences in moral perspective and field dependence and moral judgment", *Dissertation Abstract International*, Aug, Vol. 43, N. 2, p. 405-A.

Oser, F. (1980), "Stages if religious judgment", In Fowler, J. and Vergote, A. (Eds.), *Toward Moral and Religious Maturity*, Morristown, NJ: Silver Burdett.

Ostini - Remo and Ellerman D - Andrew (1997), "Clarifying the relationship between values and moral judgment", Psychological Reports, October, Vol. 81(2), pp. 691-702.

Oxford Talking Dictionary as quoted in Rangaswamy, G. (2006), "A study of moral judgment of high school pupils in relations to certain factors", Ph.D. in Education, SVU, Tirupati, p. 4.

Panigua Freddy, A. (1989), as quoted in Ayesha Noor (2001), "A comparative study of the effect of personality traits on the moral judgment of tenth standard students in Bangalore urban secondary schools", Unpublished M.Ed. Dissertation, Bangalore University, Bangalore, pp. 42-43.

Parikh (1968), "A study on development of moral judgment and its relation to family environmental factors in Indian and American families", as quoted in p. 23 of Chaya, C.V. (1993), "Moral judgment among students of eighth standard in relation to their sex, intelligence, religiosity and socio-economic status" An Unpublished M.Ed. Dissertation, Bangalore University, Bangalore.

Parmar (1986), "Study of values and aspiration of children of rural background" as quoted by Chaya, C.V. (2001), "A study of moral judgment of 10th standard students in relation to their parental behaviour, child rearing practices, emotional maturity and personality traits", Ph.D. in Education, Bangalore University, Bangalore, p. 34.

Pashupathi, M., et al. (2001), "Seeds of wisdom: adolescents' knowledge and judgment about difficult life problems", *Developmental Psychology*, May, Vol. 37(3), pp. 351-361.

Peck, R. and Havinghurst, R. (1960), "The psychology of character development", New York : John Wiley and Sons Inc.

Piaget Jean (1932, 1965, 1968), "The moral development of the child", A text book, Routledge and Keganpaul Ltd., New York.

Piaget, J. (1932), "The Moral judgment of the child", A text book, Kegan Paul, Trench, Trubner and Co., Ltd., London.

Piaget, Kathleen and Wright Lois (1998), "The moral reasoning abilities of neglected children", paper presented at the International Conference Research for Social Work Practice, Orlando, Florida, January, 26.

Popovix (1992), as quoted in Rangaswamy, G.(2006), "A study of moral judgment of high school pupils in relations to certain factors", Ph.D. in Education, SVU, Tirupati, p.73.

Portues, B., and Johnson, R.C. (1965), "Children's responses to two measures of conscience development and their relation to socio metric nomination", *Child Development*, Vol. 36, pp. 703-711.

Prabhu, K.H. (1996), "A study on the moral judgment of IX standard students in relation to their parent - child interaction, modernization and their levels of anxiety", Unpublished M.Phil. Dissertation, Bangalore University, Bangalore.

Pradhan and Pande (1996), "Moral judgment of tribal secondary school children in relation to their sex", *Indian Journal of Psychometry and Education*, January, Vol. 27(1), pp. 21-25.

Prahallada N.N. (1982), "An investigation of moral judgments of junior college students and their relationship with the SES, intelligence and personality adjustments", Ph.D in Education, Mysore University, Mysore.

Pringle, K.M., and Gooch, S. (1965), "Chosen ideal person personality development and progress in school subjects: a longitudinal study", *Human Development*, Vol. 8, pp. 161-180.

Raaijmakers, Quinten, A. W.; Engels, Rutger, C.M. E.; Van Hoof, Anne (2005), International journal of behavioral development, Vol. 29, N. 3, pp. 247-258.

Radhakrishna Commission (1948), as quoted in Sapru Alka (1982), "A study of a few socio-psychological factors in relation to moral judgment of IX standard students of a few high schools of Bangalore city", An Unpublished M.Ed. Dissertation, Bangalore University, Bangalore, p. 18.

Radhakrishnan, S. (1929), "Indian philosophy", The Macmillan Company, New York, Vol. 1, pp. 341-475.

Rajini, M.(2004), "Study habits of intermediate students in relation to certain factors", Ph.D. in Education, SVU, Tirupati.

Rangaswamy, G. (2006), "A study of moral judgment of high school pupils in relation to certain factors, Ph.D. in Education, SVU, Tirupati.

Rao (1984), "A study of moral judgment in children", as quoted by Buch, M.B. (Ed.), Research in Education, 4th Edition, p. 352.

Rao (1984), as quoted in Chaya, C.V. (2001), "A study of moral judgment of 10th standard students in relation to their parental behaviour, child rearing practices, emotional maturity and personality traits", Ph.D. in Education, Bangalore University, Bangalore, p. 83.

Rash Lall Hasting (1907), "The theory of good and evil", Oxford University press.

Ravan - Hashim Rowahan (1974), "The relationship between age, intelligence and social class to maturity level of moral judgment in children", *Dissertation Abstract International*, October, Vol. 35.

Raven, J.C. (1970), as quoted in Rangaswamy, G.(2006), "A study of moral judgment of high school pupils in relations to certain factors", Ph.D. in Education, SVU, Tirupati, p. 100.

Rest, J. Narvaez, D., Thoma, S. and Bebeau, M.(2000), "Post-conventional moral reasoning: a neo-Kohlbergian Approach", Mahway, NJ: Erlbaum Press.

Rest, J.R. (1981), "Morality", in Flaell, J. and Markmanan,E. (Eds.) "*Cognitive Development*" in Mussen, P. (Gen.Ed.), Carmichael's Manual of Child Psychology (3rd Edition), John Wiley and Sons Inc., New York.

Rest, J.R., Turiel, E. and Kohlberg, L. (1969), "Relations between level of moral judgment and preference and comprehension of the moral judgment of others", *Journal of Personality*, Vol. 37, pp. 225-252.

Richards, Herbert, C., et al. (1992), "Moral reasoning and classroom conduct: evidence of curvilinear relationship", *Merril-Palmer Quarterly*, April, Vol. 38(2), pp. 176-190.

Rule and Nesdale (1976), as quoted in Rangaswamy, G.(2006), "A study of moral judgment of high school pupils in relations to certain factors", Ph.D. in Education, SVU, Tirupati, p. 74.

Sabitha Reddy, N. (2003), "Moral judgment among students of ninth standard in relation to a few social and psychological factors", Ph.D. in Education, Bangalore University, Bangalore.

Saraswathi (1978), "Perceived maternal disciplinary practices and their relation to development of moral judgment", *Child Development*, Vol. 32, pp. 750-761.

Schliefli Andre, et al. (1985), "Does moral education improve moral judgment?", *Review of Educational Research*, Vol. 55(3), pp. 319-352.

Schoffner, Marie Forcier (1997), "The moral reasoning of gifted adolescents: its relationship with identity development, sue sensitivity and gender role flexibility", *Dissertation Abstract International*, section – B: *The Sciences and Engineering*, February, Vol. 57(8 - 13), p. 5366.

Schrmdt Paul, F. (1988), "Moral values of adolescents : public versus Christian schools", *Journal of Psychology and Christianity*, Vol. 7(3), pp. 50-54.

Schruner Greeta (1976), "Sex difference and personality variable in the moral reasoning of young adults", *Dissertation Abstract International*, January 1977, Vol. 37, No. 7, p. 4244-A.

Sears (1957), as quoted in Vanaja (1984), "A study of moral judgment among 9th and 10th standard students in relation to their self confidence, sex, Socio-economic status and the type of school", An Unpublished M.Phil. Dissertation, Bangalore University, Bangalore, p. 11.

Sears, R.R., Rau, L., and Alpert, R. (1965), "Identification and child rearing", Stanford co., Stanford University Press.

Seetharamu, A.S. (1974), "An experimental study of the problem of moral instruction in upper primary schools", second survey of research in education (1972-1978), pp. 305.

Seigal (1985), as quoted in Rangaswamy, G.(2006), "A study of moral judgment of high school pupils in relations to certain factors", Ph.D. in Education, SVU, Tirupati, p. 78.

Selman, R.(1975), "A developmental approach to inter – personal and moral awareness in young children: Some theoretical and educational implications of levels of social perspective-taking", Paper presented at the Comedian National Conference on Value Education, Toronto.

Sharma, Vandana, Kaur, Kiranjit (1992),"Moral judgment as a function of intelligence, birth order and age of the children", *Psychologia - An International Journal of Psychology in the Orient*, June, Vol. 35(2), pp. 121-124.

Shira, Haviv and Patrick, J. Leman (2004), as quoted in Rangaswamy, G.(2006), "A study of moral judgment of high school pupils in relations to certain factors", Ph.D. in Education, SVU, Tirupati, p. 74.

Shweder (1991), as quoted in Rangaswamy, G.(2006), "A study of moral judgment of high school pupils in relations to certain factors", Ph.D. in Education, SVU, Tirupati, p. 83.

Sidney Siegel (1956), "Non-parametric statistics for the behavioral schemes", A text book, McGraw-Hill book Co., Inc., New York.

Siefering (1981), "Intelligence, sex and behavioural correlates of moral reasoning of public junior high school students", *Dissertation Abstract International*, October, Vol. 42, N. 4, p. 1960-A.

Sigman Marian and Erdynast – Albert (1988), "Interpersonal understanding and moral judgment in adolescents with emotional and cognitive disorders", *Child Psychiatry and Human Development*, Vol. 19(1), pp. 36-44.

Singh (1984), as quoted in Ramakrishnaiah, V. (1996), "A study of moral judgment of IX standard urban and rural students in relation to their personality values and some selected social variables", Unpublished M.Ed. Dissertation, Bangalore University, Bangalore, p. 78-79.

Singh, R.S. (1983), as quoted by Prabhu, K.H. (1996), "A study on the moral judgment of IX standard students in relation to their parent-child interaction, modernization and their level of anxiety", Unpublished M.Ed. Dissertation, Bangalore University, Bangalore, p. 61.

Sipaur (1983), as quoted in Ramakrishnaiah, V. (1996), Á study of moral judgment of IX standard urban and rural students in relation to their personality values and some selected social variables", Unpublished M.Phil. Dissertation, Bangalore University, Bangalore, p. 70.

Skoe Eva, E. and Macia James, E. R. (1991), "A measure of care-based morality and its relation to ego identity", *Merril Palmer Quarterly*, April, Vol. 37(2), pp. 289 - 304.

Solomon Gloria, B. (1995), "The relationship between moral reasoning maturity and legitimacy judgments about gender stratification in a youth sport context", *Dissertation Abstract International*, Section A: Humanities and Social Sciences, Feb, Vol. 55(8 - A), p. 2319.

Soni (1984), "A study of moral judgment in school going children of rural area of Delhi belonging to different castes and sexes", as quoted in Chaya, C.V. (1993), "Moral judgment among students of eighth standard in relation to their sex, intelligence, religiosity and socio-economic status", An Unpublished M.Ed. Dissertation, Bangalore University, Bangalore.

Sreedharamurthy, B.N. (1984), "A study of moral judgment among IX standard high school students in relation to their religiosity", An Unpublished M.Ed. Dissertation, Bangalore University, Bangalore.

Sri Prakasha Committee (1959), as quoted in Sapru Alka (1982), "A study of a few socio - psychological factors in relation to moral judgment of IX standard students of a few high schools of Bangalore city", An Unpublished M.Ed. Dissertation, Bangalore University, Bangalore, p. 18.

Sridhar Y.N. (1994), "A study of moral judgment of high school students with reference to adult and peer influence", Ph.D in Education, Regional College of Education, NCERT, University of Mysore.

Srinivasa Rao, R., Dayakara Reddy, V. and Geethanath, P.S. (1987), "A study of moral judgment in children", UGC Major Research Project.

Stern (1921), In "Job satisfaction and teaching effectiveness of secondary school teachers", by Padmanabhaian, S. Ph.D.in Education, SVU, 1984, pp. 222.

Stiller Nancy, J. and Forrest Linda (1990), "An extension of Gilligan and Lyonbs's investigation of morality : gender differences in college students", *Journal of College Student Development*, Vol. 31(1), pp. 54-63.

Sukhia, S.P, Mehrotra, P.V. and Mehrotra, R.N. (1980), "Elements of educational research", A text book, Allied Publishers, Bombay, India, pp. 101-102.

Sullivan (1974), "Logical thinking and moral judgment in young adults", *Dissertation Abstract International*, September, 1994, Vol. 35.

Sullivan, E.V., Mc Cullough, G. and stager, M. A. (1970), "A developmental study of the relationship between conceptual, ego, and moral development", *Child Development*, Vol. 41, pp. 399-411.

Suma Rani (2001), "Moral judgment among students of IX standard in relation to their gender, type of school, urban and rural background and social maturity", An Unpublished M.Ed. Dissertation, Bangalore University, Bangalore.

Tal Eyal, Nira Liberman and Yaacov Trope (2008), *Journal of Experimental Social Psychology*, Vol. 44, I. 4, pp. 1204-1212.

Talwar, M.S. and Sheela, G. (2006), "A study of moral judgment or pre-university students in relation to gender, socio-economic status course of study, religion and moral judgment of their teachers", in Dayakara Reddy, V. and Bhaskar Rao, D. (2006), Value oriented education, Discovery Publishing House, New Delhi, pp. 324-334.

Thakur, S. and Kang (2002), "Moral values and judgment as a function of age and sex", *Indian Psychological Review*, Vol. 58, N. 1, pp. 8 - 13.

The Curriculum for the Ten Year School (1976), as quoted in Rangaswamy, G. (2006), "A study of moral judgment of high school pupils in relations to certain factors", Ph.D. in Education, SVU, Tirupati, p. 40.

The Indian Education Commission, as quoted in Rangaswamy, G. (2006), "A study of moral judgment of high school pupils in relations to certain factors", Ph.D. in Education, SVU, Tirupati, p. 41.

*The Oxford English Dictionary* (1961), Oxford University Press.

The Report of the Committee of Members of Parliament of Education (National Policy on Education) (1967), Government of India, Ministry of Education, New Delhi.

*The Report of the Committee on Religious and Moral Instructions* (1959), Government of India, Ministry of Education, New Delhi.

*The Report of the Education Commission (EC)*, (1964-66), Ministry of Education, Government of India, New Delhi.

*The Report of the Secondary Education Commission* (1952-53), Government of India, Ministry of Education, New Delhi.

*The Review Committee on National Policy on Education* (1990), Ministry of Human Resource Development, New Delhi, India .

The Secondary Education Commission (1956), as quoted in Sapru Alka (1982), "A study of a few socio-psychological factors in relation to moral judgment of IX standard students of a few high schools of Bangalore city", An

Unpublished M.Ed. Dissertation, Bangalore University, Bangalore, p. 18.

Thompson, R.I. (1932), "Honesty education-An Experimental study", Ph.D. in Education, Yale's University.

Toai Ton (1978), "Adult authority figure, grade, sex and moral judgment in Vietnamese immigrant children", *Dissertation Abstract International*, October, Vol. 39, N. 4, p. 2584-A.

Tripathi and Girishwar (1982), "Development of moral judgment in Indian children", *Indian Psychological Abstracts*, Vol. 18, N. 1, p. 193.

Tureen (1966), as quoted in Rangaswamy, G. (2006), "A study of moral judgment of high school pupils in relations to certain factors", Ph.D. in Education, SVU, Tirupati, p. 104.

Turial (1975), "Development of moral thinking in Kohlberg's theory", as quoted in Ayesha Noor (2001), "A comparative study of the effect of personality traits on the moral judgment of tenth standard students in Bangalore urban secondary schools", An Unpublished M.Ed. Dissertation, Bangalore, p. 24.

Turiel Elliot (1976), "A comparative analysis of moral knowledge and moral judgment in males and females", *Journal of Personality*, Vol. 44, June.

Turiel, Elliot (2008), *Human Development*, Vol. 51, N. 1, pp. 21-39.

Vanaia (1984), "A study of moral judgment among IX and X standard students in relation to their self-confidence, sex, socio-economic status and the type of school", An Unpublished M.Ed. Dissertation, Bangalore University, Bangalore.

Vernon (1963), as quoted in Rangaswamy, G. (2006), "A study of moral judgment of high school pupils in relations to certain factors", Ph.D. in Education, SVU, Tirupati, p. 128.

Vijaya Lakshmi Pandit, "Learning centered education", All India Association for *Educational Research*, 18th Annual Conference as International Conference, Tirunelveli, p. 176.

Vivian Ridler (1961) (Ed.), *The Oxford Dictionary*, Great Britain: Oxford University Press.

Wark and Krebs (1996, 2000), "Gender and dilemma differences in real life moral judgment", *Developmental Psychology*, March, Vol. 32(2), pp. 22-230.

Webster's Dictionary (1972), "A dictionary", Promotional Sales Book, Inc : Printed in USA.

Webster's on line Dictionary, as quoted in Rangaswamy, G. (2006), "A study of moral judgment of high school pupils in relations to certain factors", Ph.D. in Education, SVU, Tirupati, p. 5.

Westermark (1912), as quoted in Sapru Alka (1982), "A study of a few socio-psychological factors in relation to moral judgment of IX standard students of a few high schools of Bangalore city", An Unpublished M.Ed. Dissertation, Bangalore University, Bangalore, p. 13.

Wilhelm, William J., Czyzewski, Alan, B. (2006), Delta pi epsilon journal, Vol. 48, N. 3, pp. 129-143.

Winer, B. J. (1971), "Statistical principles in experimental design", A text book, McGraw-Hill Book Co., New York.

Wright and Cox (1967), "A study of the relationship between moral judgment and religion belief in a sample of English adolescents", *Journal of Social Psychology*, Vol. 72, pp. 135-144.

Yadava, Sharma and Gandhi (2001), "Aggression and moral disengagement", Inter-Personality and Clinical Studies, September, Vol. 17(2), pp. 95-99.

Yate, M.W. (1965), " Statistics in education and psychology", A text book, The Macmillan Co., New York.

Yeh Christine - Jean (1996), "A cultural perspective on interdependence in self and morality: A Japan and United States comparison", *Dissertation Abstract International*, Section A – *Humanities and Social Sciences*, Vol. 57 (2-A), p. 0594.

Young and Thomson (1984), as quoted in Sandhya, G.K. (1988), "A study of moral judgment among children of primary schools in relation to their social maturity", An Unpublished M.Ed. Dissertation, Bangalore University, Bangalore, p. 33.

Zupancic and Horvat (1990), "The role of moral judgment in child's school functioning", *Psychologiche-Beifraege*, Vol. 32 (1-2), pp. 111-118.

# INDEX

**G**



**H**



**I**



**J**



**K**

## S